Linux® Debugging and Performance Tuning

Prentice Hall
Open Source Software Development Series
Arnold Robbins, Series Editor

"Real world code from real world applications"

Open Source technology has revolutionized the computing world. Many large-scale projects are in production use worldwide, such as Apache, MySQL, and Postgres, with programmers writing applications in a variety of languages including Perl, Python, and PHP. These technologies are in use on many different systems, ranging from proprietary systems, to Linux systems, to traditional UNIX systems, to mainframes.

The **Prentice Hall Open Source Software Development Series** is designed to bring you the best of these Open Source technologies. Not only will you learn how to use them for your projects, but you will learn *from* them. By seeing real code from real applications, you will learn the best practices of Open Source developers the world over.

Titles currently in the series include:

Linux® Debugging and Performance Tuning: Tips and Techniques
Steve Best
0131492470, Paper, 10/14/2005
The book is not only a high-level strategy guide but also a book that combines strategy with hands-on debugging sessions and performance tuning tools and techniques.

Linux Programming by Example: The Fundamentals
Arnold Robbins
0131429647, Paper, 4/12/2004
Gradually, one step at a time, Robbins teaches both high level principles and "under the hood" techniques. This book will help the reader master the fundamentals needed to build serious Linux software.

The Linux® Kernel Primer: A Top-Down Approach for x86 and PowerPC Architectures
Claudia Salzberg, Gordon Fischer, Steven Smolski
0131181637, Paper, 9/21/2005
A comprehensive view of the Linux Kernel is presented in a top down approach—the big picture first with a clear view of all components, how they interrelate, and where the hardware/software separation exists. The coverage of both the x86 and the PowerPC is unique to this book.

Linux® Debugging and Performance Tuning

Tips and Techniques

Steve Best

PRENTICE HALL PTR

Prentice Hall Professional Technical Reference

Upper Saddle River, NJ • Boston • Indianapolis • San Francisco
New York • Toronto • Montreal • London • Munich • Paris
Madrid • Capetown • Sydney • Tokyo • Singapore • Mexico City

The publisher offers excellent discounts on this book when ordered in quantity for bulk purchases or special sales, which may include electronic versions and/or custom covers and content particular to your business, training goals, marketing focus, and branding interests. For more information, please contact:

U. S. Corporate and Government Sales
(800) 382-3419
corpsales@pearsontechgroup.com

For sales outside the U. S., please contact:

International Sales
international@pearsoned.com

Visit us on the Web: www.phptr.com

Pearson Education, Inc.

Rights and Contracts Department

One Lake Street

Upper Saddle River, NJ 07458

ISBN 0-13-149247-0

Text printed in the United States on recycled paper at R.R. Donnelley and Sons in Crawfordsville, Indiana.

First printing, October 2005

Library of Congress Cataloging-in-Publication Data

Best, Steve (Steve Francis), 1961-
    Linux® debugging and performance tuning : tips and techniques / Steve Best.
        p. cm.
    ISBN 0-13-149247-0
    1. Linux. 2. Operating systems (Computers) 3. Debugging in computer science. I. Title.
    QA76.76.O63B4756 2005
    005.4'32--dc22
                            2005017192

I dedicate this book to Debbi, my wonderful wife, for her support and encouragement during the adventure of writing this book.

Contents

Foreword xv

Acknowledgments xvii

About the Author xix

Introduction xxi

Chapter 1   Profiling 1

stopwatch 3

date 4

time 5

clock 6

gettimeofday 11

Performance Tuning Using GNU gprof 13

gcc Option Needed for gprof 15

    Building the sample1 Program and Using gprof 16

kprof 31

    Installation 32

    Building Graphviz, the Graph Feature 32

Summary 35

Web Resources for Profiling 36

Chapter 2   Code Coverage 37

What Is Code Coverage Analysis? 38

gcov Can't Find Logic Errors 39

Types of Code Coverage 40

gcc Options Needed for gcov 41

Summary 52

Web Resource for gcov 52

Chapter 3   GNU Debugger (gdb) **53**

Installing gdb 55

gdb Commands 56
   Some Useful gdb Commands 57
Compiling a Program That Is to Be Debugged with gdb 59

A Typical gdb Session 60
   Invoking the gdb Debugger 60
Debugging Using a Core File 63

Running the Program and Getting the Core Dump 64

Graphical gdb Interfaces 65

Data Display Debugger 66
   ddd Features 66
   Installing ddd 66
   ddd Ways to View a Program 67
Insight 70
   Insight Features 70
   Installing Insight 71
Debugging Symbols Increase the Executable's Size 77

Debugging Techniques 78

Summary 80

Web Resources for GNU Debugger 80

Chapter 4   Memory Management Debugging **81**

Dynamic Memory Functions 82

MEMWATCH 84

YAMD 86

Electric Fence 93

Valgrind 97
   Installing Valgrind 98

Losing Your Memory 101
Cache Profiling 106
Some Limitations of Valgrind 109
Summary 109
Web Resources for Memory Checkers 109

Chapter 5   System Information (/proc) 111

What Is /proc? 112
Ways an Administrator Can Use /proc 113
A Map of /proc 114
Process-Specific Subdirectories...114
Summary 148
Web Resources for /proc 149

Chapter 6   System Tools 151

Processes 152
Task States 153
Tools for Working with Processes 154
ps Reports the Process Status 154
pgrep Lists the Process IDs That Match the Input Criteria 168
pstree Displays a Tree of Processes 169
top Displays Tasks 170
strace Traces System Calls 170
The Magic Key Sequence Gets a Back Trace 174
lsof Lists Open Files 176
Network Debugging Tools 178
ifconfig Configures the Network Interface 178
arp Manipulates the System's ARP Cache 179
tcpdump Dumps Traffic on a Network 179
ethereal Interactively Browses Network Traffic 180
netstat Shows the Network Status 180
Summary 184
Web Resources for Systems Tools 185

Chapter 7   System Error Messages **187**

Kernel Files 188
    Typical Distribution /boot Layout of the Kernel Files 188
Oops Analysis 190
Building the Kernel 193
Processing the Oops Using ksymoops 196
Using gdb to Display jfs_mount 199
The gcc -S Option Generates Assembly Code 199
    Assembler Output Generated by GNU C 200
Kernel Mailing List Oops 200
    An Oops in the 3c59x Network Driver 2.4.7ac11 200
    A Linux-2.5.1-pre5 Oops 204
perror Describes a System or MySQL Error Code 208
Summary 209
Web Resources for Oops 209

Chapter 8   Event Logging **211**

Error Logging Subsystem for syslogd 213
    syslogd Key Options 213
    Remote Logging 214
    syslog.conf 214
    Changing syslogd Messages 217
    klogd 217
    Logger Command 218
    Provide Sufficient Disk Space 219
    Log File Management 221
    Debugging Using Syslog Messages 222
Error Logging Subsystem for Event Logging 226
    Event Logging Interfaces 227
    Benefits of Event-Type Logging 227
    Log Management 228
    Different Types of Event Log Records 228
    Managing the Event Log 228
    Event Logging Utilities 228
    Remote Logging 229

Setting up the Event Consolidator 230
  Forwarding Syslog Messages to the Event Log 231
  evlog Packages 231
Summary 232
Credits 232
Web Resource for Event Logging 232

Chapter 9   Linux Trace Toolkit **233**

Architecture Component Tasks 235
Package and Installation 236
Building the Kernel 240
Building LTT User-Level Tools 242
Data Acquisition 243
Recording the Data 244
Stopping Data Recording 244
Ways to Analyze Tracing Processes 245
Data Interpretation 248
  tracevisualizer 248
Tracing Example for Tarring a Subdirectory 253
Data Reviewing Text Tools 256
  tracedcore *filename* 256
  traceanalyze *filename* 257
  tracedump *filename* 258
Summary 259
Credits 259
Web Resource for the Linux Trace Toolkit 259

Chapter 10   oprofile: a Profiler Supported by the Kernel **261**

Instrumentation 262
Sampling 263
oprofile: a System-Wide Profiler 263
  Building the Kernel 264
Utilities for oprofile 267

General Profile Steps 268

Examining a Single Executable's Profile 272

Report Examples 276
    System-Wide Binary Image Summary 276
    System-Wide Symbol Summary, Including Per-Application Libraries 276

Saving Profiling Data 277

Hardware Counters 277
    Minimizing Cache Misses 278
    Padding and Aligning Structures 279
    Packing 280
    Loop Grouping 280
    Blocking 281

The Prospect Profiler 287

Summary 288

Web Resources for Profiling 289

Chapter 11   User-Mode Linux **291**

UML: Introduction to the Kernel and Root File System 293

Patching and Building the Kernel 296
    UML Kernel Options 297

Building the Kernel 303

Root Image 304

File Systems 305
    Swap Partition 306
    Setting up a gdb Session 306

Booting UML 307

A Typical gdb Session 307

GDB Thread Analysis 308

Tips 310
    Consoles and Serial Lines 310
    UML Networking Support 310
    Root Image 311
    Adding File Systems 311
    Shutting Down 312

UML Utilities 312

Summary 313

Credits 314

Web Resources for User-Mode Linux 314

Chapter 12   Dynamic Probes..**315**

Unique Aspects of Dynamic Probes 318

General Steps for Using Probes 318

Kprobes: Kernel Dynamic Probes 319

    Building the Kernel 320

    Kprobe Interfaces 321

    Registering and Unregistering Kprobes 322

Probe Example for sys_open 324

Makefile for a Basic Kernel Module 326

Finding Kprobes That Are Active on the System 328

Finding an Offset in sys_open 328

Jumper Probes 329

Uses of Kprobes 330

Successful Employment of Dprobes 331

Summary 331

Credits 331

Web Resource for Dynamic Probes 331

Chapter 13   Kernel-Level Debuggers (kgdb and kdb) **333**

kgdb 335

    kgdb Kernel Patching 336

    Checking the Null Modem Serial Cable Setup 341

    A Typical gdb Session 343

    Using kgdb to Stop and View the Kernel Source 344

    gdb Thread Analysis 347

kdb 348

    kdb Kernel Patching 348

    Building the Kernel 350

    kdb Activation 352
    kdb Commands 353
    kdb Debug Sessions 354
Summary 368
Credits 369
Web Resources for kgdb and kdb 369

Chapter 14   Crash Dump **371**

Kernel Configuration 374
    Crash Dump Kernel Options 374
Patching and Building the Kernel 376
    Building the Kernel 377
General Crash Dump Steps 379
LKCD Commands 385
System Panic and Crash Dump Taken 386
Netdump: The Network Crash Dump Facility from Both the Client
and Server 391
    Server 391
    Client 391
diskdump: a Crash Dump Facility 392
    General Steps to Configure diskdump 393
Viewing an mcore Crash Dump 393
Summary 410
Credits 411
Web Resources for Crash Dump 411

Index 413

Foreword

Debugging. That part of the job that we programmers don't enjoy, but can't avoid. (Of course, it's still not as bad as documentation.) When faced with debugging, we want the best tools we can get, and we want to know how to use them to find our problems, fix them, and get back to the fun part of our jobs (or hobbies).

That's what this book is all about: the open-source tools for finding problems and fixing them. From simple applications to kernel debugging, this book covers a wide range of the problems you may encounter and shows you what tools are out there, where to get them if you don't already have them, and how to use them. There's a lot here, even for experienced programmers.

The Linux kernel, the GDB debugger, and essentially all the tools described in this book are Free Software. The word "Free" (with a capital "F") means Free as in Freedom. In The Free Software Definition (*http://www.gnu.org/philosophy/free-sw.html*), Richard Stallman defines the freedoms that make software Free. Freedom 0 is the freedom to run the software. This is the most fundamental freedom. But immediately after that is Freedom 1, the freedom to study how a program works. This freedom is often overlooked. However, it is very important, because one of the best ways to learn how to do something is by watching other people do it. In the software world, that means reading other people's programs and seeing what they did well, as well as what they did poorly.

The freedoms of the GPL are, at least in my opinion, one of the most fundamental reasons that GNU/Linux systems have become such an important force in modern computing. Those freedoms benefit you every moment you use your GNU/Linux system, and it's a good idea to stop and think about that every once in a while.

With this book, we take advantage of Freedom 1 to give you the opportunity to study debugging and problem solving in an open-source environment. Because of Freedom 1, you will see these programs in action, and you will be able to learn from them.

And that brings me to the Prentice Hall Open-Source Software Development series, of which this book is one of the first members. The idea for the series developed from the principle that reading programs is one of the best ways to learn. Today, the world is blessed with an abundance of Free and open-source software—with source code just waiting (maybe even eager!) to be read, understood, and appreciated. The aim of the series is to be your guide up the software development learning curve, so to speak, and to help you learn by showing you as much real code as possible.

I sincerely hope that you will enjoy this book and learn a lot. I also hope that you will be inspired to carve out your own niche in the Free Software and open-source worlds, which is definitely the most enjoyable way to participate in them.

Have fun!

Arnold Robbins

Series Editor

Acknowledgments

I am deeply grateful to friends and colleagues who read drafts of the manuscript and gave me helpful comments. Arnold Robbins, Jeff Korn, and Ronald Czik read the book proposal and provided comments to make it better.

Richard J. Moore, Rob Farber, and Arnold Robbins read the manuscript, some more than once, with exceptional thoroughness. Thank you, all.

Last, but not least, thanks to the Linux developers for their relentless work in bringing these tools to the Linux environment.

Thanks to Kevin, Jeff, and Jim for finding time to fly-fish—one of my passions in life.

I would like to thank Mark L. Taub of Pearson Education for getting this book off the ground and for his continual help and advice through the development of the book.

I would also like to thank Gayle Johnson for doing a great job on copyediting and Christy Hackerd for making the production process very easy. Both Gayle and Christy have been a pleasure to work with.

About the Author

Steve Best works in the Linux Technology Center of IBM in Austin, Texas. He is currently working on Linux storage-related products. Steve has led the Journaled File System (JFS) for Linux project. Steve has worked on Linux-related projects since 1999 and has done extensive work in operating system development focusing on file systems, internationalization, and security. Steve is the author of numerous magazine articles, many presentations, and the file system chapters in *Performance Tuning Linux Servers* (Prentice Hall PTR 2005).

Introduction

Debugging and performance tuning are major parts of programming. Knowing the available tools and techniques can make this part of programming easier. This book covers debugging techniques and tools that can be used to solve both kernel and application problems on the Linux operating system.

The book includes many sample programs that demonstrate how to use the best profiling and debugging tools available for Linux. All the tools are open-source and continue to be enhanced by the open-source community.

The goal of the book is to provide you with the knowledge and skills you need to understand and solve software problems on Linux servers. It discusses techniques and tools used to capture the correct data using first failure data capture approaches.

This Book's Audience

As the Linux operating system moves further into the enterprise, the topic of being able to fix problems that arise in a timely manner becomes very important. This book helps software developers, system administrators, and service personnel find and fix that problem or capture the correct data so that the problem can be fixed. This book is intended for the person who is developing or supporting Linux applications or even the kernel.

Chapter Descriptions

This book is organized into 14 chapters, each focusing on a specific tool or set of tools. The chapters also describe the steps to build and install the tools in case your Linux distribution does not ship with that tool or if there is a later release of the tool. Most of these tools are easy to build or add to the kernel.

Chapter 1, "Profiling," discusses methods to measure execution time and real-time performance. Application performance tuning is a complex process that requires correlating pieces of data with source code to locate and analyze performance problems. This chapter shows a sample program that is tuned using a profiler called gprof and a code coverage tool called gcov.

Chapter 2, "Code Coverage," discusses coverage code that can be used to determine how well your test suites work. One indirect benefit of gcov is that its output can be used to identify which test case provides coverage for which source file. Code coverage during testing is one important measurement of software quality. Like an X-ray machine, gcov peers into your code and reports on its inner workings.

What would debugging be without a debugger? Chapter 3, "GNU Debugger (gdb)," looks at the GNU debugger. You can debug by adding printf statements to a program, but this is clumsy and very time consuming. A debugger like gdb is a much more efficient debugging tool.

Chapter 4, "Memory Management Debugging," looks at the APIs for memory management, which, although small, can give rise to a large number of disparate problems. These include reading and using uninitialized memory, reading/writing from memory past or in front of (underrun) the allocated size, reading/writing inappropriate areas on the stack, and memory leaks. This chapter covers four memory management checkers: MEMWATCH, YAMD, Electric Fence, and Valgrind. We'll review the basics, write some "buggy" code, and then use each of these tools to find the mistakes.

The /proc file system is a special window into the running Linux kernel and is covered in Chapter 5, "System Information (/proc)." The /proc file system provides a wealth of information for the Linux kernel. It offers information about each process to system-wide information about CPU, memory, file systems, interrupts, and partitions. Some of the utilities that use /proc entries to get data from the system include iostat, sar, lsdev, lsusb, lspci, vmstat, and mpstat. Each of these utilities is covered in the chapter.

Chapter 6, "System Tools," looks at various tools that can be used to pinpoint what is happening to the system and to find which component of the system is having a problem. The ps command is a valuable tool that can be used to report the status of each of the system processes. Three other process tools are covered—pgrep, pstree, and top. The strace command lets you trace system calls. The magic key sequence can provide a back trace for all the processes on the system. The lsof tool can be used to list the open files on the system. Finally, the network debugging tools ifconfig, arp, ethereal, netstat, and tcpdump are covered. They can help solve network-type problems.

Many kernel bugs show themselves as NULL pointer dereferences or other values to pointers that are incorrect. The common result of such a bug is the Oops message. Chapter 7, "System Error Messages," covers where an Oops message is stored, how to analyze the Oops, and finding the failing line of code.

An important goal of a Linux systems administrator is to ensure that his or her systems are functioning and performing 100% of the time. Applications producing error messages, file systems not having free space available, network adapter failures, hard drives producing errors, and the kernel producing errors are just a few types of problems that could possibly stop a system, impacting that goal. Chapter 8, "Event Logging," helps administrators grapple with these issues by describing Syslog and event logging.

Chapter 9, "Linux Trace Toolkit," shows how an execution trace shows exactly what scheduling decisions are made and how various management tasks are done. It captures how they are handled, how long they take, and to which process the processor has been allocated. The trace facility provides a dynamic way to gather system data. Application I/O latencies can also be identified, as well as the time when a specific application is actually reading from a disk. Certain types of locking issues also can be seen by tracing.

In short, tracing can be used to:

- Isolate and understand system problems.

- Observe system and application execution for measuring system performance.

- Permit bottleneck analysis when many processes are interacting and communicating.

The Linux Trace Toolkit (LTT) differs from strace or gprof in that LTT provides a global view of the system, including a view into the kernel.

Chapter 10, "oprofile: a Profiler Supported by the Kernel," covers the kernel profiler called oprofile. Profilers are software development tools designed to help analyze the performance of applications and the kernel. They can be used to identify sections of code that aren't performing as expected. They provide measurements of how long a routine takes to execute, how often it is called, where it is called from, and how much time it takes. Profiling is also covered in Chapter 1; one profiler in that chapter is called gprof. Another topic covered in Chapter 10 is ways to minimizing cache misses. Cache misses can be a cause of applications not performing as expected.

User-Mode Linux (UML) is covered in Chapter 11, "User-Mode Linux"; it is a fully functional Linux kernel. It runs its own scheduler and virtual memory (VM) system, relying on the host kernel for hardware support. The benefits of UML from a debugging point of view are that it lets you do kernel development and debugging at the source code level using gdb. The UML technology can be a powerful tool to reduce the time needed to debug a kernel problem and development kernel-level features.

Chapter 12, "Dynamic Probes," explains dynamic probes (Dprobes), which is a technique for acquiring diagnostic information without custom-building the component. Dynamic probes can also be used as a tracing mechanism for both user and kernel space. It can be used to debug software problems that are encountered in a production environment that can't be re-created in a test lab environment. Dprobes are particularly useful in production environments where the use of an interactive debugger is either undesirable or unavailable. Dprobes also can be used during the code development phase to cause faults or error injections into code paths that are being tested.

Chapter 13, "Kernel-Level Debuggers (kgdb and kdb)," covers two kernel-level debuggers: kgdb and kdb. kgdb is an extension to gdb that allows the gdb debugger to debug kernel-level code. One key feature of kgdb is that it allows source code-level debugging of kernel-level code. The kdb debugger allows kernel-level debugging but does not provide source-level debugging.

There are multiple ways for Linux to support a crash dump. Chapter 14, "Crash Dump," covers the different types of crash dumps. It discusses Linux Kernel Crash Dump (LKCD), Netdump, Diskdump, and mcore. Crash dump is designed to meet the needs of end users, support personnel, and systems administrators needing a reliable method of detecting, saving, and examining system problems. There are many benefits of having a bug report and dump of the problem, since the dump provides a significant amount of information about the system's state at the time of the problem.

Chapter 1

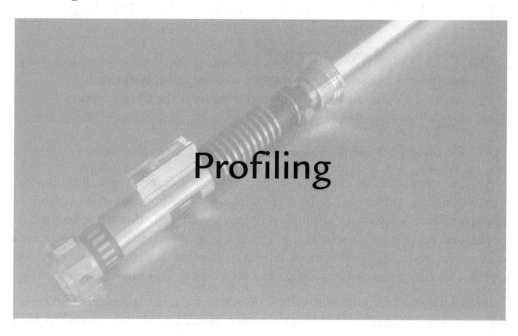

Profiling

In this chapter

- stopwatch   page 3
- date   page 4
- time   page 5
- clock   page 6
- gettimeofday   page 11
- Performance Tuning Using GNU gprof   page 13
- gcc Option Needed for gprof   page 15
- kprof   page 31
- Summary   page 35
- Web Resources for Profiling   page 36

In general, performance tuning consists of the following steps:

1. Define the performance problem.

2. Identify the bottlenecks by using monitoring and measurement tools. (This chapter focuses on measuring from the timing aspect.)

3. Remove bottlenecks by applying a tuning methodology.

4. Repeat steps 2 and 3 until you find a satisfactory resolution.

A sound understanding of the problem is critical in monitoring and tuning the system. Once the problem is defined, a realistic goal for improvement needs to be agreed on. Once a bottleneck is found, you need to verify whether it is indeed a bottleneck and devise possible solutions to alleviate it. Be aware that once a bottleneck is identified and steps are taken to relieve it, another bottleneck may suddenly appear. This may be caused by several variables in the system running near capacity.

Bottlenecks occur at points in the system where requests are arriving faster than they can be handled, or where resources, such as buffers, are insufficient to hold adequate amounts of data. Finding a bottleneck is essentially a step-by-step process of narrowing down the problem's causes.

Change only *one* thing at a time. Changing more than one variable can cloud results, since it will be difficult to determine which variable has had what effect on system performance. The general rule perhaps is better stated as "Change the minimum number of related things." In some situations, changing "one thing at a time" may mean changing multiple parameters, since changes to the parameter of interest may require changes to related parameters. One key item to remember when doing performance tuning is to start in the same state every time. Start each iteration of your test with your system in the same state. For example, if you are doing database benchmarking, make sure that you reset the values in the database to the same setting each time the test is run.

This chapter covers several methods to measure execution time and real-time performance. The methods give different types of granularity, from the program's complete execution time to how long each function in the program takes. The first three methods (**stopwatch**, **date**, and **time**) involve no changes to the program that need to be measured. The next two methods (**clock** and **gettimeofday**) need to be added directly to the program's source code. The timing routines could be coded to be on or off, depending on whether the collection of performance measurements is needed all the time or just when the program's performance is in question. The last method requires the application to be compiled with an additional compiler flag that allows the compiler to add the performance measurement directly to the code. Choosing one method over another can depend on whether the application's source code is available. Analyzing the source code with gprof is a very effective way to see which function is using a large percentage of the overall time spent executing the program.

Application performance tuning is a complex process that requires correlating many types of information with source code to locate and analyze performance problem bottlenecks. This chapter shows a sample program that we'll tune using gprof and gcov.

stopwatch

The stopwatch uses the chronograph feature of a digital watch. The steps are simple. Reset the watch to zero. When the program begins, start the watch. When the program ends, stop the watch. The total execution time is shown on the watch. Figure 1.1 uses the file system benchmark **dbench**. The stopwatch starts when dbench is started, and it stops when the program dbench is finished.

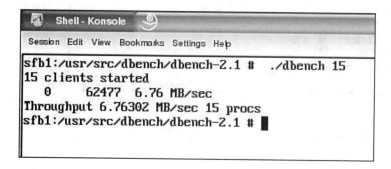

FIGURE 1.1
Timing dbench with **stopwatch**.

Using the digital stopwatch method, the dbench program execution time came out to be 13 minutes and 56 seconds, as shown in Figure 1.2.

00:13.56

FIGURE 1.2
The execution time is shown on the watch.

date

The **date** command can be used like a stopwatch, except that it uses the clock provided by the system. The **date** command is issued before the program is run and right after the program finishes. Figure 1.3 shows the output of the **date** command and the dbench program, which is a file system benchmark program. The execution time is 29 minutes and 59 seconds. This is the difference between the two times shown in the figure (17:52:24 − 17:22:25 = 29 minutes 59 seconds).

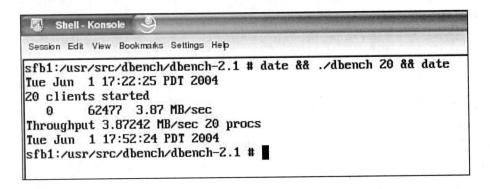

FIGURE 1.3
Using **date** to measure dbench timing.

time

The **time** command can be used to measure the execution time of a specified program. When the program finishes, **time** writes a message to standard output, giving timing statistics about the program that was run. Figure 1.4 shows the timing for the list directory contents command (**ls**) with the **-R** option, which recursively lists subdirectories.

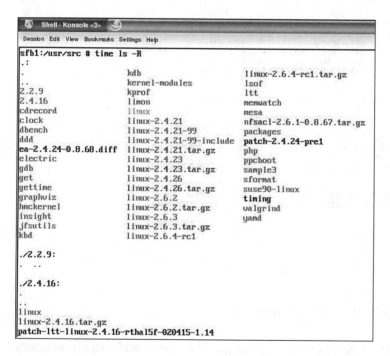

FIGURE 1.4
Timing the **ls** command with **time**.

Figure 1.5 shows the finishing up of the ls command and the three timings (**real**, **user**, and **sys**) produced by time.

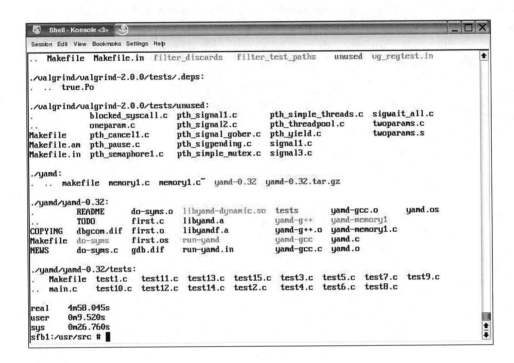

FIGURE 1.5
The results of timing the **ls** command with **time**.

The output from time produces three timings. The first is **real**, which indicates that 4 minutes and 58.045 seconds elapsed during the execution of the **ls** command, that the CPU in user space (**user**) spent 9.520 seconds, and that 26.760 seconds were spent executing system (**sys**) calls.

clock

The **clock()** function is a way to measure the time spent by a section of a program. The sample program shown in Listing 1.2, called sampleclock, measures two **for** loops. The first **for** loop is on line 27 of the sampleclock program, and the second is on line 69. The **delay_time** on lines 17 and 56 calculates how long the **clock ()** call takes. The makefile shown in Listing 1.1 can be used to build the sampleclock program.

Listing 1.1

The Makefile for the sampleclock Program

```
Makefile for sampleclock program
CC = g++
CFLAGS = -g -Wall


sampleclock: sampleclock.cc
    $(CC) $(CFLAGS) sampleclock.cc -o sampleclock


clean:
    rm -f *.o sampleclock
```

Listing 1.2

sampleclock.cc

```
1   #include <iostream>
2   #include <ctime>
3   using namespace std;
4
5   // This sample program uses the clock() function to measure
6   // the time that it takes for the loop part of the program
7   // to execute
8
9   int main()
10  {
11  clock_t start_time ,finish_time;
12
13    // get the delay of executing the clock() function
14
15    start_time = clock();
16    finish_time = clock();
17    double delay_time = (double)(finish_time - start_time);
18
19      cout<<"Delay time:"<<(double)delay_time<<" seconds."
        <<endl;
20
21    // start timing
22
23    start_time = clock();
24
25    // Begin the timing
26
27    for (int i = 0; i < 100000; i++)
28      {
```

```
29    cout <<"In:"<<i<<" loop" << endl;
30    }
31
32 // End the timing
33
34 // finish timing
35
36 finish_time = clock();
37
38 // compute the running time without the delay
39
40 double elapsed_iter_time = (double)(finish_time - start_
     time);
41 elapsed_iter_time -= delay_time;
42
43 // convert to second format
44
45 double elapsed_time = elapsed_iter_time / CLOCKS_PER_SEC;
46
47 // output the time elapsed
48
49 cout<<"Elapsed time:"<<(double)elapsed_time<<" seconds."
     <<endl;
50
51 // get the delay of executing the clock() function
52
53
54 start_time = clock();
55 finish_time = clock();
56 delay_time = (double)(finish_time - start_time);
57
58 cout<<"Delay time:"<<(double)delay_time<<" seconds."<<endl;
59
60 // now see what results we get by doing the measurement
61 // of the loop by cutting the loop in half
62
63 // start timing
64
65 start_time = clock();
66
67 // Begin the timing
68
69 for (int i = 0; i < 50000; i++)
70    {
71    cout <<"In:"<<i<<" loop" << endl;
72    }
73
74 // End the timing
75
76 // finish timing
77
78 finish_time = clock();
79
```

```
80   // compute the running time without the delay
81
82   elapsed_iter_time = (double)(finish_time - start_time);
83   elapsed_iter_time -= delay_time;
84
85   // convert to second format
86
87   elapsed_time = elapsed_iter_time / CLOCKS_PER_SEC;
88
89   // output the time elapsed.
90
91   cout<<"Elapsed time:"<<(double)elapsed_time<<" seconds."
       <<endl;
92
93   return 0;
94
95 }
```

The sampleclock.cc program can be built by executing the **make** command. Figure 1.6 shows the building and running of the sampleclock program.

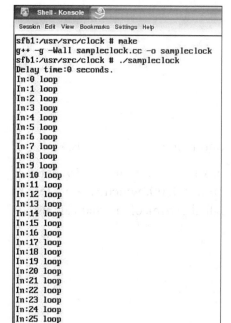

FIGURE 1.6
Building and running sampleclock.

Figure 1.7 shows the elapsed time for the first loop as 3.11 seconds.

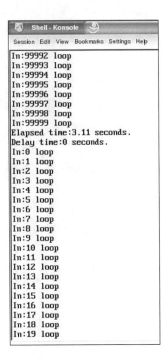

```
Shell - Konsole
Session Edit View Bookmarks Settings Help
In:99992 loop
In:99993 loop
In:99994 loop
In:99995 loop
In:99996 loop
In:99997 loop
In:99998 loop
In:99999 loop
Elapsed time:3.11 seconds.
Delay time:0 seconds.
In:0 loop
In:1 loop
In:2 loop
In:3 loop
In:4 loop
In:5 loop
In:6 loop
In:7 loop
In:8 loop
In:9 loop
In:10 loop
In:11 loop
In:12 loop
In:13 loop
In:14 loop
In:15 loop
In:16 loop
In:17 loop
In:18 loop
In:19 loop
```

FIGURE 1.7
The timing for loop 1.

Figure 1.8 shows the elapsed time for the second loop as 1.66 seconds.

So the sampleclock program takes 3.11 seconds to execute the first **for** loop of 100000 and 1.66 seconds for the second **for** loop of 50000, which is very close to half of the time. Now let's look at another API called gettimeofday that can also be used to time functions in a program.

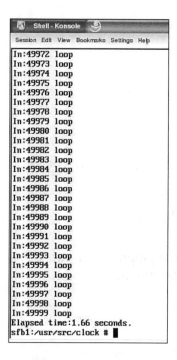

FIGURE 1.8
The timing for loop 2.

gettimeofday

gettimeofday() returns the current system clock time. The return value is a list of two integers indicating the number of seconds since January 1, 1970 and the number of microseconds since the most recent second boundary.

The sampletime code shown in Listing 1.3 uses gettimeofday to measure the time it takes to sleep for 200 seconds. The gettimeofday routine could be used to measure how long it takes to write or read a file. Listing 1.4 is the pseudocode that could be used to time a write call.

Listing 1.3

sampletime.c

```
1    #include <stdio.h>
2    #include <sys/time.h>
3
```

```
4    struct timeval start, finish ;
5    int msec;
6
7    int main ()
8    {
9     gettimeofday (&start, NULL);
10
11    sleep (200); /* wait ~ 200 seconds */
12
13    gettimeofday (&finish, NULL);
14
15    msec = finish.tv_sec * 1000 + finish.tv_usec / 1000;
16    msec -= start.tv_sec * 1000 + start.tv_usec / 1000;
17
18    printf("Time: %d milliseconds\n", msec);
19   }
```

Figure 1.9 shows the building of sampletime.c and the program's output. Using gettimeofday, the time for the sleep call on line 11 is 200009 milliseconds.

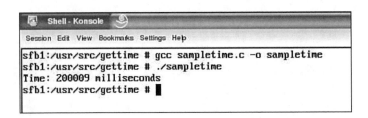

FIGURE 1.9
Timing using **gettimeofday**.

Listing 1.4 shows pseudocode for measuring the write call with the gettimeofday API. The gettimeofday routine is called before the write routine is called to get the start time. After the write call is made, gettimeofday is called again to get the end time. Then the **elapse_time** for the write can be calculated.

Listing 1.4

Pseudocode for Timing Write Code

```
1    /* get time of day before writing */
2       if ( gettimeofday( &tp_start, NULL ) == -1 )
3          {
4          /* error message gettimeofday failed */
```

```
5        }
6    /* calculate  elapse_time_start  */
7    /* write to disk */
8    for ( i = 0; i < count; i++ )
9        {
10              if ( write( fd, buf, buf_size ) == 0 )
11              {
12                  /* error message write failed */
13              }
14       }
15   /* get time of day after write */
16   if ( gettimeofday( &tp_end, NULL ) == -1 )
17       {
18          /* error message gettimeofday failed */
19       }
20   /* calculate elapse_time_new */
21   elapse_time = elapse_time_new - elapse_time_start;
22   /* compute throughput */
23   printf( "elapse time for write: %d \n", elapse_time );
```

Raw timings have limited usage when looking for performance issues. Profilers can help pinpoint the parts of your program that are using the most time.

Performance Tuning Using GNU gprof

A profiler provides execution profiles. In other words, it tells you how much time is being spent in each subroutine or function. You can view two kinds of extreme profiles: a sharp profile and a flat profile.

Typically, scientific and engineering applications are dominated by a few routines and give sharp profiles. These routines are usually built around linear algebra solutions. Tuning code should focus on the most time-consuming routines and can be very rewarding if successful.

Programs with flat profiles are more difficult to tune than ones with sharp profiles. Regardless of the code's profile, a subroutine (function) profiler, gprof, can provide a key way to tune applications.

Profiling tells you where a program is spending its time and which functions are called while the program is being executed. With profile information, you can determine which pieces of the program are slower than expected. These sections of the code can be good candidates to be rewritten to make the program execute faster. Profiling is also the best way to determine how often each function is called. With this information, you can determine which function will give the most performance boost by changing the code to perform faster.

The profiler collects data during the program's execution. Having a complete analysis of the program helps you ensure that all its important paths are while the program is being profiled. Profiling can also be used on programs that are very complex. This could be another way to learn the source code in addition to just reading it. Now let's look at the steps needed to profile a program using gprof:

- Profiling must be enabled when compiling and linking the program.

- A profiling data file is generated when the program is executed.

- Profiling data can be analyzed by running gprof.

    gprof can display two different forms of output:

- A flat profile displays the amount of time the program went into each function and the number of times the function was executed.

- A call graph displays details for each function, which function(s) called it, the number of times it was called, and the amount of time that was spent in the subroutines of each function. Figure 1.10 shows part of a call graph.

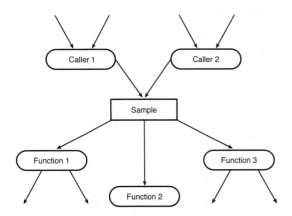

FIGURE 1.10
A typical fragment of a call graph.

gprof is useful not only to determine how much time is spent in various routines, but also to tell you which routines call (invoke) other routines. Suppose you examine gprof's output and see that xyz is consuming a lot of time, but the output doesn't tell you which routine is calling xyz. If there were a call tree, it would tell you where the calls to xyz were coming from.

gcc Option Needed for gprof

Before programs can be profiled using gprof, they must be compiled with the -**pg** gcc option. To get complete information about gprof, you can use the command **info gprof** or **man gprof**.

Listing 1.5 shows the benefits that profiling can have on a small program. The sample1 program prints the prime numbers up to 50,000. You can use the output from gprof to increase this program's performance by changing the program to sample2, shown later in Listing 1.8.

Listing 1.5

sample1.c

```
1   #include <stdlib.h>
2   #include <stdio.h>
3
4   int prime (int num);
5
6   int main()
7   {
8     int i;
9     int colcnt = 0;
10    for (i=2; i <= 50000; i++)
11      if (prime(i)) {
12        colcnt++;
13        if (colcnt%9 == 0) {
14          printf("%5d\n",i);
15          colcnt = 0;
16        }
17      else
18          printf("%5d ", i);
19      }
20    putchar('\n');
21    return 0;
22  }
23
24  int prime (int num) {
25      /* check to see if the number is a prime? */
26      int i;
27      for (i=2; i < num; i++)
28      if (num %i == 0)
29        return 0;
30      return 1;
31  }
```

Building the sample1 Program and Using gprof

The sample1.c program needs to be compiled with the option **-pg** to have profile data generated, as shown in Figure 1.11.

Shell - Konsole

Session Edit View Bookmarks Settings Help

```
sfb1:/usr/src/sample1 # gcc -pg -o sample1 sample1.c
sfb1:/usr/src/sample1 # ./sample1
    2    3    5    7   11   13   17   19   23
   29   31   37   41   43   47   53   59   61
   67   71   73   79   83   89   97  101  103
  107  109  113  127  131  137  139  149  151
  157  163  167  173  179  181  191  193  197
  199  211  223  227  229  233  239  241  251
  257  263  269  271  277  281  283  293  307
  311  313  317  331  337  347  349  353  359
  367  373  379  383  389  397  401  409  419
  421  431  433  439  443  449  457  461  463
  467  479  487  491  499  503  509  521  523
  541  547  557  563  569  571  577  587  593
  599  601  607  613  617  619  631  641  643
  647  653  659  661  673  677  683  691  701
  709  719  727  733  739  743  751  757  761
  769  773  787  797  809  811  821  823  827
  829  839  853  857  859  863  877  881  883
  887  907  911  919  929  937  941  947  953
  967  971  977  983  991  997 1009 1013 1019
 1021 1031 1033 1039 1049 1051 1061 1063 1069
 1087 1091 1093 1097 1103 1109 1117 1123 1129
 1151 1153 1163 1171 1181 1187 1193 1201 1213
 1217 1223 1229 1231 1237 1249 1259 1277 1279
 1283 1289 1291 1297 1301 1303 1307 1319 1321
 1327 1361 1367 1373 1381 1399 1409 1423 1427
 1429 1433 1439 1447 1451 1453 1459 1471 1481
 1483 1487 1489 1493 1499 1511 1523 1531 1543
 1549 1553 1559 1567 1571 1579 1583 1597 1601
```

FIGURE 1.11
Building and running sample1.

When the sample1 program is run, the gmon.out file is created.

To view the profiling data, the gprof utility must be on your system. If your system is **rpm**-based, the **rpm** command shows the version of gprof, as shown in Figure 1.12.

FIGURE 1.12
The version of gprof.

gprof is in the binutils package. For you to use the utility, the package must be installed on your system. One useful gprof option is **-b**. The **-b** option eliminates the text output that explains the data output provided by gprof:

```
# gprof -b ./sample1
```

The output shown in Listing 1.6 from gprof gives some high-level information like the total running time, which is 103.74 seconds. The main routine running time is 0.07 seconds, and the prime routine running time is 103.67 seconds. The prime routine is called 49,999 times.

Listing 1.6

Output from gprof for sample1

```
Flat profile:

Each sample counts as 0.01 seconds.
  %      cumulative    self              self     total
 time     seconds     seconds    calls  ms/call  ms/call  name
99.93     103.67      103.67     49999    2.07     2.07    prime
 0.07     103.74       0.07                                main


                  Call graph


granularity: each sample hit covers 4 byte(s) for 0.01% of
103.74 seconds

index % time     self   children     called     name
                                                   <spontaneous>
[1]     100.0    0.07    103.67                  main [1]
                 103.67    0.00   49999/49999       prime [2]
```

```
----------------------------------------------------------
                103.67     0.00    49999/49999   main [1]
[2]      99.9   103.67     0.00    49999          prime [2]
----------------------------------------------------------

Index by function name

    [1] main                          [2] prime
```

Next we can use the gcov program to look at the actual number of times each line of the program was executed. (See Chapter 2, "Code Coverage," for more about gcov.)

We will build the sample1 program with two additional options—**-fprofile-arcs** and **-ftest-coverage**, as shown in Figure 1.13. These options let you look at the program using gcov, as shown in Figure 1.14.

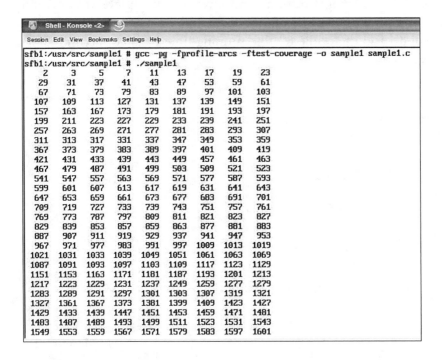

FIGURE 1.13
Building sample1 with gcov options.

FIGURE 1.14
Running sample1 and creating gcov output.

Running gcov on the source code produces the file sample1.c.gcov. It shows the actual number of times each line of the program was executed. Listing 1.7 is the output of gcov on sample1.

Listing 1.7

Output from gcov for sample1

```
  -:      0:Source:sample1.c
  -:      0:Graph:sample1.bbg
  -:      0:Data:sample1.da
  -:      1:#include <stdlib.h>
  -:      2:#include <stdio.h>
  -:      3:
  -:      4:int prime (int num);
  -:      5:
  -:      6:int main()
  1:      7: {
```

```
      1:      8:    int i;
      1:      9:    int colcnt = 0;
  50000:     10:    for (i=2; i <= 50000; i++)
  49999:     11:      if (prime(i)) {
   5133:     12:        colcnt++;
   5133:     13:        if (colcnt%9 == 0) {
    570:     14:    printf("%5d\n",i);
    570:     15:    colcnt = 0;
      -:     16:      }
      -:     17:    else
   4563:     18:      printf("%5d ", i);
      -:     19:      }
      1:     20:        putchar('\n');
      1:     21:        return 0;
      -:     22: }
      -:     23:
  49999:     24:int prime (int num) {
      -:     25:        /* check to see if the number is a prime?
                      */
  49999:     26:    int i;
121337004:   27:    for (i=2; i < num; i++)
121331871:   28:    if (num %i == 0)
  44866:     29:      return 0;
   5133:     30:    return 1;
      -:     31:      }
      -:     32:
```

There are 5,133 prime numbers. The expensive operations in the routine prime are the **for** loop (line 27) and the **if** statement (line 28). The "hot spots" are the loop and the **if** test inside the prime routine. This is where we will work to increase the program's performance. One change that will help this program is to use the **sqrt()** function, which returns the nonnegative square root function of the number passed in. sample2, shown inListing 1.8, has been changed to use the **sqrt** function in the newly created function called **faster**.

Listing 1.8

sample2.c

```
1 #include <stdlib.h>
2 #include <stdio.h>
3 #include <math.h>
4
5 int prime (int num);
6 int faster (int num);
7
8 int main()
9 {
```

```
10    int i;
11    int colcnt = 0;
12    for (i=2; i <= 50000; i++)
13      if (prime(i)) {
14        colcnt++;
15      if (colcnt%9 == 0) {
16         printf("%5d\n",i);
17         colcnt = 0;
18      }
19      else
20         printf("%5d ", i);
21      }
22      putchar('\n');
23      return 0;
24 }
25
26 int prime (int num) {
27     /* check to see if the number is a prime? */
28     int i;
29     for (i=2; i <= faster(num); i++)
30     if (num %i == 0)
31        return 0;
32     return 1;
33 }
34
35 int faster (int num)
36 {
37   return (int) sqrt( (float) num);
38 }
```

Now you can build the sample2 program (see Figure 1.15) and use gprof to check how long the program will take to run (see Figure 1.16). Also, the gcov output shows the reduced number of times each line needs to be executed. In Listing 1.9, the total running time has been reduced from 103.74 seconds to 2.80 seconds.

Listing 1.9 shows the output of gprof for the sample2 program.

Listing 1.9

Output from gprof for sample2

```
Flat profile:

Each sample counts as 0.01 seconds.
 %       cumulative    self                       self      total
time      seconds     seconds     calls       us/call    us/call    name
52.68      1.48        1.48       1061109        1.39       1.39     faster
46.61      2.78        1.30         49999       26.10      55.60     prime
 0.71      2.80        0.02                                          main
```

```
Call graph


granularity: each sample hit covers 4 byte(s) for 0.36% of 2.80
seconds

index   % time    self  children     called      name
                                                  <spontaneous>
[1]      100.0    0.02    2.78                   main [1]
                  1.30    1.48   49999/49999        prime [2]
-----------------------------------------------------------------
                  1.30    1.48   49999/49999        main [1]
[2]       99.3    1.30    1.48   49999            prime [2]
                  1.48    0.00   1061109/1061109      faster [3]
-----------------------------------------------------------------
                  1.48    0.00   1061109/1061109    prime [2]
[3]       52.7    1.48    0.00   1061109          faster [3]
-----------------------------------------------------------------


Index by function name

[3] faster                        [1] main                         [2]
prime
```

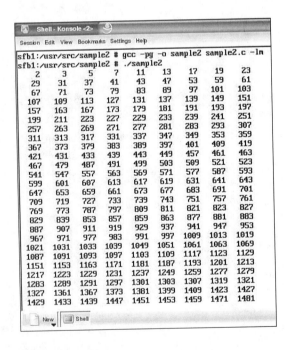

FIGURE 1.15
Building and running sample2.

FIGURE 1.16
Using gprof on sample2.

Now we'll run gcov on the sample2 program, as shown in Figures 1.17 and 1.18.

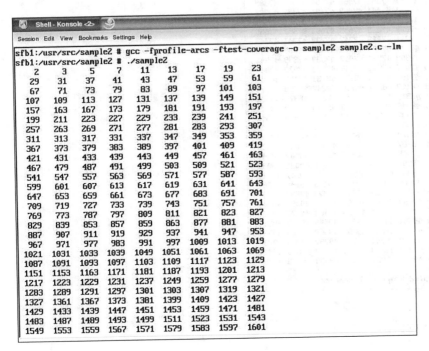

FIGURE 1.17
Building sample2 with gcov and running sample2.

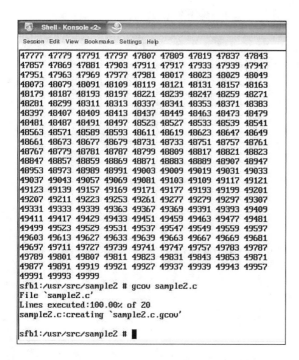

FIGURE 1.18
Running sample2 and getting gcov output.

Listing 1.10 shows gcov output for the sample2 program.

Listing 1.10

Output of sample2.c.gcov

```
    -:      0:Source:sample2.c
    -:      0:Graph:sample2.bbg
    -:      0:Data:sample2.da
    -:      1:#include <stdlib.h>
    -:      2:#include <stdio.h>
    -:      3:#include <math.h>
    -:      4:
    -:      5:int prime (int num);
    -:      6:int faster (int num);
    -:      7:
    -:      8:int main()
    1:      9:{
    1:     10:    int i;
    1:     11:    int colcnt = 0;
50000:     12:    for (i=2; i <= 50000; i++)
```

```
49999:    13:      if (prime(i)) {
 5133:    14:          colcnt++;
 5133:    15:          if (colcnt%9 == 0) {
  570:    16:printf("%5d\n",i);
  570:    17:colcnt = 0;
    -:    18:          }
    -:    19:      else
 4563:    20:         printf("%5d ", i);
    -:    21:      }
    1:    22:          putchar('\n');
    1:    23:          return 0;
    -:    24: }
    -:    25:
49999:    26:int prime (int num) {
    -:    27:      /* check to see if the number is a
               prime? */
49999:    28:      int i;
1061109:  29:      for (i=2; i <= faster(num); i++)
1055976:  30:      if (num %i == 0)
44866:    31:          return 0;
 5133:    32:      return 1;
    -:    33:      }
    -:    34:
    -:    35:int faster (int num)
1061109:  36: {
1061109:  37:  return (int) sqrt( (float) num);
    -:    38: }
    -:    39:
```

The **for** loop in the prime routine has been reduced from 121 million executions to 1 million executions. Therefore, the total time has been reduced from 103.74 seconds to 2.80 seconds.

The tools gprof and gcov helped find the "hot spots" in this sample program. After the "hot spots" were found, the program was changed to increase its overall performance. It is interesting how changing a few lines of code can have a great impact on a program's performance.

Listing 1.11, sample3.cpp, has three different functions (1, 2, and 3). It shows a more complex use of profiling, with both flat and graphic profiles. We'll also use kprof, which can use gprof output. It presents the information in list or tree views, which make the information easier to understand when programs are more complicated. Let's start by building the sample3.cpp program and displaying the flat and graphic profiles and then displaying the data using kprof.

Listing 1.11

sample3.cpp

```
1   #include <iostream>
2
3   void function1(){
4       for(int i=0;i<1000000;i++);
5   }
6
7   void function2(){
8       function1();
9       for (int i=0;i<2000000;i++);
10  }
11
12  void function3(){
13      function1();
14      function2();
15      for (int i=0;i<3000000;i++);
16          function1();
17  }
18
19  int main(){
20      for(int i=0;i<10;i++)
21      function1();
22
23      for (int i=0;i<5000000;i++);
24
25      for(int i=0;i<10;i++)
26          function2();
27          for(int i=0; i<13;i++);
28              {
29              function3();
30              function2();
31              function1();
32              }
33  }
```

Figure 1.19 shows the commands used to build and run the sample3 program. gprof is also run on sample3 to get the profile data from sample3.

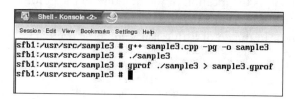

FIGURE 1.19
Building and capturing gprof output for sample3.

We won't use the **-b** option on the gprof output on the sample3 program so that we can see all the descriptive information that gprof can display.

The sample3.gprof should look similar to this:

```
Flat profile:
Each sample counts as 0.01 seconds.
%       cumulative    self                self     total
time    seconds       seconds   calls     ms/call  ms/call   name
43.36   4.21          4.21      12        0.35     0.52      function2()
42.84   8.37          4.16      25        0.17     0.17      function1()
 8.65   9.21          0.84                                   main
 5.15   9.71          0.50      1         0.50     1.35      function3()
 0.00   9.71          0.00      1         0.00     0.00      global constructors
                                                             keyed to function1()
 0.00   9.71          0.00      1         0.00     0.00
__static_initialization_and_destruction_0(int, int)
```

Field	Description
% time	The percentage of the program's total running time used by this function.
cumulative seconds	A running sum of the number of seconds accounted for by this function and those listed above it.
self seconds	The number of seconds accounted for by this function alone. This is the major sort for this listing.
calls	The number of times this function was invoked if this function is profiled; otherwise, it is blank.
self ms/call	The average number of milliseconds spent in this function per call if this function is profiled; otherwise, it is blank.
total ms/call	The average number of milliseconds spent in this function and its descendents per call if this function is profiled; otherwise, it is blank.
name	The function's name. This is the minor sort for this listing. The index shows the location of the function in the gprof listing. If the index is in parentheses, it shows where it would appear in the gprof listing if it were to be printed.

```
Call graph (explanation follows)
granularity: each sample hit covers 4 byte(s) for 0.10% of 9.71 seconds
index   % time  self    children    called      name
                                                <spontaneous>
[1]     100.0   0.84    8.87                    main [1]
                3.86    1.83        11/12           function2() [2]
```

```
                      1.83    0.00       11/25                   function1() [3]
                      0.50    0.85        1/1                    function3() [4]
           --------------------------------------
                      0.35    0.17        1/12                   function3() [4]
                      3.86    1.83       11/12                   main [1]
[2]        63.9       4.21    2.00       12           function2() [2]
                      2.00    0.00       12/25                   function1() [3]
           --------------------------------------
                      0.33    0.00        2/25                   function3() [4]
                      1.83    0.00       11/25                   main [1]
                      2.00    0.00       12/25                   function2() [2]
[3]        42.8       4.16    0.00       25           function1() [3]
           --------------------------------------
                      0.50    0.85        1/1                    main [1]
[4]        13.9       0.50    0.85        1            function3() [4]
                      0.35    0.17        1/12                   function2() [2]
                      0.33    0.00        2/25                   function1() [3]
           --------------------------------------
                      0.00    0.00        1/1                    __do_global_ctors_aux [13]
[11]        0.0       0.00    0.00        1            global constructors keyed to
function1() [11]
                      0.00    0.00        1/1
__static_initialization_and_destruction_0(int, int) [12]
           --------------------------------------
                      0.00    0.00        1/1                    global constructors keyed to
function1() [11]
[12]        0.0       0.00    0.00        0.00                   1
__static_initialization_and_destruction_0(int, int) [12]
           --------------------------------------
```

This table describes the program's call tree. It is sorted by the total amount of time spent in each function and its children.

Each entry in this table consists of several lines. The line with the index number at the left margin lists the current function. The lines above it list the functions that called this function, and the lines below it list the functions this one called.

You see the following:

Field	Description
index	A unique number given to each element of the table. Index numbers are sorted numerically. The index number is printed next to every function name so that it is easier to look up the function in the table.
% time	The percentage of the total time that was spent in this function and its children. Note that due to different viewpoints, functions excluded by options, and so on, these numbers *do not* add up to 100%.

Field	Description
self	The total amount of time spent in this function.
children	The total amount of time propagated into this function by its children.
called	The number of times the function was called. If the function called itself recursively, the number includes only nonrecursive calls and is followed by a + and the number of recursive calls.
name	The name of the current function. The index number is printed after it. If the function is a member of a cycle, the cycle number is printed between the function's name and the index number.

For the function's parents, the fields have the following meanings:

Field	Description
self	The amount of time that was propagated directly from the function into this parent.
children	The amount of time that was propagated from the function's children into this parent.
called	The number of times this parent called the function and the total number of times the function was called. Recursive calls to the function are not included in the number after the /.
name	The parent's name. The parent's index number is printed after it. If the parent is a member of a cycle, the cycle number is printed between the name and the index number.

If the function's parents cannot be determined, the word <spontaneous> is printed in the name field, and all the other fields are blank.

For the function's children, the fields have the following meanings:

Field	Description
self	The amount of time that was propagated directly from the child into the function.
children	The amount of time that was propagated from the child's children to the function.

| called | The number of times the function called this child and the total number of times the child was called. Recursive calls by the child are not listed in the number after the /. |
| name | The child's name. The child's index number is printed after it. If the child is a member of a cycle, the cycle number is printed between the name and the index number. |

If the call graph has any cycles (circles), there is an entry for the cycle as a whole. This entry shows who called the cycle (as parents) and the members of the cycle (as children). The + recursive calls entry shows how many function calls were internal to the cycle. The calls entry for each member shows, for that member, how many times it was called from other members of the cycle.

```
Index by function name
[11] global constructors keyed to function1() [3] function1() [4] function3()
[12] __static_initialization_and_destruction_0(int, int) [2] function2() [1]
main
```

kprof

kprof is a graphical tool that displays the execution profiling output generated by the gprof profiler. kprof presents the information in list or tree view, which makes the information easy to understand.

kprof has the following features:

- *Flat* profile view displays all functions and methods and their profiling information. (See Figure 1.22 for a view of this functionality.)

- *Hierarchical* profile view displays a tree for each function and method with the other functions and methods it calls as subelements. (See Figure 1.23 for a view of this functionality.)

- *Graph* view is a graphical representation of the call tree. It requires Graphviz to work. (See Figure 1.24 for a view of this functionality.)

- Right-clicking a function or method displays a pop-up with the *list of callers and called functions*. You can go to one of these functions directly by selecting it in the pop-up menu. (See Figure 1.22 for a view of this functionality.)

Installation

We've nstalled the kprof-1.4.2-196.i586.rpm that comes with the distribution. The following **rpm** command displays the version of the kprof application:

```
% rpm -qf /opt/kde3/bin/kprof

kprof-1.4.2-196
```

Building Graphviz, the Graph Feature

kprof supports a graph feature, but before it can be used, the Graphviz program must be built. See the Graphviz URL in the section "Web Resources for Profiling" at the end of this chapter to download the source code for Graphviz.

The version of source code for Graphviz that will be built for this section is version 1.12. The tar file graphviz-1.12.tar.gz can be downloaded.

The next steps expand the source tree. Then, using the **make** and **make install** commands, the program is built and installed to the proper location on your system, as shown in Figure 1.20.

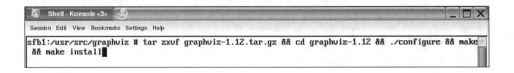

FIGURE 1.20
Building and installing Graphviz.

After Graphviz is installed, kprof uses it to create the Graph View that can be seen in Figure 1.24.

To use kprof, the **-b** option is needed. The following command uses gprof with the **-b** option on the sample3 program. gprof's output is saved to the sample3.prof1 file:

```
% gprof -b sample3 >sample3.prof1
```

The next step is to start kprof:

```
% kprof
```

After kprof loads, select File, Open to bring the sample3 gprof output into kprof. Figure 1.21 shows the open dialog box.

FIGURE 1.21
The open dialog box.

Figure 1.22 shows the flat profile view of the sample3 program. This screen shot also shows that function1 is called by function2, function3, and main.

Function/Method	Count	Total (s)	%	Self (s)	Total ms/call	Self ms/call	
__static_initialization...	1	9.700	0.000	0.000	0.000	0.000	
function1	25	8.360	42.780	4.150	0.170		Called By
function2	12	4.210	43.400	4.210	0.520		function3()
function3	1	9.700	5.150	0.500	1.350		main
global constructors k...	1	9.700	0.000	0.000	0.000		function2()
main	0	9.200	8.660	0.840	0.000		

FIGURE 1.22
The flat profile view.

Figure 1.23 shows the hierarchical profile view of the sample3 program.

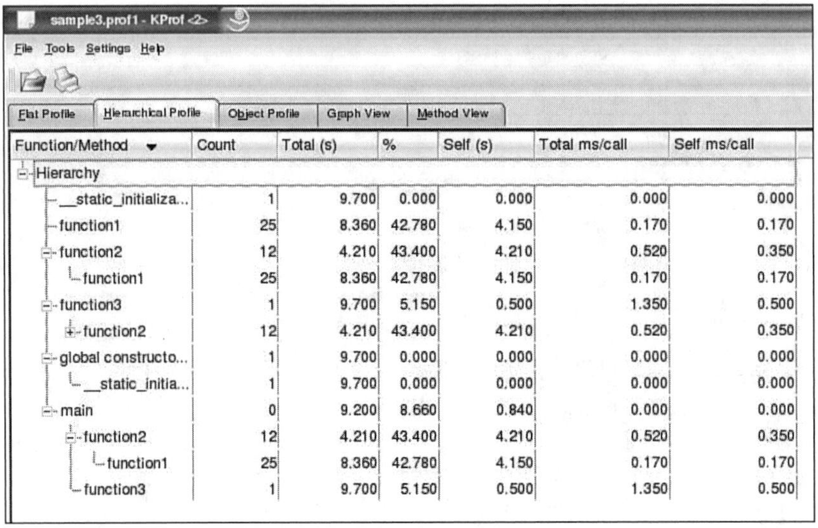

FIGURE 1.23
The hierarchical profile view.

Figure 1.24 shows the graph view of the sample3 program. The graph view uses Graphviz. This view shows that function1 is called by main, function2, and function3. It also shows that function2 is called by main and function3 and that function3 is called only by main.

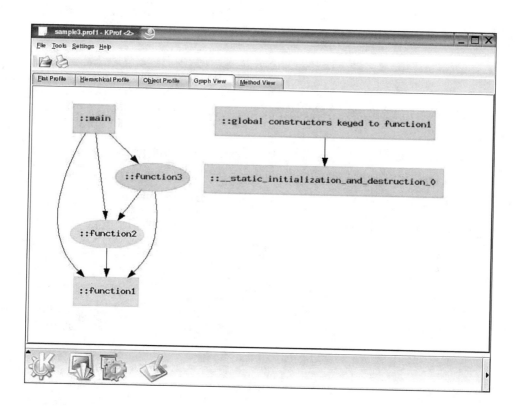

FIGURE 1.24
The graph view.

Summary

This chapter covered five methods of timing programs or functions inside of programs. The first three methods were **stopwatch**, **date**, and **time**. These three methods are ways to measure the total time that the program takes to execute. These methods require no modifications to the program to measure the time spent by the program. The **clock** and **gettimeofday** routines can be added to parts of a program to measure the time spent doing a section of the program. Finally, the gprof profiler and kprof can be used to profile sample programs.

Web Resources for Profiling

URL	Description
http://www.gnu.org/software/binutils/manual/ gprof-2.9.1/gprof.html	Documentation for gprof
http://kprof.sourceforge.net/	kprof home page
http://www.research.att.com/sw/tools/graphviz/ download.html	graphviz home page
http://samba.org/ftp/tridge/dbench/	dbench download page

Chapter 2

Code Coverage

In this chapter

- What Is Code Coverage Analysis?   page 38
- gcov Can't Find Logic Errors   page 39
- Types of Code Coverage   page 40
- gcc Options Needed for gcov   page 41
- Summary   page 52
- Web Resource for gcov   page 52

Before releasing any code, developers usually test their work to tune performance and prove that the software works as intended. But often, validation is quite difficult, even if the application is simple.

For example, the venerable UNIX/Linux ls utility is conceptually quite simple, yet its many options and the myriad vagaries of the underlying file system make validating ls quite a challenge.

To help validate the operation of their code, developers often rely on test suites to either simulate or re-create operational scenarios. If the test suite is thorough, all the code's features can be exercised and be shown to work.

But how thorough is thorough? In theory, a completely thorough test suite would test all circumstances, validate all the results, and exercise every single line of code, demonstrating that no code is "dead." Dead code is a favorite hiding place for pesky bugs. Results can be validated in any number of ways, because output typically is tangible in one form or another, but how is it possible to make sure that all your code was executed? Use GNU's gcov.

Like an X-ray machine, gcov peers into your code and reports on its inner workings. And gcov is easy to use. You simply compile your code with gcc and two extra options, and your code automatically generates data that highlights statement-by-statement runtime coverage. Best of all, gcov is readily available: if gcc is installed, gcov is also available, because gcov is a standard part of the GNU development tools.

The next section looks at code coverage analysis and shows you how to use gcov to improve the quality of your code and the quality and thoroughness of your test suites.

What Is Code Coverage Analysis?

As mentioned, it's ideal to find dead code and get rid of it. In some cases, it's appropriate to remove dead code because it's unneeded or obsolete. Dead code can't cause a programming error, but it's a good idea to find code that can no longer be executed and remove it. Removing the dead code increases the source code's readability.

In other cases, the test suite itself may have to be expanded to be more thorough. *Code coverage analysis* is the (often iterative) process of finding and targeting "dead" or unexercised code. It's characterized by the following steps:

1. Find the areas of a program not exercised by the test suite.

2. Create additional test cases to exercise the code, thereby increasing code coverage.

3. Determine a quantitative measure of code coverage, which is an indirect measure of the program's quality.

Code coverage analysis is also useful to identify which test cases are appropriate to run when changes are made to a program and to identify which test cases do not increase coverage.

gcov Can't Find Logic Errors

Unfortunately, code coverage analysis doesn't find logic errors. Consider the following code:

```
10:  rc = call_to_xx ();
11:  if (rc == ERROR_FATAL)
12:    exit(2);    /* exit with error code 2 */
13:  else
14:    /* continue on */
```

When the code coverage was checked for this snippet of code, the output from the test coverage tool stated that line 11 was never true, so the exit with error code 2 wasn't tested. The apparently obvious test case to write is a scenario in which the operation fails with ERROR_FATAL. That seems to be sufficient—*unless* the call to call_to_xx routine returns other error conditions. For example, if call_to_xx returns ERROR_HANDLE, the new test would not cover the code completely.

Instead, the code should have been written to handle both error conditions— ERROR_FATAL and ERROR_HANDLE:

```
10:  rc  = call_to_xx ();
11:  if (rc == ERROR_FATAL)
12:    exit(2);    /* exit with error code 2 */
13:  else if (rc == ERROR_HANDLE)
14:    /* handle this error condition */
15:  else
16:    /* continue on */
```

The test suite should check that the code handles ERROR_HANDLE correctly. But no test does that for this error condition.

No test coverage tool will tell you that this is needed. It can't. The test coverage tool can only identify the coverage on the existing code.

Types of Code Coverage

gcov can measure many different types of code coverage. This section briefly discusses the most common and useful two: branch coverage and loop coverage.

Branch coverage verifies that every branch has been taken in all directions. Similarly, *loop coverage* tries to verify that all paths through a loop have been tried. Loop coverage sounds complex, but it can be done by satisfying just three conditions:

- The loop condition yields false, so the body is not executed.

- The loop condition is true the first time and then is false, so the body is executed only once.

- The loop condition is true at least two times, causing the loop to execute twice.

For example, in the following code snippet:

```
routine Example_function(number)
{
  if (number % 2) == 0)
    printf("even \n");
  for (;number < 9; number++){
    printf("number is %d\n", number);
  }
}
```

the **if** statement must be tested with both odd and even numbers. The **for** statement must be tested with two numbers, such that the condition (**number < 9**) is true and false, respectively. Therefore, the following three tests would achieve complete test coverage for the routine just shown:

```
Example_function(11);
Example_function(6);
Example_function(8);
```

Figure 2.1 shows the steps of creating gcov output.

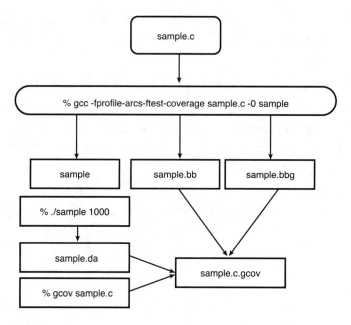

FIGURE 2.1
The steps to create gcov output.

gcc Options Needed for gcov

Before programs can use gcov, they must be compiled with two gcc options: **–fprofile-arcs** and **–ftest-coverage**. These options cause the compiler to insert additional code into the object files.

With **-fprofile-arcs**, gcc creates a program flow graph for each function of a program and then finds a spanning tree for the graph. Only arcs that are not on the spanning tree have to be instrumented: the compiler adds code to count how many times these arcs are executed. When an arc is the only exit or only entrance to a block, the instrumentation code can be added to the block; otherwise, a new basic block must be created to hold the instrumentation code.

Then, when the code runs, it generates two files—*sourcename*.bb and *source-name*.bbg, where *sourcename* is the name of your source code file.

The *.bb file has a list of source files, functions within the file, and line numbers corresponding to each block in the source file. The *.bbg file contains a list of the program flow arcs for all the functions.

Executing a gcov-enabled program also causes the dumping of counter information into a *sourcename*.da file when the program exits.

gcov uses the *.bbg, *.bb, and *.da files to reconstruct program flow and create a listing of the code that highlights how many times each line was executed. Let's try using gcov on the sample.c program.

Compile the file sample.c, shown in Listing 2.1, with the options **–fprofile-arcs**, **–ftest-coverage**, and **–g**. The **-g** option allows the program to be debugged using the gdb debugger.

Listing 2.1

sample.c: a Test Program

```
1   #include <stdlib.h>
2   #include <stdio.h>
3
4
5
6   int main(argc, argv)
7        int argc;
8        char **argv;
9   {
10  int x, y;
11  int arraysize;
12  int **array;
13  if (argc != 2) {
14    printf("Usage: %s Enter arraysize value \n",argv[0]);
15    exit(-1);
16
17  }
18  else {
19    arraysize = atoi (argv[1]);
20    if (arraysize <= 0) {
21      printf("Array size must be larger than 0 \n");
22      exit(-1);
23    }
```

```
24  }
25
26  array = (int **) malloc (arraysize*sizeof (int *));
27
28  printf("Creating an %d by %d array \n", arraysize,
       arraysize);
29
30  if (array == NULL) {
31    printf("Malloc failed for array size %d \n", arraysize);
32    exit(-1);
33  }
34  for (x=0; x < arraysize; x++) {
35    array[x] = (int *) malloc (arraysize*sizeof (int));
36    if (array[x] == NULL) {
37      printf("Failed malloc for array size %d \n",
         arraysize);
38      exit(-1);
39    }
40  }
41
42
43    exit(0);
44  }
```

Figure 2.2 shows the sample.c program.

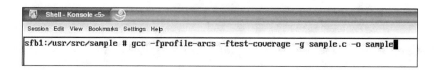

FIGURE 2.2
Building the sample.c program.

Now you're ready to see how much coverage each test case provides. Run the sample application with an input of 1000.

As shown in Figure 2.3, the application says "Creating an 1000 by 1000 array" and creates a new file called sample.da. Next, run gcov on the source code. (If your application has more than one source file, run gcov on all the source files.)

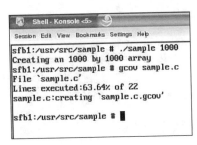

FIGURE 2.3
Creating an 1000 by 1000 array.

The input of 1000 gives the sample program 63.64% of coverage. So the main line path through the sample program is about 63% of the code.

The gcov command also creates the file sample.c.gcov, shown in Listing 2.2. In the listing, a ##### marker indicates that the associated line of source code hasn't been executed.

Listing 2.2

sample.c.gcov After Running the Application with Input 1000

```
    -:      0:Source:sample.c
    -:      0:Graph:sample.bbg
    -:      0:Data:sample.da
    -:      1:
    -:      2:#include <stdlib.h>
    -:      3:#include <stdio.h>
    -:      4:
    -:      5:
    -:      6:
    -:      7:int main(argc, argv)
    -:      8:    int argc;
    -:      9:    char **argv;
    1:     10:{
    1:     11:  int x, y;
    1:     12:  int arraysize;
    1:     13:  int **array;
    1:     14:  if (argc != 2) {
#####:     15:    printf("Usage: %s Enter arraysize value
                      \n",argv[0]);
#####:     16:    exit(-1);
```

```
  -  :  17:
  -  :  18:  }
  -  :  19:  else {
  1  :  20:    arraysize = atoi (argv[1]);
  1  :  21:    if (arraysize <= 0) {
#####:  22:      printf("Array size must be larger than 0
             \n");
#####:  23:      exit(-1);
  -  :  24:    }
  -  :  25:  }
  -  :  26:
  1  :  27:  array = (int **) malloc (arraysize*sizeof
             (int *));
  -  :  28:
  1  :  29:  printf("Creating an %d by %d array \n",
             arraysize, arraysize);
  -  :  30:
  1  :  31:  if (array == NULL) {
#####:  32:    printf("Malloc failed for array size %d
             \n", arraysize);
#####:  33:    exit(-1);
  -  :  34:  }
1001 :  35:  for (x=0; x < arraysize; x++) {
1000 :  36:    array[x] = (int *) malloc (arraysize*sizeof
             (int));
1000 :  37:    if (array[x] == NULL) {
#####:  38:      printf("Failed malloc for array size %d
             \n", arraysize);
#####:  39:      exit(-1);
  -  :  40:    }
  -  :  41:  }
  -  :  42:
  -  :  43:
  1  :  44:    exit(0);
  -  :  45:}
```

Next, run the sample program with no input, and then run gcov again, as shown in Figure 2.4.

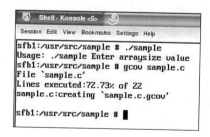

FIGURE 2.4

Running the sample program again.

The no input case gives the sample program 81.82% of coverage, as shown in Figure 2.5. The gcov runs are cumulative. You can see that after three runs the percentage of coverage is 81.82%. So the no input case has bumped up the coverage by 9.09% (81.82 – 72.73 = 9.09).

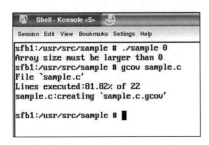

FIGURE 2.5
81.82% coverage.

Now run the sample program with the parameter 0, and run gcov again.

Now comes the interesting part of testing this program. There are two **malloc()** error conditions; both must be tested to get 100% coverage of this code. Let's use the gdb debugger to simulate the **malloc()** failures. Let's set a break point and then create each error condition. The following gdb commands create the first error condition, as shown in Figures 2.6 and 2.7. For additional information about gdb, see Chapter 3, "GNU Debugger (gdb)."

- The **list** command displays the source code for sample program. The **list** command is entered three times.

- The **break 30** command sets the break point on line 30.

- The **run 1** command starts the program executing with 1 as the input to the program.

- The **print array** command shows the value of the **array** variable, which in this example is 0x804c050.

- The **set array=0** command sets the value of the **array** variable to 0.

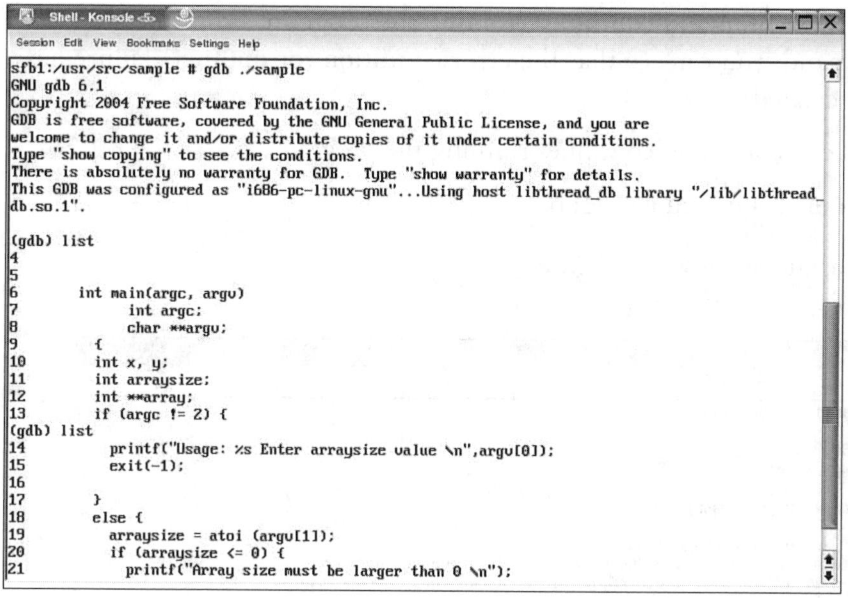

FIGURE 2.6
The sample program.

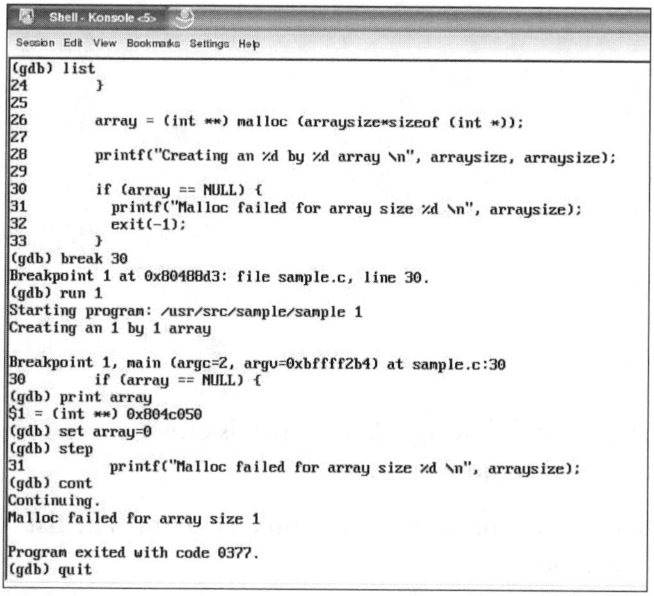

FIGURE 2.7
The sample program (continued).

- The **step** command continues running the program. From the **step** command, you can see that the error condition for **malloc()** failure has been created.
- The **cont** command continues running the program.
- The **quit** command ends gdb.

Run gcov again, as shown in Figure 2.8.

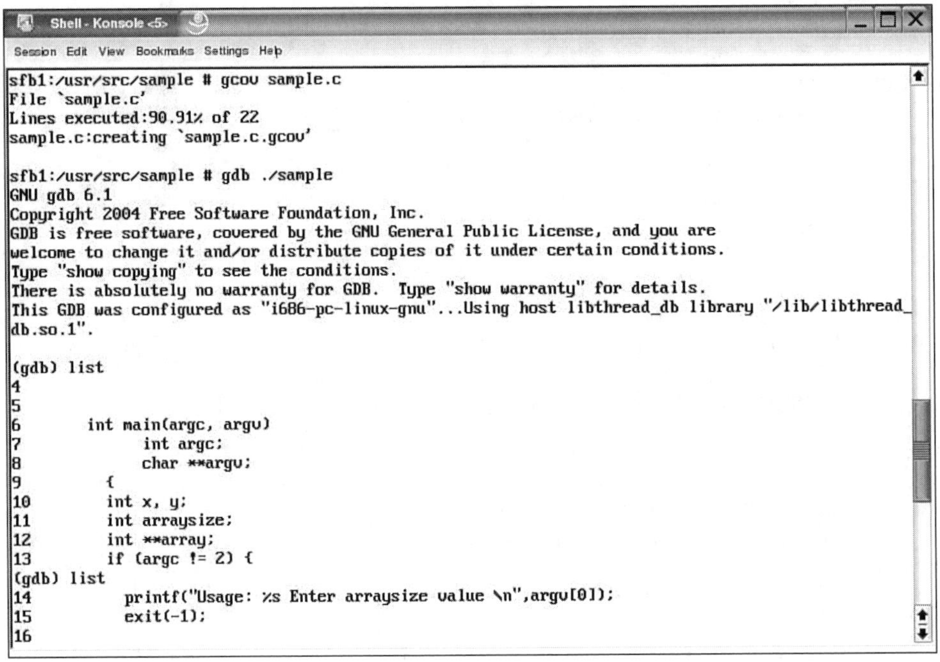


```
sfb1:/usr/src/sample # gcov sample.c
File `sample.c'
Lines executed:90.91% of 22
sample.c:creating `sample.c.gcov'

sfb1:/usr/src/sample # gdb ./sample
GNU gdb 6.1
Copyright 2004 Free Software Foundation, Inc.
GDB is free software, covered by the GNU General Public License, and you are
welcome to change it and/or distribute copies of it under certain conditions.
Type "show copying" to see the conditions.
There is absolutely no warranty for GDB.  Type "show warranty" for details.
This GDB was configured as "i686-pc-linux-gnu"...Using host libthread_db library "/lib/libthread_
db.so.1".

(gdb) list
4
5
6       int main(argc, argv)
7            int argc;
8            char **argv;
9         {
10        int x, y;
11        int arraysize;
12        int **array;
13        if (argc != 2) {
(gdb) list
14          printf("Usage: %s Enter arraysize value \n",argv[0]);
15          exit(-1);
16
```

FIGURE 2.8
Running gcov again.

One more test needs to be run. The following gdb commands create the second error condition, as shown in Figures 2.8 through 2.10:

- The **list** command displays the source code for sample program. The **list** command is entered four times.
- The **break 36** command sets the break point on line 36.

- The **run 1** command starts the program executing with 1 as the input to the program.

- The **print array[0]** command shows the value of the **array** variable, which in this example is 0x804c060.

- The **set array[0]=0** command sets the value of the **array** variable to 0.

- The **step** command continues running the program. From the **step** command you can see that the error condition for **malloc()** failure has been created.

- The **cont** command continues running the program.

- The **quit** command ends gdb.

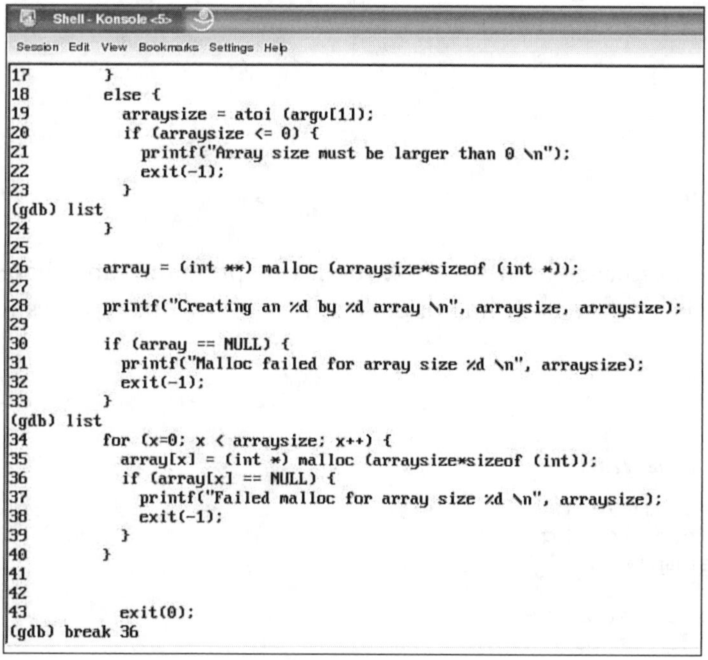

```
Shell - Konsole <5>

Session  Edit  View  Bookmarks  Settings  Help
17              }
18              else {
19                  arraysize = atoi (argv[1]);
20                  if (arraysize <= 0) {
21                      printf("Array size must be larger than 0 \n");
22                      exit(-1);
23                  }
(gdb) list
24              }
25
26              array = (int **) malloc (arraysize*sizeof (int *));
27
28              printf("Creating an %d by %d array \n", arraysize, arraysize);
29
30              if (array == NULL) {
31                  printf("Malloc failed for array size %d \n", arraysize);
32                  exit(-1);
33              }
(gdb) list
34              for (x=0; x < arraysize; x++) {
35                  array[x] = (int *) malloc (arraysize*sizeof (int));
36                  if (array[x] == NULL) {
37                      printf("Failed malloc for array size %d \n", arraysize);
38                      exit(-1);
39                  }
40              }
41
42
43              exit(0);
(gdb) break 36
```

FIGURE 2.9

Running gcov again (continued).

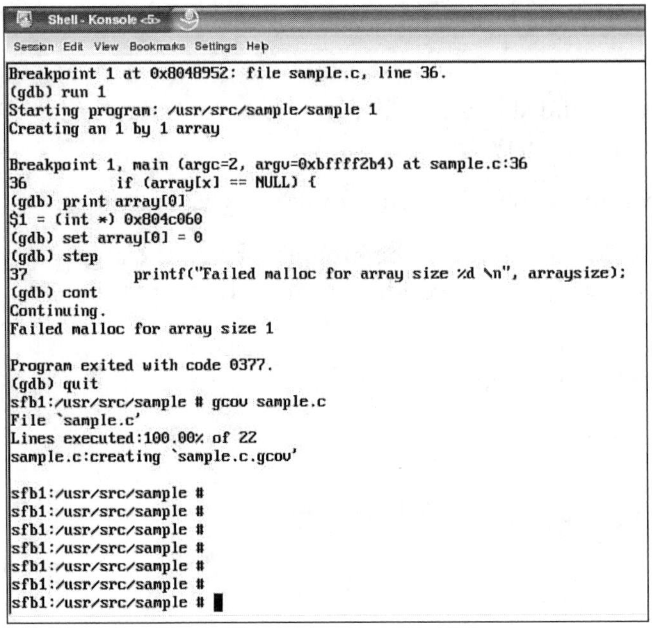

FIGURE 2.10
Running gcov again (continued).

Listing 2.3 shows no lines flagged with #####, so all this program's lines have been executed. The number before each line of code tells you how many times it was executed.

Listing 2.3

sample.c.gcov After the Five Tests

```
        -:      0:Source:sample.c
        -:      0:Graph:sample.bbg
        -:      0:Data:sample.da
        -:      1:
        -:      2:#include <stdlib.h>
        -:      3:#include <stdio.h>
        -:      4:
        -:      5:
        -:      6:
        -:      7:int main(argc, argv)
        -:      8:    int argc;
        -:      9:    char **argv;
```

```
    5:    10:{
    5:    11:    int x, y;
    5:    12:    int arraysize;
    5:    13:    int **array;
    5:    14:    if (argc != 2) {
    1:    15:       printf("Usage: %s Enter arraysize value
                    \n",argv[0]);
    1:    16:       exit(-1);
    -:    17:
    -:    18:    }
    -:    19:    else {
    4:    20:       arraysize = atoi (argv[1]);
    4:    21:       if (arraysize <= 0) {
    1:    22:          printf("Array size must be larger than 0
                       \n");
    1:    23:          exit(-1);
    -:    24:       }
    -:    25:    }
    -:    26:
    3:    27:    array = (int **) malloc (arraysize*sizeof (int
                 *));
    -:    28:
    3:    29:    printf("Creating an %d by %d array \n", array
                 size, arraysize);
    -:    30:
    3:    31:    if (array == NULL) {
    1:    32:       printf("Malloc failed for array size %d \n",
                    arraysize);
    1:    33:       exit(-1);
    -:    34:    }
 1002:    35:    for (x=0; x < arraysize; x++) {
 1001:    36:       array[x] = (int *) malloc (arraysize*sizeof
                    (int));
 1001:    37:       if (array[x] == NULL) {
    1:    38:          printf("Failed malloc for array size %d
                       \n", arraysize);
    1:    39:          exit(-1);
    -:    40:       }
    -:    41:    }
    -:    42:
    -:    43:
    1:    44:       exit(0);
    -:    45:}
```

Summary

gcov determines how well your test suites exercise your code. One indirect benefit of gcov is that its output can be used to identify which test case provides coverage for each source file. With that information, you can select a subset of the test suite to validate changes in the program. Thorough code coverage during testing is one measurement of software quality.

Web Resource for gcov

URL	Description
http://gcc.gnu.org/onlinedocs/gcc/Gcov.html#Gcov	Documentation for gcov

## Chapter 3

GNU Debugger (gdb)

In this chapter

- Installing gdb — page 55
- gdb Commands — page 56
- Compiling a Program That Is to Be Debugged with gdb — page 59
- A Typical gdb Session — page 60
- Debugging Using a Core File — page 63
- Running the Program and Getting the Core Dump — page 64
- Graphical gdb Interfaces — page 65
- Data Display Debugger — page 66
- Insight — page 70
- Debugging Symbols Increase the Executable's Size — page 77
- Debugging Techniques — page 78
- Summary — page 80
- Web Resources for GNU Debugger — page 80

The very basic debug method is adding **printf**() statements to a program. This method can work in several types of problems that need to be debugged. One issue with debugging with **printf**() is that it is very time-consuming. A debugger like gdb lets you view the program in a more expedited way.

The purpose of the GNU debugger, gdb, is to examine what is going on inside a program that needs to be debugged. gdb provides a text-based user interface, and it can be used to debug programs written in several languages (C, C++, and others). Graphical user interfaces (GUIs) can be used with gdb. Two of the GUIs for gdb are Data Display Debugger (ddd) and Insight. Both are covered in this chapter.

The gdb source-code debugger is available for Linux and other UNIXs. gdb can be used to perform the following operations, which are helpful in the process of debugging a compiled program:

- **Setting break points:** Program execution can be temporarily suspended at specified points (called break points). At a break point the program is stopped, and specific values can be displayed to determine their correctness. Upon program suspension, the programmer can interact with gdb and use its full set of commands to investigate the performance of the executing program before resuming program execution. A break point can be conditional. For example, if you want to see how a loop runs when hi-lo is 1, you tell gdb to break when **lo==(hi-1)**. The command to do this is as follows:

    ```
    (gdb) condition 1 lo==(hi-1)
    ```

- **Hardware watch points**: Some processors can use the hardware to watch a small set of memory locations to see when they change. Since the checking is done by hardware, the program runs at full speed until the memory location is modified. At this point the debugger stops and tells you which instruction modified which memory address and what the old and new values are for that address. As an example, assume you want to know when the low-memory global **TheMem** is changing. Here is how it might look under gdb:

    ```
    (gdb) watch TheMem
    Hardware watchpoint 1: TheMem
    (gdb) c
    Continuing.
    Hardware watchpoint 1: TheMem
    ```

```
Old value = 0
New value = 768
C_FirstMenu (mid=3) at menu1.c:577
```

At the first (gdb) prompt, you tell gdb that you want to be alerted whenever the expression **TheMem** changes. gdb watches that expression with a hardware watch point, so it assigns watch point 1 to the task.

- **Displaying program values and attributes:** gdb can be instructed to display the current contents of variables as the program executes.

- **Step through a program line by line:** Each line of the executable program can be executed one line at a time.

- **Stack frame:** Each time a program performs a function call, the information about where in your program the call was made from is saved in a block of data called a *stack frame*, or *frame* for short. Each frame is the data associated with one call to one function. The frame contains the arguments given to the function, the function's local variables, and the address where the function is executing. All the stack frames are allocated in a region of memory called the *call stack*. The basic commands to operate frames are **frame**, **info frame**, and **backtrace**.

You can tell GDB to switch from frame 0 to frame 1 using the **frame** command with the frame number as the argument. This gives you access to the variables in frame 1. As you can guess, after switching frames, you can't access variables stored in frame 0.

The gdb package comes with information on all the features. You can view this information by typing **info gdb** after the gdb package has been installed. The debugger also comes with a quick reference card in the file gdb-x.x/doc/refcard.ps.

Installing gdb

gdb is generally distributed as source code, archived, and compressed into a single file using the tar and gzip utilities. Once the source code is in hand, the user typically decompresses, configures, compiles, and installs the programs. Most, if not all, Linux distributions ship a version of the gdb package, but the steps to install and build it are listed here.

Figure 3.1 shows all the steps to decompress and then build and install gdb.

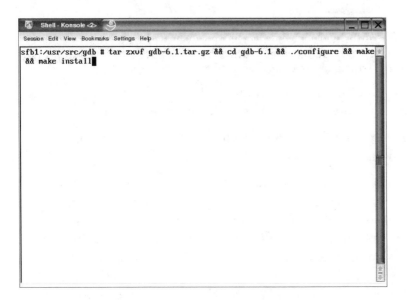

FIGURE 3.1
Building gdb.

gdb Commands

gdb can start to debug an application by using the command **gdb executable_file name**. gdb loads the executable's symbols. Then the display prompt is available to start using the debugger.

There are three ways to view a process with this debugger:

- Use the **attach** command to view a running process. **attach** stops the process.

- Use the **run** command to start the program.

- Look at an existing core file to determine the state the process was in when it crashed or was killed. To view a core file, start gdb with the command **gdb executable_file corefile**.

Before the program is run or before attaching it to a running program, list the source code where the bug is believed to be, and then set break points to start debugging the program. The "Debugging with gdb" link listed in the "Web

Resources for GNU Debugger" section at the end of this chapter contains a detailed tutorial on using gdb. gdb also includes extensive online help, which you can view using the **help** command.

Some Useful gdb Commands

Many gdb commands have abbreviations, as shown in the following list:

Command	Abbreviation	Description
attach	at	Attaches to a running process.
backtrace	bt	Prints a stack trace.
break	b	Sets a break point.
clear		Clears a break point.
continue	c	Allows the program to continue executing.
delete		Clears a break point by number.
detach		Detaches from the currently attached process.
display		Displays the value of an expression every time execution stops.
finish		Runs to the end of the function and displays return values of that function.
help		Displays help for gdb commands.
jump		Jumps to an address and continues the execution there.
listl		Lists the next 10 lines.
next	n	Steps to the next machine language instruction.
print	p	Prints the value of an expression.
run	r	Runs the current program from the start.
set		Changes the value of a variable.
step	s	Steps the program instruction by instruction.
where	w	Prints a stack trace.

Listing 3.1 has an error built into it to demonstrate some of gdb's features. Let's run the gdb-sample1 program without the debugger and see the error message. Figure 3.2 shows the building of gdb-sample1 and running the program without using gdb.

Listing 3.1

Sample Program (gdb-sample1.c)

```
1   int Change_Value = 0;
2
3   int  Sum_it (int, int);
4   void error_with_code (void);
5
6   /***************************************/
7   /*                                     */
8   /* main () - main routine              */
9   /*                                     */
10  /***************************************/
11
12  int main (void)
13  {
14      int Arg_1 = 20, Arg_2 = 40;
15      int i;
16
17
18      for (i = 0; i < 10; i++) {
19          if (Arg_1 > Arg_2)
20              Arg_2 = Sum_it (Arg_1, Arg_2);
21          else
22              Arg_1 = Sum_it (Arg_1, Arg_2);
23      }
24
25      error_with_code ();
26
27  }   /* End of main() */
28
29
30  /******************************************************/
31  /*                                                    */
32  /* Sum_it() - This routine adds two numbers and returns the
result */
33  /*                                                    */
34  /******************************************************/
35  int Sum_it (int a, int b)
36
37  {
38      return a+b;
39
40  } /* End of Sum_it */
41
42
43
44  /******************************************************/
45  /*                                                    */
46  /* error_with_code() - This routine has an intended bug.
*/
```

```
47 /*
*/
48
/**************************************************************
*/
49 void error_with_code(void)
50 {
51    int divide_value;
52    int result;
53
54    divide_value = Change_Value;
55    result = 10 / divide_value;
56    return ;
57
58 } /* End of error_with_code() */
```

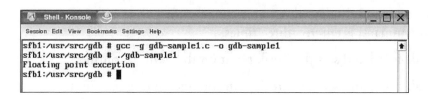

FIGURE 3.2
Building and running gdb-sample1.c.

Compiling a Program That Is to Be Debugged with gdb

The source code of the program that is to be debugged using gdb must first be successfully compiled. Once the program source code compiles successfully, compile it one more time using the **-g** compiler option:

```
g++ -g source_code_file.cpp
```

or

```
gcc -g source_code_file.c
```

> NOTE   g++ is the GNU C++ compiler, and gcc is the GNU C compiler.

Using the **-g** compiler option causes the compiler to build special symbols and tables of data that gdb needs for subsequent debugging.

A Typical gdb Session

Invoking the gdb Debugger

After compiling the source code file with the **-g** option, you are ready to use gdb and start debugging the program. To invoke gdb enter

```
gdb executable_file
```

where *executable_file* is the name of the compiled executable form of the program (which is a.out unless you have changed its name).

Now let's look at the sample program gdb-sample1.c using gdb. Figures 3.3 through 3.5 show the starting of gdb and the following gdb commands:

- The **list** command displays the source code for the gdb-sample1 program. The **list** command is entered three times.

- The **break** command sets the break point on the **Sum_it** routine.

- The **break** command sets the break point on line 26 of gdb-sample1.

- The **run** command starts the program executing. The break point at the **Sum_it** routine is hit.

- The **backtrace** command shows the back trace of where the **Sum_it** routine is called from. In this case it is called from line 40 of main. The **Sum_it** parameters are a = 20 and b = 40.

- The **delete** command removes the first break point on the **Sum_it** routine.

- The **cont** command starts the program executing until the second break point at line 26 is hit.

- The **cont** command starts the program executing until the program has Arithmetic exception on line 57.

- The **print** command displays the variable **divide_value**, which has a value of 0. The error in the program is caused by trying to divide 10 by 0 and store that result in a variable called **result**.

- The **print** command displays the **Change_Value** variable.

- The **run** command starts the program again. The program stops when it hits the break point on the **error_with_code** routine.

- The **set** command changes the variable **Change_Value** to the correct value of 10. This is how the program should have been coded.

- The **s** command steps one line of code.

- The **print** command displays the value of the **result** variable, which is 1.

- The **cont** command continues running the program.

- The **quit** command exits gdb.

```
Shell - Konsole <2>
Session  Edit  View  Bookmarks  Settings  Help
sfb1:/usr/src/gdb # gdb gdb-sample1
GNU gdb 6.1
Copyright 2004 Free Software Foundation, Inc.
GDB is free software, covered by the GNU General Public License, and you are
welcome to change it and/or distribute copies of it under certain conditions.
Type "show copying" to see the conditions.
There is absolutely no warranty for GDB.  Type "show warranty" for details.
This GDB was configured as "i686-pc-linux-gnu"...Using host libthread_db library
 "/lib/libthread_db.so.1".

(gdb) list
6
7       /*********************************************************************/
8       /*                                                                 */
9       /* main () - main routine                                          */
10      /*                                                                 */
11      /*********************************************************************/
12
13      int main ()
14      {
15          int Arg_1 = 20, Arg_2 = 40;
(gdb) list
16          int i;
17
18
19          for (i = 0; i < 10; i++) {
20              if (Arg_1 > Arg_2)
21                  Arg_2 = Sum_it (Arg_1, Arg_2);
22              else
23                  Arg_1 = Sum_it (Arg_1, Arg_2);
```

FIGURE 3.3
gdb-sample1 gdb commands.

```
 Shell - Konsole <2>
Session  Edit  View  Bookmarks  Settings  Help
24              }
25
(gdb) list
26              error_with_code ();
27
28       }  /* End of main() */
29
30
31
32       /**********************************************************************/
33       /*                                                                  */
34       /* Sum_it() - This routine adds two numbers and returns the result.*/
35       /*                                                                  */
(gdb) break Sum_it
Breakpoint 1 at 0x804837c: file gdb-sample1.c, line 40.
(gdb) break 26
Breakpoint 2 at 0x8048372: file gdb-sample1.c, line 26.
(gdb) run
Starting program: /usr/src/gdb/gdb-sample1

Breakpoint 1, Sum_it (a=20, b=40) at gdb-sample1.c:40
40              return a+b;
(gdb) backtrace
#0  Sum_it (a=20, b=40) at gdb-sample1.c:40
#1  0x08048365 in main () at gdb-sample1.c:23
(gdb) delete 1
(gdb) cont
Continuing.

Breakpoint 2, main () at gdb-sample1.c:26
```

FIGURE 3.4

gdb-sample1 gdb commands.

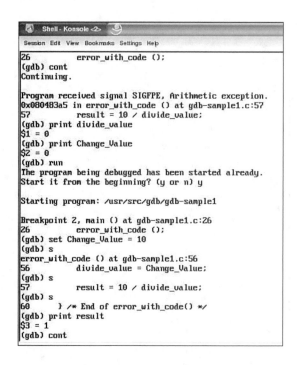

```
26            error_with_code ();
(gdb) cont
Continuing.

Program received signal SIGFPE, Arithmetic exception.
0x080483a5 in error_with_code () at gdb-sample1.c:57
57            result = 10 / divide_value;
(gdb) print divide_value
$1 = 0
(gdb) print Change_Value
$2 = 0
(gdb) run
The program being debugged has been started already.
Start it from the beginning? (y or n) y

Starting program: /usr/src/gdb/gdb-sample1

Breakpoint 2, main () at gdb-sample1.c:26
26            error_with_code ();
(gdb) set Change_Value = 10
(gdb) s
error_with_code () at gdb-sample1.c:56
56            divide_value = Change_Value;
(gdb) s
57            result = 10 / divide_value;
(gdb) s
60      } /* End of error_with_code() */
(gdb) print result
$3 = 1
(gdb) cont
```

FIGURE 3.5
gdb-sample1 gdb commands.

Debugging Using a Core File

For a user mode application to be able to create a core file, the system limit on the size of the core files must be greater than 0.

The default core file size is 0. When the core file size is 0, the system does not allow a core dump. Figure 3.6 shows that the core file size is 0 using the **ulimit** command with the -a option. To change the core file to 500,000, use the **ulimit -c** option.

FIGURE 3.6
Viewing and changing the core file size.

Running the Program and Getting the Core Dump

Now that core dump functionality has been enabled, Figure 3.7 shows debugging the gdb-sample1 program with a core file. The first step is to use gdb-sample1 as the program to be debugged. The next command, **core-file**, says to use the file named core as the core dump. The gdb session using the core dump file identifies that the error occurred in routine **error_with_code** at line 57. Next, looking at the variable **divide_value**, you see that it has a value of 0, which is the reason this program took the Arithmetic exception on line 57. The program is doing a divide by 0.

```
Shell - Konsole <2>
Session  Edit  View  Bookmarks  Settings  Help
sfb1:/usr/src/gdb # gdb
GNU gdb 6.1
Copyright 2004 Free Software Foundation, Inc.
GDB is free software, covered by the GNU General Public License, and you are
welcome to change it and/or distribute copies of it under certain conditions.
Type "show copying" to see the conditions.
There is absolutely no warranty for GDB.  Type "show warranty" for details.
This GDB was configured as "i686-pc-linux-gnu".
(gdb) file gdb-sample1
Reading symbols from gdb-sample1...done.
Using host libthread_db library "/lib/libthread_db.so.1".
(gdb) core-file core
Core was generated by `./gdb-sample1'.
Program terminated with signal 8, Arithmetic exception.
warning: current_sos: Can't read pathname for load map: Input/output error

Reading symbols from /lib/i686/libc.so.6...done.
Loaded symbols for /lib/i686/libc.so.6
Reading symbols from /lib/ld-linux.so.2...done.
Loaded symbols for /lib/ld-linux.so.2
#0  0x080483a5 in error_with_code () at gdb-sample1.c:57
57              result = 10 / divide_value;
(gdb) print divide_value
$1 = 0
(gdb) list gdb-sample1.c:57
52      {
53              int divide_value;
54              int result;
55
56              divide_value = Change_Value;
57              result = 10 / divide_value;
58              return ;
59
```

FIGURE 3.7
Using gdb on a core dump file.

Linux can create core files named core.PID, where PID is the process ID of the process that dumped the core. This feature can be set using the kernel **sysctl** command for the **core_uses_pid** field. The default coredump filename is core. By setting **core_uses_pid** to 1, the coredump filename becomes core.PID. If **core_pattern** does not include %p (the default does not) and **core_uses_pid** is set, .PID is appended to the filename.

Graphical gdb Interfaces

Once gdb is working on your system, its text console is fast and easy to use. It is a bit outdated, though. Fortunately, several free graphical add-ons are easy to use. These enhancements all use a running instance of gdb itself as the low-level debugger. We'll cover two of the graphical interfaces—Data Display Debugger (ddd) and Insight.

Data Display Debugger

The ddd is a mature, high-quality X Window-based graphical gdb interface. ddd provides an easy-to-navigate graphical data display that allows sophisticated data structure visualization with just a few mouse clicks.

ddd Features

Besides "classic" front-end features such as viewing source code, ddd provides a graphical data display, where data structures are displayed as graphs. A simple mouse click lets you dereference pointers or view structure contents, updated each time the program stops. Using ddd, you can view the application's data easily, not just by watching it execute lines of source code.

Other ddd features include the following:

- Debugging of programs written in C, C++, Ada, Fortran, Java, Perl, Pascal, Modula-2, and Modula-3
- Machine-level debugging
- Hypertext source navigation and lookup
- Break point, back trace, and history editors
- Preferences and settings editors
- Program execution in a terminal emulator window
- Debugging on a remote host
- Online manual
- Interactive help on the Motif user interface

Installing ddd

ddd is generally distributed as source code, archived, and compressed into a single file using the tar and gzip utilities. Once the source code is in hand, the user typically decompresses, configures, compiles, and installs the program. Most, if not all,

Linux distributions ship a version of the ddd package, but the steps to install and build it are listed next. You'll download version 3.3.8 of ddd and use that version throughout this chapter. Follow these steps to install ddd:

1. Extract ddd-3.8.8.tar.gz:

```
# tar xzvf ddd-3.8.8.tar.gz
# cd ddd-3.8.8
# ./configure
```

   configure looks at the machine's setup and creates the proper local environment in which to build ddd.

2. Tell ddd to compile and install:

```
# make
# make install
```

ddd Ways to View a Program

There are three different ways to invoke ddd:

- ddd executable_file
- ddd executable_file core
- ddd executable_file process_id

The file named core is produced whenever a program has an error and crashes. The core file contains useful information about the program's status during the error that generates the crash. If your system does not generate core dumps, look at the environment variables for the core (refer to Figure 3.6). (**ulimit -a** shows all of them. You also can use **ulimit -c** *value* to define the maximum core file size.)

The *process id* allows you to inspect the program during runtime.

Figure 3.8 shows an example of using ddd on the program gdb-sample1.

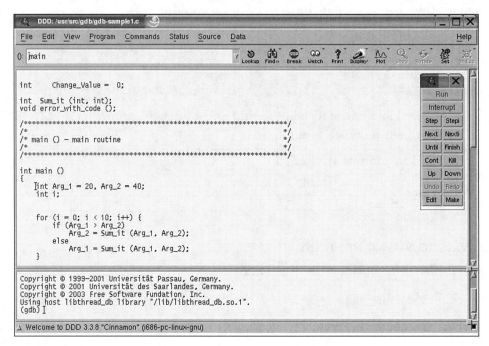

FIGURE 3.8
Using ddd on gdb-sample1.

Figure 3.9 shows the running of gdb-sample1 with the exception on line 57.

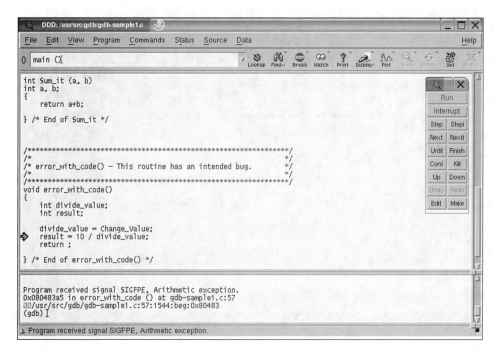

FIGURE 3.9
gdb-sample1 exception.

ddd has some nice features. If you right-click **main**, the following pull-down menu appears:

Print **main**

Display **main**

Print ***main**

Display ***main**

What is **main**

Lookup **main**

Break at **main**

Clear at **main**

Figure 3.10 shows the result of choosing the option Break at **main**.

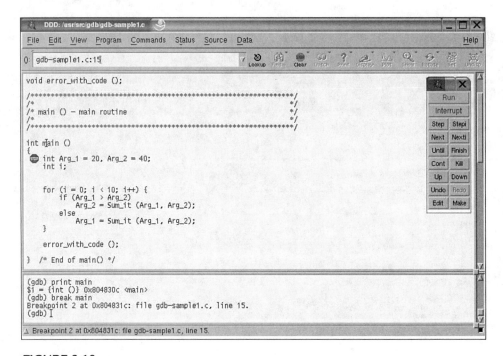

FIGURE 3.10
A break point at **main**.

Insight

Insight is a graphical enhancement to gdb. In contrast to ddd, Insight's graphics are from Tcl/Tk instead of X Window. Furthermore, Insight is compiled into gdb (rather than its running gdb as a subprocess, the way ddd does). This improves its performance and makes its communications with gdb more interactive.

Insight Features

Insight has the following features:

- Source window
- Dialog boxes for the Source window
- Stack window

- Registers window

- Memory window

- Watch Expressions window

- Local Variables window

- Break points window

- Console window

- Function Browser window

- Threads window

- Help window

- Memory window

- Source search widget

- Source window cache (for faster navigation, searches, and settings)

- Function browser window (a user interface feature to examine functions in source code)

- Special right-click mouse features for better and faster access to debugger GUI features

Installing Insight

Insight generally is distributed as source code, archived, and compressed into a single file using the tar and gzip utilities. Once the source code is in hand, the user typically decompresses, configures, compiles, and installs the programs. Most, if not all, Linux distributions ship a version of the Insight package, but the steps to install and build it are listed next. You'll download version 6.1 of Insight and use that version throughout this chapter. Follow these steps to install Insight:

1. Decompress insight-6.1.tar.gz:

```
# tar xzvf insight-6.1.tar.gz
# cd insight-6.1
# ./configure
```

configure looks at the machine's setup and creates the proper local environment in which to build Insight.

2. Tell Insight to compile and install:

```
# make
# make install
```

Figure 3.11 shows gdb-sample1.

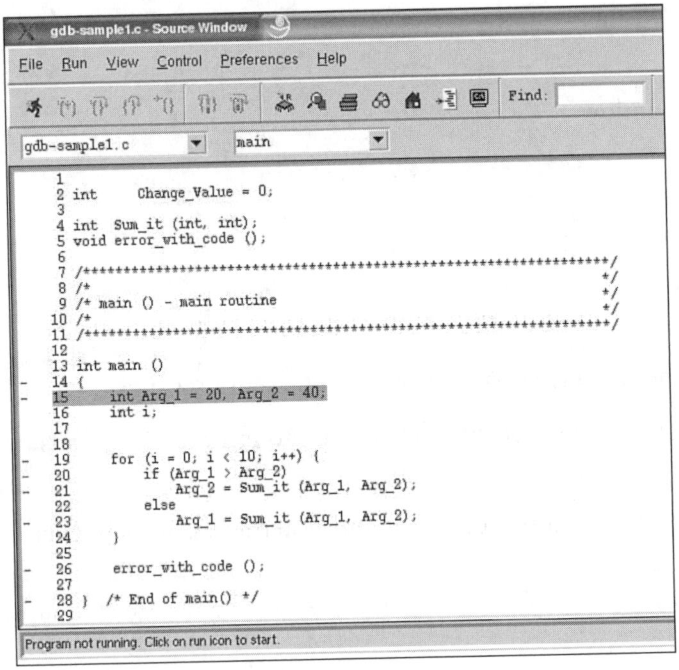

FIGURE 3.11
Using gdb-sample1.

Now let's look at using Insight to debug threaded programs.

Listing 3.2 is a sample program that uses **pthread_create** to create a new thread of control that executes concurrently with the calling thread. The gdb-sample2.c program creates two threads by using the **pthread_create** API. The first thread uses the **Thread_function1** routine, and the second thread uses the **Thread_function2** routine. This sample program shows the different commands that are used when programs have multiple threads. Figure 3.12 shows the output from gdb-sample2.

Listing 3.2

gdb-sample2.c

```
1  #include <stdio.h>
2  #include <pthread.h>
3  #include <unistd.h>
4  void* Thread_function1(void * arg)
5  {
6   unsigned int i=1;
7      while(i < 11)
8      {
9              printf("Child Thread Iteration %d\n",i);
10             i++;
11     if(i%2)
12             sleep(2);
13     else
14             sleep(1);
15     }
16     return arg;
17 }
18 void* Thread_function2(void * arg)
19 {
20   unsigned int i=1;
21   while(i < 11)
22   {
23     printf("Child Thread 2 Iteration %d\n",i);
24     i++;
25     if(i%2)
26             sleep(2);
27     else
28             sleep(1);
29   }
30   return arg;
31 }
32 int main (int argc, char *argv[])
33 {
34     pthread_t thread;
35     pthread_t thread2;
36     if(pthread_create(&thread,NULL,Thread_function1,NULL))
37     {
38     return(1);
39     }
40     if(pthread_create(&thread2,NULL,Thread_function2,NULL))
41     {
42     return(1);
43     }
44     unsigned int i = 1;
45     while(i < 11)
46     {
47        printf("Main Loop Iteration %d\n",i);
```

```
48        i++;
49        if(i%2)
50             sleep(1);
51        else
52             sleep(2);
53        }
54      return 0;
55 }
```

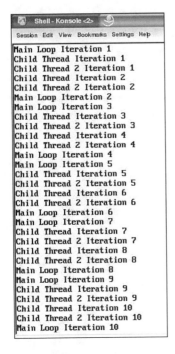

```
Main Loop Iteration 1
Child Thread Iteration 1
Child Thread 2 Iteration 1
Child Thread Iteration 2
Child Thread 2 Iteration 2
Main Loop Iteration 2
Main Loop Iteration 3
Child Thread Iteration 3
Child Thread 2 Iteration 3
Child Thread Iteration 4
Child Thread 2 Iteration 4
Main Loop Iteration 4
Main Loop Iteration 5
Child Thread Iteration 5
Child Thread 2 Iteration 5
Child Thread Iteration 6
Child Thread 2 Iteration 6
Main Loop Iteration 6
Main Loop Iteration 7
Child Thread Iteration 7
Child Thread 2 Iteration 7
Child Thread Iteration 8
Child Thread 2 Iteration 8
Main Loop Iteration 8
Main Loop Iteration 9
Child Thread Iteration 9
Child Thread 2 Iteration 9
Child Thread Iteration 10
Child Thread 2 Iteration 10
Main Loop Iteration 10
```

FIGURE 3.12
Output from gdb-sample2.

Now let's look at the sample program gdb-sample2.c using gdb. Figures 3.13 through Figure 3.15 show the starting of gdb and the following gdb commands:

- The **run** command starts the program. You can press Ctrl-C to break in and stop the program's execution. Four threads are created—16384, 32769, 16386, and 32771.

- The **info threads** command displays the program's threads.

- The **thread** 4 command switches to that thread.

- The **where** command displays a back trace for thread 4.

- The **thread** 3 command switches to that thread.

- The **where** command displays a back trace for thread 3.

- The **thread** 2 command switches to that thread.

- The **where** command displays a back trace for thread 2.

- The **thread** 1 command switches to that thread.

- The **where** command displays a back trace for thread 1.

- The **list** command for gdb-sample2.c.52 sees where thread 1 called the routine **sleep** from.

- The **list** command for gdb-sample2.c.14 sees where thread 3 called the routine **sleep** from.

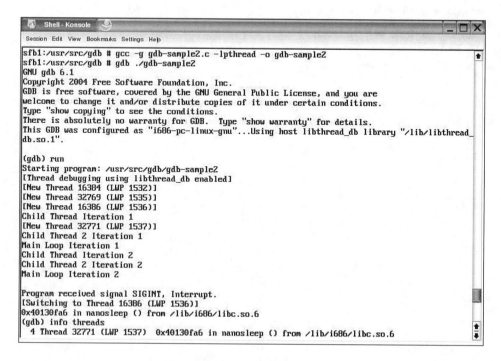

FIGURE 3.13

Building gdb-sample2 and running it under gdb.

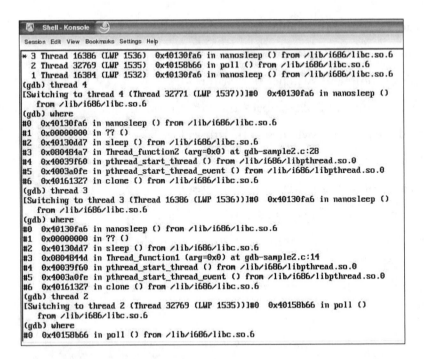

```
    Shell - Konsole

 Session Edit View Bookmarks Settings Help

* 3 Thread 16386 (LWP 1536)  0x40130fa6 in nanosleep () from /lib/i686/libc.so.6
  2 Thread 32769 (LWP 1535)  0x40158b66 in poll () from /lib/i686/libc.so.6
  1 Thread 16384 (LWP 1532)  0x40130fa6 in nanosleep () from /lib/i686/libc.so.6
(gdb) thread 4
[Switching to thread 4 (Thread 32771 (LWP 1537))]#0  0x40130fa6 in nanosleep ()
    from /lib/i686/libc.so.6
(gdb) where
#0  0x40130fa6 in nanosleep () from /lib/i686/libc.so.6
#1  0x00000000 in ?? ()
#2  0x40130dd7 in sleep () from /lib/i686/libc.so.6
#3  0x080484a7 in Thread_function2 (arg=0x0) at gdb-sample2.c:28
#4  0x40039f60 in pthread_start_thread () from /lib/i686/libpthread.so.0
#5  0x4003a0fe in pthread_start_thread_event () from /lib/i686/libpthread.so.0
#6  0x40161327 in clone () from /lib/i686/libc.so.6
(gdb) thread 3
[Switching to thread 3 (Thread 16386 (LWP 1536))]#0  0x40130fa6 in nanosleep ()
    from /lib/i686/libc.so.6
(gdb) where
#0  0x40130fa6 in nanosleep () from /lib/i686/libc.so.6
#1  0x00000000 in ?? ()
#2  0x40130dd7 in sleep () from /lib/i686/libc.so.6
#3  0x0804844d in Thread_function1 (arg=0x0) at gdb-sample2.c:14
#4  0x40039f60 in pthread_start_thread () from /lib/i686/libpthread.so.0
#5  0x4003a0fe in pthread_start_thread_event () from /lib/i686/libpthread.so.0
#6  0x40161327 in clone () from /lib/i686/libc.so.6
(gdb) thread 2
[Switching to thread 2 (Thread 32769 (LWP 1535))]#0  0x40158b66 in poll ()
    from /lib/i686/libc.so.6
(gdb) where
#0  0x40158b66 in poll () from /lib/i686/libc.so.6
```

FIGURE 3.14
thread and **where** commands.

Now that you know some useful gdb threading commands, such as **info threads** and **thread**, you should be able to debug multithreaded programs.

```
#1  0x40039a8e in __pthread_manager () from /lib/i686/libpthread.so.0
#2  0x40039d63 in __pthread_manager_event () from /lib/i686/libpthread.so.0
#3  0x40161327 in clone () from /lib/i686/libc.so.6
(gdb) thread 1
[Switching to thread 1 (Thread 16384 (LWP 1532))]#0  0x40130fa6 in nanosleep ()
    from /lib/i686/libc.so.6
(gdb) where
#0  0x40130fa6 in nanosleep () from /lib/i686/libc.so.6
#1  0x00000000 in ?? ()
#2  0x40130dd7 in sleep () from /lib/i686/libc.so.6
#3  0x0804854f in main (argc=1, argv=0xbffff2b4) at gdb-sample2.c:52
(gdb) list gdb-sample2.c:52
47          while(i < 110)
48          {
49              printf("Main Loop Iteration %d\n",i);
50              i++;
51              if(i%2)
52                  sleep(1);
53              else
54                  sleep(2);
55          }
56          return 0;
(gdb) list gdb-sample2.c:14
9           while(i < 110)
10          {
11              printf("Child Thread Iteration %d\n",i);
12              i++;
13              if(i%2)
14                  sleep(2);
15              else
```

FIGURE 3.15
Viewing threads.

Debugging Symbols Increase the Executable's Size

Most programs and libraries are, by default, compiled with debugging symbols included (with gcc's **-g** option). This means that, when debugging a program or library that was compiled with debugging information included, the debugger can give not only memory addresses but also the names of the routines and variables.

Including these debugging symbols, however, enlarges a program or library significantly. To give you an idea of how much space these symbols occupy, an lsof binary with debugging symbols is 209,229 bytes, and an lsof binary without debugging symbols is 103,894 bytes.

Sizes may vary somewhat, but when you compare programs with and without debugging symbols, the difference can be a factor between 2 and 4. Programs can be built with debugging symbols included. Then, if the symbols are unneeded, you can remove them using the **strip** command. Figure 3.16 shows the last part of building lsof with the -**g** option added to CFLAGS. Also shown is the size of the lsof program before and after the symbols have been removed.

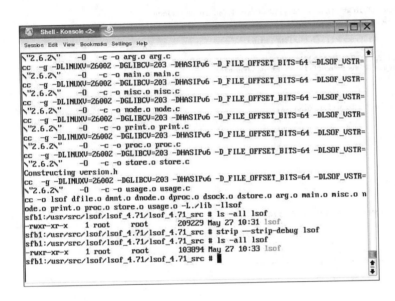

FIGURE 3.16
The **strip** command to remove symbols.

Debugging Techniques

Now let's look at some helpful hints for debugging an application more quickly.

When debugging, it is often a good practice to stop program execution at the bottom of a function so that a **print** or multiple displays can be done to see the current values stored in the data the function has altered. There is no simple built-in gdb statement to do this, but you can do the following:

1. Do a **list funct_name**, and find the number of the line (**line#**) in that function where the function **end-block-delimiter** (}) is.

2. Set a break point at each of these line numbers using the following:
    ```
    "break <line#>"
    ```

Use the line numbers that were identified in step 1. When the **run** command is issued in the debugger, the program execution stops at the end of each function in the program. At that time you can do a **print** to examine the values currently stored in program data objects (global, local, or parameters passed into the function).

You can find out where a program is crashing. A **segmentation fault - core dumped** message, a **bus error** message, and other such messages indicate that the logic at some point in a program is incorrect. For this reason, the program execution cannot continue—that is, the program stops running, or a crash happens.

To find out the exact line of source code that caused your program to crash, do the following:

1. Compile your program using the **-g** compiler option if this hasn't already been done.

2. Enter **gdb executable_file** from the Linux command line.

3. Enter the **run** command. The program begins executing and stops at the first line of code that has an error (the program may have more than one runtime error).

4. Enter the gdb command **list**. In most cases, gdb lists the line of code that caused the program to crash.

5. Edit the source code, and go to the line of code just specified. Fix the logical error and then recompile and run the program to see if things are now working correctly.

Do the following to step through the entire program:

1. Start the executable code by using gdb.

2. Enter **break main** from the gdb command line.

3. Enter **run** from the gdb command line. The program begins executing. Execution stops on line 1 of main.

4. Repeatedly enter **step** from the gdb command line. At each step, you can execute a **print** command to see the values of variables as the program executes.

Summary

This chapter covered gdb and two GUIs for gdb—ddd and Insight—both of which reduce debugging time. One way that they can do this is by displaying the value of the variable when you move the mouse over that variable. When gdb is used, the **print** command must be invoked to display the variable's value. The user can see much more information at one time. The GUI interface is more intuitive, and data structures are easier to visualize.

Web Resources for GNU Debugger

URL	Description
http://www.gnu.org/software/gdb/gdb.html	gdb
http://sources.redhat.com/gdb/current/onlinedocs/ gdb.html#SEC_Top	Debugging with gdb
http://www.gnu.org/software/ddd/	ddd
http://sources.redhat.com/insight/	Insight

Chapter 4

Memory Management Debugging

In this chapter

- Dynamic Memory Functions   page 82
- MEMWATCH   page 84
- YAMD   page 86
- Electric Fence   page 93
- Valgrind   page 97
- Summary   page 109
- Web Resources for Memory Checkers   page 109

Dynamic memory allocation seems straightforward enough: Memory is allocated on demand—using **malloc**() or one of its variants—and memory is freed when it's no longer needed. Memory management would be that easy if programmers never made mistakes. Alas, we do make mistakes (from time to time), so memory management problems do occur.

For example, a *memory leak* occurs when memory is allocated but never freed. Leaks can obviously be caused by a **malloc**() without a corresponding **free**(), but leaks can also be inadvertently caused if a pointer to dynamically allocated memory is deleted, lost, or overwritten. *Memory corruption* can occur when allocated (and in use) memory is overwritten accidentally or when using statically allocated memory and stack variables (especially if a pointer to stack-allocated memory is returned to a calling method). Buffer overruns—caused by writing past the end of a block of allocated memory—frequently corrupt memory.

Regardless of the root cause, memory management errors can have unexpected, even devastating effects on application and system behavior. With dwindling available memory, processes and entire systems can grind to a halt, while corrupted memory often leads to spurious crashes. System security is also susceptible to buffer overruns. Worse, it might take days before evidence of a real problem appears. Today, it's common for Linux systems to have a gigabyte of main memory. If a program leaks a small amount of memory, it takes some time before the application and system show symptoms of a problem. Memory management errors can be quite insidious and very difficult to find and fix.

This chapter covers four memory-management checkers: MEMWATCH, YAMD, Electric Fence, and Valgrind. All these tools can help detect common memory management errors. We'll review the basics, write some "buggy" code, and then use each of these tools to find the mistakes.

Dynamic Memory Functions

Of all the library calls (libc) in Linux, only four manage memory: **malloc**(), **calloc**(), **realloc**(), and **free**(). All these functions have prototypes in the stdlib.h include file.

malloc() allocates a memory block that is uninitialized. Its prototype is

```
void* malloc(size_t size)
```

The single argument is the number of bytes of memory to allocate.

If the allocation is successful, **malloc()** returns a pointer to the memory. If memory allocation fails for some reason (for example, if the system is out of memory), **malloc()** returns a NULL pointer.

calloc() allocates an array in memory and initializes all the memory to 0 (with **malloc()**, the allocated memory is uninitialized). Here's the prototype:

```
void* calloc(size_t nmemb, size_t size)
```

The first argument is the number of elements in the array, and the second argument is the size (in bytes) of each element. Like **malloc()**, **calloc()** returns a pointer if the memory allocation was successful, and NULL otherwise.

realloc() is defined as

```
void* realloc (void *ptr, size_t size)
```

realloc() changes the size of the object referenced by the pointer to a new size specified by the second argument. **realloc()** returns a pointer to the moved block of memory.

free() deallocates a memory block. It takes a pointer as an argument, as shown in its prototype, and releases that memory:

```
void free (void *ptr),
```

While the API for memory management is unusually small, the number and kind of memory errors that can occur are substantial. They include:

- Reading and using uninitialized memory
- Reading and writing memory after it has been freed
- Reading and writing from memory after or in front of (underrun) the allocated size
- Reading and writing inappropriate areas on the stack
- Memory leaks

The use of pointers can cause problems in all types of memory. In addition, indexes into statically allocated arrays can cause corruption. Stack issues can also cause problems with some compilers. Returning a pointer to a stack variable in a function is a big no-no.

MEMWATCH

MEMWATCH, written by Johan Lindh, is an open-source memory error-detection tool for C. It can be downloaded from www.linkdata.se/sourcecode.html. By simply adding a header file to your code and defining MEMWATCH in your gcc command, you can track memory leaks and corruptions in a program. MEMWATCH supports ANSI C; provides a log of the results; and detects double frees, erroneous frees, unfreed memory, overflow and underflow, and so on. To follow the example shown next, download a version of MEMWATCH. The example uses version 2.71. Figure 4.1 shows the unpacking of the tar file. Listing 4.1 is the sample source code that is used with MEMWATCH.

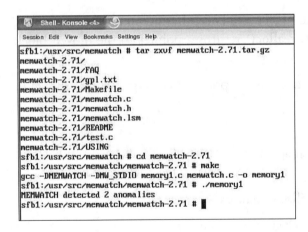

FIGURE 4.1
Unpacking the MEMWATCH tar file and building memory1.c.

Listing 4.1

Memory Sample (memory1.c)

```
1 #include <stdlib.h>
2 #include <stdio.h>
3 #include "memwatch.h"
```

```
4
5  int main(void)
6  {
7    char *ptr1;
8    char *ptr2;
9
10   ptr1 = malloc(512);
11   ptr2 = malloc(512);
12
13   ptr2 = ptr1;
14   free(ptr2);
15   free(ptr1);
16 }
```

The only change to this sample code is to add the memwatch.h include on line 3 so that MEMWATCH can be enabled. Also, two compile-time flags—-DMEMWATCH and -DMW_STDIO—need to be added to the compile statement for each source file in the program.

The code shown in Listing 4.1 allocates two 512-byte blocks of memory (lines 10 and 11), and then the pointer to the first block is set to the second block (line 13). As a result, the address of the second block is lost, and a memory leak occurs.

Now compile the memwatch.c file, which is part of the MEMWATCH package with the sample source code (memory1.c) shown in Listing 4.1. The following is a sample makefile for building memory1.c. memory1 is the executable produced by this makefile:

```
gcc -DMEMWATCH -DMW_STDIO memory1.c memwatch.c -o memory1
```

Figure 4.1 shows that running program memory1 captures two memory-management anomalies. The MEMWATCH package comes with a FAQ and a test.c sample program that shows another sample program where MEMWATCH catches memory management errors.

MEMWATCH creates a log called memwatch.log. Figure 4.2 displays this log file, which is created by running the memory1 program.

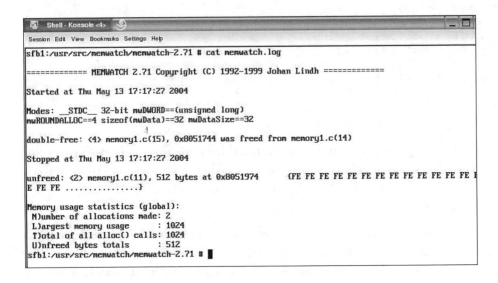

```
sfb1:/usr/src/memwatch/memwatch-2.71 # cat memwatch.log

============= MEMWATCH 2.71 Copyright (C) 1992-1999 Johan Lindh =============

Started at Thu May 13 17:17:27 2004

Modes: __STDC__ 32-bit mwDWORD==(unsigned long)
mwROUNDALLOC==4 sizeof(mwData)==32 mwDataSize==32

double-free: <4> memory1.c(15), 0x8051744 was freed from memory1.c(14)

Stopped at Thu May 13 17:17:27 2004

unfreed: <2> memory1.c(11), 512 bytes at 0x8051974    {FE FE FE FE FE FE FE FE FE FE FE FE FE F
E FE FE ...............}

Memory usage statistics (global):
 N)umber of allocations made: 2
 L)argest memory usage      : 1024
 T)otal of all alloc() calls: 1024
 U)nfreed bytes totals      : 512
sfb1:/usr/src/memwatch/memwatch-2.71 #
```

FIGURE 4.2
Displaying the log file.

MEMWATCH tells you which line has the problem. For a free of an already freed pointer, it identifies that condition. The same goes for unfreed memory. The section at the end of the log displays statistics, including how much memory was leaked, how much was used, and the total amount allocated.

In Figure 4.2 you can see that the memory management errors occur on line 15, which shows that there is a double free of memory. The next error is a memory leak of 512 bytes, and that memory is allocated in line 11.

YAMD

Written by Nate Eldredge, the YAMD package finds dynamic memory allocation-related problems in C and C++. The latest version of YAMD is 0.32. You can download yamd-0.32.tar.gz from www.cs.hmc.edu/~nate/yamd/. Execute a **make** command to build the program, and then execute a **make install** command to install the program and set up the tool.

Once YAMD has been downloaded, use it on yamd-memory1.c. Listing 4.2 is the same program as Listing 4.1, but without the memwatch.h include.

Listing 4.2

Memory Sample (yamd-memory1.c)

```
1  #include <stdlib.h>
2  #include <stdio.h>
3
4  int main(void)
5  {
6     char *ptr1;
7     char *ptr2;
8
9     ptr1 = malloc(512);
10    ptr2 = malloc(512);
11
12    ptr2 = ptr1;
13    free(ptr2);
14    free(ptr1);
15 }
```

Figure 4.3 shows the steps to unpack the yamd-0.32.tar.gz file and build YAMD.

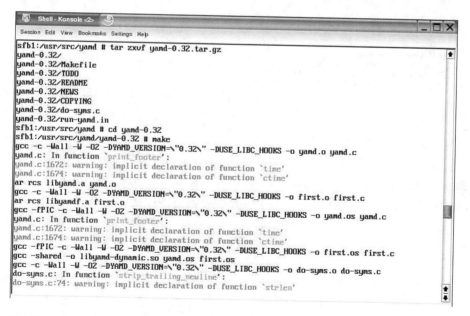

FIGURE 4.3
Unpacking the YAMD tar file and building YAMD.

> NOTE   Figures 4.3 and 4.4 have warnings. These warnings won't cause a
> problem with the building of YAMD.

Figure 4.4 continues to show YAMD building. The **make install** command is
used to install YAMD.

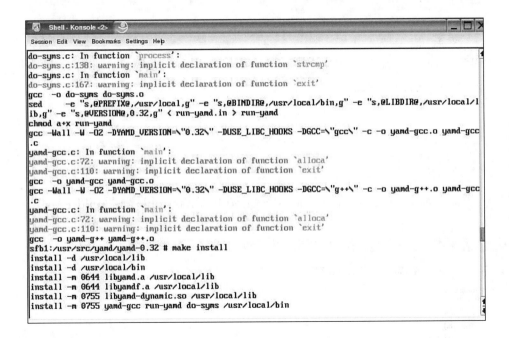

FIGURE 4.4
Building and installing YAMD.

Figure 4.5 shows the gcc command used to build the program yamd-memory1.
The program yamd-memory1 is started using **./run-yamd**.

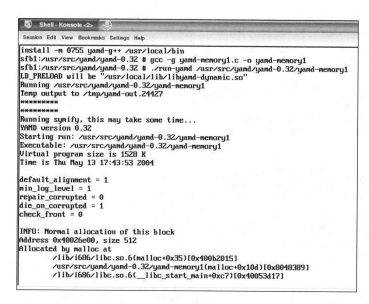

FIGURE 4.5
Building and running yamd-memory1.

Figure 4.6 shows the output from YAMD on program yamd-memory1. The first memory management error of multiple freeing is displayed.

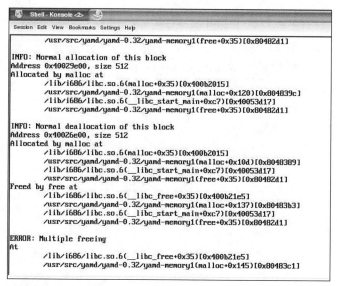

FIGURE 4.6
YAMD output.

Figure 4.7 shows the continuation of the output from YAMD on program yamd-memory1. The second memory management error of a memory leak is displayed.

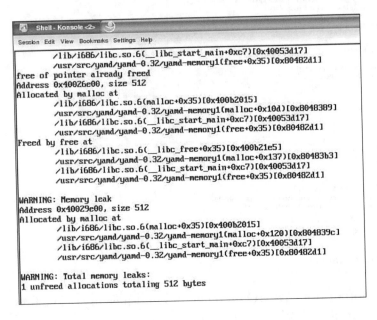

FIGURE 4.7
YAMD output (continued).

Figure 4.8 shows the continuation of the output from YAMD on program yamd-memory1. A summary of the memory allocations is displayed.

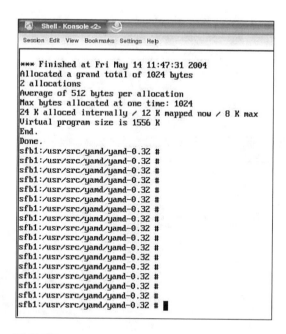

FIGURE 4.8
Summary of the YAMD output.

YAMD shows that the memory has already been freed and that a memory leak exists. Let's try YAMD on the sample program shown in Listing 4.3.

Listing 4.3

Memory Code (yamd-memory2.c)

```
1   #include <stdlib.h>
2   #include <stdio.h>
3
4  int main(void)
5  {
6      char *ptr1;
7      char *ptr2;
8      char *chptr;
9      int i = 1;
10     ptr1 = malloc(512);
11     ptr2 = malloc(512);
12     chptr = (char *)malloc(512);
13     for (i; i <= 512; i++) {
14       chptr[i] = 'S';
15     }
```

```
16      free(ptr2);
17      free(ptr1);
18    free(chptr);
19  }
```

Figure 4.9 shows the output.

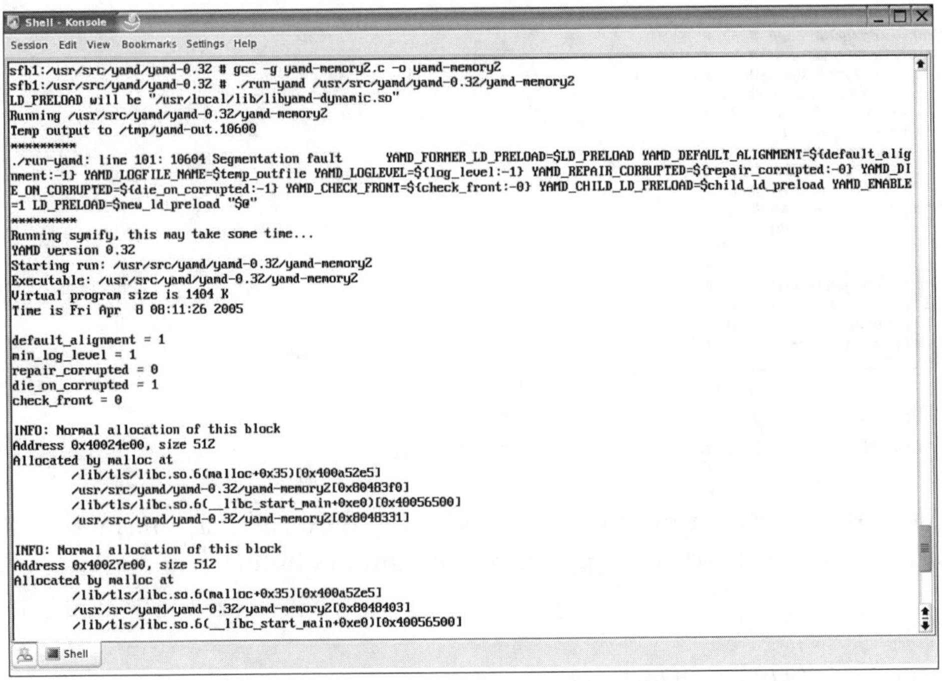

FIGURE 4.9
Building yamd-memory2 and YAMD output.

The command **run-yamd** starts YAMD for the program yamd-memory2. Figure 4.10 shows the output from using YAMD on the sample program yamd-memory2. YAMD shows that there is an out-of-bounds condition in the **for** loop on line 14.

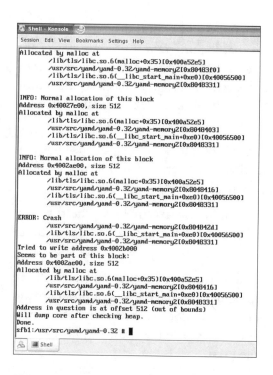

FIGURE 4.10
YAMD output showing a memory management overrun.

MEMWATCH and YAMD are both useful debugging tools that require different approaches. With MEMWATCH, the include file memwatch.h and two compile-time flags are needed. YAMD requires only the **-g** option for the **link** statement.

Electric Fence

Most Linux distributions include the Electric Fence package; it can also be downloaded from http://perens.com/FreeSoftware/. Electric Fence is a **malloc**() debugging library written by Bruce Perens. It allocates protected memory just after the memory the program allocates. If a fencepost error occurs (running off the end of an array), the program immediately exits with a protection error. By combining Electric Fence with gdb, you can track down exactly what line tried to access the protected memory. Electric Fence can also detect memory leaks.

To use Electric Fence, you must add the **-lefence** and **-g** options to the program's makefile. One side effect of Electric Fence is that the program runs more slowly and uses more memory. The main side effect is that if something is wrong with memory accesses (such as out-of-bounds array accesses), the program has a segmentation fault where the memory problem is. Therefore, gdb or ddd needs to be used to identify the memory problems.

The main advantage of using Electric Fence is that it exposes "hidden" bugs that can silently wreak havoc in programs and that can later lead to inexplicable segmentation faults (these problems can be very hard to find).

Listing 4.4 is a makefile that is set up to build two executables. The first executable, efence_test, is built with Electric Fence, and the second is built without Electric Fence.

One reason to create two executables is that running Electric Fence results in overhead. It would be great to find and fix memory problems with a program and then, when the program is placed into production, to not use the version of the program with Electric Fence built in. In the case of the makefile shown in Listing 4.4, the executable without Electric Fence is called test.

Listing 4.4

Makefile for malloc_test.c

```
1 CC =gcc
2
3 all: efence_test test
4
5 efence_test:
6       $(CC) -g -o efence_test malloc_test.c -lefence
7
8 test:
9       $(CC) -g -o test malloc_test.c
10
11 clean:
12      rm -rf efence_test
13      rm -rf test
```

The malloc_test.c code, shown in Listing 4.5, contains a memory error. Can you tell on which line the error occurs?

Listing 4.5

malloc_test.c

```
1   #include<stdlib.h>
2
3   int main (void)
4   {
5     const int SIZE = 20;
6     char *xx;
7     int i = 0;
8     xx  = (char *) malloc (SIZE);
9     for (i ; i <= SIZE; i++) {
10      xx[i] = 2;
11    }
12  }
```

Electric Fence can!

Electric Fence is a link-in replacement for **malloc()** that highlights bugs like the one shown here to be automatically caught at runtime. The problem with bad pointers is that they probably point to data near where they should point. If they point off into the blue, a core dump happens with or without Electric Fence. However, if they point nearer to your own data, the machine probably will keep running in an undefined state until the program accesses the incorrect memory.

In Figure 4.11, the **make** command is used to build malloc_test.c. Next, the test program, which is malloc_test.c without Electric Fence built in, is run, and no errors are displayed. ddd is used to start the efence_test program. Figure 4.12 shows an overrun error caught by Electric Fence. Line 10 is where the error occurs when the loop counter **i** equals 20.

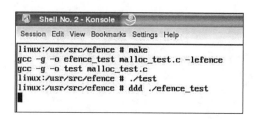

FIGURE 4.11
Building malloc_test and starting ddd.

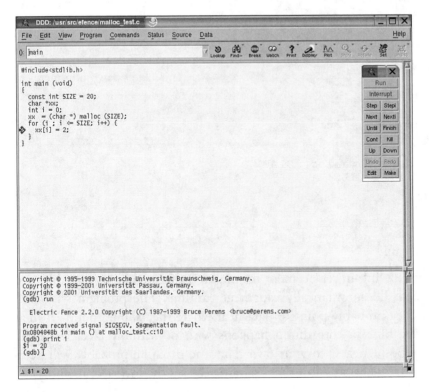

FIGURE 4.12
ddd with efence_test.

Listing 4.6 contains the fix to the **for** loop to remove the overrun error found by
Electric Fence on line 10. The loop has been changed from **i <= SIZE** to **i < SIZE**.

Listing 4.6

malloc_test-fixed.c

```
1   #include<stdlib.h>
2
3   int main (void)
4   {
5     const int SIZE = 20;
6     char *xx;
7     int i = 0;
8     xx   = (char *) malloc (SIZE);
9     for (i ; i < SIZE; i++) {
10        xx[i] = 2;
11    }
12  }
```

Chasing Memory Overruns

It is not good to be in a situation where an allocation overrun happens after thousands of memory management calls. I've spent many long hours tracking down odd memory corruption problems. One problem application worked on our development workstation but would fail after 2,000 calls to **malloc()** on the new product workstation. The real problem was an overrun around call 1,000. The new system had the problem because the reserved **malloc()** area was laid out differently, so the offending memory was located at a different place and destroyed something different when it did the overrun.

I solved this problem using many different techniques—one using a debugger, and another adding tracing to the source code. I started to look at memory debugging tools around this time, looking to solve these types of problems faster and more efficiently. One of the first things I do when starting a new project is run the memory checkers in this chapter to see if they can pinpoint possible memory management problems. Memory leaks are a common problem in applications, but you can use the tools described in this chapter to find and solve them.

Valgrind

Valgrind was written by Julian Seward; it's available under the GNU Public License. Valgrind is closely tied to the operating system architecture and currently is supported only on Linux x86 machines. There is a port of Valgrind to the PowerPC architecture, and a patch for this is available under the Related Projects link on the Valgrind web site. Valgrind works on machines with kernels from the 2.4.x and 2.6.x series and glibc 2.2.x and 2.3.x. When a program is run under Valgrind's control, all writes and reads of memory are looked at, and calls to **malloc()/new()/free()/delete()** are intercepted. As a result, Valgrind can detect problems such as:

- Use of uninitialized memory
- Reading and writing memory after it has been freed
- Reading and writing from memory past the allocated size
- Reading and writing inappropriate areas on the stack
- Memory leaks

- Passing of uninitialized and/or unaddressable memory

- Mismatched use of **malloc/new/new** [] versus **free/delete/delete** []

When a program is run under Valgrind, all memory reads and writes are inspected, and all calls to **malloc()/new()** and **free()/delete()** are intercepted.

Installing Valgrind

You can download the source for Valgrind from http://valgrind.org/. Download the latest stable release (or the latest development release, depending on your sense of adventure) and build the software.

Figure 4.13 shows two commands. **bunzip2** unzips the valgrind-2.0.0.tar file. **tar** expands the Valgrind files.

FIGURE 4.13
Unpacking the Valgrind tar file.

Figure 4.14 shows three commands. **./configure** sets up the build environment for the Valgrind package. **make** and **make install** build and install the Valgrind libraries and executables.

FIGURE 4.14
Building and installing Valgrind.

One great feature of Valgrind is that it doesn't require building (or rebuilding) the application in any special way. Simply place Valgrind in front of the program that needs to be inspected. For example, the command **valgrind ls -all**, shown in Figure 4.15, inspects and monitors the **ls** command. (Running this command on SuSE 9.0 showed no errors.)

```
 Shell - Konsole <2>
Session  Edit  View  Bookmarks  Settings  Help
linux:/usr/src/valgrind # valgrind ls -all
==21212== Memcheck, a.k.a. Valgrind, a memory error detector for x86-linux.
==21212== Copyright (C) 2002-2003, and GNU GPL'd, by Julian Seward.
==21212== Using valgrind-2.0.0, a program supervision framework for x86-linux.
==21212== Copyright (C) 2000-2003, and GNU GPL'd, by Julian Seward.
==21212== Estimated CPU clock rate is 2418 MHz
==21212== For more details, rerun with: -v
==21212==
total 4114
drwxr-xr-x    3 root     root         184 May 16 13:05 .
drwxr-xr-x   11 root     root         552 May 16 12:54 ..
-rwxr-xr-x    1 root     root         375 May 16 12:55 valgrind-1.c
drwxrwxrwx   14 best     users       1512 May 16 13:32 valgrind-2.0.0
-rwxr-xr-x    1 root     root     4198400 May 16 12:55 valgrind-2.0.0.tar
-rwxr-xr-x    1 root     root         321 May 16 12:55 valgrind-2.c
==21212==
==21212== ERROR SUMMARY: 0 errors from 0 contexts (suppressed: 0 from 0)
==21212== malloc/free: in use at exit: 12206 bytes in 17 blocks.
==21212== malloc/free: 45 allocs, 28 frees, 25062 bytes allocated.
==21212== For a detailed leak analysis,  rerun with: --leak-check=yes
==21212== For counts of detected errors, rerun with: -v
linux:/usr/src/valgrind # ▮
```

FIGURE 4.15
valgrind ls -all.

When it finds a problem, the Valgrind output has the following format:

```
==20691== 8192 bytes in 1 blocks are definitely lost in loss record 1 of 1
==20691==    at 0x40048434: malloc (vg_clientfuncs.c:100)
==20691==    by 0x806910C: fscklog_init (fsckwsp.c:2491)
==20691==    by 0x806E7D0: initial_processing (xchkdsk.c:2101)
==20691==    by 0x806C70D: main (xchkdsk.c:289)
```

The ==*xxxxx*== string prefixes each line of Valgrind-specific output. (Application-specific output does not have this prefix.) In the sample output shown here, 20691 is the process ID. The message indicates that there is a memory leak of 8,192 bytes and provides diagnostics and a kind of trace to direct you to the error. The second and subsequent lines indicate that the memory was initially allocated on line 2491 in the routine **fscklog_init()** (in the file fsckwsp.c). **fscklog_init()** was called from **initial_processing()** at line 2101, and **main()** called **initial_processing()**. By the way, if **fscklog_init()** is called more than once in the **initial_processing()** routine, the line number clearly identifies which call caused the problem.

Losing Your Memory

Valgrind can be used to find some common memory errors. The first sample program, valgrind-1.c, shown in Listing 4.7, has more than one memory leak. The code shown in Listing 4.7 allocates two 512-byte blocks of memory and then sets the pointer to the second block to the first block. As a result, the address of the second block is lost, causing a memory leak. Also, 512 10-byte blocks of memory are never freed. This memory is allocated by the call to the **get_mem** routine.

Listing 4.7

valgrind-1.c, a Program with a Memory Leak

```
1    #include <stdlib.h>
2    #include <stdio.h>
3    void get_mem()
4    {
5      char *ptr;
6      ptr = (char *) malloc (10);   /* memory not freed */
7    }
8    int main(void)
9    {
10     char *ptr1, *ptr2;
11     int i;
12     ptr1 = (char *) malloc (512);
13     ptr2 = (char *) malloc (512);
14     ptr2 = ptr1;
15     free(ptr2);
16     free(ptr1);
17     for ( i = 0; i < 512; i++) {
18         get_mem();
19       }
20   }
```

Compile and analyze valgrind-1.c using the commands shown at the top of Figure 4.16.

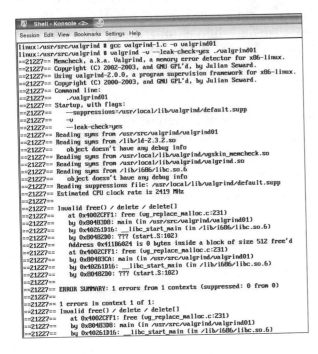

FIGURE 4.16
Building valgrind-1.c and memory leak output.

Valgrind produces the output shown in Figures 4.16 and 4.17, correctly identifying the 512-byte and 10-byte memory leaks. The **-v** option provides verbose feedback, and the **—leak-check=yes** option searches for memory leaks when the client program exits.

FIGURE 4.17
More memory leak output from valgrind-1.

valgrind-2.c, shown in Listing 4.8, demonstrates another common memory error: reading beyond the end of an array of bytes. Again, build the sample code and run Valgrind to analyze it.

Listing 4.8

valgrind-2.c, a Program That Tries to Access Memory Beyond the End of an Array

```
1 #include <stdlib.h>
2 #include <stdio.h>
3
4 int main(void)
5 {
6   char *chptr;
7   char *chptr1;
8   int i   = 1;
9   chptr   = (char *) malloc(512);
```

```
10 chptr1 = (char *) malloc (512);
11      for (i; i <= 513; i++) {
12         chptr[i] = '?';
13         chptr1[i] = chptr[i];
14      }
15
16   free(chptr1);
17   free(chptr);
18 }
```

As you can see from the output shown in Figure 4.18, references to element 513 in the two arrays cause a write error, a read error, and another write error. The message **Address 0x411B6224 is 0 bytes after a block of size 512 alloc'd** indicates that there is no storage beyond the end of the array of 512 bytes.

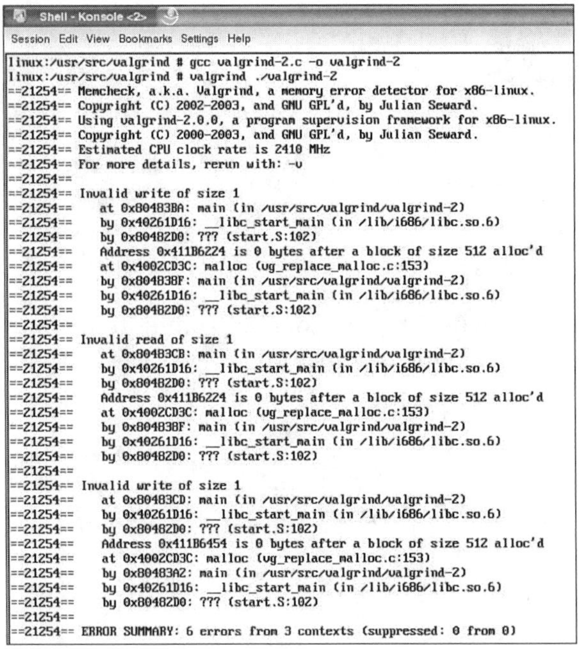

FIGURE 4.18
Building valgrind-2.c and Valgrind output.

Finally, to see how Valgrind finds invalid use of uninitialized memory, let's look at the results of analyzing the Journaled File System's (JFS) fsck utility. As before, you run fsck under the auspices of Valgrind.

The command **valgrind -v —leak-check=yes fsck.jfs /dev/hdb2** is used to check for problems on the fsck.jfs utility, as shown in Figure 4.19.

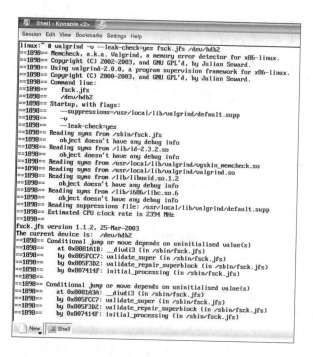

FIGURE 4.19

A snippet of the output for the Journaled File System utility fsck.jfs.

The **validate_super()** routine can be found in the jfsutils package in jfsutils-1.x.x/fsck/fsckmeta.c. Listing 4.9 shows a portion of the code.

Listing 4.9

A Code Snippet from fsckmeta.c

```
int validate_super(int which_super)
{
  int64_t bytes_on_device;

    /* get physical device size */
                 vfs_rc = ujfs_get_dev_size(Dev_IOPort,
bytes_on_device);
  .
  .
  .
```

```
dev_blks_on_device = bytes_on_device / Dev_blksize; /* Line
    2331 */
if (sb_ptr->s_pbsize != Dev_blksize) {
```

The output from Valgrind indicates that an uninitialized variable is used on line 2331. That's the line that says **dev_blks_on_device = bytes_ on_device / Dev_blksize**. As you can see, **bytes_on_device** is not set before it is used. Using Valgrind, this memory management problem was identified and fixed before an end user ever came across it.

Cache Profiling

Valgrind can also perform cache simulations and annotate your source line by line with the number of cache misses. In particular, it records the following:

- L1 instruction cache reads and misses

- L1 data cache reads and read misses and writes and write misses

- L2 unified cache reads and read misses and writes and write misses

L1 is a small amount of static RAM (SRAM) memory that's used as a cache. L1 temporarily stores instructions and data, ensuring that the processor has a steady supply of data to process while memory catches up on delivering new data. L1 is integrated or packaged within the same module as the processor. Level 2 caching is performed in L2.

Valgrind's cachegrind tool is used to do cache profiling—you use it just like valgrind. For example, the following command can be used to look at the fsck.jfs program:

```
valgrind —skin=cachegrind fsck.jfs -n -v /dev/hdb2
```

The output of cachegrind is collected in the file cachegrind.out.pid. Sample output from analyzing fsck.jfs is shown in Figures 4.20 and 4.21.

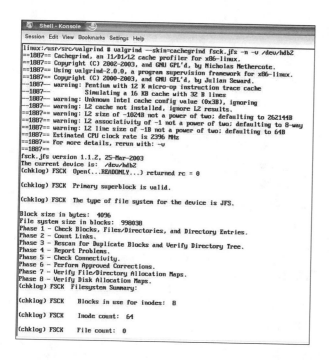

FIGURE 4.20
cachegrind's analysis of fsck.jfs.

The output uses the following abbreviations for recorded events:

Abbreviation	Description
Ir	I cache reads (instructions executed)
I1mr	I1 cache read misses
I2mr	L2 cache instruction read misses
Dr	D cache reads (memory reads)
D1mr	D1 cache read misses
D2mr	L2 cache data read misses
Dw	D cache writes (memory writes)
D1mw	D1 cache write misses
D2mw	L2 cache data write misses

```
Shell - Konsole
Session  Edit  View  Bookmarks  Settings  Help

(chklog) FSCK    Block count: 998038

(chklog) FSCK    Free block count: 993705

(chklog)    3992152 kilobytes total disk space.

(chklog)          0 kilobytes in 1 directories.

(chklog)          0 kilobytes in 0 user files.

(chklog)          0 kilobytes in extended attributes

(chklog)          0 kilobytes in access control lists

(chklog)      17332 kilobytes reserved for system use.

(chklog)    3974820 kilobytes are available for use.

File system checked READ ONLY.
File system is clean.
(chklog) FSCK  processing terminated: 5/16/2004 18.8.27  with return code: 0  exit code: 0.

==1915==
==1915== I   refs:      29,369,425
==1915== I1  misses:         4,425
==1915== L2i misses:         2,049
==1915== I1  miss rate:       0.1%
==1915== L2i miss rate:       0.0%
==1915==
==1915== D   refs:      19,466,490 (18,016,969 rd + 1,449,521 wr)
==1915== D1  misses:        17,564 (     9,187 rd +     8,377 wr)
==1915== L2d misses:         9,852 (     3,404 rd +     6,448 wr)
==1915== D1  miss rate:       0.0% (       0.0% +       0.5% )
==1915== L2d miss rate:       0.0% (       0.0% +       0.4% )
==1915==
==1915== L2 refs:         21,989 (    13,612 rd +     8,377 wr)
==1915== L2 misses:        11,901 (     5,453 rd +     6,448 wr)
==1915== L2 miss rate:       0.0% (       0.0% +       0.4% )
linux:/usr/src/valgrind #
```

FIGURE 4.21
cachegrind's analysis of fsck.jfs (continued).

You can annotate the output from cachegrind using **cg_annotate -pid 1915**.

cg_annotate produces output like that shown in Listing 4.10. It shows one annotation for the routine **dmap_pmap_verify**(). The entry states that 88,405,584 instructions of 99,813,615 total instructions were spent in **dmap_pmap_verify**(). This information is invaluable for deciding where to tune the program. You can also further annotate **dmap_pmap_verify**() to find the actual instructions executed in that routine.

Listing 4.10

Annotation of One Entry of cachegrind for fsck.jfs

Ir	I1mr	I2mr	Dr	D1mr	D2mr	Dw	D1mw	D2mw
88,405,584	23	23	61,740,960	14,535	98	576,828	9	9
fsckbmap.c:dmap_pmap_verify								

For a complete description of cachegrind, see the Valgrind user manual in docs/index.html in the Valgrind distribution.

Some Limitations of Valgrind

You should be aware of two issues when analyzing an application with Valgrind. First, an application running under Valgrind consumes more memory. Second, your program will run slower. However, these two minor annoyances shouldn't stop you from using this powerful memory management debugging tool.

Several projects use or have used Valgrind, including OpenOffice, StarOffice, AbiWord, Koffice, Evolution, Mozilla, and Opera. For a complete list of projects, see the Valgrind web site.

Summary

This chapter looked at four different memory checkers: MEMWATCH, YAMD, Electric Fence, and Valgrind. All these memory checkers can be integrated into any small or large project. They are valuable tools that can uncover memory management problems without large integration effort. It would be easy to set up the project's makefile to include one of the memory checkers. An example of how to change a makefile to add Electric Fence was shown in Listing 4.4.

Web Resources for Memory Checkers

URL	Description
http://www.linkdata.se/sourcecode.html	MEMWATCH
http://www.cs.hmc.edu/~nate/yamd/	YAMD
http://perens.com/FreeSoftware/	Electric Fence
http://valgrind.org/	Valgrind web page

Chapter 5

System Information (/proc)

In this chapter

- What Is /proc?   page 112
- Ways an Administrator Can Use /proc   page 113
- A Map of /proc   page 114
- Summary   page 148
- Web Resources for /proc   page 149

A wealth of information is provided by the /proc file system for the Linux kernel, from information about each process to system-wide information about CPU, memory, file systems, interrupts, and partitions. This chapter covers the /proc file system to help you see the overall information that a running system can provide. The two different types of information in the /proc file system are read-only and writeable. The writeable information can be changed on-the-fly. If you change the value of a /proc entry, the system feature could perform in a different way.

The /proc file system is a special window into the running Linux kernel. Each file under /proc is tied to a kernel that provides the file's information on-the-fly when the file is read. Many utilities rely on /proc to gather system-type information. Some of the utilities that use /proc entries include iostat, sar, lsdev, lsusb, lspci, vmstat, and mpstat. This chapter covers each of these utilities.

What Is /proc?

The /proc file system is a reflection of the system in memory. It can be used as a hierarchal view of the system. The goal of the /proc file system is to provide an easy view of the kernel resources and components. You also can use /proc to view information about the processes that are currently running on the system. A second goal of /proc is to present information about the system in a readable way instead of getting this type of information through API system calls.

There is a close relationship between /proc and **sysctl** functions. In general, all **sysctl** functions are also represented under /proc/sys/ as a proc file system entry. The /proc file system entries are not stored on a nonvolatile medium such as a file system; the entries are generated on-the-fly. In other words, every time the read method for the associated file is invoked, the entries are provided. This results in much freedom in how output is represented to the user. The /proc file system is a file system in the sense that it provides an interface to the user that resembles the normal file system interface of any other file system, allowing access via **open**, **read**, **write**, and **close**.

/proc has two basic interface types: binary and character-based. Most interfaces are text-mode. In cases where binary interfaces are used, usually both types are implemented at the same time. For user-space applications, it is generally simpler to interface with the binary version rather than with text mode, since in the latter case parsing (or at least scanning fixed-format input lines) would be required. On the other hand, binary interfaces are not well-suited for direct interpretation by humans.

Ways an Administrator Can Use /proc

/proc can be used for the following types of system-related tasks:

- Performance and memory information

- Viewing and modifying runtime parameters

- Viewing hardware information

- Viewing and modifying network parameters

- Viewing statistical information

> NOTE You must be careful when changing parameters through the /proc interface.

Figure 5.1 shows a view of a /proc file system for a typical system. This is a snapshot of a SuSE x86 version 9.0 system.

```
    Shell - Konsole <7>

Session Edit  View  Bookmarks  Settings  Help

sfb1:/proc # ls
.         12616   19090   3928   4487   4519   4551   driver       misc
..        1268    2       3929   4490   4520   5      execdomains  modules
1         1276    21803   3968   4493   4522   6      filesystems  mounts
10        14656   21964   3970   4502   4523   6861   fs           net
104       15160   3       3971   4506   4526   6862   ide          partitions
1081      15161   3799    3972   4507   4529   8      interrupts   self
1084      15185   3851    3973   4509   4530   9      iomem        slabinfo
11        15858   3857    3974   4510   4534   buddyinfo ioports    stat
1167      15859   3886    4      4511   4538   bus      irq         sys
1189      15876   3922    4391   4512   4539   cmdline  kallsyms    sysrq-trigger
12        16090   3923    4392   4513   4541   cpuinfo  kcore       sysvipc
12146     16091   3924    4436   4514   4543   devices  kmsg        tty
12147     16833   3925    4466   4515   4544   diskstats loadavg    uptime
12607     16948   3926    4467   4516   4546   dma      locks       version
12608     19089   3927    4484   4518   4547   dri      meminfo     vmstat
sfb1:/proc # 
```

FIGURE 5.1

A view of a typical /proc file system.

A Map of /proc

The following is a brief description of files and directories in the /proc file system. The system shown has the 2.6 kernel and is Linux on an Intel Pentium processor. The **cat** command is used throughout this chapter to display the files in the /proc file system. The entries that are covered are related to debugging or performance tuning, so not all the /proc entries are discussed in this chapter.

Process-Specific Subdirectories

Each process subdirectory has the following entries:

Entry	Description
auxv	ELF auxiliary vector
cmdline	Command-line arguments
cwd	Link to the current working directory
environ	Shows all environment variables known to the process
exe	Link to the executable of this process
fd	Entries of all open files
maps	Memory maps for executables and libraries
mem	Memory for this process
mounts	Mounted file systems
root	Link to the process's root directory
stat	Process status in readable format
statm	Process memory information
status	Process status
wchan	Process predecode for a process's wait channel (wchan)

All the processes running on the machine have entries defined by /proc/*process id*. For an example of the type of process data that can be shown on a system, you can look at the init process, which has a process ID (PID) of 1 (see Figure 5.2).

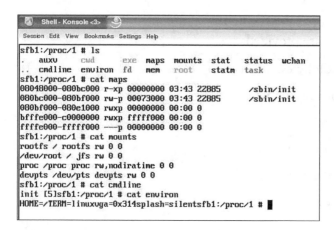

FIGURE 5.2
maps, **mounts**, **cmdline**, and **environ** for PID 1.

Figure 5.3 shows the status for PID 1. This is where the **ps** command captures data for each process. For additional information about the **ps** command, see Chapter 6, "System Tools."

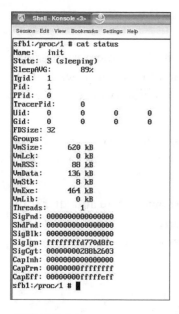

FIGURE 5.3
Status for PID 1.

You can see the process memory usage using the **statm** entry, as shown in Figure 5.4. The following seven values are provided:

- Total program size in kilobytes
- Size of memory portions in kilobytes
- Number of shared pages
- Number of pages that are code
- Number of pages of data/stack
- Number of library pages
- Number of dirty pages

FIGURE 5.4
statm for PID 1.

Figure 5.4 shows that the program's total size is 155 KB. The memory portion's size is 22 KB. The number of shared pages is 119. The number of pages that are code is 119. There are 0 pages of data/stack. The number of library pages is 36. The number of dirty pages is 0.

The **ps** command can be used to display an application's memory usage. The following example looks at three applications and their memory usage. **ps** captures the memory usage by using the /proc/statm fields.

The memory usages of OpenOffice and Mozilla are shown before and after some typical uses of these applications. For OpenOffice the **vsize** starts out as 143976 and grows to 323336, and **rss** starts out as 51996 and grows to 234440.

This example shows the starting of OpenOffice:

```
$ ps -eo"comm,vsize,rss" | grep soffice
soffice.bin     143976 51996
```

The following shows the opening of a 10-page document with a simple layout (26,060 characters):

```
$ ps -eo"comm,vsize,rss" | grep soffice
soffice.bin     157708 68780
```

You see the following after entering **gert** and right-clicking to get corrections:

```
$ ps -eo"comm,vsize,rss" | grep soffice
soffice.bin     323336 234440
```

Here's an example of starting Mozilla:

```
$ ps -eo"comm,vsize,rss" | grep mozilla
mozilla-bin     97084 29392
```

After a few web pages are viewed, the memory usage grows to the following:

```
$ ps -eo"comm,vsize,rss" | grep mozilla
mozilla-bin     142016 44528
```

buddyinfo

buddyinfo contains information about the buddy allocator. This file is used primarily to diagnose memory fragmentation issues. Using the buddy algorithm, each column represents the number of pages of a certain order (a certain size) that are available at any given time. A standard /proc/buddyinfo file looks similar to Figure 5.5. In this case, two chunks of 2^2***PAGE_SIZE** of memory are available in **ZONE_DMA**, and 144 chunks of 2^4***PAGE_SIZE** of memory are available in **ZONE_NORMAL**. The DMA row references the first 16 MB on a system, the HighMem row references all memory greater than 4 GB on a system, and the Normal row references all memory in between.

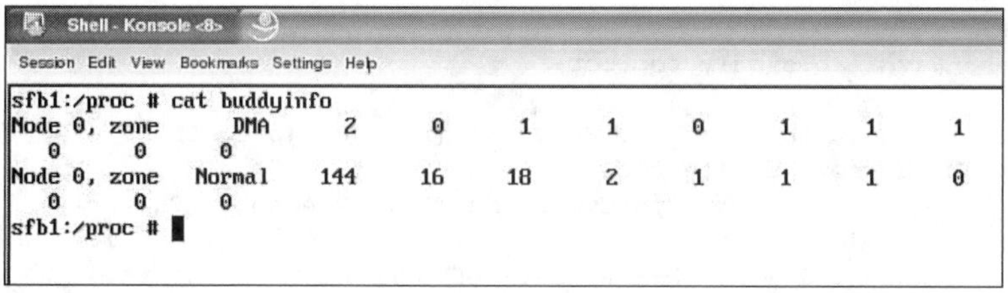

FIGURE 5.5
A standard /proc/buddyinfo file.

bus

The bus directory contains information specific to the various buses available on the system. For example, on a standard system containing USB and PCI buses, current data on each of these buses is available in a subdirectory of the same name within /proc/bus/, such as /proc/bus/pci/.

The subdirectories and files available within /proc/bus/ vary depending on the devices connected to the system.

For example, the /proc/bus/usb/ subdirectory contains files that track the various devices on any USB buses, as well as the drivers required for them.

lsusb

lsusb is a utility for displaying information about all USB buses in the system and all devices connected to them. The lsusb utility uses the /proc/bus/usb information to display USB bus information.

lspci

lspci is a utility for displaying information about all PCI buses in the system and all devices connected to them. The lspci utility uses the /proc/bus/pci information to display PCI bus information. A useful option is **-vv**, which displays everything that each PCI device can provide about itself. Here's some sample output from a six-way server:

```
best@build1:~$ lspci -vv
00:00.0 Host bridge: IBM: Unknown device 0302 (rev 02)
        Control: I/O- Mem+ BusMaster+ SpecCycle- MemWINV- VGASnoop- ParErr+
Stepping- SERR+ FastB2B-
        Status: Cap+ 66Mhz+ UDF- FastB2B+ ParErr- DEVSEL=slow >TAbort- <TAbort-
<MAbort+ >SERR- <PERR-
        Latency: 100
        Capabilities: <available only to root>

00:01.0 VGA compatible controller: S3 Inc. Savage 4 (rev 06) (prog-if 00 [VGA])
        Subsystem: IBM: Unknown device 01c5
        Control: I/O+ Mem+ BusMaster+ SpecCycle- MemWINV- VGASnoop- ParErr+
Stepping- SERR- FastB2B-
        Status: Cap+ 66Mhz- UDF- FastB2B- ParErr- DEVSEL=medium >TAbort-
<TAbort- <MAbort- >SERR- <PERR-
        Latency: 248 (1000ns min, 63750ns max), cache line size 10
        Interrupt: pin A routed to IRQ 0
        Region 0: Memory at fbf80000 (32-bit, non-prefetchable) [size=512K]
        Region 1: Memory at f0000000 (32-bit, prefetchable) [size=128M]
```

```
        Expansion ROM at <unassigned> [disabled] [size=64K]
        Capabilities: <available only to root>

00:02.0 Bridge: IBM: Unknown device 010f
        Subsystem: IBM: Unknown device 0113
        Control: I/O+ Mem+ BusMaster+ SpecCycle- MemWINV- VGASnoop- ParErr+
Stepping- SERR+ FastB2B+
        Status: Cap+ 66Mhz- UDF- FastB2B- ParErr- DEVSEL=medium >TAbort-
<TAbort- <MAbort- >SERR- <PERR-
        Latency: 103 (1000ns min, 2000ns max), cache line size 10
        Interrupt: pin A routed to IRQ 17
        BIST result: 00
        Region 0: [virtual] Memory at fbc00000 (64-bit, non-prefetchable)
[size=2M]
        Region 2: I/O ports at 1800 [size=128]
        Expansion ROM at <unassigned> [disabled] [size=2M]

00:03.0 Ethernet controller: Intel Corp. 82557 [Ethernet Pro 100] (rev 08)
        Subsystem: IBM: Unknown device 024d
        Control: I/O+ Mem+ BusMaster+ SpecCycle- MemWINV+ VGASnoop- ParErr+
Stepping- SERR+ FastB2B-
        Status: Cap+ 66Mhz- UDF- FastB2B+ ParErr- DEVSEL=medium >TAbort-
<TAbort- <MAbort- >SERR- <PERR-
        Latency: 100 (2000ns min, 14000ns max), cache line size 10
        Interrupt: pin A routed to IRQ 42
        Region 0: Memory at fbf7f000 (32-bit, non-prefetchable) [size=4K]
        Region 1: I/O ports at 1880 [size=64]
        Region 2: Memory at fbe00000 (32-bit, non-prefetchable) [size=1M]
        Capabilities: <available only to root>

00:04.0 SCSI storage controller: Adaptec 7892P (rev 02)
        Subsystem: IBM: Unknown device 0201
        Control: I/O- Mem+ BusMaster+ SpecCycle- MemWINV+ VGASnoop- ParErr+
Stepping- SERR+ FastB2B-
        Status: Cap+ 66Mhz+ UDF- FastB2B+ ParErr- DEVSEL=medium >TAbort-
<TAbort- <MAbort- >SERR- <PERR-
        Latency: 100 (10000ns min, 6250ns max), cache line size 10
        Interrupt: pin A routed to IRQ 41
        BIST result: 00
        Region 0: I/O ports at 1900 [disabled] [size=256]
        Region 1: Memory at fbf7e000 (64-bit, non-prefetchable) [size=4K]
        Expansion ROM at <unassigned> [disabled] [size=128K]
        Capabilities: <available only to root>

00:06.0 Class 0808: IBM: Unknown device 0246
        Subsystem: IBM: Unknown device 0247
        Control: I/O- Mem- BusMaster+ SpecCycle- MemWINV- VGASnoop- ParErr+
Stepping+ SERR+ FastB2B-
        Status: Cap- 66Mhz- UDF- FastB2B- ParErr- DEVSEL=medium >TAbort-
<TAbort- <MAbort- >SERR- <PERR-
        Latency: 100 (32000ns min, 32000ns max)
```

```
00:0f.0 ISA bridge: ServerWorks OSB4 South Bridge (rev 50)
        Subsystem: ServerWorks OSB4 South Bridge
        Control: I/O+ Mem+ BusMaster+ SpecCycle- MemWINV- VGASnoop- ParErr+
Stepping- SERR+ FastB2B-
        Status: Cap- 66Mhz- UDF- FastB2B- ParErr- DEVSEL=medium >TAbort-
<TAbort- <MAbort- >SERR- <PERR-
        Latency: 0

00:0f.1 IDE interface: ServerWorks OSB4 IDE Controller (prog-if 8a [Master SecP
PriP])
        Control: I/O+ Mem- BusMaster+ SpecCycle- MemWINV- VGASnoop- ParErr+
Stepping- SERR+ FastB2B-
        Status: Cap- 66Mhz- UDF- FastB2B- ParErr- DEVSEL=medium >TAbort-
<TAbort- <MAbort- >SERR- <PERR-
        Latency: 100
        Region 4: I/O ports at 0700 [size=16]

00:0f.2 USB Controller: ServerWorks OSB4/CSB5 OHCI USB Controller (rev 04)
(prog-if 10 [OHCI])
        Subsystem: ServerWorks OSB4/CSB5 OHCI USB Controller
        Control: I/O+ Mem+ BusMaster+ SpecCycle- MemWINV+ VGASnoop- ParErr+
Stepping- SERR+ FastB2B-
        Status: Cap- 66Mhz- UDF- FastB2B+ ParErr- DEVSEL=medium >TAbort-
<TAbort- <MAbort- >SERR- <PERR-
        Latency: 96 (20000ns max)
        Interrupt: pin A routed to IRQ 16
        Region 0: Memory at fbf7d000 (32-bit, non-prefetchable) [size=4K]

01:00.0 Host bridge: IBM: Unknown device 0302 (rev 02)
        Control: I/O- Mem+ BusMaster+ SpecCycle- MemWINV- VGASnoop- ParErr+
Stepping- SERR+ FastB2B-
        Status: Cap+ 66Mhz+ UDF- FastB2B+ ParErr- DEVSEL=slow >TAbort- <TAbort-
<MAbort+ >SERR- <PERR-
        Latency: 100
        Capabilities: <available only to root>

01:04.0 Ethernet controller: BROADCOM Corporation: Unknown device 16a7 (rev 02)
        Subsystem: BROADCOM Corporation: Unknown device 0009
        Control: I/O- Mem+ BusMaster+ SpecCycle- MemWINV+ VGASnoop- ParErr+
Stepping- SERR+ FastB2B-
        Status: Cap+ 66Mhz+ UDF- FastB2B+ ParErr- DEVSEL=medium >TAbort-
<TAbort- <MAbort- >SERR- <PERR-
        Latency: 96 (16000ns min), cache line size 10
        Interrupt: pin A routed to IRQ 20
        Region 0: Memory at efff0000 (64-bit, non-prefetchable) [size=64K]
        Expansion ROM at <unassigned> [disabled] [size=64K]
        Capabilities: <available only to root>

0a:00.0 Host bridge: IBM: Unknown device 0302 (rev 02)
        Control: I/O- Mem+ BusMaster+ SpecCycle- MemWINV- VGASnoop- ParErr+
Stepping- SERR+ FastB2B-
```

```
          Status: Cap+ 66Mhz+ UDF- FastB2B+ ParErr- DEVSEL=slow >TAbort- <TAbort-
<MAbort+ >SERR- <PERR-
          Latency: 100
          Capabilities: <available only to root>

0a:01.0 RAID bus controller: IBM ServeRAID-3x (rev 10)
          Subsystem: IBM: Unknown device 022e
          Control: I/O+ Mem+ BusMaster+ SpecCycle- MemWINV- VGASnoop- ParErr+
Stepping- SERR+ FastB2B-
          Status: Cap+ 66Mhz- UDF- FastB2B- ParErr- DEVSEL=medium >TAbort-
<TAbort- <MAbort- >SERR- <PERR-
          Latency: 100 (32000ns min, 32000ns max), cache line size 10
          Interrupt: pin A routed to IRQ 29
          Region 0: I/O ports at 3000 [size=256]
          Region 1: Memory at ebf00000 (32-bit, non-prefetchable) [size=1M]
          Expansion ROM at <unassigned> [disabled] [size=32K]
          Capabilities: <available only to root>

0a:02.0 RAID bus controller: IBM ServeRAID-3x (rev 10)
          Subsystem: IBM: Unknown device 022e
          Control: I/O+ Mem+ BusMaster+ SpecCycle- MemWINV- VGASnoop- ParErr+
Stepping- SERR+ FastB2B-
          Status: Cap+ 66Mhz- UDF- FastB2B- ParErr- DEVSEL=medium >TAbort-
<TAbort- <MAbort- >SERR- <PERR-
          Latency: 100 (32000ns min, 32000ns max), cache line size 10
          Interrupt: pin A routed to IRQ 33
          Region 0: I/O ports at 3100 [size=256]
          Region 1: Memory at ebe00000 (32-bit, non-prefetchable) [size=1M]
          Expansion ROM at <unassigned> [disabled] [size=32K]
          Capabilities: <available only to root>
```

cmdline

cmdline is the kernel command line. This file shows the parameters passed to the Linux kernel when it is started. A standard /proc/cmdline file looks similar to Figure 5.6.

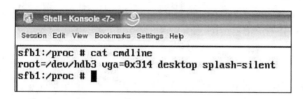

FIGURE 5.6
A standard /proc/cmdline file.

cpuinfo

cpuinfo contains information about the CPU. This is a collection of CPU and system architecture-dependent items. For each supported architecture a different list can be provided. Two common entries are **processor**, which gives the number of CPUs, and **bogomips**, a system constant that is calculated during kernel initialization. A standard /proc/cpuinfo file looks similar to Figure 5.7.

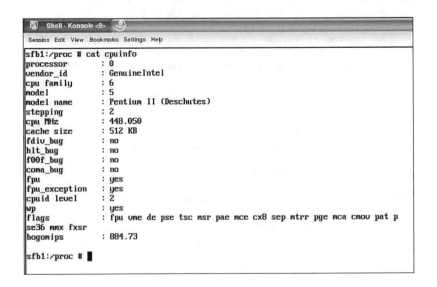

FIGURE 5.7
A standard /proc/cpuinfo file.

diskstats

diskstats provides a view of the disks and/or partitions on the system. The iostat and sar utilities use the diskstats /proc entry to capture the data display in these utilities. Let's take a closer look at both of these utilities.

iostat

The Linux iostat utility analyzes and reports on I/O and CPU utilization and allocation by providing a simultaneous interval-by-interval profile of disk and CPU usage. This utility can indicate which system resource might be limiting overall system performance if used during heavy workloads or periods of inadequate system performance. Once the system bottleneck is identified, directed actions can be taken to improve system performance. iostat uses /proc/diskstats, /proc/stat, /proc/partitions, and /proc/sys to get its information.

The **iostat** command monitors system input and output device loading by observing the time the devices are active in relation to their average transfer rates. The command generates reports that can be used to change the system configuration to better balance the input and output load between the physical disks.

As with most monitoring commands, the first line of iostat output reflects a summary of statistics since boot time. To look at meaningful real-time data, run iostat with a time stamp and look at the lines that report summaries over the time stamp intervals. iostat can provide a way to balance the load among the physical hard drives by viewing statistics from bytes read from or written to the drive.

When bytes are either read or written, iostat reports the following information:

- **tps**—Number of transfers per second.
- **device**—Disk device name
- **Blk_read/s**—Amount of data read from the device, expressed in number of blocks per second.
- **Blk_wrtn/s**—Amount of data written to the device, expressed in number of blocks per second.
- **Blk_read**—Total number of blocks read.
- **Blk_wrtn**—Total number of blocks written.
- **kB_read/s**—Amount of data read from the device, expressed in kilobytes per second.
- **kB_wrtn/s**—Amount of data written from the device, expressed in kilo bytes per second.
- **kB_read**—Total number of kilobytes read.
- **kB_wrtn**—Total number of kilobytes written.
- **rrqm/s**—Number of read requests merged per second that were issued to the device.
- **wrqm/s**—Number of write requests merged per second that were issued to the device.
- **r/s**—Number of read requests that were issued to the device per second.

- **w/s**—Number of write requests that were issued to the device per second.

- **rsec/s**—Number of sectors read from the device per second.

- **wsec/s**—Number of sectors written to the device per second.

- **rkB/s**—Number of kilobytes read from the device per second.

- **wkB/s**—Number of kilobytes written to the device per second.

- **avgrp-sz**—Average size (in sectors) of requests that were issued to the device.

- **avgqu-sz**—Average queue length.

iostat displays statistics about the disk subsystem that are more detailed than those displayed by vmstat. Here's some sample iostat output:

```
best@build1:~$ iostat
Linux 2.4.27-2-686-smp (build1)     05/11/05

avg-cpu:  %user   %nice   %sys   %idle
           1.54    3.03   1.74   93.68


Device:            tps   Blk_read/s   Blk_wrtn/s   Blk_read    Blk_wrtn
dev8-0            1.77        69.23       119.87   341187484   590771256
dev8-1           94.93       863.24       439.24  4254606666  2164837392
dev8-2           16.83       147.99       263.66   729402674  1299470184
dev8-3            9.16        80.77       153.83   398101034   758163712
dev8-4           29.44       264.56       371.61  1303919362  1831506272
```

iostat's **-x** option displays extended disk statistics:

```
best@build1:~$ iostat -x
Linux 2.4.27-2-686-smp (build1)     05/11/05

avg-cpu:  %user   %nice   %sys   %idle
           1.54    3.03   1.74   93.68


Device:    rrqm/s wrqm/s  r/s   w/s rsec/s  wsec/s    rkB/s    wkB/s avgrq-sz
avgqu-sz   await  svctm  %util
/dev/scsi/host0/bus0/target12/lun0/disc
           7.81  14.08  0.87  0.89  69.23  119.87    34.61    59.93   107.33
0.50  281.92  59.07   1.04
/dev/scsi/host0/bus0/target12/lun0/part1
           7.74  14.07  0.85  0.89  68.73  119.74    34.36    59.87   108.44
0.49  284.08  59.34   1.03
/dev/scsi/host0/bus0/target12/lun0/part2
           0.03   0.01  0.02  0.00   0.42    0.13     0.21     0.06    23.40
0.00  126.27  53.18   0.01
/dev/scsi/host1/bus0/target0/lun0/disc
```

```
           136.91  39.92 79.94 14.97  435.72  435.72   217.86    217.86      9.18
2.57   91.82  24.88  23.61
/dev/scsi/host1/bus0/target0/lun0/part1
           136.88  39.92 79.94 14.97  435.72  435.72   217.86    217.86      9.18
2.57   91.82  24.88  23.61
/dev/scsi/host1/bus0/target1/lun0/disc
             5.95  28.70 12.57  4.22  147.99  263.66    74.00    131.83     24.52
4.36   292.87  30.05   5.04
/dev/scsi/host1/bus0/target1/lun0/part1
             5.92  28.70 12.57  4.22  147.94  263.66    73.97    131.83     24.52
4.36   292.88  30.05   5.04
/dev/scsi/host1/bus0/target2/lun0/disc
             3.32  16.85  6.79  2.36   80.77  153.83    40.39     76.91     25.64
2.67   291.59  38.11   3.49
/dev/scsi/host1/bus0/target2/lun0/part1
             3.31  16.85  6.79  2.36   80.75  153.83    40.37     76.91     25.63
2.67   291.59  38.11   3.49
/dev/scsi/host2/bus0/target0/lun0/disc
            11.36  38.74 21.72  7.65  264.56  371.60   132.28    185.80     21.65
4.36   189.96  33.83   9.94
/dev/scsi/host2/bus0/target0/lun0/part1
            11.34  38.74 21.72  7.65  264.53  371.60   132.27    185.80     21.65
4.36   189.96  33.83   9.94
```

iostat can be used to measure the results of tuning a system by load-balancing between disks on a system. The following example shows that dev8-1 starts out with 0 **Blk_wrtn**, and after the workload has finished the **Blk_wrtn** has increased to 6129208. It also shows that device dev8-0 has a very small amount of activity.

Here's iostat before the workload:

```
Linux 2.4.21-1.1931.2.349.2.2.entsmp 05/09/2005

Device:            tps   Blk_read/s   Blk_wrtn/s   Blk_read   Blk_wrtn
dev8-0          164.69      1312.58       361.87     150002      41354
dev8-1            2.81         5.71         0.00        652          0
```

Here's iostat after the workload:

```
Linux 2.4.21-1.1931.2.349.2.2.entsmp 05/09/2005

Device:            tps   Blk_read/s   Blk_wrtn/s   Blk_read   Blk_wrtn
dev8-0           55.12       410.41       146.44     152426      54386
dev8-1          341.88      2828.43     16502.98    1050478    6129208
```

Now we tune this system to balance the reads and writes from dev8-0 and dev8-1 and then rerun iostat to determine the effectiveness of the balancing. After the system balancing, dev8-0 has **Blk_read** as 1253186 and dev8-1 has **Blk_read** as 1051798. For **Blk_wrtn**, dev8-0 has 6209198 and dev8-1 has 6138576. The workload balancing was very effective in that roughly the same number of reads and writes occurred for each device.

Here's iostat after the workload balancing:

```
Linux 2.4.21-1.1931.2.349.2.2.entsmp 02/09/2004

Device:           tps   Blk_read/s   Blk_wrtn/s   Blk_read   Blk_wrtn
dev8-0         121.60       612.59      3035.21    1253186    6209198
dev8-1         110.10       514.15      3000.69    1051798    6138576
```

sar

The sar utility with the **-b** option reports the I/O and transfer rate. **sar -b** reports the following I/O rates:

- **tps**—Number of transfers per second issued to the device.

- **rtps**—Total number of read requests per second to the device.

- **wtps**—Total number of write requests per second to the device.

- **bread/s**—Total amount of data read from the device in blocks per second.

- **bwrtn/s**—Total amount of data written to the device in blocks per second.

Here's sample output from **sar -b**:

```
bbest@build1:~$ sar -b
Linux 2.4.27-2-686-smp (build1)      05/12/05

00:05:01         tps      rtps      wtps    bread/s    bwrtn/s
00:15:01       60.99     37.96     23.02    1273.06     603.01
00:25:01       75.21     51.50     23.71    1864.94     646.64
00:35:01       20.34      0.12     20.21       3.10     593.95
00:45:01       35.19      5.21     29.99      43.17     790.30
00:55:01       54.86     27.86     27.01     892.61     734.99
01:05:01      134.89    112.51     22.38    4048.51     665.93
01:15:01        9.40      0.01      9.39       0.05     233.52
01:25:01       63.17     46.68     16.48    1006.31     500.63
01:35:01       16.00      0.00     16.00       0.16     462.36
01:45:01       23.46      3.14     20.32      25.19     655.67
01:55:01       30.76      0.04     30.72       1.13     948.36
02:05:01       21.82      0.01     21.81       0.07     600.12
02:15:01       30.21      3.11     27.10     122.32     830.31
02:25:01       44.35      6.68     37.67     146.25    1159.22
02:35:01       26.62      0.09     26.54       2.55     822.39
02:45:01       26.40      1.70     24.71      18.27     792.12
```

The sar output shows that the peak of 1159.22 bwrtn/s (the total amount of data written to the device in blocks per second) occurred on the system at 02:25:01.

A standard /proc/diskstats file looks similar to Figure 5.8.

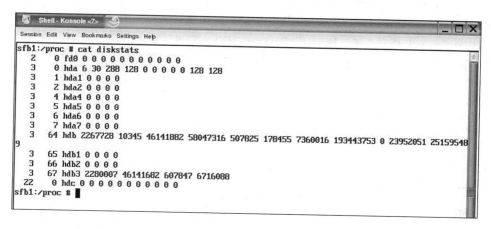

FIGURE 5.8
A standard /proc/diskstats file.

interrupts

interrupts provides information about the number of interrupts per IRQ on the x86 architecture. A standard /proc/interrupts file looks similar to Figure 5.9. Each number in the far-left column represents the interrupt that is being used.

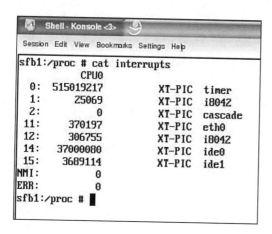

FIGURE 5.9
A standard /proc/interrupts file.

lsdev

lsdev displays information about installed hardware. lsdev acquires information about your computer's installed hardware from the interrupts, ioports, and DMA files in the /proc directory, thus displaying an overview of which hardware uses what I/O addresses and what IRQ and DMA channels. Here's some sample output from lsdev:

```
best@build1:~$ lsdev
Device            DMA   IRQ   I/O Ports
--------------------------------------

Adaptec                       1900-19ff
aic7xxx                 41
cascade            4     2
dma                           0080-008f
dma1                          0000-001f
dma2                          00c0-00df
eepro100                       1880-18bf
eth0                    42
fpu                           00f0-00ff
IBM                           1800-187f 3000-30ff 3100-31ff
Intel                         1880-18bf
ips               29 33        3000-30ff    3100-31ff
keyboard                 1    0060-006f
PCI                           0cf8-0cff
pic1                          0020-003f
pic2                          00a0-00bf
rtc                      8    0070-007f
serial                        03f8-03ff
ServerWorks                   0700-070f
timer                    0    0040-005f
vga+                          03c0-03df
```

kallsyms

kallsyms provides symbols exported by the kernel.

kcore

This file represents the system's physical memory. It is stored in the core file format.

kmsg

kmsg is kernel messages that are still buffered. The dmesg utility can print or control the still-buffered kernel messages.

loadavg

loadavg is the system load average for 1, 5, and 15 minutes. The first value is the load average for 1 minute. The second value is the load average for 5 minutes. The third value is the load average for 15 minutes. The fourth value is the number of currently ready-to-run threads and the total number of threads in the machine. The fifth value is the PID of the most-recently-created thread.

A standard /proc/loadavg file looks similar to Figure 5.10.

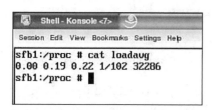

FIGURE 5.10
A standard /proc/loadavg file.

meminfo

meminfo contains information about memory usage, both physical and swap. It reports valuable information about the current utilization of RAM on the system:

- **MemTotal**—Total usable RAM.

- **MemFree**—The sum of LowFree + HighFree.

- **Buffers**—Memory in the buffer cache.

- **Cached**—Memory in the page cache (doesn't SwapCache).

- **SwapCached**—Memory that once was swapped out.

- **Active**—Memory that has been used more recently and usually is not reclaimed unless absolutely necessary.

- **Inactive**—Memory that has been less recently used.

- **HighTotal**—The total amount of memory in the high region. Highmem is all memory above (approximately) 860 MB of physical RAM.

- **HighFree**—High region free memory.

- **LowTotal**—The total amount of non-highmem memory.

- **LowFree**—The amount of free memory in the low memory region.

- **SwapTotal**—The total amount of swap memory.

- **SwapFree**—The total amount of free swap memory.

- **Dirty**—Memory waiting to get written back to the disk.

- **Writeback**—Memory that is actively being written back to the disk.

- **Mapped**—Files that have been mmapped.

- **Slab**—In-kernel data structures cache.

- **Committed_AS**—An estimate of how much RAM is needed to make a 99.99% guarantee that there is never an OOM (out of memory) for this workload. Normally the kernel overcommits memory. So if you do a 1 GB **malloc**, for example, nothing happens, really. Only when you start *using* that **malloc** memory do you get real memory on demand, and just as much as needed. Other cases might include when a file is mmapped that's shared only when a write to the file occurs and a private copy of that data is created. Normally it is shared between processes. The **Committed_AS** is a guesstimate of how much RAM/swap is needed in the worst case.

- **PageTables**—The amount of memory dedicated to the lowest level of page tables.

- **VmallocTotal**—The total size of the **vmalloc** memory area.

- **VmallocUsed**—The amount of **vmalloc** area that is used.

- **VmallocChunk**—The largest contiguous block of **vmalloc** area that is free.

A standard /proc/meminfo file looks similar to Figure 5.11.

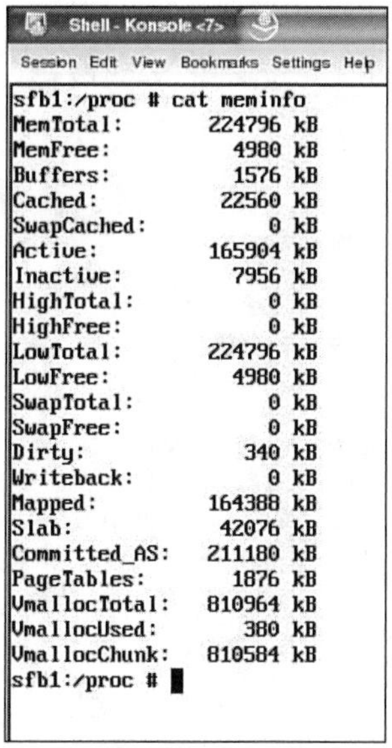

FIGURE 5.11
A standard /proc/meminfo file.

vmstat

vmstat is a program that gives you a quick look at statistics about memory, CPU, and disk subsystems. vmstat is generally executed for a short period of time so that you can see a trend in the utilization of the subsystem you are interested in. Often vmstat helps you know where to investigate when a system is not performing as expected. The **vmstat** command provides data that can help you find unusual system activity such as high page faults or excessive context switches, which can degrade your system performance.

The vmstat utility reports certain kernel statistics kept about process, virtual memory, disk, trap, and CPU activity. vmstat uses /proc/meminfo to get some of its information. It is useful to tune a system. Let's take a look at a desktop system and a heavily used server.

The following output is from a lightly used desktop:

```
best@sfb1:~> vmstat
procs ------memory----- --swap-- ---io-- —system- --cpu--
 r  b   swpd   free   buff  cache   si   so   bi   bo   in   cs us sy id wa
 0  1      0   1648  17436  26416    0    0    7    3   11    9 18  6 74  1
```

The following output is from a more heavily used server:

```
best@build1:~$ vmstat 5
   procs           memory              swap      io       system      cpu
 r  b  w   swpd   free   buff   cache   si  so   bi   bo    in    cs   us sy id
18  0  0  11524 391348 270652 1641016   0   0    6  4216  279  1897   90 10  0
21  0  0  11524 391468 269848 1659776   0   0    1  4356  289  2015   89 11  0
18  0  0  11524 362604 270404 1678080   0   0    2  3989  269  1853   91  9  0
21  0  0  11524 345720 271072 1696108   0   0   14  4794  401  1788   89 11  0
18  0  0  11524 249360 269888 1716568   0   0   14  5045  305  1797   88 12  0
19  0  0  11524 241992 270440 1735688   0   0    1  4219  246  1892   90 10  0
19  0  1  11524 248128 271064 1754072   0   0    0  4086  242  1971   91  9  0
19  0  0  11524 245132 271660 1769716   0   0   48  4299  260  2072   90 10  0
18  0  0  11524 213600 270796 1777648   0   0    1  2234  208  2061   92  8  0
```

The following output is the same server without the load on it:

```
best@build1:~$ vmstat 5
   procs           memory              swap      io       system      cpu
 r  b  w   swpd   free   buff   cache   si  so   bi    bo   in    cs   us sy id
 0  1  0  17192  81828 178624 2331504   0   0  8110  125 3230  2521   1  3 96
 0  3  0  17192  81736 177644 2332428   0   0  9606  186 3583  3101   1  3 96
 0  4  0  17192  81848 176608 2329160   0   0  9583  898 3861  3429   4  5 91
 0  1  0  17192  82972 175404 2334892   0   0 10415  123 3809  3006   2  3 95
 0  0  0  17192  82820 174048 2336660   0   0  9845  100 3632  3044   1  3 95
```

The fields are as follows:

- procs shows the number of processes that are ready and running (r), blocked (b), or swapped out (w).

- memory shows the amounts of swap (swpd), free (free), buffered (buff), and cached memory (cache) in kilobytes.

- swap shows in kilobytes per second the amount of memory swapped in (si) from disk and swapped out (so) to disk.

- io shows the number of blocks sent (bi) and received (bo) to and from block devices per second.

- system shows the number of interrupts (in) and context switches (cs) per second.

- cpu shows the percentage of total CPU time in terms of user (us), system (sy), and idle (id) time.

The procs r number is the number of processes that are in the run queue. The run queue number shows how many processes are ready to be executed but that cannot be run because another process needs to finish. With a lightly loaded system, this number is usually in the range of 0 to 3. With a more heavily used system, this number will be above 15.

Other interesting values are the system numbers for in and cs. The in value is the number of interrupts per second a system is getting. A system servicing a significant network or disk I/O will have high values here, because interrupts are generated every time something is read from or written to the network or disk subsystem. The cs value is the number of context switches. Some reasons why context switches occur are as follows:

- Rescheduling, requiring switches between processes

- Kernel calls, requiring switching between process and kernel space

- Interrupts, requiring switching between process and kernel space

Context switches are the main cause of both latency and CPU load. Use vmstat to monitor and evaluate system activity. For example, if the value for free is small and accompanied by high values for swap (si and so), you have excessive paging and swapping due to physical memory shortage.

If the value of so is consistently high, the system may have either insufficient swap space or physical memory. Use the **free** command to see your memory and swap space configurations. Use the **swapon -s** command to display your swap device configuration. Use the **iostat** command to see which disk is being used the most.

free

free displays the amount of free and used memory in the system:

```
best@build1:~$ free
            total      used      free    shared   buffers    cached
Mem:      3090816   2844796    246020         0     35052   1918428
-/+ buffers/cache:    891316   2199500
Swap:     2097136     25632   2071504
```

mpstat

mpstat is a program that lets you see statistics about processor utilization. mpstat provides an option that lets you display statistics for a specific CPU on multiprocessor systems. The mpstat fields have the following meanings:

- **CPU**—The processor number. The keyword **all** indicates that statistics are calculated as averages among all processors.

- **%user**—The percentage of CPU utilization that occurred while executing at the user level (application).

- **%nice**—The percentage of CPU utilization that occurred while executing at the user level with the nice priority.

- **%system**—The percentage of CPU utilization that occurred while executing at the system level (kernel).

- **%idle**—The percentage of time that the CPU(s) were idle and the system did not have an outstanding disk I/O request.

- **intr/s**—The total number of interrupts received per second by the CPU(s).

Here's some sample mpstat output:

```
best@build1:~$ mpstat -P ALL 2 5
Linux 2.4.27-2-686-smp (build1)     05/11/05
13:06:54    CPU   %user   %nice %system    %idle    intr/s
13:06:56    all    7.44    0.00    2.81    89.75    481.50
13:06:56      0   48.50    0.00    2.00    49.50    481.50
13:06:56      1    0.00    0.00    0.50    99.50    481.50
13:06:56      2    0.00    0.00    0.50    99.50    481.50
13:06:56      3    0.00    0.00    0.00   100.00    481.50
13:06:56      4   11.00    0.00   19.00    70.00    481.50
13:06:56      5    0.00    0.00    0.00   100.00    481.50
13:06:56      6    0.00    0.00    0.50    99.50    481.50
```

net

net contains information about the network layer(s). This directory provides various networking parameters and statistics:

- **arp**—The Address Resolution Protocol (ARP) table.
- **dev_mcast**—Displays the various Layer 2 multicast groups each device is listening to.
- **mcfilter**—Multicast filter.
- **netstat**—Network statistics.
- **raw**—Raw device statistics.
- **rt_cache**—Routing cache.
- **snmp**—Information for SNMP data.
- **softnet_stat**—Softnet statistics.
- **udp**—UDP sockets.
- **dev**—Network devices with statistics.
- **igmp**—IGMP multicast information.
- **netlink**—List of **PF_NETLINK** sockets.
- **packet**—Packet information.
- **route**—IP routing information.
- **rt_cache_stat**—Routing cache.
- **sockstat**—Socket statistics.
- **tcp**—TCP socket information.
- **unix**—UNIX domain socket information.

Standard /proc/net/netstat, route, and sockstat files look similar to Figure 5.12.

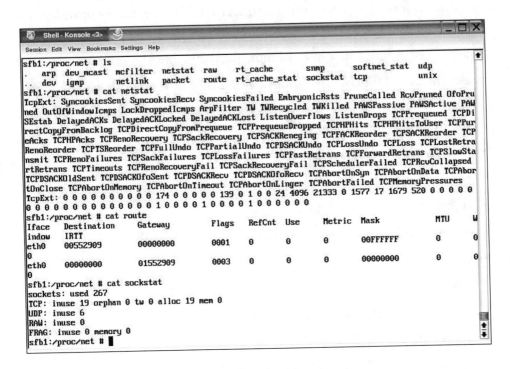

FIGURE 5.12
Standard /proc/net/netstat, route, and sockstat files.

slabinfo

slabinfo provides information about memory usage at the slab level. It provides information about objects in the Linux kernel (buffer heads, inodes, dentries, and so on) that have their own cache and gives statistics about the caches. A standard /proc/slabinfo file looks similar to Figure 5.13.

```
sfb1:/proc # cat slabinfo
slabinfo - version: 2.0 (statistics)
# name            <active_objs> <num_objs> <objsize> <objperslab> <pagesperslab> : tunables <batc
hcount> <limit> <sharedfactor> : slabdata <active_slabs> <num_slabs> <sharedavail> : globalstat <
listallocs> <maxobjs> <grown> <reaped> <error> <maxfreeable> <freelimit> : cpustat <allochit> <al
locmiss> <freehit> <freemiss>
unix_sock            226    280    548    7    1 : tunables   32   16    0 : slabdata     40
40      0 : globalstat   43286    308   447  362    0    3   39 : cpustat  13061   4389  17197
  27
tcp_tw_bucket          0      0    100   39    1 : tunables   32   16    0 : slabdata      0
 0      0 : globalstat    1360     29    68   68    0    0   71 : cpustat     79     85    164
   0
tcp_bind_bucket       19    127     28  127    1 : tunables   32   16    0 : slabdata      1
 1      0 : globalstat    1616     39     1    0    0    0  159 : cpustat    105    101    187
   0
tcp_open_request       0      0     68   56    1 : tunables   32   16    0 : slabdata      0
 0      0 : globalstat     896     16    56   56    0    0   88 : cpustat      5     56     61
   0
inet_peer_cache        0      0     52   72    1 : tunables   32   16    0 : slabdata      0
 0      0 : globalstat     160     16    10   10    0    0  104 : cpustat      0     10     10
   0
ip_fib_hash            9    127     28  127    1 : tunables   32   16    0 : slabdata      1
 1      0 : globalstat      32     20     1    0    0    0  159 : cpustat      7      2      0
   0
ip_dst_cache           9     15    260   15    1 : tunables   32   16    0 : slabdata      1
 1      0 : globalstat   97646     75  1459 1456    0    0   47 : cpustat   2698   8821  11508
   2
arp_cache              1     21    188   21    1 : tunables   32   16    0 : slabdata      1
 1      0 : globalstat    7856     19   410  409    0    0   53 : cpustat    243    491    733
   0
```

FIGURE 5.13
A standard /proc/slabinfo file.

stat

stat provides general statistics about the system, such as CPU, interrupts, and context switches.

iostat uses /proc/stats to get some of its information. For details about iostat, see the "iostat" section.

The stat fields are as follows:

- **cpu**—The number of jiffies spent in user, nice, system, idle, iowait, irq, and softirq.
- **cpu0**—Per-CPU statistics.
- **intr**—The number of interrupts received.
- **ctxt**—The number of context switches.

- **btime**—Boot time.

- **processes**—The number of forks.

- **procs_running**—The number of running processes.

- **procs_blocked**—The number of blocked processes.

A standard /proc/stat file looks similar to Figure 5.14.

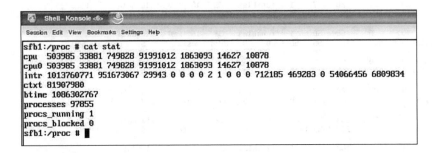

FIGURE 5.14
A standard /proc/stat file.

sys

The sys directory allows some of the parameters within the kernel to be changed without rebooting the system. To change a value, echo the new value into the file. Note that the change applies only to this boot of the system. A boot script can be created to change the value if the change to the parameter needs to be permanent.

dev/fs

dev/fs provides information about file system-type structures. The fields are as follows:

- **aio-max-nr**—Maximum number of aio requests.

- **aio-nr**—Number of events on the io_setup system call for all active aio contexts.

- **dentry-state**—Information about directory entries.

- **dir-notify-enable**—Directory notification.

- **file-max**—The maximum number of open files.

- **file-nr**—Open files.

- **inode-nr**—The number of inodes the system has allocated and free inodes.

- **inode-state**—Allocated and free inodes and five additional values.

- **lease-break-time**—Lease time.

- **leases-enable**—Lease enabled.

- **overflowgid**—Defines the group ID.

- **overflowuid**—Defines the user ID.

- **binfmt_misc**—The ability to register additional binary formats.

A standard /proc/sys/fs file looks similar to Figure 5.15.

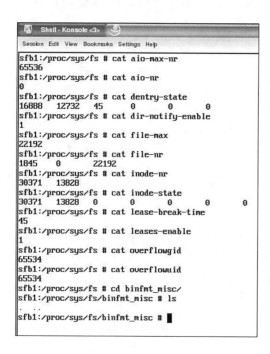

FIGURE 5.15
A standard /proc/sys/fs file.

To change file-max from what it is now on this system (22192) to 30000, do an echo to file-max, as shown in Figure 5.16.

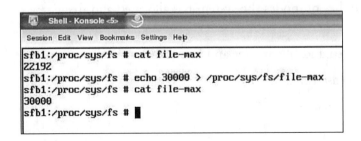

FIGURE 5.16
Changing file-max.

/sys/kernel

/sys/kernel provides information about the kernel using the following fields (see Figure 5.17):

- **cad_pid**—Ctrl-Alt-Delete PID.

- **cap-bound**—Capability bounding set.

- **core_pattern**—String pattern for core filenames.

- **core_uses_pid**—Use PID for the core filename.

- **ctrl-alt-del**—Tells how Ctrl-Alt-Delete is processed.

- **domainname**—The system's domain name.

- **hostname**—The system's hostname.

- **hotplug**—The utility configuration name when the system configuration changes (the default is /sbin/hotplug).

- **msgmax**—The maximum size of any message sent from one process to another.

- **msgmnb**—The maximum number of bytes in a single message queue.

- **msgmni**—The maximum number of message queue identifiers.

- **ngroups_max**—The maximum number of groups.

- **osrelease**—The kernel release number.

- **ostype**—The operating system.

- **overflowgid**—The overflow group ID.

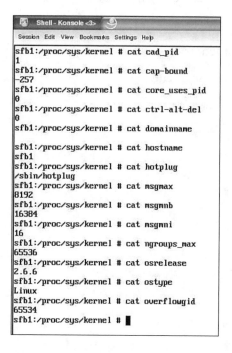

FIGURE 5.17
A standard /proc/sys/kernel file.

/sys/kernel provides several more fields, as shown in Figure 5.18:

- **overflowuid**—The overflow user ID.

- **panic**—Defines how many seconds the kernel postpones rebooting the system when a kernel panic is experienced.

- **panic_on_oops**—Defines whether the kernel will panic on an Oops.

- **pid_max**—The maximum number of PIDs.

- **printk**—Controls a variety of settings related to printing error messages.

- **printk_ratelimit**—The **printk** rate limit.

- **printk_ratelimit_burst**—The **printk** rate burst limit.

- **rtsig-max**—The maximum number of POSIX real-time (queued) signals that can be outstanding in the system.

- **rtsig-nr**—The number of real-time signals currently queued.

- **sem**—Semaphore limits.

- **shmall**—The maximum size of shared memory.

- **shmmax**—The maximum shared memory segment.

- **shmmni**—Shared memory array identifiers.

- **sysrq**—SysRq is enabled.

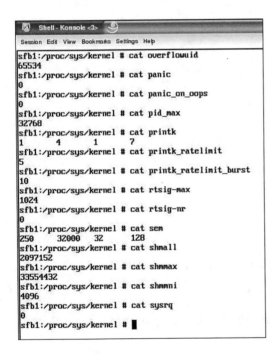

FIGURE 5.18
A standard /proc/sys/kernel file.

/sys/kernel provides the additional information shown in Figure 5.19:

- **tainted**—Specifies whether the kernel has loaded tainted modules.

- **threads-max**—The maximum number of threads.

- **version**—How many times the kernel has been built from this source base. The date following it indicates when the kernel was built.

- **pty**—A directory with information about the number of UNIX 98 pseudoterminals.

- **random**—This directory contains various parameters controlling the operation of the file /dev/random.

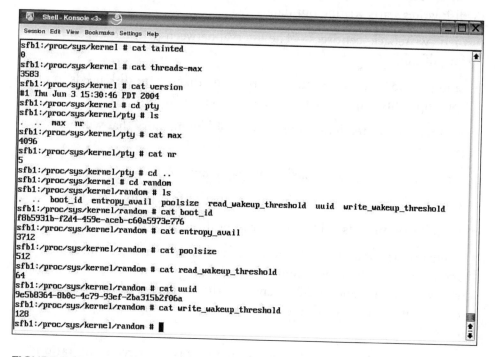

FIGURE 5.19
A standard /proc/sys/kernel file.

/sys/vm

/sys/vm is the virtual memory subsystem. The files in this directory can be used to tune the kernel's virtual memory subsystem. The fields are as follows:

- **block_dump**—When this flag is set, can be used to debug why a disk needs to spin up.

- **dirty_back_ground_ratio**—The number of pages at which the pdflush daemon will start writing out dirty data.

- **dirty_expire_centisecs**—When dirty data is old enough to be written out by the pdflush daemon.

- **dirty_ratio**—The number of pages at which a process that is generating disk writes starts writing out data.

- **dirty_writeback_centisecs**—The interval between periodic wake-ups for pdflush.

- **laptop_mode**—Used to minimize the time that a hard disk needs to be spun up. This helps conserve battery power on laptops.

- **lower_zone_protection**—The amount of low memory that will be protected.

- **max_map_count**—The maximum map count.

- **min_free_kbytes**—The minimum number of free kilobytes.

- **nr_pdflush_threads**—The number of pdflush threads.

- **overcommit_memory**—The kernel supports three overcommit handling modes. 0 means that overcommits of address space are refused. 1 means no overcommit handling. 2 means that the system's total address space commit is not permitted to exceed swap plus a configurable percentage of RAM.

- **overcommit_ratio**—If **overcommit_memory** is 2, **overcommit_ratio** is the configurable percentage of RAM.

- **page-cluster**—The number of pages that are written to swap at a time.

- **swappiness**—Determines the amount of swapping.

A standard /proc/sys/vm file looks similar to Figure 5.20.

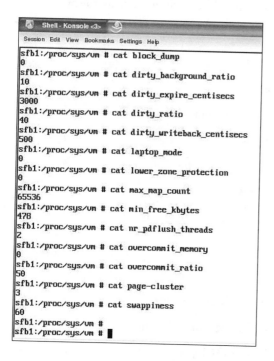

FIGURE 5.20
A standard /proc/sys/vm file.

sysrq-trigger

sysrq-trigger triggers sysrq functions.

Magic SysRq is a key combination directly intercepted by the kernel. Among other things, it can be used to perform an emergency shutdown. It is described in Documentation/sysrq.txt. Magic SysRq is invoked as Alt-SysRq-*command*. The SysRq key is also labeled as Print Screen. Writing a character to this has the same effect as pressing Alt-SysRq-*that character*.

This makes SysRq facilities available to remote users. It is useful when access to the keyboard is unavailable. A useful debug key is Alt-SysRq-T, which shows information about the tasks currently running. Each process has a stack trace of the process displayed.

/proc/vmstat

vmstat reports on the global page accounting. The variables are as follows:

- **nr_dirty**—Dirty writeable pages.
- **nr_writeback**—Pages under writeback.
- **nr_unstable**—NFS unstable pages.
- **nr_page_table_pages**—Pages used for pagetables.
- **nr_mapped**—Mapped into pagetables.
- **nr_slab**—In slab.
- **pgpgin**—Disk reads.
- **pgpgout**—Disk writes.
- **pswpin**—Swap reads.
- **pswpout**—Swap writes.
- **pgalloc_high**—Page allocations in the high region.
- **pgalloc_normal**—Page allocations in the normal region.
- **pgalloc_dma**—Page allocations in the DMA region.
- **pgfree**—Page freeing.
- **pgactivate**—Pages moved from inactive to active.
- **pgdeactivate**—Pages moved from active to inactive.
- **pgfault**—Faults (major and minor).
- **pgmajfault**—Faults (major only).
- **pgrefill_high**—Inspected in **refill_inactive_zone**.
- **pgrefill_normal**—Inspected in **refill_normal_zone**.
- **pgrefill_dma**—Inspected in **refill_dma_zone**.
- **pgsteal_high**—Total highmem pages reclaimed.
- **pgsteal_normal**—Total normal pages reclaimed.
- **pgsteal_dma**—Total DMA pages reclaimed.
- **pgscan_kswapd_high**—Total highmem pages scanned by kswapd.

- **pgscan_kswapd_normal**—Total normal pages scanned by kswapd.
- **pgscan_kswapd_dma**—Total DMA pages scanned by kswapd.
- **pgscan_direct_high**—Total highmem pages scanned.
- **pgscan_direct_normal**—Total normal pages scanned.
- **pgscan_direct_dma**—Total DMA pages scanned.
- **pginodesteal**—Pages reclaimed via inode freeing.
- **slabs_scanned**—Slab objects scanned.
- **kswapd_steal**—Pages reclaimed by kswapd.
- **kswapd_inodesteal**—Reclaimed via kswapd inode freeing.
- **pageoutrun**—kswapd's calls to page reclaim.
- **allocstall**—Direct reclaim calls.
- **pgrotated**—Pages rotated to tail of the LRU.

Figures 5.21 and 5.22 show standard /proc/vmstat files.

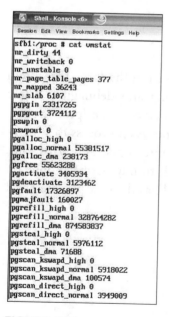

FIGURE 5.21
A standard /proc/vmstat file.

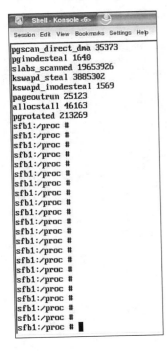

FIGURE 5.22
A standard /proc/vmstat file.

Summary

This chapter covered the system information available from the /proc file system and some of the key commands for performance tuning and debugging. These commands use the /proc entries to display system information. The /proc file system has a wealth of information—from information about each process to system-wide information about CPU, memory, file systems, interrupts, and partitions. Some of the /proc file system parameters can be tuned. If tuning has been done on a running kernel, make sure that each file that was tuned has the new parameter set by adding it to the distribution sysctl.conf file.

Web Resources for /proc

URL	Description
http://www.kernel.org	Kernel source. Several files in the /Documentation directory of the kernel source provide more information about each /proc entry. The proc.txt file in the /filesystems directory is one such example of a file that contains additional information about the /proc file system.
http://perso.wanadoo.fr/sebastien.godard/	sysstat utilities (iostat, sar, sadf, mpstat, and sa). The sysstat utilities are a collection of performance-monitoring tools for Linux. These tools get their system information from the /proc file system.

## Chapter 6

System Tools

In this chapter

- Processes   page 152
- Task States   page 153
- Tools for Working with Processes   page 154
- strace Traces System Calls   page 170
- The Magic Key Sequence Gets a Back Trace   page 174
- lsof Lists Open Files   page 176
- Network Debugging Tools   page 178
- Summary   page 184
- Web Resources for System Tools   page 185

This chapter covers various tools that can be used to pinpoint what is happening to the system and to find which component of the system is having a problem. The **ps** command can be used to report the process status. Two sample programs will be used to view the process's status using the **ps** command. One of the sample programs will be changed to create a hang condition, and you will view this condition using the **ps** command. Other process tools that are covered include pgrep, pstree, top, and strace. strace intercepts and records the system calls that are called by a process and the signals that are received by a process. The name of each system call, its arguments, and its return value are printed to standard error or to the file you specify with the -**o** option. The magic key sequence (a set of keyboard keys you press) is provided by the Linux kernel; it gives you a way to get a back trace of all the processes on the system. The lsof tool can be used to list the open files on a system. Finally, the network debugging tools ifconfig, arp, ethereal, netstat, and tcpdump are covered.

Processes

Linux manages the processes in the system by having each process be represented by a **task_struct** data structure, which is dynamically allocated by the kernel. The **task_struct** is defined in the /usr/src/linux-2.6.x/include/linux/sched.h file in the kernel source tree. The maximum number of processes/threads created is limited by memory and is set up in /usr/src/linux-2.6.x/kernel/fork.c in the routine **fork_init**. The default for the maximum number of threads is created by the following source code:

```
/*
 * The default maximum number of threads is set to a safe
 * value: the thread structures can take up at most half
 * of memory. */

    max_threads = mempages / (THREAD_SIZE/PAGE_SIZE) / 8;
```

You can change the maximum number of threads on-the-fly by changing the /proc/sys/kernel/threads-max file. The default for one of my systems is 3583. You can change **threads-max** using the **echo** command. For example, if the value needs to be 4096, the **echo** command shown in Figure 6.1 can be used.

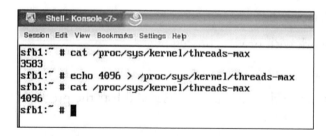

FIGURE 6.1
Viewing and changing **threads-max**.

The kernel manages each process by assigning the process to a task state. *Process* and *task* have the same meaning throughout this chapter.

Task States

Six task states are defined in the file named sched.h, which is located in the /usr/src/linux-2.6.x/include/linux/sched.h subdirectory in the kernel source tree:

- **TASK_RUNNING** means that the task is in the run queue (either executing on the CPU or waiting to be executed).

- **TASK_INTERRUPTIBLE** means that the task is waiting for a signal or resource (sleeping). The process is suspended (sleeps) until some condition becomes true.

- **TASK_UNINTERRUPTIBLE** means that the task is waiting for a resource (sleeping). It is in the same "wait queue" as the preceding state, except that delivering a signal to the sleeping process leaves its state unchanged. This process state is seldom used. However, it is valuable under certain specific conditions in which a process must wait until a given event occurs without being interrupted.

- **TASK_STOPPED** means that the task is being debugged.

- **TASK_ZOMBIE** means that the task child is without a parent. Process execution is terminated, but the parent process has not yet issued a **wait()**.

- **TASK_DEAD** means that the task is in the process of dying.

Tools for Working with Processes

Several tools allow a user to work with or view processes:

- ps reports the status of one or more processes.
- pgrep looks through the currently running processes and lists the process IDs, which match the input criteria.
- pstree displays the tree of running processes.
- top displays the processes that are using the most CPU resources. The top output is periodically updated.

ps Reports the Process Status

The ps (process status) program provides a snapshot of information for processes currently executing on Linux systems. A variety of command-line options control which processes this program reports and what information it reports about each. For details of all the options and output values, consult the ps man page. The following options are particularly useful when investigating processes:

- **a** elects all the processes on a terminal and shows those of other users.
- **e** displays information about all processes.
- **f** provides a full listing.
- **u** selects all processes owned by *username*.
- **x** selects processes without controlling ttys.

To view all the options for ps, you can use the **man ps** command to view the man page.

The output from the **ps au** option is displayed in the following columns:

- USER is the username for the running process.
- PID is the process ID.
- %CPU is the CPU utilization.
- %MEM is the memory utilization.

- VSZ is the virtual memory size.
- RSS is the resident set size—the number of kilobytes of program in memory.
- TTY specifies which terminal the process was started from.
- STAT is the process state.
- START is the start time.
- TIME is the execution time.
- COMMAND is the command name.

The process state codes have the following meanings. They are taken from the ps man page:

- D means uninterruptible sleep (can be waiting on I/O).
- R means runnable (on the run queue).
- S means sleeping.
- T means traced or stopped.
- W means paging.
- X means dead.
- Z means a defunct ("zombie") process.

For BSD formats and when a STAT is displayed, additional symbols can be displayed:

- W means no resident pages.
- < means a high-priority process.
- N means a low-priority task.
- L means pages locked into memory.

Figure 6.2 shows sample output from the **ps au** command. It has 11 tasks. The first PID is 3942, and the last PID is 31386. The user root started all the tasks. All the tasks are in the S (sleeping) state except the **ps au**, which is in the R (runnable) state.

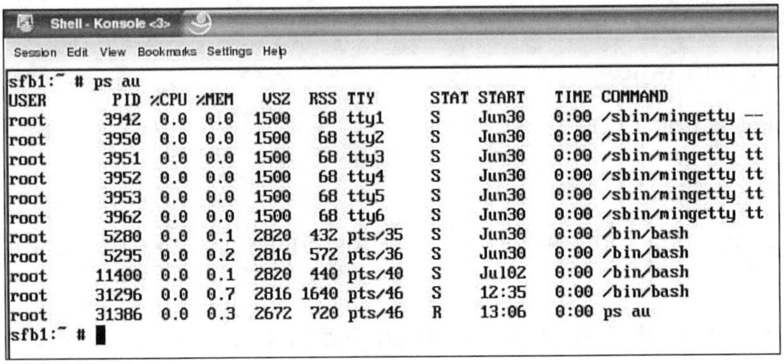

```
  Shell - Konsole <3>
Session  Edit  View  Bookmarks  Settings  Help

sfb1:~ # ps au
USER       PID %CPU %MEM   VSZ   RSS TTY     STAT START   TIME COMMAND
root      3942  0.0  0.0  1500    68 tty1    S    Jun30   0:00 /sbin/mingetty --
root      3950  0.0  0.0  1500    68 tty2    S    Jun30   0:00 /sbin/mingetty tt
root      3951  0.0  0.0  1500    68 tty3    S    Jun30   0:00 /sbin/mingetty tt
root      3952  0.0  0.0  1500    68 tty4    S    Jun30   0:00 /sbin/mingetty tt
root      3953  0.0  0.0  1500    68 tty5    S    Jun30   0:00 /sbin/mingetty tt
root      3962  0.0  0.0  1500    68 tty6    S    Jun30   0:00 /sbin/mingetty tt
root      5280  0.0  0.1  2820   432 pts/35  S    Jun30   0:00 /bin/bash
root      5295  0.0  0.2  2816   572 pts/36  S    Jun30   0:00 /bin/bash
root     11400  0.0  0.1  2820   440 pts/40  S    Jul02   0:00 /bin/bash
root     31296  0.0  0.7  2816  1640 pts/46  S    12:35   0:00 /bin/bash
root     31386  0.0  0.3  2672   720 pts/46  R    13:06   0:00 ps au
sfb1:~ # 
```

FIGURE 6.2
Viewing the system with the **ps au** command.

Let's look at the sample program ps-test.c, shown in Listing 6.1. We'll look at this program with the **ps** command to view the different threads while the program runs. ps-test.c is a multiple-thread program that uses **pthread_mutex_lock** and **pthread_mutex_unlock** to serialize **dlsym** and **dlopen** calls. Let's define some of the APIs that ps-test.c uses.

Mutex objects are intended to serve as a low-level primitive from which other thread synchronization functions can be built. The mutex object referenced by **mutex** is locked by calling **pthread_mutex_lock**(). If the mutex is already locked, the calling thread blocks until the mutex becomes available. This operation returns with the mutex object referenced by **mutex** in the locked state with the calling thread as its owner. The **pthread_mutex_unlock**() function releases the mutex object referenced by **mutex**.

dlopen() makes an executable object file available to the calling program. The **dlsysm**() function allows a process to obtain the address of a symbol defined within an object made accessible through a **dlopen**() call.

We'll also change ps-test2.c to remove the **pthread_mutex_unlock** call to cause the program to hang and then look at the threads with the **ps** command to verify that the program is hung.

Listing 6.1

ps-test.c

```
1    #include <pthread.h>
2    #include <dlfcn.h>
3    #include <dirent.h>
4
5    pthread_mutex_t mutex1 = PTHREAD_MUTEX_INITIALIZER;
6    void *
7    lookup_thread (void *handle)
8    {
9        while (1) {
10               pthread_mutex_lock( &mutex1 );
11               dlsym (handle, "main");
12               pthread_mutex_unlock( &mutex1 );
13   }
14
15       return NULL;
16   }
17
18
19   int
20   main (int argc, char **argv)
21   {
22       pthread_t loader;
23       DIR *d;
24       struct dirent *dent;
25       char *so;
26
27 pthread_create (&loader, NULL, lookup_thread, dlopen (NULL,
RTLD_NOW));
28 d = opendir ("/usr/lib");
29       while ((dent = readdir (d))) {
30               so = strstr (dent->d_name, ".so");
31               if (!so || so[3])
32                   continue;
33
34               printf ("%s\n", dent->d_name);
35               pthread_mutex_lock( &mutex1 );
36               dlopen (dent->d_name, RTLD_NOW | RTLD_GLOBAL);
37               pthread_mutex_unlock( &mutex1 );
38       }
39
40       printf ("we have finished!\n");
41       return 0;
42   }
```

Figure 6.3 shows typical output from the sample ps-test.c program.

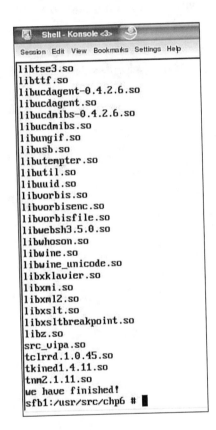

FIGURE 6.3
Sample output for ps-test.

Figure 6.4 shows typical output of looking at the ps-test.c program using ps aux and grep to filter the ps output to show only the ps-test threads. ps-test creates three threads. The first thread, 11242, is shown as R (runnable) and changes to D (unin-terruptible sleep) in the fifth view of the threads. The second thread, 11243, is shown to be in the S (sleeping) state in all five views of the threads. The third thread, 11244, is shown to be in the S state in the first and second views. In the third and fourth views it moves to the R state. In the fifth view, the third thread moves back to S. The output of ps for ps-test shows that the program is still active and that all the threads appear to be in an acceptable state.

```
sfb1:~ # ps aux | grep ps-test
root    11242  0.0  1.6 24524  3692 pts/46  R  07:35  0:00 ./ps-test
root    11243  0.0  1.6 24524  3692 pts/46  S  07:35  0:00 ./ps-test
root    11244  0.0  1.6 24524  3692 pts/46  S  07:35  0:00 ./ps-test
root    11246  0.0  0.2  1764   572 pts/47  S  07:35  0:00 grep ps-test
sfb1:~ # ps aux | grep ps-test
root    11242  0.0  2.8 32416  6416 pts/46  R  07:35  0:00 ./ps-test
root    11243  0.0  2.8 32416  6416 pts/46  S  07:35  0:00 ./ps-test
root    11244  0.0  2.8 32416  6416 pts/46  S  07:35  0:01 ./ps-test
root    11248  0.0  0.2  1764   572 pts/47  S  07:35  0:00 grep ps-test
sfb1:~ # ps aux | grep ps-test
root    11242  0.0  4.2 32948  9492 pts/46  R  07:35  0:01 ./ps-test
root    11243  0.0  4.2 32948  9492 pts/46  S  07:35  0:00 ./ps-test
root    11244  0.0  4.2 32948  9492 pts/46  R  07:35  0:02 ./ps-test
root    11250  0.0  0.2  1764   572 pts/47  S  07:35  0:00 grep ps-test
sfb1:~ # ps aux | grep ps-test
root    11242  0.0  5.7 43544 12968 pts/46  R  07:35  0:02 ./ps-test
root    11243  0.0  5.7 43544 12968 pts/46  S  07:35  0:00 ./ps-test
root    11244  0.0  5.7 43544 12968 pts/46  R  07:35  0:06 ./ps-test
root    11252  0.0  0.2  1764   572 pts/47  S  07:35  0:00 grep ps-test
sfb1:~ # ps aux | grep ps-test
root    11242  0.0  7.3 65248 16516 pts/46  D  07:35  0:05 ./ps-test
root    11243  0.0  7.3 65248 16516 pts/46  S  07:35  0:00 ./ps-test
root    11244  0.0  7.3 65248 16516 pts/46  S  07:35  0:15 ./ps-test
root    11254  0.0  0.2  1764   572 pts/47  S  07:36  0:00 grep ps-test
sfb1:~ # █
```

FIGURE 6.4
Viewing ps-test with the **ps aux** option.

Another option with using ps to check if the threads are still in an acceptable state is the -fp option, as shown in Figure 6.5. You want to know if the thread's time value increases, and both 28447 and 28449 do this. The thread 28447 time increases from 00:00:04 to 00:00:06. The thread 28449 time increases from 00:00:14 to 00:00:23.

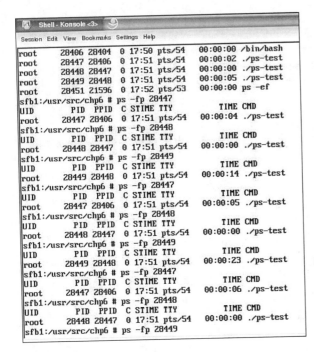

FIGURE 6.5
Viewing ps-test threads with ps and the **-fp** PID option.

The sample program ps-test has multiple threads and uses **pthread_mutex_lock**
and **pthread_mutex_unlock** to serialize the calls between **dlsym** and **dlopen**. The
new ps-test2.c has been changed to cause a deadlock by commenting out line 37.
The deadlock is caused by not doing a **pthread_mutex_unlock** after the **dlopen**.
Listing 6.2, ps-test2, views the state of the three threads with ps.

Listing 6.2

ps-test2.c

```
1   #include <pthread.h>
2   #include <dlfcn.h>
3   #include <dirent.h>
4
5   pthread_mutex_t mutex1 = PTHREAD_MUTEX_INITIALIZER;
6   void *
7   lookup_thread (void *handle)
8   {
```

```
9        while (1) {
10               pthread_mutex_lock( &mutex1 );
11               dlsym (handle, "main");
12               pthread_mutex_unlock( &mutex1 );
13  }
14
15      return NULL;
16  }
17
18
19  int
20  main (int argc, char **argv)
21  {
22      pthread_t loader;
23      DIR *d;
24      struct dirent *dent;
25      char *so;
26
27  pthread_create (&loader, NULL, lookup_thread, dlopen (NULL,
RTLD_NOW));
28  d = opendir ("/usr/lib");
29      while ((dent = readdir (d))) {
30               so = strstr (dent->d_name, ".so");
31               if (!so || so[3])
32                   continue;
33
34               printf ("%s\n", dent->d_name);
35               pthread_mutex_lock( &mutex1 );
36               dlopen (dent->d_name, RTLD_NOW | RTLD_GLOBAL);
37               // cause a dead lock pthread_mutex_unlock( &mutex1
);
38      }
39
40      printf ("we have finished!\n");
41      return 0;
42  }
```

Building and Running ps-test2

The building of ps-test2 needs two libraries—dl and pthread. Building and running ps-test2 can show output similar to Figure 6.6.

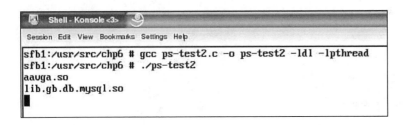

FIGURE 6.6
Building and running ps-test2.

The ps-test2 program looks to be hung. When you view it using ps, as shown in Figure 6.7, you can see that all three threads are in S (sleeping) state. The four views shown aren't normal when compared to the ps output from ps-test. In that output, the threads moved from S to R state.

```
sfb1:~ # ps aux | grep ps-test
root     17999  0.0  0.3 12060   852 pts/46   S   09:44  0:00 ./ps-test2
root     18000  0.0  0.3 12060   852 pts/46   S   09:44  0:00 ./ps-test2
root     18001  0.0  0.3 12060   852 pts/46   S   09:44  0:00 ./ps-test2
root     18031  0.0  0.2  1764   572 pts/50   S   09:50  0:00 grep ps-test
sfb1:~ # ps aux | grep ps-test
root     17999  0.0  0.3 12060   852 pts/46   S   09:44  0:00 ./ps-test2
root     18000  0.0  0.3 12060   852 pts/46   S   09:44  0:00 ./ps-test2
root     18001  0.0  0.3 12060   852 pts/46   S   09:44  0:00 ./ps-test2
root     18033  0.0  0.2  1764   572 pts/50   S   09:50  0:00 grep ps-test
sfb1:~ # ps aux | grep ps-test
root     17999  0.0  0.3 12060   852 pts/46   S   09:44  0:00 ./ps-test2
root     18000  0.0  0.3 12060   852 pts/46   S   09:44  0:00 ./ps-test2
root     18001  0.0  0.3 12060   852 pts/46   S   09:44  0:00 ./ps-test2
root     18035  0.0  0.2  1764   572 pts/50   S   09:50  0:00 grep ps-test
sfb1:~ # ps aux | grep ps-test
root     17999  0.0  0.3 12060   852 pts/46   S   09:44  0:00 ./ps-test2
root     18000  0.0  0.3 12060   852 pts/46   S   09:44  0:00 ./ps-test2
root     18001  0.0  0.3 12060   852 pts/46   S   09:44  0:00 ./ps-test2
root     18037  0.0  0.2  1764   572 pts/50   S   09:51  0:00 grep ps-test
sfb1:~ #
```

FIGURE 6.7
Viewing ps-test with the **ps aux** command.

Now let's use the **ps -fp** command to look at the three threads of ps-test2. Figure 6.8 shows that none of the three threads increases in time. All three of the threads start out with the time 00:00:00 and keep the same value of 00:00:00 through the different samplings.

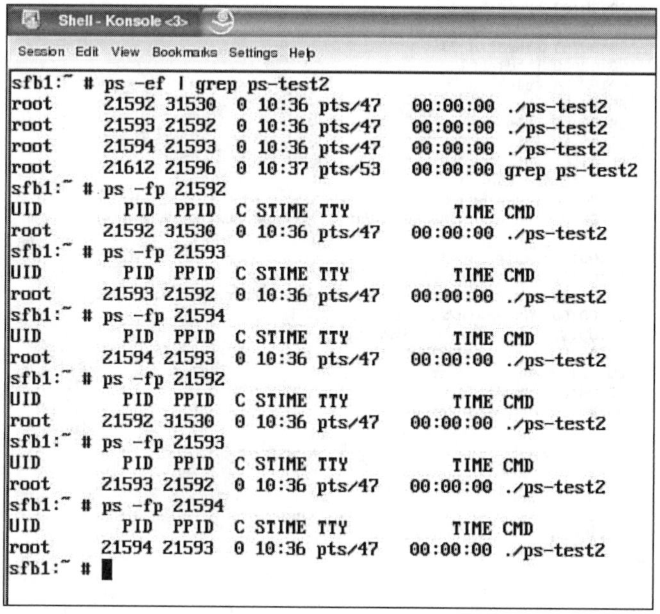

```
Shell - Konsole <3>

Session  Edit  View  Bookmarks  Settings  Help
sfb1:~ # ps -ef | grep ps-test2
root      21592 31530  0 10:36 pts/47    00:00:00 ./ps-test2
root      21593 21592  0 10:36 pts/47    00:00:00 ./ps-test2
root      21594 21593  0 10:36 pts/47    00:00:00 ./ps-test2
root      21612 21596  0 10:37 pts/53    00:00:00 grep ps-test2
sfb1:~ # ps -fp 21592
UID        PID  PPID  C STIME TTY          TIME CMD
root      21592 31530  0 10:36 pts/47    00:00:00 ./ps-test2
sfb1:~ # ps -fp 21593
UID        PID  PPID  C STIME TTY          TIME CMD
root      21593 21592  0 10:36 pts/47    00:00:00 ./ps-test2
sfb1:~ # ps -fp 21594
UID        PID  PPID  C STIME TTY          TIME CMD
root      21594 21593  0 10:36 pts/47    00:00:00 ./ps-test2
sfb1:~ # ps -fp 21592
UID        PID  PPID  C STIME TTY          TIME CMD
root      21592 31530  0 10:36 pts/47    00:00:00 ./ps-test2
sfb1:~ # ps -fp 21593
UID        PID  PPID  C STIME TTY          TIME CMD
root      21593 21592  0 10:36 pts/47    00:00:00 ./ps-test2
sfb1:~ # ps -fp 21594
UID        PID  PPID  C STIME TTY          TIME CMD
root      21594 21593  0 10:36 pts/47    00:00:00 ./ps-test2
sfb1:~ # █
```

FIGURE 6.8
Viewing ps-test2 with the **ps -fp** PID command.

You can filter the output of the **ps** command in a few different ways. The first does a sort on the first and second field. Figure 6.9 shows typical output from sorting the first and second field.

```
 Shell - Konsole <7>                                                             _ □ X
Session Edit View Bookmarks Settings Help
sfb1:~ # ps -ef | sort +0 -1 | more
UID        PID  PPID  C STIME TTY       TIME CMD
bin       1163     1  0 Jun30 ?      00:00:00 /sbin/portmap
lp        1242     1  0 Jun30 ?      00:00:45 /usr/sbin/cupsd
postfix   3830  3825  0 Jun30 ?      00:00:10 qmgr -l -t fifo -u
postfix  21029  3825  0 08:11 ?      00:00:00 pickup -l -t fifo -u
root         1     0  0 Jun30 ?      00:00:18 init [5]
root         2     1  0 Jun30 ?      00:00:00 [ksoftirqd/0]
root         3     1  0 Jun30 ?      00:00:00 [events/0]
root         4     3  0 Jun30 ?      00:00:49 [kblockd/0]
root         5     3  0 Jun30 ?      00:00:00 [khelper]
root         6     3  0 Jun30 ?      00:02:24 [pdflush]
root         8     1  0 Jun30 ?      00:08:22 [kswapd0]
root         9     3  0 Jun30 ?      00:00:00 [aio/0]
root        10     1  0 Jun30 ?      00:00:13 [jfsIO]
root        11     1  0 Jun30 ?      00:01:06 [jfsCommit]
root        12     1  0 Jun30 ?      00:00:00 [jfsSync]
root       104     1  0 Jun30 ?      00:00:00 [kseriod]
root      1055     1  0 Jun30 ?      00:00:03 /sbin/syslogd -a /var/lib/dhcp/dev/log -a /var/li
b/named/dev/log
root      1058     1  0 Jun30 ?      00:00:00 /sbin/klogd -c 1 -2
root      1149     1  0 Jun30 ?      00:00:00 /sbin/resmgrd
root      1243     1  0 Jun30 ?      00:00:00 /usr/sbin/sshd -o PidFile=/var/run/sshd.init.pid
root      3773     1  0 Jun30 ?      00:00:00 /usr/sbin/xinetd
root      3825     1  0 Jun30 ?      00:00:37 /usr/lib/postfix/master
root      3859     1  0 Jun30 ?      00:00:00 /opt/kde3/bin/kdm
root      3899     1  0 Jun30 ?      00:00:30 /usr/sbin/cron
root      3901     1  0 Jun30 ?      00:00:07 /usr/sbin/nscd
root      3908  3901  0 Jun30 ?      00:00:12 /usr/sbin/nscd
sfb1:~ # █
```

FIGURE 6.9
Using the **ps -ef** command and sorting the output.

The second view shows all the emacs processes. Figure 6.10 shows typical output from viewing all the emacs processes.

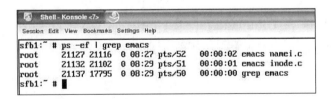

```
 Shell - Konsole <7>
Session Edit View Bookmarks Settings Help
sfb1:~ # ps -ef | grep emacs
root      21127 21116  0 08:27 pts/52   00:00:02 emacs namei.c
root      21132 21102  0 08:29 pts/51   00:00:01 emacs inode.c
root      21137 17795  0 08:29 pts/50   00:00:00 grep emacs
sfb1:~ # █
```

FIGURE 6.10
Using the **ps -ef** command to view all emacs processes.

There are two emacs processes. PID 21127 is viewing the namei.c file. PID 21132 is viewing the inode.c file.

The next example shows a deadlock in the JFS file system while running a program called fstest. Most of the file system processes are waiting on txBeginAnon. This is not the normal case. Listing 6.3 shows the output of ps. Jon Nelson submitted this problem to the JFS mailing list. With the information provided, we were able to determine why the file system was waiting on txBeginAnon. It turned out we were running out of transaction locks (tlocks). The **wchan** option is the most interesting option for finding the location of the hang in this case. If this is a kernel address, ps uses /proc/kallsyms to find the nearest symbolic location. In this case PIDs 6595 through 6644 are all waiting on txBeginAnon.

Listing 6.3

ps Command Showing a Deadlock in JFS

```
Included below is the output of:
ps -eo pid,wchan:14,comm | grep -E 'fstest|find'
========================================
 6594 wait          fstest
 6595 txBeginAnon   fstest
 6596 txBeginAnon   fstest
 6597 txBeginAnon   fstest
 6598 txBeginAnon   fstest
 6599 txBeginAnon   fstest
 6600 txBeginAnon   fstest
 6601 txBeginAnon   fstest
 6603 txBeginAnon   fstest
 6604 txBeginAnon   fstest
 6605 txBeginAnon   fstest
 6606 txBeginAnon   fstest
 6607 txBeginAnon   fstest
 6608 txBeginAnon   fstest
 6609 txBeginAnon   fstest
 6610 txBeginAnon   fstest
 6611 txBeginAnon   fstest
 6612 txBeginAnon   fstest
 6613 txBeginAnon   fstest
 6614 txBeginAnon   fstest
 6615 txBeginAnon   fstest
 6616 txBeginAnon   fstest
 6617 txBeginAnon   fstest
 6618 txBeginAnon   fstest
 6619 txBeginAnon   fstest
 6620 txBeginAnon   fstest
 6621 txBeginAnon   fstest
```

```
6622 txBeginAnon      fstest
6623 txBeginAnon      fstest
6624 txBeginAnon      fstest
6625 txBeginAnon      fstest
6626 txBeginAnon      fstest
6627 txBeginAnon      fstest
6628 txBeginAnon      fstest
6629 txBeginAnon      fstest
6630 txBeginAnon      fstest
6631 txLockAlloc      fstest
6632 txBeginAnon      fstest
6633 txBeginAnon      fstest
6634 txBeginAnon      fstest
6635 txBeginAnon      fstest
6636 txBeginAnon      fstest
6637 txBeginAnon      fstest
6638 txBeginAnon      fstest
6639 txBeginAnon      fstest
6640 txBeginAnon      fstest
6641 txBeginAnon      fstest
6642 txBeginAnon      fstest
6643 txBeginAnon      fstest
6644 txBeginAnon      fstest
6755 -                find
```

The ps Option to Show the Syscall Currently Being Executed

The next ps command shows every process with the PID number, % of CPU, memory size, name, and what syscall the process is currently executing. The output is similar to this:

```
best@sfb1:~> ps -eo pid,%cpu,vsz,args,wchan
 PID %CPU   VSZ COMMAND           WCHAN
   1  0.0   588 init [5]          select
   2  0.0     0 [ksoftirqd/0]     ksoftirqd
   3  0.0     0 [events/0]        worker_thread
   4  0.0     0 [khelper]         worker_thread
   5  0.0     0 [kblockd/0]       worker_thread
  25  0.0     0 [pdflush]         pdflush
  26  0.0     0 [pdflush]         pdflush
  28  0.0     0 [aio/0]           worker_thread
  27  0.0     0 [kswapd0]         kswapd
  29  0.0     0 [jfsIO]           jfsIOWait
  30  0.0     0 [jfsCommit]       jfs_lazycommit
  31  0.0     0 [jfsSync]         jfs_sync
 101  0.0     0 [kseriod]         serio_thread
1012  0.0  2500 /bin/bash /sbin/  wait
1015  0.0  1360 logger -t /sbin/  pipe_wait
1057  0.0  2500 /bin/bash /etc/h  wait
```

```
1058   0.0   1360 logger -t /etc/h pipe_wait
1152   0.0   1412 [hwscand]        msgrcv
1382   0.0   1436 /sbin/syslogd -a select
1385   0.0   2232 /sbin/klogd -c 1 syslog
1441   0.0   1420 /sbin/portmap    poll
1447   0.0   1588 /sbin/resmgrd    poll
1513   0.0   4640 /usr/sbin/sshd - select
5452   0.0   6340 /usr/sbin/cupsd  select
5469   0.0 42624 /usr/sbin/nscd   wait_for_packet
5525   0.0   2596 /opt/kde3/bin/kd select
5562   0.0   4036 /usr/lib/postfix select
5600   0.0   1980 /usr/sbin/xinetd select
5626   0.0   1396 /usr/sbin/cron   nanosleep
```

How to Start a New Process

One way to start a new process is to use the **system** call. **system** executes a shell command. The prototype for the **system** call is as follows:

```
int system(const char *string);
```

Listing 6.4 uses the **system** call to start the **ps** command using the **au** option.

Listing 6.4

test-system.c

```
1 #include <stdlib.h>
2 #include <stdio.h>
3
4 int main ()
5 {
6       printf("Before ps\n");
7       system("ps au");
8       printf("After ps\n");
9 }
```

If you build and run the test-system program, the output is similar to Figure 6.11.

```
 Shell - Konsole <4>
Session Edit View Bookmarks Settings Help
sfb1:/usr/src/chp6 # gcc test-system.c -o test-system
sfb1:/usr/src/chp6 # ./test-system
Before ps
USER       PID %CPU %MEM   VSZ  RSS TTY     STAT START   TIME COMMAND
root      3942  0.0  0.0  1500   84 tty1    S    Jun30   0:00 /sbin/mingetty --
root      3950  0.0  0.0  1500   84 tty2    S    Jun30   0:00 /sbin/mingetty tt
root      3951  0.0  0.0  1500   84 tty3    S    Jun30   0:00 /sbin/mingetty tt
root      3952  0.0  0.0  1500   84 tty4    S    Jun30   0:00 /sbin/mingetty tt
root      3953  0.0  0.0  1500   84 tty5    S    Jun30   0:00 /sbin/mingetty tt
root      3962  0.0  0.0  1500   84 tty6    S    Jun30   0:00 /sbin/mingetty tt
root      5280  0.0  0.1  2820  448 pts/35  S    Jun30   0:00 /bin/bash
root      5295  0.0  0.2  2816  452 pts/36  S    Jun30   0:00 /bin/bash
root      8755  0.0  2.1 10944 4876 pts/36  S    Jul01   0:28 emacs
root      8758  0.0  0.1  2820  448 pts/37  S    Jul01   0:00 /bin/bash
root      8768  0.0  0.4  2820 1028 pts/38  S    Jul01   0:00 /bin/bash
root     10944  0.0  0.7  2820 1580 pts/39  S    07:54   0:00 /bin/bash
root     10952  0.0  0.7  4856 1712 pts/39  S    07:54   0:00 ssh screensrc@mcp
root     11073  0.0  0.4  2472  924 pts/38  S    08:32   0:00 su
root     11074  0.0  0.7  2820 1636 pts/38  S    08:32   0:00 bash
root     11167  0.0  0.1  1352  312 pts/38  S    09:06   0:00 ./test-system
root     11168  0.0  0.3  2672  720 pts/38  R    09:06   0:00 ps au
After ps
sfb1:/usr/src/chp6 # ▮
```

FIGURE 6.11
test-system output.

pgrep Lists the Process IDs That Match the Input Criteria

The pgrep utility examines the active processes on the system and reports the process IDs of the processes whose attributes match the criteria specified on the command line.

All the criteria have to match. For example, **pgrep -u root httpd** lists only the processes that are called **httpd** and that are owned by **root**. On the other hand, **pgrep -u root,best** lists the processes owned by **root** or **best**.

pgrep without options and just a process name looks in the process queue to see whether a process by a particular name is running. If it finds the requested process, it returns the process ID. For example, this system has four bash processes running with PIDs of 5280, 5295, 8758, and 11400, as shown in Figure 6.12.

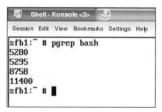

FIGURE 6.12
Viewing a system with pgrep.

The command **pgrep bash** is easy and quick to interpret to see "if bash is running."

pstree Displays a Tree of Processes

pstree shows running processes as a tree. pstree visually merges identical branches by putting them in square brackets and prefixing them with the repetition count. It has several options to select criteria and to change the output style. To view all the options for pstree, you can view the man page using the command **man pstree**. Figure 6.13 shows sample pstree output for a system.

FIGURE 6.13
Viewing a system with pstree.

top Displays Tasks

top provides a dynamic, rolling display of processes on a running Linux system. It also displays other information about the system's overall health, including load averages and memory utilization. Figure 6.14 shows sample output from top.

```
 Shell - Konsole <4>                                                      _ □ X
 Session  Edit  View  Bookmarks  Settings  Help
Tasks:  92 total,   1 running,  91 sleeping,   0 stopped,   0 zombie
Cpu(s):   0.3% user,   0.7% system,   0.0% nice,  97.5% idle,   1.4% IO-wait
Mem:   224796k total,   221404k used,     3392k free,     3688k buffers
Swap:       0k total,        0k used,       0k free,    33360k cached

  PID USER      PR  NI  VIRT  RES  SHR S %CPU %MEM    TIME+  COMMAND
11438 root      16   0  1872  848 1688 R 10.5  0.4  0:00.13 top
    1 root      16   0   620   88  476 S  0.0  0.0  0:06.99 init
    2 root      34  19     0    0    0 S  0.0  0.0  0:00.02 ksoftirqd/0
    3 root       5 -10     0    0    0 S  0.0  0.0  0:00.08 events/0
    4 root       5 -10     0    0    0 S  0.0  0.0  0:05.99 kblockd/0
    5 root       6 -10     0    0    0 S  0.0  0.0  0:00.23 khelper
    6 root      15   0     0    0    0 S  0.0  0.0  0:05.01 pdflush
    7 root      15   0     0    0    0 S  0.0  0.0  0:25.72 pdflush
    9 root      15 -10     0    0    0 S  0.0  0.0  0:00.00 aio/0
    8 root      15   0     0    0    0 S  0.0  0.0  0:58.23 kswapd0
   10 root      15   0     0    0    0 S  0.0  0.0  0:01.76 jfsIO
   11 root      15   0     0    0    0 S  0.0  0.0  0:08.51 jfsCommit
   12 root      25   0     0    0    0 S  0.0  0.0  0:00.00 jfsSync
  104 root      18   0     0    0    0 S  0.0  0.0  0:00.00 kseriod
 1055 root      16   0  1564  260 1396 S  0.0  0.1  0:00.35 syslogd
 1058 root      16   0  2392 1004 1348 S  0.0  0.4  0:00.34 klogd
 1149 root      17   0  1716  116 1552 S  0.0  0.1  0:00.00 resmgrd
sfb1:~ #
```

FIGURE 6.14
Viewing a system with top.

strace Traces System Calls

strace intercepts and records the system calls that are called by a process and the signals that are received by a process. The name of each system call, its arguments, and its return value are printed on standard error or to the file specified with the -**o** option. strace receives information from the kernel; it does not require the kernel to be built in any special way. The trace information can be useful to debug applications. Figure 6.15 uses strace on a ping operation for the hostname **steveb**. The output of strace is captured in the file called output011.

```
sfb1:~ # strace -o output011 ping steveb
PING steveb.austin.ibm.com (9.41.85.27) 56(84) bytes of data.
64 bytes from steveb.austin.ibm.com (9.41.85.27): icmp_seq=1 ttl=64 time=5.36 ms
64 bytes from steveb.austin.ibm.com (9.41.85.27): icmp_seq=2 ttl=64 time=2.33 ms

--- steveb.austin.ibm.com ping statistics ---
2 packets transmitted, 2 received, 0% packet loss, time 1001ms
rtt min/avg/max/mdev = 2.339/3.851/5.363/1.512 ms
sfb1:~ #
```

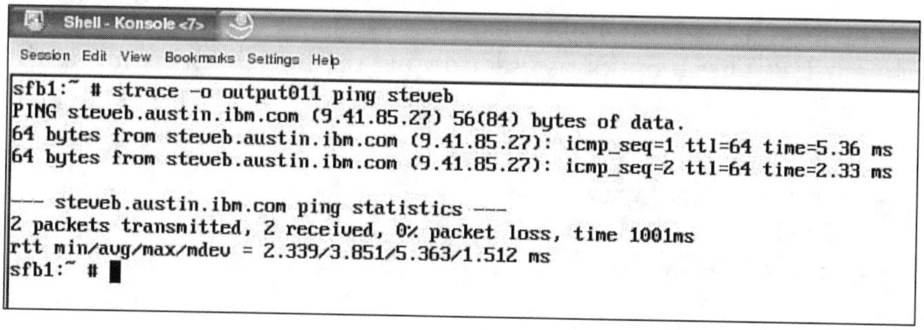

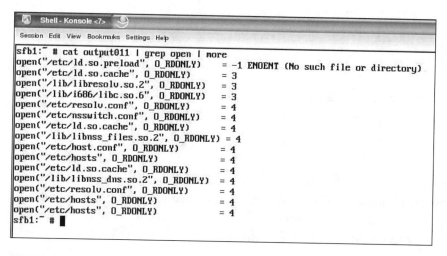

FIGURE 6.15
Using strace to capture system calls for ping.

As you can imagine, the output of strace for even a small program contains a significant amount of data. Figure 6.16 uses grep to filter the output and display just the open calls. This strace output has 15 open calls. The first is for the file /etc/ld.so.preload. The result returned by **open** is the file descriptor.

```
sfb1:~ # cat output011 | grep open | more
open("/etc/ld.so.preload", O_RDONLY)      = -1 ENOENT (No such file or directory)
open("/etc/ld.so.cache", O_RDONLY)        = 3
open("/lib/libresolv.so.2", O_RDONLY)     = 3
open("/lib/i686/libc.so.6", O_RDONLY)     = 3
open("/etc/resolv.conf", O_RDONLY)        = 4
open("/etc/nsswitch.conf", O_RDONLY)      = 4
open("/etc/ld.so.cache", O_RDONLY)        = 4
open("/lib/libnss_files.so.2", O_RDONLY) = 4
open("/etc/host.conf", O_RDONLY)          = 4
open("/etc/hosts", O_RDONLY)              = 4
open("/etc/ld.so.cache", O_RDONLY)        = 4
open("/lib/libnss_dns.so.2", O_RDONLY)    = 4
open("/etc/resolv.conf", O_RDONLY)        = 4
open("/etc/hosts", O_RDONLY)              = 4
open("/etc/hosts", O_RDONLY)              = 4
sfb1:~ #
```

FIGURE 6.16
Viewing strace output for open calls.

Tracing the first sample program in this chapter, ps-test.c, is the next example for strace (see Figure 6.17). The **-o** option is used to store the trace information in the out01 file.

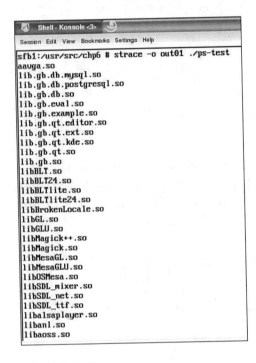

FIGURE 6.17
strace of ps-test.

The following is sample strace output from the file out01, which is the strace from the ps-test program. The first system call is **execve**, and the last system call for the snippet of this strace is the **open** call for /lib/i686/libthread.so.0. The bold words are the system calls at the start of the strace for this program.

```
execve("./ps-test", ["./ps-test"], [/* 71 vars */]) = 0
uname({sys="Linux", node="sfb1", ...})  = 0
brk(0)                                    = 0x804a000
old_mmap(NULL, 4096, PROT_READ|PROT_WRITE, MAP_PRIVATE|MAP_ANONYMOUS, -1, 0) =
0x40019000
open("/etc/ld.so.preload", O_RDONLY)    = -1 ENOENT (No such file or directory)
open("/etc/ld.so.cache", O_RDONLY)      = 3
fstat64(3, {st_mode=S_IFREG|0644, st_size=102934, ...}) = 0
old_mmap(NULL, 102934, PROT_READ, MAP_PRIVATE, 3, 0) = 0x4001a000
```

```
close(3)                            = 0
open("/lib/libdl.so.2", O_RDONLY)   = 3
read(3, "\177ELF\1\1\1\0\0\0\0\0\0\0\0\0\3\0\3\0\1\0\0\0\220\34"..., 512) = 512
fstat64(3, {st_mode=S_IFREG|0755, st_size=13625, ...}) = 0
old_mmap(NULL, 8632, PROT_READ|PROT_EXEC, MAP_PRIVATE, 3, 0) = 0x40034000
old_mmap(0x40036000, 4096, PROT_READ|PROT_WRITE, MAP_PRIVATE|MAP_FIXED, 3,
0x2000) = 0x40036000
close(3)                            = 0
open("/lib/i686/libpthread.so.0", O_RDONLY) = 3
```

strace can be a very effective way to debug an application if you think a system call is failing.

In Listing 6.5, a format of a partition is failing. The listing shows the start of the strace on calls being made by the file system (mkfs) utility. By using strace, you can determine which call is causing the problem.

Listing 6.5

Start of the strace on mkfs

```
execve("/sbin/mkfs.jfs", ["mkfs.jfs", "-f", "/dev/test1"], &
...
 open("/dev/test1", O_RDWR|O_LARGEFILE) = 4
 stat64("/dev/test1", {st_mode=&, st_rdev=makedev(63, 255),
...}) = 0
 ioctl(4, 0x40041271, 0xbfffe128) = -1 EINVAL (Invalid
argument)
 write(2, "mkfs.jfs: warning - cannot setb" ..., 98mkfs.jfs:
warning -
 cannot set blocksize on block device /dev/test1: Invalid
argument )
  = 98
 stat64("/dev/test1", {st_mode=&, st_rdev=makedev(63, 255),
...}) = 0
 open("/dev/test1", O_RDONLY|O_LARGEFILE) = 5
 ioctl(5, 0x80041272, 0xbfffe124) = -1 EINVAL (Invalid
argument)
 write(2, "mkfs.jfs: can\'t determine device"..., ..._exit(1)
  = ?
```

Listing 6.5 shows that the **ioctl** call caused the mkfs program to fail. The **BLKGETSIZE64 ioctl** is failing. (**BLKGETSIZE64** is defined in the source code that calls **ioctl**.) The **BLKGETSIZE64 ioctl** is being added to all the devices in Linux, and in this case, the logical volume manager does not support it yet. Therefore, the **mkfs** code was changed to call the older **ioctl** call if the **BLKGET-SIZE64 ioctl** call fails; this allows **mkfs** to work with the logical volume manager.

Listing 6.5 is a real-life example of a strace sent in by a user of the JFS file system that I've worked on. The strace for this problem gave us the information we needed to solve this problem in an efficient manner.

The Magic Key Sequence Gets a Back Trace

This section looks at getting a back trace for all processes on a system. A back trace can be an effective way to identify which process is hung on a system.

If your Linux system is hanging but your keyboard is still functioning, use the following method to help resolve the source of the hang. These steps perform a back trace of the current running process and all processes using the magic key sequence:

1.   The kernel that is running on the system must be built with **CONFIG_MAGIC_SYS-REQ** enabled. The system must also be in text mode. Pressing Ctrl-Alt-F1 places the system in text mode. Pressing Ctrl-Alt-F7 places the system back in X Window.

2.   While in text mode, press Alt-ScrollLock followed by Ctrl-ScrollLock. These magic keystrokes give you a stack trace of the currently running processes and all processes, respectively.

3.   Look in the system's /var/log/messages file for the back trace. If everything is set up correctly, the system should have converted the symbolic kernel addresses.

The following two figures show snippets of the back trace from the /var/log/messages file. This back trace is for processes of the ps-test2 program, which has a hang caused by the removal of a **pthread_mutex_unlock**. See Listing 6.2 for the source of this program. Three processes make up the ps-test2 program. The back trace for the first process shows that **copy_from_user+56/96** was the last routine called (see Figure 6.18). The back trace for the second process shows that **__mod_timer+840/1680** was the last routine called (see Figure 6.19).

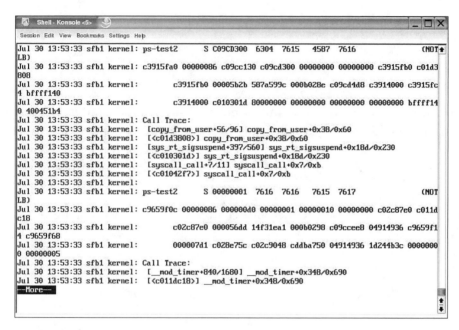

FIGURE 6.18
Back trace of ps-test2, part 1.

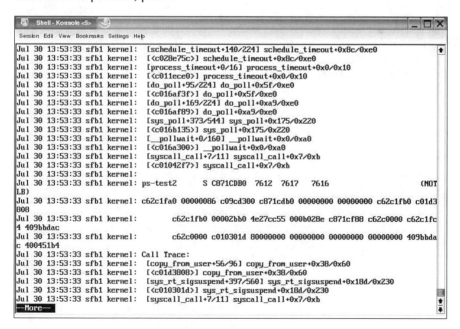

FIGURE 6.19
Back trace of ps-test2, part 2.

The back trace for the third process shows that copy_from_user+56/96 was the last routine called.

lsof Lists Open Files

lsof is a Linux diagnostic tool. Its name stands for list open files, and it does just that. It lists information about any files that are open by processes currently running on the system. It can also list communications open by each process. Figures 6.20 and 6.21 show sample output for lsof on one of my systems. lsof displays eight columns:

- COMMAND contains the first nine characters of the process name.
- PID is the process ID number.
- USER is the user ID number or login name of the user process.
- FD is the file descriptor.
- TYPE is the type of node associated with the file.
- DEVICE contains the device numbers.
- SIZE is the file's size or its offset in bytes.
- NODE NAME is the node number of a local file.

For a more complete description of these columns and options, view the lsof man page using **man lsof**.

```
Shell - Konsole <5>
Session Edit View Bookmarks Settings Help
sfb1:~ # lsof
COMMAND      PID    USER   FD    TYPE     DEVICE     SIZE      NODE NAME
init           1    root  cwd     DIR       3,67     4096         2 /
init           1    root  rtd     DIR       3,67     4096         2 /
init           1    root  txt     REG       3,67   490240     22885 /sbin/init
init           1    root   10u   FIFO       3,67             323606 /dev/initctl
ksoftirqd      2    root  cwd     DIR       3,67     4096         2 /
ksoftirqd      2    root  rtd     DIR       3,67     4096         2 /
events/0       3    root  cwd     DIR       3,67     4096         2 /
events/0       3    root  rtd     DIR       3,67     4096         2 /
kblockd/0      4    root  cwd     DIR       3,67     4096         2 /
kblockd/0      4    root  rtd     DIR       3,67     4096         2 /
khelper        5    root  cwd     DIR       3,67     4096         2 /
khelper        5    root  rtd     DIR       3,67     4096         2 /
pdflush        6    root  cwd     DIR       3,67     4096         2 /
pdflush        6    root  rtd     DIR       3,67     4096         2 /
kswapd0        8    root  cwd     DIR       3,67     4096         2 /
kswapd0        8    root  rtd     DIR       3,67     4096         2 /
aio/0          9    root  cwd     DIR       3,67     4096         2 /
aio/0          9    root  rtd     DIR       3,67     4096         2 /
jfsIO         10    root  cwd     DIR       3,67     4096         2 /
jfsIO         10    root  rtd     DIR       3,67     4096         2 /
jfsCommit     11    root  cwd     DIR       3,67     4096         2 /
jfsCommit     11    root  rtd     DIR       3,67     4096         2 /
jfsSync       12    root  cwd     DIR       3,67     4096         2 /
jfsSync       12    root  rtd     DIR       3,67     4096         2 /
kseriod      104    root  cwd     DIR       3,67     4096         2 /
kseriod      104    root  rtd     DIR       3,67     4096         2 /
syslogd     1055    root  cwd     DIR       3,67     4096         2 /
syslogd     1055    root  rtd     DIR       3,67     4096         2 /
```

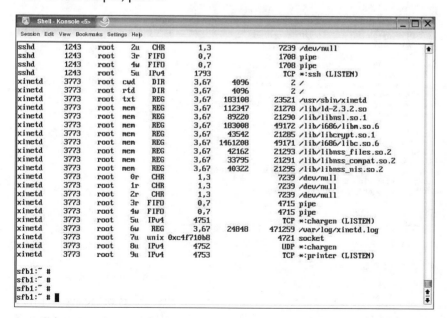

FIGURE 6.20
View of lsof output, part 1.

```
Shell - Konsole <5>
Session Edit View Bookmarks Settings Help
sshd       1243    root    2u    CHR        1,3               7239 /dev/null
sshd       1243    root    3r   FIFO        0,7               1708 pipe
sshd       1243    root    4w   FIFO        0,7               1708 pipe
sshd       1243    root    5u   IPv4       1793                TCP *:ssh (LISTEN)
xinetd     3773    root  cwd     DIR       3,67      4096        2 /
xinetd     3773    root  rtd     DIR       3,67      4096        2 /
xinetd     3773    root  txt     REG       3,67    183108    23521 /usr/sbin/xinetd
xinetd     3773    root  mem     REG       3,67    112347    21278 /lib/ld-2.3.2.so
xinetd     3773    root  mem     REG       3,67     89220    21290 /lib/libnsl.so.1
xinetd     3773    root  mem     REG       3,67    183008    49172 /lib/i686/libm.so.6
xinetd     3773    root  mem     REG       3,67     43542    21285 /lib/libcrypt.so.1
xinetd     3773    root  mem     REG       3,67   1461208    49171 /lib/i686/libc.so.6
xinetd     3773    root  mem     REG       3,67     42162    21293 /lib/libnss_files.so.2
xinetd     3773    root  mem     REG       3,67     33795    21291 /lib/libnss_compat.so.2
xinetd     3773    root  mem     REG       3,67     40322    21295 /lib/libnss_nis.so.2
xinetd     3773    root    0r    CHR        1,3               7239 /dev/null
xinetd     3773    root    1r    CHR        1,3               7239 /dev/null
xinetd     3773    root    2r    CHR        1,3               7239 /dev/null
xinetd     3773    root    3r   FIFO        0,7               4715 pipe
xinetd     3773    root    4w   FIFO        0,7               4715 pipe
xinetd     3773    root    5u   IPv4       4751                TCP *:chargen (LISTEN)
xinetd     3773    root    6w    REG       3,67     24848   471259 /var/log/xinetd.log
xinetd     3773    root    7u   unix 0xc4f710b8               4721 socket
xinetd     3773    root    8u   IPv4       4752                UDP *:chargen
xinetd     3773    root    9u   IPv4       4753                TCP *:printer (LISTEN)

sfb1:~ #
sfb1:~ #
sfb1:~ #
sfb1:~ #
```

FIGURE 6.21
View of lsof output, part 2.

Network Debugging Tools

This section covers the network debugging tools ifconfig, arp, tcpdump, ethereal, and netstat. The ifconfig tool is used to assign an address or configure network interface parameters. The arp tool lets you manipulate the system Address Resolution Protocol (ARP) cache. The tcpdump program can let you view packets over the Ethernet. The ethereal tool allows interactive browsing of network traffic. The **netstat** command symbolically displays the contents of various network-related data structures.

ifconfig Configures the Network Interface

The ifconfig utility assigns an address to a network interface and configures network interface parameters. The ifconfig utility can be used at boot time to define the network address of each interface present on a machine. It may also be used at a later time to redefine an interface's address or other parameters. Figure 6.22 shows that this system's IP address is 9.41.85.43. There are 21,116 receive packets and 606 transmit packets. There are 2,176,802 receive bytes and 468,411 transmit bytes.

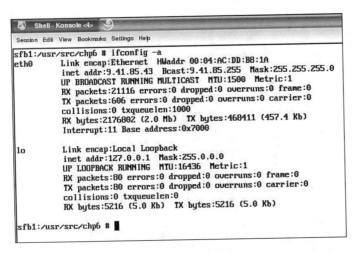

FIGURE 6.22
Sample output for ifconfig.

ifconfig can be used without parameters to check on the status of network links. It can be used to determine if transmit (TX) or receive (RX) errors are occurring. Figure 6.22 shows no transmit or receive errors.

arp Manipulates the System's ARP Cache

The **arp** command is used to view and change the address resolution table (ARP). The ARP, also called the ARP cache, lists all the data link protocols-to-IP mappings for the network. This command lets you view and modify the ARP cache. With the **arp** command, you can display the ARP cache, add ARP entries, and delete ARP entries. Figure 6.23 shows a sample of an ARP cache.

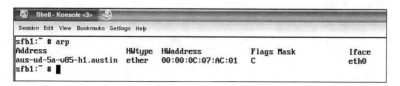

FIGURE 6.23
Displaying the ARP cache.

tcpdump Dumps Traffic on a Network

With the tcpdump program you can view all or only certain packets going over the Ethernet. tcpdump can be used to debug network problems. Figure 6.24 shows how to use tcpdump to sniff the device eth0.

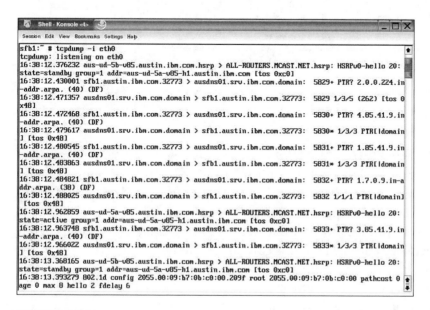

FIGURE 6.24
Sample output for tcpdump.

ethereal Interactively Browses Network Traffic

ethereal is a GUI network protocol analyzer. It lets you interactively browse packet data from a live network or from a previously saved capture file. Figure 6.25 shows a typical screen for the ethereal program.

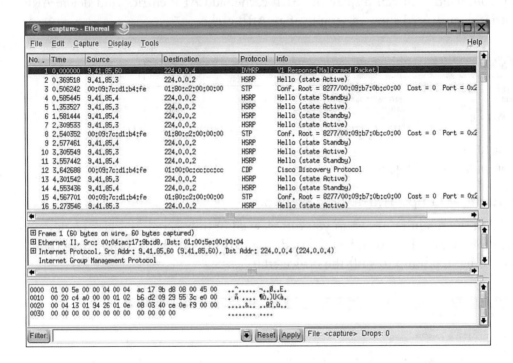

FIGURE 6.25
The ethereal program.

netstat Shows the Network Status

The **netstat** command symbolically displays the contents of various network-related data structures. It has a number of output formats, depending on the options for the information presented. The first form of the command displays a list of active sockets for each protocol. The second form presents the contents of one of the other network data structures according to the option selected. Using the third form, with a wait interval specified, netstat continuously displays information regarding packet traffic on the configured network interfaces. The fourth form displays statistics about the named protocol.

Figure 6.26 displays sample output from netstat using the **-an** option. This option can be used to retrieve the current Internet connections and to check if any program is waiting for an incoming connection. These programs are called servers because they are used to retrieve information from your system. Figures 6.26 and 6.27 show output from **netstat -an** from one of my systems. Your systems could have similar output. Figure 6.27 shows sample output from the active sockets.

```
Shell - Konsole <4>
Session Edit View Bookmarks Settings Help
sfb1:~ # netstat -an
Active Internet connections (servers and established)
Proto Recv-Q Send-Q Local Address          Foreign Address        State
tcp        0      0 0.0.0.0:2401            0.0.0.0:*              LISTEN
tcp        0      0 0.0.0.0:515             0.0.0.0:*              LISTEN
tcp        0      0 0.0.0.0:37              0.0.0.0:*              LISTEN
tcp        0      0 0.0.0.0:7               0.0.0.0:*              LISTEN
tcp        0      0 0.0.0.0:9098            0.0.0.0:*              LISTEN
tcp        0      0 0.0.0.0:11              0.0.0.0:*              LISTEN
tcp        0      0 0.0.0.0:13              0.0.0.0:*              LISTEN
tcp        0      0 0.0.0.0:15              0.0.0.0:*              LISTEN
tcp        0      0 0.0.0.0:111             0.0.0.0:*              LISTEN
tcp        0      0 0.0.0.0:6000            0.0.0.0:*              LISTEN
tcp        0      0 0.0.0.0:5810            0.0.0.0:*              LISTEN
tcp        0      0 0.0.0.0:5811            0.0.0.0:*              LISTEN
tcp        0      0 0.0.0.0:19              0.0.0.0:*              LISTEN
tcp        0      0 0.0.0.0:21              0.0.0.0:*              LISTEN
tcp        0      0 0.0.0.0:5910            0.0.0.0:*              LISTEN
tcp        0      0 0.0.0.0:22              0.0.0.0:*              LISTEN
tcp        0      0 0.0.0.0:5911            0.0.0.0:*              LISTEN
tcp        0      0 0.0.0.0:631             0.0.0.0:*              LISTEN
tcp        0      0 127.0.0.1:25            0.0.0.0:*              LISTEN
udp        0      0 0.0.0.0:7               0.0.0.0:*
udp        0      0 0.0.0.0:13              0.0.0.0:*
udp        0      0 0.0.0.0:19              0.0.0.0:*
udp        0      0 0.0.0.0:37              0.0.0.0:*
udp        0      0 0.0.0.0:111             0.0.0.0:*
udp        0      0 0.0.0.0:631             0.0.0.0:*
Active UNIX domain sockets (servers and established)
Proto RefCnt Flags       Type      State       I-Node Path
```

FIGURE 6.26
Viewing output with the **netstat -an** command, part 1.

```
 Shell - Konsole <4>                                              _ □ X
Session Edit View Bookmarks Settings Help
unix  2      [ ACC ]   STREAM    LISTENING   7101   /tmp/mcop-root/sfb1_austin_ibm_com-118b-
410989e5
unix  10     [ ]        DGRAM                 1629   /dev/log
unix  2      [ ACC ]   STREAM    LISTENING   6959   /tmp/ksocket-root/kdeinit-:0
unix  2      [ ACC ]   STREAM    LISTENING   5085   /var/run/.nscd_socket
unix  2      [ ACC ]   STREAM    LISTENING   1669   /var/run/.resmgr_socket
unix  2      [ ACC ]   STREAM    LISTENING   6766   /tmp/.X11-unix/X0
unix  2      [ ACC ]   STREAM    LISTENING   6929   /tmp/ssh-XtdP4425/agent.4425
unix  2      [ ACC ]   STREAM    LISTENING   6996   /tmp/ksocket-root/klauncherafM9Gb.slave-
socket
unix  2      [ ACC ]   STREAM    LISTENING   4889   public/cleanup
unix  2      [ ACC ]   STREAM    LISTENING   4896   private/rewrite
unix  2      [ ACC ]   STREAM    LISTENING   4900   private/bounce
unix  2      [ ACC ]   STREAM    LISTENING   4904   private/defer
unix  2      [ ACC ]   STREAM    LISTENING   4908   public/flush
unix  2      [ ACC ]   STREAM    LISTENING   4912   private/proxymap
unix  2      [ ACC ]   STREAM    LISTENING   4916   private/smtp
unix  2      [ ACC ]   STREAM    LISTENING   4920   private/relay
unix  2      [ ACC ]   STREAM    LISTENING   4924   public/showq
unix  2      [ ACC ]   STREAM    LISTENING   4928   private/error
unix  2      [ ACC ]   STREAM    LISTENING   4932   private/local
unix  2      [ ACC ]   STREAM    LISTENING   4936   private/virtual
unix  2      [ ACC ]   STREAM    LISTENING   4940   private/lmtp
unix  2      [ ACC ]   STREAM    LISTENING   4944   private/maildrop
unix  2      [ ACC ]   STREAM    LISTENING   6969   /tmp/.ICE-unix/dcop4476-1091144159
unix  2      [ ACC ]   STREAM    LISTENING   4948   private/cyrus
unix  2      [ ACC ]   STREAM    LISTENING   4952   private/uucp
unix  2      [ ACC ]   STREAM    LISTENING   4956   private/ifmail
unix  2      [ ACC ]   STREAM    LISTENING   4960   private/bsmtp
unix  2      [ ACC ]   STREAM    LISTENING   4964   private/vscan
```

FIGURE 6.27
Viewing output with the **netstat -an** command, part 2.

The next option for netstat is **-tap**, which is a good way to determine what programs are serving from your system (see Figure 6.28). It can be used to look for rogue connections to your server. One way to look for rogue connections is to check the local address for nonnormal ports. Once a nonnormal port is found, the PID and program name can be used to investigate the program and see why it is being served from your system.

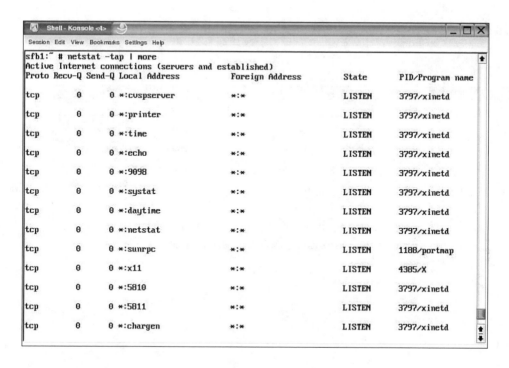

FIGURE 6.28
Sample output for **netstat -tap**, part 1.

The last tcp entry in Figure 6.29 shows that an ftp session is active on this system.

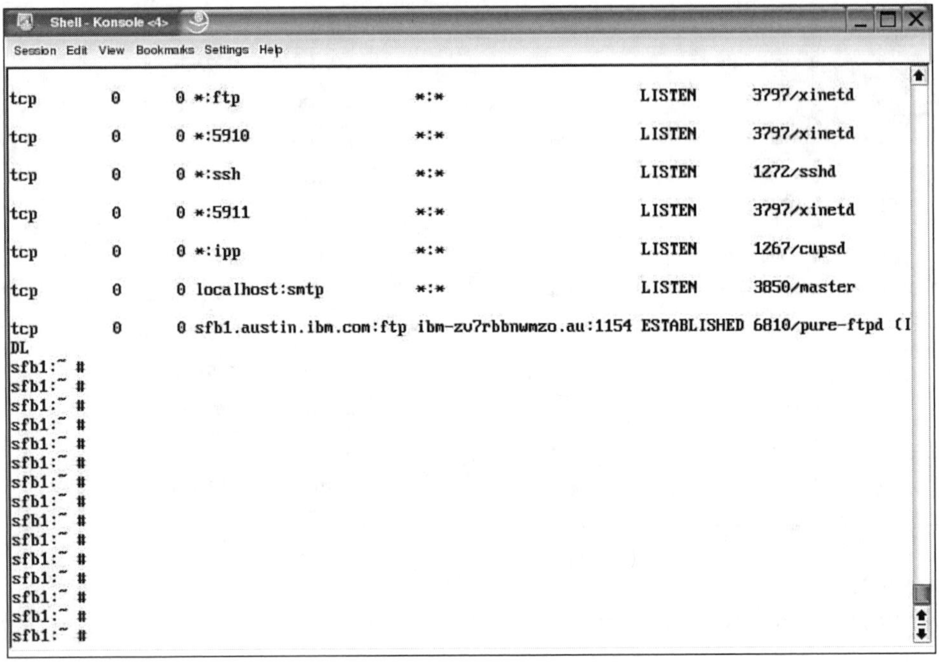

```
 Shell - Konsole <4>
Session  Edit  View  Bookmarks  Settings  Help

tcp       0       0 *:ftp                   *:*              LISTEN      3797/xinetd
tcp       0       0 *:5910                  *:*              LISTEN      3797/xinetd
tcp       0       0 *:ssh                   *:*              LISTEN      1272/sshd
tcp       0       0 *:5911                  *:*              LISTEN      3797/xinetd
tcp       0       0 *:ipp                   *:*              LISTEN      1267/cupsd
tcp       0       0 localhost:smtp          *:*              LISTEN      3850/master
tcp       0       0 sfb1.austin.ibm.com:ftp ibm-zu7rbbnumzo.au:1154 ESTABLISHED 6810/pure-ftpd (I
DL
sfb1:~ #
sfb1:~ #
sfb1:~ #
sfb1:~ #
sfb1:~ #
sfb1:~ #
sfb1:~ #
sfb1:~ #
sfb1:~ #
sfb1:~ #
sfb1:~ #
sfb1:~ #
sfb1:~ #
sfb1:~ #
```

FIGURE 6.29
Sample output for **netstat -tap**, part 2.

Summary

This chapter looked at various tools that can be used to pinpoint what is happening to the system and to find which component of the system is having a problem. The **ps** command is a valuable tool that can be used to report the status of each system process. The other process tools that were covered are pgrep, pstree, and top. The **strace** command allows the tracing of system calls. The magic key sequence can provide a back trace for all the processes on the system. The lsof tool can be used to list the open files on the system. The network debugging tools ifconfig, arp, tcpdump, ethereal, and netstat also were covered. They can help solve network-type problems.

Web Resources for Systems Tools

URL	Description
http://sourceforge.net/projects/psmisc/	ps
http://sourceforge.net/projects/strace/	strace
http://ethereal.com/	ethereal
http://www.tcpdump.org/	tcpdump
http://www.tazenda.demon.co.uk/phil/net-tools/	netstat, arp, ifconfig
http://people.freebsd.org/~abe/	lsof

Chapter 7

System Error Messages

In this chapter

- Kernel Files   page 188
- Oops Analysis   page 190
- Processing the Oops Using ksymoops   page 196
- Using gdb to Display jfs_mount   page 199
- The gcc -S Option Generates Assembly Code   page 199
- Kernel Mailing List Oops   page 200
- perror Describes a System or MySQL Error Code   page 208
- Summary   page 209
- Web Resources for Oops   page 209

Many kernel bugs show themselves as NULL pointer dereferences or other values to pointers that are incorrect. The common result of such a bug is the Oops message. This chapter covers where an Oops message is stored, how to analyze the Oops, and how to find the failing line of code. We'll create an Oops by changing the mount code of the Journaled File System (JFS), which is one of the file systems available in the Linux kernel. After the Oops is created, we'll show the steps needed to process the Oops and find the failing line of code in JFS. Also shown are a couple of Oops that were posted to the kernel mailing list. The solution to each Oops is explained.

perror is a useful command that shows the text for an error number. This chapter shows some examples of using **perror** to determine the cause of a program's failure to work.

Before we look at an Oops message, let's look at the kernel's key files. Some of these files are used to process an Oops message.

Kernel Files

This section describes the kernel files that end up in the /boot directory of a typical system.

Typical Distribution /boot Layout of the Kernel Files

The layout of the /boot directory is from SuSE x86 9.0. It shows a similar naming of kernel, System.map, and config as described next.

The vmlinuz file, shown in Figure 7.1, is the kernel executable. It is located in the /boot directory. Most distributions create a symbolic link for the kernel executable and call the kernel something like vmlinuz-2.4.21-99. This shows that the kernel's level is 2.4.21 and that the kernel's build level is 99. So this kernel is based on kernel level 2.4.21 from www.kernel.org, and the distribution built this version of the kernel 99 times before it was shipped.

The vmlinux file, shown in Figure 7.1, is the uncompressed version of the built kernel; vmlinuz is the compressed kernel that is bootable. The x86 kernel makes a file called bzImage, which is created in the /usr/src/linux-2.4.21/arch/i386/boot directory. The normal process is to copy the bzImage file to /boot and to configure the boot loader grub or lilo so that the new kernel is one of the kernels that can be booted from the boot loader menu. The standard method to add the bzImage to the /boot directory is by using the **cp** command. Copy the /usr/src/linux/arch/i386/ boot/bzImage from the kernel source tree to the /boot directory, and give it an appropriate new name:

```
# cp /usr/src/linux/arch/i386/boot/bzImage /boot/vmlinuz-kernel.version.number
```

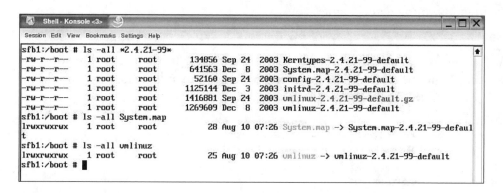

FIGURE 7.1
vmlinux and vmlinuz files.

Config File

The kernel config file is stored in the /usr/src/linux-2.4.21 directory and has the filename .config. Every time the kernel is compiled and built and installed to the /boot directory, it is a good practice to place the corresponding .config in /boot. Sometimes the .config file is requested when you report a kernel bug, so having it in a standard place on your system is a useful practice to follow.

```
# cp /usr/src/linux/.config /boot/.config-kernel.version.number
```

System.map

System.map is a list of functions or symbols available in the kernel. It contains information about the entry points of the functions compiled into the kernel, along with debug information. It is created by the **nm** command in the kernel makefile. The following is the **nm** command from the makefile that creates the kernel map file:

```
$(NM) $@ | grep -v '\(compiled\)\|\(\.o$$\)\|\( [aUw]
\)\|\(\.\.ng$$\)\|\(LASH[RL]DI\)' | sort > System.map
```

The **nm** command prints formatted listings of the symbol tables for each file specified. A file can be a relocatable object file, or it can be an archive. **nm**'s function is to display an object file's symbol table. If the System.map file changes, copy /usr/src/linux/System.map from the kernel source tree to the /boot directory, and give it an appropriate new name:

```
# cp /usr/src/linux/System.map /boot/System.map-kernel.version.number
```

After the kernel and System.map have been copied to the /boot directory, the symlinks should be created. The following two **ln** commands create the symlinks for the kernel and the System.map files:

```
# cd /boot
# ln -s vmlinuz-kernel.version.number vmlinuz
# ln -s System.map-kernel.version.number System.map
```

Programs That Use System.map

Several programs use the System.map file to resolve addresses to function names. Having a function name makes it easier and faster to debug kernel-related problems. The following programs use System.map:

- klogd is the kernel log daemon.

- ps reports the process status, used to produce the wchan field.

- Oops processing decodes the back trace.

Oops Analysis

The Oops (or panic) message contains details of a system failure, such as the contents of CPU registers. With Linux, the traditional method of debugging a system crash has been to analyze the details of the Oops message sent to the system console at the time of the crash. After the Oops message is captured, the message can be passed to the ksymoops utility, which attempts to convert the code to instructions and maps stack values to kernel symbols. In many cases, this is enough information for a programmer to determine a possible cause of the failure. Note that the Oops message does not include a core file. Also note that for the 2.6.x level of the kernel, the ksymoops utility doesn't need to be used to view the Oops. The 2.6.x level of the kernel already decodes the Oops, converts the code to instructions, and maps stack values to kernel symbols.

Let's say your system has just created an Oops message. As the author of the code, you should process the Oops and determine what caused it, or you should process the Oops and give the code's developer this information so that the bug can be solved in a timely manner. The Oops message is one part of the equation, but it is not helpful unless you run it through the ksymoops program. Figure 7.2 shows the process of formatting an Oops message.

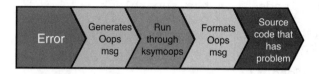

FIGURE 7.2
Formatting an Oops message.

ksymoops needs several items: Oops message output; the System.map file from the kernel that is running; and /proc/ksyms, vmlinuz, and /proc/modules. Additional instructions on how to use ksymoops in the kernel source tree appear in the /usr/src/linux/Documentation/Oops-tracing.txt file and in the ksymoops man page. ksymoops disassembles the code section, points to the failing instruction, and displays a back trace section that shows how the code was called.

Let's create an Oops by changing the source code for the JFS system. We'll add three lines to the ifs_mount_c code shown in Listing 7.1 to force an Oops.

Listing 7.1

Modified jfs_mount.c Code

```
68 /*
69  * NAME: jfs_mount(sb)
70  *
71  * FUNCTION: vfs_mount()
72  *
73  * PARAMETER: sb - super block
74  *
75  * RETURN:-EBUSY - device already mounted or open for write
```

```
76   *            -EBUSY - cvrdvp already mounted
77   *            -EBUSY - mount table full
78   *            -ENOTDIR - cvrdvp not directory on a device mount
79   *            -ENXIO - device open failure
80   */
81   int jfs_mount(struct super_block *sb)
82   {
83      int rc = 0;   /* Return code */
84      struct jfs_sb_info *sbi = JFS_SBI(sb);
85      struct inode *ipaimap = NULL;
86      struct inode *ipaimap2 = NULL;
87      struct inode *ipimap = NULL;
88      struct inode *ipbmap = NULL;
89      int *ptr; /* line 1 added */
90      /*
91       * read/validate superblock
92       * (initialize mount inode from the superblock)
93       */
94      if ((rc = chkSuper(sb))) {
95             goto errout20;
96      }
97      ptr = 0; /* line 2 added */
98      printk(" jfs %d \n", *ptr); /* line 3 added */
99
```

So we have changed the JFS file system code to create a NULL pointer reference by adding the three lines of code to the mount code of JFS. The new lines of code are lines 89, 97, and 98.

To build the changed file system code, the first step is to make sure that the JFS file system is configured for the kernel. One way to check the kernel config is to use the **make xconfig** command in the directory of the kernel source tree—usually /usr/src/linux. The kernel source on this system is 2.4.27.

The JFS file system kernel menu in Figure 7.3 shows all the JFS options turned on that will be built directly into the kernel. A check mark in the configure menu means that the option will be built directly into the kernel. A period in the configure menu means that the option will be built as a module for the kernel. No mark in the configure menu means that the option hasn't been turned on.

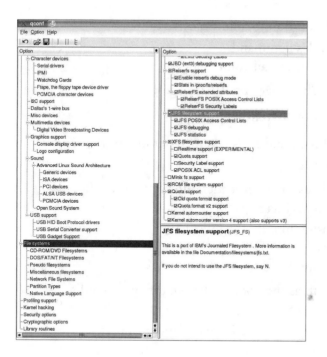

FIGURE 7.3
The JFS kernel menu.

Building the Kernel

The following steps show you how to build the kernel (for i386):

1. Issue the **make xconfig** command.

2. Under "Filesystems," do the following:
   a. Select "JFS filesystem support."
   b. Configure other kernel settings as needed.

3. Save and exit.

4. Issue the **make clean** command.

5. Issue the **make bzImage** command.

6. If modules need to be built, do the following:
    a. Issue the **make modules** command.
    b. Issue the **make modules install** command.

7. Enter **cp arch/i386/boot/bzImage /boot/bzImage-jfs**.

8. Enter **cp System.map /boot/System.map-jfs**.

9. Enter **rm /boot/System.map and ln -s /boot/System.map-jfs System.map**.

10. If the system is using lilo as the boot loader, modify your configuration to boot from /boot/bzImage-jfs.

    For example, if you're using lilo, do the following:
    a. Modify /etc/lilo.conf.
    b. Run lilo to read the modified lilo.conf.

11. If the system is using grub as the boot loader, modify your configuration to boot from /boot/bzImage-jfs.

    For example, if you're using grub, modify /boot/grub/menu.lst.

12. Reboot.

The next step is to check the kernel's level and make sure that the JFS-supported kernel is the one that is running. The **uname** command does not directly show that JFS support is built into the kernel, but the following example shows that level 2.4.27 of the kernel is running. The **uname -a** command displays the kernel's level. The output should be similar to the following:

```
Linux sfb1 2.4.27 #1 Wed Oct 27 02:08:30 UTC 2004 i686 i686 i386 GNU/Linux
```

If you mount the file system using /dev/hda1 as the JFS device and /jfs as the mount point, a segment failure similar to Figure 7.4 is displayed.

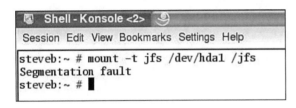

FIGURE 7.4
A segment failure.

The Oops message shown in Listing 7.2 is directly from /var/log/messages; it hasn't been processed by ksymoops. You can see that this information isn't as helpful as Listing 7.3, which has the Oops message processed by ksymoops.

Listing 7.2

Oops Directly from /ar/log/messages

```
Aug  9 10:24:41 steveb kernel: Unable to handle kernel NULL
pointer dereference at virtual address 00000000
Aug  9 10:24:41 steveb kernel:  printing eip:
Aug  9 10:24:41 steveb kernel: c01874e5
Aug  9 10:24:41 steveb kernel: *pde = 00000000
Aug  9 10:24:41 steveb kernel: Oops: 0000
Aug  9 10:24:41 steveb kernel: CPU:    0
Aug  9 10:24:41 steveb kernel: EIP:     0010:[jfs_mount+37/704]
Not tainted
Aug  9 10:24:41 steveb kernel: EIP:     0010:[<c01874e5>]
Not tainted
Aug  9 10:24:41 steveb kernel: EFLAGS: 00013246
Aug  9 10:24:41 steveb kernel: eax: d734c800     ebx: 00000000
ecx: cee40000    edx: cee63b44
Aug  9 10:24:41 steveb kernel: esi: d734c800     edi: d7ee01d4
ebp: 00000000    esp: cee2fe64
Aug  9 10:24:41 steveb kernel: ds: 0018    es: 0018    ss: 0018
Aug  9 10:24:41 steveb kernel: Process mount (pid: 1083, stack-
page=cee2f000)
Aug  9 10:24:41 steveb kernel: Stack: 00001000 00000000
d734c800 d7ee01d4 00000000 00000000 c0183fdc d734c800
Aug  9 10:24:41 steveb kernel:        d734c800 00001000
00000000 00000000 00000002 00000000 c027f230 00000000
Aug  9 10:24:41 steveb kernel:        d734c800 c01363b7
d734c800 00000000 00000000 c027f230 c027f230 00000000
Aug  9 10:24:41 steveb kernel: Call Trace:
[jfs_read_super+172/624] [get_sb_bdev+359/560] [alloc_vfsm-
nt+121/176] [do_kern_mount+215/256] [do_add_mount+101/320]
Aug  9 10:24:41 steveb kernel: Call Trace:    [<c0183fdc>]
[<c01363b7>] [<c0146299>] [<c0136687>] [<c01471b5>]
Aug  9 10:24:41 steveb kernel:    [do_mount+354/384]
[copy_mount_options+77/160] [sys_mount+123/192]
[system_call+51/64]
Aug  9 10:24:41 steveb kernel:       [<c0147492>] [<c01472dd>]
[<c014780b>] [<c0106cc3>]
Aug  9 10:24:41 steveb kernel:
Aug  9 10:24:41 steveb kernel: Code: 8b 2d 00 00 00 00 55 68
67 09 25 c0 e8 0a c1 f8 ff 6a 00 6a
```

Processing the Oops Using ksymoops

The system that this Oops came from has a standard /boot directory where System.map has a symlink to System.map-2.4.27. If you have a standard /boot setup, all the ksymoops program needs as input is what file contains the Oops message. In Figure 7.5, the Oops message is taken directly from the /var/log /messages file.

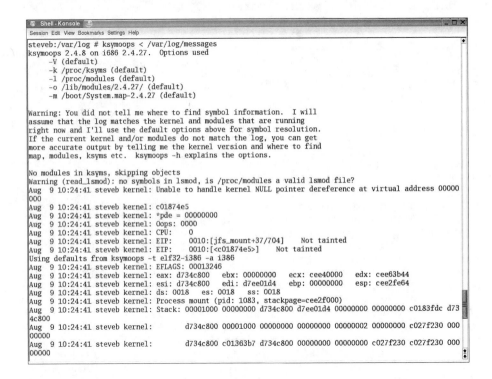

FIGURE 7.5
The Oops message comes from /var/log/messages.

The complete Oops message as processed by ksymoops is shown in Listing 7.3.

Listing 7.3

Oops Messages After Being Processed by ksymoops

```
10:24:41 steveb kernel: Unable to handle kernel NULL pointer
dereference at virtual address 00000000
Aug  9 10:24:41 steveb kernel: c01874e5
Aug  9 10:24:41 steveb kernel: *pde = 00000000
```

```
Aug  9 10:24:41 steveb kernel: Oops: 0000
Aug  9 10:24:41 steveb kernel: CPU:    0
Aug  9 10:24:41 steveb kernel: EIP:     0010:[jfs_mount+37/704]
Not tainted
Aug  9 10:24:41 steveb kernel: EIP:     0010:[<c01874e5>]
Not tainted
Using defaults from ksymoops -t elf32-i386 -a i386
Aug  9 10:24:41 steveb kernel: EFLAGS: 00013246
Aug  9 10:24:41 steveb kernel: eax: d734c800    ebx: 00000000
ecx: cee40000    edx: cee63b44
Aug  9 10:24:41 steveb kernel: esi: d734c800    edi: d7ee01d4
ebp: 00000000    esp: cee2fe64
Aug  9 10:24:41 steveb kernel: ds: 0018    es: 0018    ss: 0018
Aug  9 10:24:41 steveb kernel: Process mount (pid: 1083, stack-
page=cee2f000)
Aug  9 10:24:41 steveb kernel: Stack: 00001000 00000000
d734c800 d7ee01d4 00000000 00000000 c0183fdc d734c800
Aug  9 10:24:41 steveb kernel:          d734c800 00001000
00000000 00000000 00000002 00000000 c027f230 00000000
Aug  9 10:24:41 steveb kernel:          d734c800 c01363b7
d734c800 00000000 00000000 c027f230 c027f230 00000000
Aug  9 10:24:41 steveb kernel: Call Trace:
[jfs_read_super+172/624] [get_sb_bdev+359/560] [alloc_vfsm-
nt+121/176] [do_kern_mount+215/256] [do_add_mount+101/320]
Aug  9 10:24:41 steveb kernel: Call Trace:    [<c0183fdc>]
[<c01363b7>] [<c0146299>] [<c0136687>] [<c01471b5>]
Aug  9 10:24:41 steveb kernel:    [<c0147492>] [<c01472dd>]
[<c014780b>] [<c0106cc3>]
Aug  9 10:24:41 steveb kernel: Code: 8b 2d 00 00 00 00 55 68
67 09 25 c0 e8 0a c1 f8 ff 6a 00 6a


>>EIP; c01874e5 <jfs_mount+25/2c0>    <=====

Trace; c0183fdc <jfs_read_super+ac/270>
Trace; c01363b7 <get_sb_bdev+167/230>
Trace; c0146299 <alloc_vfsmnt+79/b0>
Trace; c0136687 <do_kern_mount+d7/100>
Trace; c01471b5 <do_add_mount+65/140>
Trace; c0147492 <do_mount+162/180>
Trace; c01472dd <copy_mount_options+4d/a0>
Trace; c014780b <sys_mount+7b/c0>
Trace; c0106cc3 <system_call+33/40>

Code;  c01874e5 <jfs_mount+25/2c0>
00000000 <_EIP>:
Code;  c01874e5 <jfs_mount+25/2c0>    <=====
   0:    8b 2d 00 00 00 00
                                       mov    0x0,%ebp    <=====
Code;  c01874eb <jfs_mount+2b/2c0>
   6:    55
                                       push   %ebp
Code;  c01874ec <jfs_mount+2c/2c0>
   7:    68 67 09 25 c0
                                       push   $0xc0250967
Code;  c01874f1 <jfs_mount+31/2c0>
```

```
   c:     e8 0a c1 f8 ff                        call    fff8c11b
<_EIP+0xfff8c11b>
Code;   c01874f6 <jfs_mount+36/2c0>
  11:     6a 00                                 push    $0x0
Code;   c01874f8 <jfs_mount+38/2c0>
  13:     6a 00                                 push    $0x0
```

Next you need to determine which line of code is causing the problem in **jfs_mount**. The Oops message tells you that the problem is caused by the instruction at offset 25. To find out where in the **jfs_mount** routine offset 25 is, you can use the objdump utility on the jfs_mount.o file and look at offset 25. objdump is used to disassemble a module function and see what assembler instructions are created by the C source code. Figure 7.6 shows what is displayed from objdump. Next you can look at C code for **jfs_mount** and see that the null pointer was caused by line 98. Offset 25 is important because that is the location the Oops message identified as the cause of the problem.

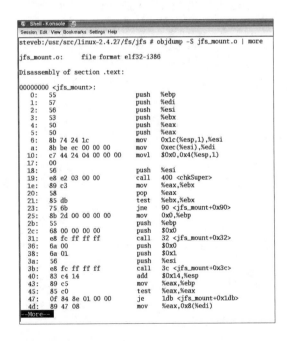

FIGURE 7.6
Assembler listing of jfs_mount.

Using gdb to Display jfs_mount

Another way to disassemble the **jfs_mount** code is to use gdb, as shown in Figure 7.7. The **jfs_mount** source code is in the kernel source tree and is located in the /usr/src/linux-2.4.27/fs/jfs/jfs_mount.c file. So the first step is to start gdb with input as fs/jfs/jfs_mount.o and to use gdb's **disassemble** function to display the **jfs_mount** routine.

```
Shell - Konsole
Session Edit View Bookmarks Settings Help
steveb:/usr/src/linux-2.4.27 # gdb fs/jfs/jfs_mount.o
GNU gdb 5.3
Copyright 2002 Free Software Foundation, Inc.
GDB is free software, covered by the GNU General Public License, and you are
welcome to change it and/or distribute copies of it under certain conditions.
Type "show copying" to see the conditions.
There is absolutely no warranty for GDB.  Type "show warranty" for details.
This GDB was configured as "i586-suse-linux"...(no debugging symbols found)...
(gdb) disassemble jfs_mount
Dump of assembler code for function jfs_mount:
0x0 <jfs_mount>:        push    %ebp
0x1 <jfs_mount+1>:      push    %edi
0x2 <jfs_mount+2>:      push    %esi
0x3 <jfs_mount+3>:      push    %ebx
0x4 <jfs_mount+4>:      push    %eax
0x5 <jfs_mount+5>:      push    %eax
0x6 <jfs_mount+6>:      mov     0x1c(%esp,1),%esi
0xa <jfs_mount+10>:     mov     0xec(%esi),%edi
0x10 <jfs_mount+16>:    movl    $0x0,0x4(%esp,1)
0x18 <jfs_mount+24>:    push    %esi
0x19 <jfs_mount+25>:    call    0x400 <chkSuper>
0x1e <jfs_mount+30>:    mov     %eax,%ebx
0x20 <jfs_mount+32>:    pop     %eax
0x21 <jfs_mount+33>:    test    %ebx,%ebx
0x23 <jfs_mount+35>:    jne     0x90 <jfs_mount+144>
0x25 <jfs_mount+37>:    mov     0x0,%ebp
0x2b <jfs_mount+43>:    push    %ebp
0x2c <jfs_mount+44>:    push    $0x0
0x31 <jfs_mount+49>:    call    0x32 <jfs_mount+50>
0x36 <jfs_mount+54>:    push    $0x0
0x38 <jfs_mount+56>:    push    $0x1
0x3a <jfs_mount+58>:    push    %esi
0x3b <jfs_mount+59>:    call    0x3c <jfs_mount+60>
0x40 <jfs_mount+64>:    add     $0x14,%esp
0x43 <jfs_mount+67>:    mov     %eax,%ebp
0x45 <jfs_mount+69>:    test    %eax,%eax
0x47 <jfs_mount+71>:    je      0x1db <jfs_mount+475>
```

FIGURE 7.7
Using gdb.

An additional way to disassemble source code is to use the **gcc -S** option when compiling the source code.

The gcc -S Option Generates Assembly Code

Compilers for high-level languages such as C and C++ can translate high-level language into assembly code. The GNU C and C++ compiler option of -S generates assembly code equivalent to that of the corresponding source program.

Assembler Output Generated by GNU C

Listing 7.4 is sample program that adds together integers i and j and places the sum into integer p. Listing 7.5 shows the file add.s generated by **gcc -S add.c**. Note that add.s has been edited to remove many assembler directives (mostly for alignments and other things of that sort). The comments in Listing 7.5 show how the C code matches up to the assembler code.

Listing 7.4

add.c

```
int add (int i, int j)
{
        int p = i + j;
        return p;
```

Listing 7.5

add.s

```
add:
        pushl %ebp
        movl %esp,%ebp
        subl $4,%esp             // create space for integer p
        movl 8(%ebp), %edx       // 8(%ebp) refers to i
        addl 12(%ebp), %edx      // 12(%ebp) refers to j
        movl %edx, -4(%ebp)      // -4(%ebp) refers to p
        movl -4(%ebp), %eax      // store return value in eax
        leave                    // e.g. to movl %ebp, %esp, popl
%ebp ret
```

Kernel Mailing List Oops

The kernel mailing list is one of the ways that problems are reported to developers of the kernel. This section looks at two Oops examples that were sent to the kernel mailing list. For each Oops, the developer used the Oops message to determine what was causing the problem. The developer provided a source code change to fix both of these problems. Sometimes the Oops message is an effective way to debug kernel-related problems.

An Oops in the 3c59x Network Driver 2.4.7ac11

The Oops in the 3c59x network driver comes directly from the kernel mailing list. Just looking at the Oops and using the developer's knowledge of the code can

solve some types of problems. Wichert Akkerman reported this Oops on the kernel
mailing list on August 24, 2001. Alan Cox replied to Wichert with a proposed fix,
and the problem was resolved when Wichert tried out Alan's fix. The following is
the Oops for the 3c59x driver:

```
Subject : Oops in 3c59x driver 2.4.7ac11
From: Wichert Akkerman
Date: Fri Aug 24 2001 - 19:00:22 EST
CPU: 0
EIP: 0010:[<c01d27c3>]
Using defaults from ksymoops -t elf32-i386 -a i386
EFLAGS: 00010246
eax: 000005dc ebx: c2f5c6e0 ecx: 00000006 edx: cae12712
esi: c1e12812 edi: c5fd4870 ebp: c5fd4940 esp: c125be70
ds: 0018 es: 0078 ss: 0018
Process kpnpbios (pid: 2, stackpage=c125b000)
Stack: c2f5c6e0 c5fd4800 c5fd4800 c8875003 c2f5c6e0 c5fd4800 00000020 c5fd4800
       0000000b 0000e601 000005ea 42413938 0000001f 600085ea 00001800 00000017
       c88748a0 c5fd4800 c335e240 04000001 0000000b c125bf34 c12437f0 c1243760
Call Trace: [<c8875003>] [<c88748a0>] [<c01c58c>] [<c010802d>] [<c010818e>]
   [<c010a0ee>] [<c01b8634>] [<c0110018>] [<c01b8811>] [<c0105454>]
Code: f3 a6 74 04 c6 43 6a 03 0f b7 42 0c 86 c4 0f b7 c0 3d ff 05
>>EIP; c01d27c3 <eth_type_trans+6b/a8> <=====
Trace; c8875003 <[3c59x]boomerang_rx+23b/3ec>
Trace; c88748a0 <[3c59x]boomerang_interrupt+120/38c>
Trace; 0c01c58c Before first symbol
Trace; c010802d <handle_IRQ_event+35/60>
Trace; c010818e <do_IRQ+6e/b0>
Trace; c010a0ee <call_do_IRQ+5/b>
Trace; c01b8634 <pnp_bios_dock_station_info+98/e8>
Trace; c0110018 <do_release+78/b8>
Trace; c01b8811 <pnp_dock_thread+59/c8>
Trace; c0105454 <kernel_thread+28/38>
Code; c01d27c3 <eth_type_trans+6b/a8>
00000000 <_EIP>:
Code; c01d27c3 <eth_type_trans+6b/a8> <=====
   0: f3 a6 repz cmpsb %es:(%edi),%ds:(%esi) <=====
Code; c01d27c5 <eth_type_trans+6d/a8>
   2: 74 04 je 8 <_EIP+0x8> c01d27cb <eth_type_trans+73/a8>
Code; c01d27c7 <eth_type_trans+6f/a8>
   4: c6 43 6a 03 movb $0x3,0x6a(%ebx)
Code; c01d27cb <eth_type_trans+73/a8>
   8: 0f b7 42 0c movzwl 0xc(%edx),%eax
Code; c01d27cf <eth_type_trans+77/a8>
   c: 86 c4 xchg %al,%ah
Code; c01d27d1 <eth_type_trans+79/a8>
   e: 0f b7 c0 movzwl %ax,%eax
Code; c01d27d4 <eth_type_trans+7c/a8>
  11: 3d ff 05 00 00 cmp $0x5ff,%eax
 <0>Kernel panic: Aiee, killing in interrupt handler!
```

It is always a good idea to describe what is going on in the system that might be causing the Oops. Wichert described the system activity as follows:

The description of the problem was the machine died in the middle of transferring a large chunk of data (500 MB or so) via ssh. It did that twice in a row, so it seems to be reproducible.

Alan said that an IRQ happened during a PnPBIOS call, and this is what caused the problem. Alan's fix was to change the semaphore in /drivers/pnp/pnp_bios.c to a **spinlock_irqsave** and **__cli/spin_unlock_irqrestore** to see if the crashes would go away. Wichert reported back to Alan that his fix worked.

A spinlock is a lock in which the thread simply waits in a loop ("spins"), repeatedly checking until the lock becomes available. This is also known as "busy waiting" because the thread remains active but isn't performing a useful task. Once acquired, spinlocks are held until they are released or the thread blocks ("goes to sleep").

The complete discussion of this problem can be viewed on the archive of the kernel mailing list. See the section "Web Resources for Oops" at the end of this chapter for the URL.

This problem was fixed using a patch. Listing 7.6 shows a method of creating a patch. The basics of patching are that a diff file is created and then applied to the source code using the **patch** command.

Listing 7.6 has two directories, A and B, and each has a copy of the code. Directory A has the original code, and directory B has the changed code. If both directories are in /home, change to the /home directory and execute the **diff** command.

Listing 7.6

Creating a Patch

```
% cd /home
% diff -urN A B > patch.diff
```

Listing 7.7 shows the actual patch that fixed the problem. A + in front of a line of source code means that the line has been added to the file. A – in front of a line of source code means that the line has been removed from the file.

Listing 7.7

Fix to pnp_bios.c

```
diff -Nur /usr/src/linux-2.4.7/drivers/pnp/pnp_bios.c
/usr/src/linux/drivers/pnp/pnp_bios.c
-- /usr/src/linux-2.4.7/drivers/pnp/pnp_bios.c  2004-08-11
16:38:55.239893160 -0700
+++ /usr/src/linux/drivers/pnp/pnp_bios.c  2004-08-12
08:15:00.146529520 -0700
@@ -43,6 +43,7 @@
 #include <linux/pci.h>
 #include <linux/kmod.h>
 #include <linux/completion.h>
+#include <linux/spinlock.h>

 /* PnPBIOS signature: "$PnP" */
 #define PNP_SIGNATURE    (('$' << 0) + ('P' << 8) + ('n' <<
16) + ('P' << 24))
@@ -155,20 +156,26 @@
 u32 pnp_bios_fault_eip;
 u32 pnp_bios_is_utter_crap = 0;

+static spinlock_t pnp_bios_lock;
+
 static inline u16 call_pnp_bios(u16 func, u16 arg1, u16 arg2,
u16 arg3,
                                         u16 arg4, u16 arg5, u16
arg6, u16 arg7)
 {
+       unsigned long flags;
        u16 status;
+
        /*
         *      PnPBIOS is generally not terribly re-entrant.
         *      Also don't rely on it to save everything correctly
+        *
+        *      On some boxes IRQs during PnPBIOS calls seem fatal
         */
-       static DECLARE_MUTEX(pnp_bios_sem);

        if(pnp_bios_is_utter_crap)
                return PNP_FUNCTION_NOT_SUPPORTED;

-       down(&pnp_bios_sem);
+       spin_lock_irqsave(&pnp_bios_lock, flags);
+       __cli();
        __asm__ __volatile__(
                "pushl %%ebp\n\t"
                "pushl %%edi\n\t"
```

```
@@ -198,7 +205,7 @@
                "i" (0)
                "memory"x
        );
-       up(&pnp_bios_sem);
+       spin_unlock_irqrestore(&pnp_bios_lock, flags);


@@ -567,6 +575,8 @@
        u8 sum;
        int i, length;

+       spin_lock_init(&pnp_bios_lock);
+
        if(pnp_bios_disabled)
        {
                printk(KERN_INFO "PNP BIOS services disabled.\n");
@@ -662,6 +672,46 @@
        }
 }
```

A Linux-2.5.1-pre5 Oops

The following is an Oops that was sent to the kernel mailing list by Udo A. Steinberg. This is another example where a developer looked at the Oops and determined what was causing the problem. The start of the discussion about this problem is available in the kernel mailing list archive. See the section "Web Resources for Oops" at the end of this chapter for the URL.

```
ksymoops 2.4.1 on i686 2.5.1-pre5. Options used
     -V (default)
     -k /proc/ksyms (default)
     -l /proc/modules (default)
     -o /lib/modules/2.5.1-pre5/ (default)
     -m /boot/System.map-2.5.1-pre5 (specified)
Unable to handle kernel NULL pointer dereference at virtual address 00000028
c01d0538
*pde = 00000000
Oops: 0000
CPU: 0
EIP: 0010:[<c01d0538>] Not tainted
Using defaults from ksymoops -t elf32-i386 -a i386
EFLAGS: 00010286
eax: 00000000 ebx: c1be11c0 ecx: 00000030 edx: 00000200
esi: 00000001 edi: c1be14c0 ebp: c10688ac esp: cac1bdb0
ds: 0018 es: 0018 ss: 0018
Process kdeinit (pid: 223, stackpage=cac1b000)
```

```
Stack: 00000030 00000001 c1be11c0 00000000 c0135af7 00000001 c1be11c0 c010820c
       0000000b c1101ad4 000001f0 00000020 00000a0e c010a238 c1101ad4 c1be14c0
       c10688ac c1be14c0 c0135b5c c1be14c0 000001f0 00000018 00000018 fffff0b
Call Trace: [<c0135af7>] [<c010820c>] [<c010a238>] [<c0135b5c>] [<c01346bc>]
   [<c012c328>] [<c012c5e0>] [<c012c64c>] [<c012cf51>] [<c012d19c>] [<c012d230>]
   [<c013f8d3>] [<c02638d5>] [<c022177f>] [<c013fb03>] [<c013fed2>] [<c01c9b5f>]
   [<c0106d1b>]
Code: 8b 48 28 66 c1 ea 09 0f b7 d2 0f af 53 04 89 10 0f b7 53 0c
>>EIP; c01d0538 <submit_bh+48/d0> <=====
Trace; c0135af7 <sync_page_buffers+97/b0>
Trace; c010820c <do_IRQ+7c/b0>
Trace; c010a238 <call_do_IRQ+5/d>
Trace; c0135b5c <try_to_free_buffers+4c/100>
Trace; c01346bc <try_to_release_page+1c/50>
Trace; c012c328 <shrink_cache+188/310>
Trace; c012c5e0 <shrink_caches+50/90>
Trace; c012c64c <try_to_free_pages+2c/50>
Trace; c012cf51 <balance_classzone+51/190>
Trace; c012d19c <__alloc_pages+10c/190>
Trace; c012d230 <__get_free_pages+10/20>
Trace; c013f8d3 <__pollwait+33/90>
Trace; c02638d5 <unix_poll+25/a0>
Trace; c022177f <sock_poll+1f/30>
Trace; c013fb03 <do_select+f3/200>
Trace; c013fed2 <sys_select+292/4a0>
Trace; c01c9b5f <keyboard_interrupt+f/20>
Trace; c0106d1b <system_call+33/38>
Code; c01d0538 <submit_bh+48/d0>
0000000000000000 <_EIP>:
Code; c01d0538 <submit_bh+48/d0> <=====
   0: 8b 48 28 mov 0x28(%eax),%ecx <=====
Code; c01d053b <submit_bh+4b/d0>
   3: 66 c1 ea 09 shr $0x9,%dx
Code; c01d053f <submit_bh+4f/d0>
   7: 0f b7 d2 movzwl %dx,%edx
Code; c01d0542 <submit_bh+52/d0>
   a: 0f af 53 04 imul 0x4(%ebx),%edx
Code; c01d0546 <submit_bh+56/d0>
   e: 89 10 mov %edx,(%eax)
Code; c01d0548 <submit_bh+58/d0>
  10: 0f b7 53 0c movzwl 0xc(%ebx),%edx
```

The problem was that the **bio_alloc()** routine was not waiting on the reserved pool for free entries, even though **__GFP_WAIT** was set. It was also determined that there was no need for **__GFP_IO** in that case. Jens Axboe created the patch shown in Listing 7.8 that fixed this Oops.

Listing 7.8

Fix to bio.c

```
--- /opt/kernel/linux-2.5.1-pre5/fs/bio.c   Tue Dec   4 04:42:00
2001
+++ fs/bio.c  Tue Dec   4 04:45:56 2001
@@ -35,7 +35,7 @@
 #include <asm/uaccess.h>

 kmem_cache_t *bio_cachep;
-static spinlock_t __cacheline_aligned bio_lock =
SPIN_LOCK_UNLOCKED;
+static spinlock_t __cacheline_aligned_in_smp bio_lock =
SPIN_LOCK_UNLOCKED;
 static struct bio *bio_pool;
 static DECLARE_WAIT_QUEUE_HEAD(bio_pool_wait);
 static DECLARE_WAIT_QUEUE_HEAD(biovec_pool_wait);
@@ -74,7 +74,7 @@
        struct bio *bio;

        if ((bio = bio_pool)) {
-               BUG_ON(bio_pool_free <= 0);
+               BIO_BUG_ON(bio_pool_free <= 0);
                bio_pool = bio->bi_next;
                bio->bi_next = NULL;
                bio_pool_free—;
@@ -90,7 +90,7 @@

        spin_lock_irqsave(&bio_lock, flags);
        bio = __bio_pool_get();
-       BUG_ON(!bio && bio_pool_free);
+       BIO_BUG_ON(!bio && bio_pool_free);
        spin_unlock_irqrestore(&bio_lock, flags);

        return bio;
@@ -121,8 +121,7 @@
        }
 }

-#define BIO_CAN_WAIT(gfp_mask)   \
-       (((gfp_mask) & (__GFP_WAIT | __GFP_IO)) == (__GFP_WAIT |
__GFP_IO))
+#define BIO_CAN_WAIT(gfp_mask)   ((gfp_mask) & __GFP_WAIT)

 static inline struct bio_vec *bvec_alloc(int gfp_mask, int nr,
int *idx)
 {
@@ -198,13 +197,15 @@
 {
```

```
         struct biovec_pool *bp = &bvec_list[bio->bi_max];

-        BUG_ON(bio->bi_max >= BIOVEC_NR_POOLS);
+        BIO_BUG_ON(bio->bi_max >= BIOVEC_NR_POOLS);

         /*
          * cloned bio doesn't own the veclist
          */
-        if (!(bio->bi_flags & (1 << BIO_CLONED)))
+        if (!(bio->bi_flags & (1 << BIO_CLONED))) {
+                kmem_cache_free(bp->bp_cachep, bio->bi_io_vec);
+                wake_up_nr(&bp->bp_wait, 1);
+        }

         bio_pool_put(bio);
 }
@@ -212,13 +213,13 @@
 inline void bio_init(struct bio *bio)
 {
         bio->bi_next = NULL;
-        atomic_set(&bio->bi_cnt, 1);
         bio->bi_flags = 0;
         bio->bi_rw = 0;
         bio->bi_vcnt = 0;
         bio->bi_idx = 0;
         bio->bi_size = 0;
         bio->bi_end_io = NULL;
+        atomic_set(&bio->bi_cnt, 1);
 }

 static inline struct bio *__bio_alloc(int gfp_mask,
bio_destructor_t *dest)
@@ -314,14 +315,13 @@
 **/
 void bio_put(struct bio *bio)
 {
-        BUG_ON(!atomic_read(&bio->bi_cnt));
+        BIO_BUG_ON(!atomic_read(&bio->bi_cnt));

         /*
          * last put frees it
          */
         if (atomic_dec_and_test(&bio->bi_cnt)) {
-                BUG_ON(bio->bi_next);
-
+                BIO_BUG_ON(bio->bi_next);
                 bio_free(bio);
         }
 }
```

perror Describes a System or MySQL Error Code

The perror utility can display a description of a system error code.

You can find out what the error code means by checking your system's documentation or by using perror. perror prints a description of a system error code. In Figure 7.8, perror is invoked without a parameter. Also shown is descritive text for error codes 1 and 2.

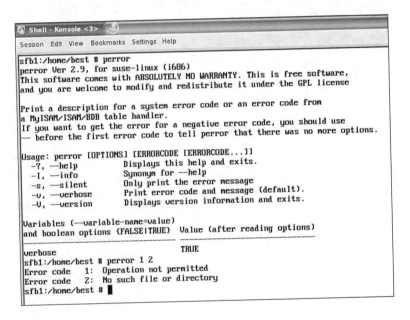

```
Shell - Konsole <3>

Session  Edit  View  Bookmarks  Settings  Help

sfb1:/home/best # perror
perror Ver 2.9, for suse-linux (i686)
This software comes with ABSOLUTELY NO WARRANTY. This is free software,
and you are welcome to modify and redistribute it under the GPL license

Print a description for a system error code or an error code from
a MyISAM/ISAM/BDB table handler.
If you want to get the error for a negative error code, you should use
-- before the first error code to tell perror that there was no more options.

Usage: perror [OPTIONS] [ERRORCODE [ERRORCODE...]]
  -?, --help        Displays this help and exits.
  -I, --info        Synonym for --help
  -s, --silent      Only print the error message
  -v, --verbose     Print error code and message (default).
  -V, --version     Displays version information and exits.

Variables (--variable-name=value)
and boolean options {FALSE|TRUE}  Value (after reading options)
-------------------------------------------------------------------
verbose                           TRUE
sfb1:/home/best # perror 1 2
Error code   1: Operation not permitted
Error code   2: No such file or directory
sfb1:/home/best # 
```

FIGURE 7.8
perror, explaining error codes.

Sometimes, seeing a useful description of an error code can help you determine the problem an application is having. The following example shows that the database test is having a problem during the creation process.

Execute the following command:

```
echo "drop database test;" | /usr/local/mysql/bin/mysql -u root
```

Then execute this command:

```
/usr/local/mysql/bin/mysql -u root < /usr/local/mysql/db_backup/dump-
test.courses.sql
```

The first commands in the SQL command are as follows:

```
CREATE DATABASE /*!32312 IF NOT EXISTS*/ test;
USE test;
```

The database is dumped successfully, but when the second command is run, the following error is displayed:

```
ERROR 1006 at line 11: Can't create database 'test'. (errno: 28)
```

Now let's see what perror tells us about error 28:

```
# perror 28

Error code  28:  No space left on device
```

In this situation, the MySQL program did not find sufficient free space to create the database.

Summary

The Oops message is one way the kernel can show you that one of its components has a NULL or invalid pointer. Using an Oops message that has been run through the ksymoops utility, you can determine the failing line of code. Knowing the failing line of code is one step in solving a kernel problem; some problems can be solved with just this type of information. You have seen from the two real Oops examples shown in this chapter that developers can provide source code fixes just by having the information provided by the Oops message.

Web Resources for Oops

URL	Description
http://www.kernel.org	Kernel source tree
http://jfs.sourceforge.net/	JFS for the Linux web site
http://www.uwsg.iu.edu/hypermail/linux/kernel/0108.3/0163.html	Oops in 3c59x driver
http://www.uwsg.iu.edu/hypermail/linux/kernel/0112.0/0670.html	Oops Linux-2.5.1-pre5

Chapter 8

Event Logging

In this chapter

- Error Logging Subsystem for syslogd   page 213
- Error Logging Subsystem for Event Logging   page 226
- Setting up the Event Consolidator   page 230
- Summary   page 232
- Credits   page 232
- Web Resource for Event Logging   page 232

Often if something doesn't work as expected, you might not see an error message. In most cases the message is there, but you have to know where to look. This chapter walks through Syslog and event logging, which are two of the error logging subsystems in Linux. It is good to have an overview of how the logging systems are set up so that you know that on the system you are debugging the logs are rotated daily. With this type of information, you might want to look at a log that was produced days ago to determine when an error started to happen.

If the system you are debugging is using Syslog, the kernel, modules, and daemon's log messages are included in the /var/log/messages file. This is an ordinary text file you can look at as root. Since you usually want to see only the last few lines and the messages file becomes quite large, use **tail /var/log/messages**. Using the -**f** option even allows you to follow changes made to that file in real time.

Notice that the /var/log directory also contains other significant helpful log files, like boot.log and boot.msg. boot.msg contains boot messages or further subdirectories that contain logs for running services like cups/, httpd/, and apache2/. Whereas the messages file usually gives a short summary of system messages, these other logs should be checked for more detailed messages by specific services.

An important goal of a Linux systems administrator is to ensure that the systems he or she administers function and perform 100% of the time. Applications producing error messages, file systems not having free space available, network adapter failures, hard drives producing errors, and the kernel producing an error are just a few types of errors that could possibly stop a system, impacting that goal.

This chapter covers Syslog and event logging. A key feature of event logging is that it provides standard calls for a single system-wide log to which all event entries are written. Keeping all event entry records intact through a single logical mechanism allows an implementation to monitor and analyze events in a system-wide view, which can help determine where faults may exist. Logging is a good security monitoring tool as well.

Event logging in Linux is based on the POSIX standard 1003.25. This standard provides for logging of binary data to enable more efficient processing of log events. With just textual data, hardware sense data and other binary failure cannot be supported, and logging and viewing of these types of events are limited. The standard supports logging of textual data, and in this respect it is compatible with the logging found in the Syslog implementation. In Linux, the most commonly used logging facilities are printk/klog (for logging kernel events) and Syslog (for logging nonkernel events), which collectively can be referred to as syslogd. Syslog has been the standard where system events or errors have been recorded. This chapter shows how event logging is an improvement from Syslog. Both Syslog and event logging events can be a key factor in finding and then fixing a system problem.

Error Logging Subsystem for syslogd

On most Linux systems, system events (information or errors) are still managed by the Syslog daemon, called syslogd. Kernel logging is supported by the klogd utility, which allows kernel logging to be supported either stand-alone or as a client of syslogd. Every logged message contains a time stamp and a hostname field. The main configuration file, /etc/syslog.conf, controls the messages that pass from the kernel, daemons, and user applications to the console and log files. /etc/syslog.conf is read at startup and when syslogd receives a HUP signal. A HUP signal causes a restart of the process from the beginning (reloading any config files it uses).

syslogd Key Options

The most significant options are as follows:

- **-h** causes the log daemon to forward any remote messages it receives to forwarding hosts.

- **-l hostlist** logs only the simple hostname (such as sfb), not the full name (such as sfb.austin.ibm.com).

- **-r** enables the receipt of messages from the network using an Internet domain socket with the Syslog service.

- **-s domainlist** specifies a domain name that should be stripped off before logging.

Remote Logging

The syslogd facility has network support, which allows messages to be forwarded from one node running syslogd to another node running syslogd. These messages are then logged to a file. The -r option allows this syslogd to listen to the network. syslogd listens on a socket for locally generated log messages and then forwards the messages to other hosts. One use of forwarding messages to another host is in a local network. A central log server could have all the important information on one machine.

syslog.conf

The syslog.conf file is the main configuration file for the syslogd. It identifies rules for logging.

Each rule consists of two fields—the selector field and the action field. The selector field states a pattern of facilities and priorities belonging to the specified action.

Understanding Facilities and Priorities

The selector field consists of two parts—a facility code and a severity code. The names listed here correspond to the **LOG_** values in /usr/include/sys/syslog.h.

The following keywords define the message's severity:

- **emerg** means that the system is unusable.
- **alert** means that action must be taken immediately.
- **crit** specifies a critical condition.
- **err** is an error condition.
- **warning** is a warning condition.
- **notice** is a normal but significant condition.
- **info** is informational.
- **debug** is the debug level.

The facility code identifies the subsystem that created the message. It is one of the following keywords:

- **kern** is the kernel message.

- **user** is the user-level message.

- **mail** is the mail system.

- **daemon** is the system daemon.

- **auth** is the security authorization message.

- **syslog** is messages generated internally by syslogd.

- **lpr** is the line printer.

- **news** is network news.

- **uucp** is the UUCP system.

- **cron** is the clock daemon.

- **authpriv** is the security/authorization message.

- **ftp** is the ftp daemon.

Actions

The action field describes the log file where the message will be written. A log file can be a file, or it can be one of the following:

- Named pipe

- Console/terminal

- Remote host

- List of users

- All users currently logged on

The behavior of syslogd is that all messages of a certain priority and higher are logged according to a given action. Listing 8.1 shows an example of the syslog.conf file.

Listing 8.1

Sample syslog.conf File

```
# /etc/syslog.conf - Configuration file for syslogd(8)
#
# For info about the format of this file, see "man
syslog.conf".
#

#
#
# print most on tty10 and on the xconsole pipe
#
kern.warning;*.err;authpriv.none    /dev/tty10
kern.warning;*.err;authpriv.none    |/dev/xconsole
*.emerg                  *

# enable this if you want the root to be informed
# immediately, e.g. of logins
#*.alert              root


#
# all email messages in one file
#
mail.*              -/var/log/mail
mail.info           -/var/log/mail.info
mail.warning        -/var/log/mail.warn
mail.err            /var/log/mail.err


#
# all news-messages
#
# these files are rotated and examined by "news.daily"
news.crit       -/var/log/news/news.crit
news.err        -/var/log/news/news.err
news.notice     -/var/log/news/news.notice
# enable this if you want to keep all news messages
# in one file
#news.*                    -/var/log/news.all


#
# Warnings in one file
#
*.=warning;*.=err       -/var/log/warn
*.crit                  /var/log/warn

#
```

```
# save the rest in one file
#
*.*;mail.none;news.none              -/var/log/messages

#
# enable this if you want to keep all messages
# in one file
#*.*                                 -/var/log/allmessages

#
# Some foreign boot scripts require local7
#
local0,local1.*                      -/var/log/localmessages
local2,local3.*                      -/var/log/localmessages
local4,local5.*                      -/var/log/localmessages
local6,local7.*                      -/var/log/localmessages
```

Changing syslogd Messages

The following rule tells syslogd to write all emergency messages to all currently logged-in users:

```
# Emergency messages will be displayed to all users
#
*.=emerg                         *
```

See the syslog.conf man page for more complete descriptions and examples of how to set up different options.

klogd

klogd can log messages to a specific file with the **-f** option or use the default option, where messages are logged through syslogd. When the kernel messages are directed through syslogd, klogd assigns the Syslog priority if a priority value is provided. The value of each priority is defined in /usr/src/linux/include/linux/kernel.h. The priorities are as follows:

- emerg (0) means that the system is unusable.

- alert (1) means that action must be taken immediately.

- crit (2) indicates a critical condition.

- err (3) is an error condition.

- warning (4) is a warning condition.

- notice (5) is a normal but significant condition.

- info (6) is an informational condition.

- debug (7) is the debug level.

By looking at the kernel's source code, you can see that this method of logging errors is very prevalent. An example of **KERN_EMERG** is in the /usr/src/linux/arch/i386/kernel/irq.c file at line 314, which uses the following log message that the IRQ will be disabled:

```
305 desc->irq_count = 0;
306 if (desc->irqs_unhandled > 99900) {
307    /*
308     * The interrupt is stuck
309     */
310    __report_bad_irq(irq, desc, action_ret);
311    /*
312     * Now kill the IRQ
313     */
314    printk(KERN_EMERG "Disabling IRQ #%d\n", irq);
315    desc->status |= IRQ_DISABLED;
316    desc->handler->disable(irq);
```

See the klogd man page for more complete descriptions and examples of how to set up different options.

Logger Command

If changes are made to Syslog, you can use the **logger** command to see if Syslog is still set up correctly. The **logger** command is a shell command interface to Syslog. Figure 8.1 uses the -i option, which adds the process ID to the entry, and the -p option, which adds a priority. The text for the entry is **log entry test2**. The **tail** command lets you view the last few records in the /var/log/messages file. It shows that the last entry is **log entry test2**. The process ID for the entry that was written by the logger command is 17218.

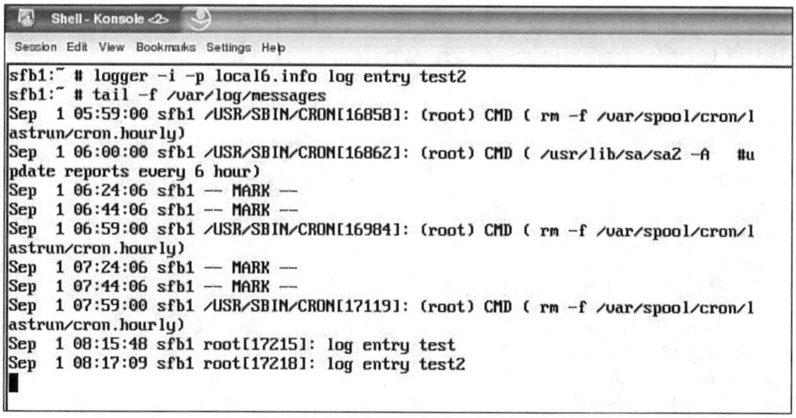
Shell - Konsole
Session Edit View Bookmarks Settings Help
sfb1:~ # logger -i -p local6.info log entry test2
sfb1:~ # tail -f /var/log/messages
Sep 1 05:59:00 sfb1 /USR/SBIN/CRON[16858]: (root) CMD (rm -f /var/spool/cron/lastrun/cron.hourly)
Sep 1 06:00:00 sfb1 /USR/SBIN/CRON[16862]: (root) CMD (/usr/lib/sa/sa2 -A #update reports every 6 hour)
Sep 1 06:24:06 sfb1 -- MARK --
Sep 1 06:44:06 sfb1 -- MARK --
Sep 1 06:59:00 sfb1 /USR/SBIN/CRON[16984]: (root) CMD (rm -f /var/spool/cron/lastrun/cron.hourly)
Sep 1 07:24:06 sfb1 -- MARK --
Sep 1 07:44:06 sfb1 -- MARK --
Sep 1 07:59:00 sfb1 /USR/SBIN/CRON[17119]: (root) CMD (rm -f /var/spool/cron/lastrun/cron.hourly)
Sep 1 08:15:48 sfb1 root[17215]: log entry test
Sep 1 08:17:09 sfb1 root[17218]: log entry test2

FIGURE 8.1
The **logger** command.

See the logger man page for more complete descriptions and examples of how to set up different options.

Provide Sufficient Disk Space

One key aspect of any type of disk logging is that there must be sufficient disk space to store all the desired log messages. The required space depends on the configuration and system disk utilization. One key feature of syslogd that helps reduce the number of logged messages per event is that if it sees a flood of identical messages, it reduces the duplicates by capturing them in one message. A count of those duplicates is logged.

In Figure 8.2, the 23 log entry messages are identical. By using the prevent log flood feature of syslogd, only two messages are written to the log.

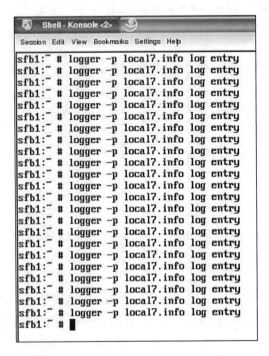

FIGURE 8.2
Identical log entry messages.

Two messages are written to the log after 23 identical messages have been sent to syslogd. Figure 8.3 shows the /var/log/messages file after these messages have been sent to syslogd.

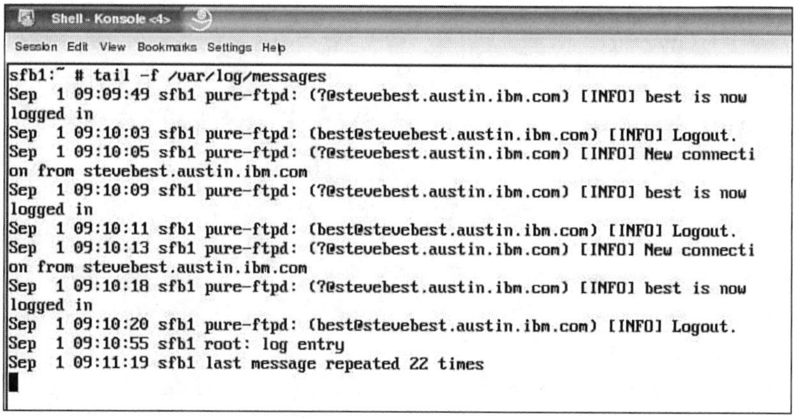

FIGURE 8.3
The /var/log/messages file.

Log File Management

One method to control managing log files is the use of the **logrotate** command. It enables automatic rotation, compression, removal, and mailing of log files. Each log file may be handled daily, weekly, monthly, or if the file grows to a predetermined size. The **logrotate** command can typically be run as a daily cron job.

Actions that occur by **logrotate** are defined in configuration files. Listing 8.2 shows an example of a default configuration file. The default configuration file is located in /etc and is named logrotate.conf.

Listing 8.2

Typical logrotate.conf

```
# see "man logrotate" for details
# rotate log files weekly
weekly

# keep 4 weeks worth of backlogs
rotate 4

# create new (empty) log files after rotating old ones
create

# uncomment this if you want your log files compressed
#compress
```

```
# uncomment these to switch compression to bzip2
#compresscmd /usr/bin/bzip2
#uncompresscmd /usr/bin/bunzip2

# RPM packages drop log rotation information into this directory
include /etc/logrotate.d

# no packages own wtmp — we'll rotate them here
#/var/log/wtmp {
#    monthly
#    create 0664 root utmp
#    rotate 1
#}

# system-specific logs may be also be configured here.
```

Debugging Using Syslog Messages

Now that we have finished going over Syslog and its available features, let's look at the types of problems that can show up in the logs. The following example has kernel component-related messages. We'll walk through messages 1 through 5 to show where in the kernel these messages originate.

```
1 May 28 11:29:50 hpcdhm05-cntrl kernel: hda: timeout waiting for DMA
2 May 28 11:29:50 hpcdhm05-cntrl kernel: ide_dmaproc: chipset supported
  ide_dma_timeout func only: 14
3 May 28 11:29:50 hpcdhm05-cntrl kernel: hda: status timeout: status=0xd0 {Busy}
4 May 28 11:29:50 hpcdhm05-cntrl kernel: hda: drive not ready for command
5 May 28 11:29:50 hpcdhm05-cntrl kernel: ide0: reset: success
6 May 28 11:29:52 hpcdhm05-cntrl init: Id "bpal" respawning too fast: disabled
  for 5 minutes
7 May 28 11:30:11 hpcdhm05-cntrl modprobe: modprobe: Can't locate module net-pf-
10
8 May 28 11:31:01 hpcdhm05-cntrl kernel: hda: timeout waiting for DMA
9 May 28 11:31:01 hpcdhm05-cntrl kernel: ide_dmaproc: chipset supported
  ide_dma_timeout func only: 14
10 May 28 11:31:01 hpcdhm05-cntrl kernel: hda: status timeout: status=0xd0 { 4
Busy }
11 May 28 11:31:01 hpcdhm05-cntrl kernel: hda: drive not ready for command
12 May 28 11:31:01 hpcdhm05-cntrl kernel: ide0: reset: success
13 May 28 11:33:36 hpcdhm05-cntrl xlog_stage_one[1828]: file_copy failed for
comp
   log, rc = 2, crc = d
14 May 28 11:34:33 hpcdhm05-cntrl kernel: hda: timeout waiting for DMA
15 May 28 11:34:33 hpcdhm05-cntrl kernel: ide_dmaproc: chipset supported
   ide_dma_timeout func
16 only: 14
```

```
17 May 28 11:34:33 hpcdhm05-cntrl kernel: hda: status timeout: status=0xd0 {
   Busy }
18 May 28 11:34:33 hpcdhm05-cntrl kernel: hda: drive not ready for command
19 May 28 11:34:33 hpcdhm05-cntrl kernel: ide0: reset: success
[1]                     [2]                 [3]               [4]
```

Each entry in the log file contains the following information:

[1]   Date and time

[2]   Hostname

[3]   Component

[4]   Message

Optionally, there could be a priority entry field between the component and message.

Message 1 states that the IDE device driver had an issue with DMA (direct memory access). DMA channels are system pathways used by many devices to transfer information directly to and from memory.

The message is **timeout waiting for DMA.** Listing 8.3 shows that the source for this Syslog message is in the kernel source tree /usr/src/linux/drivers/ide/ide.c on line 1551.

Listing 8.3

ide.c (ide_dma_timeout_retry)

```
1538 void ide_dma_timeout_retry(ide_drive_t *drive)
1539 {
1540         ide_hwif_t *hwif = HWIF(drive);
1541         struct request *rq;
1542
1543         /*
1544          * end current dma transaction
1545          */
1546         (void) hwif->dmaproc(ide_dma_end, drive);
1547
1548     /*
1549      * complain a little; later we might remove some of
this verbosity
1550      */
1551         printk("%s: timeout waiting for DMA\n",
drive->name);
1552         (void) hwif->dmaproc(ide_dma_timeout, drive);
1553
```

```
1554    /*
1555    * disable dma for now, but remember that we did so
because of
1556    * a timeout — we'll reenable after we finish this next
request
1557    * (or rather the first chunk of it) in pio
1558    */
```

Message 2 states that the IDE device driver has an informative message—**ide_dmaproc: chipset supported ide_dma_timeout func only: 14**. Listing 8.4 shows that the source of this Syslog message is in the kernel source tree /usr/src/linux/drivers/ide/ide_dma.c on line 760.

Listing 8.4

ide_dma.c (ide_dmaproc)

```
622 int ide_dmaproc (ide_dma_action_t func, ide_drive_t *drive)
623 {

758             case ide_dma_retune:
759             case ide_dma_lostirq:
760     printk("ide_dmaproc: chipset supported %s func only:
%d\n", ide_dmafunc_verbose(func),   func);
761             return 1;
```

Message 3 states that the IDE device driver had an error in the **ide_wait_stat** routine, with the text of the message being **status timeout: status=0xd0 {Busy}**. Listing 8.5 shows that the source of this Syslog message is in the kernel source tree /usr/src/linux/drivers/ide/ide.c on line 1098.

Listing 8.5

ide.c (ide_wait_stat)

```
1079 int ide_wait_stat (ide_startstop_t *startstop, ide_drive_t
*drive,
                        byte good, byte bad, unsigned long
timeout) {
1080    byte stat;
1081    int i;
1082    unsigned long flags;
1083
1084    /* bail early if we've exceeded max_failures */
1085    if (drive->max_failures && (drive->failures > drive-
max_failures)){
1086            *startstop = ide_stopped;
1087            return 1;
```

```
1088    }
1089
1090    udelay(1);     /* spec allows drive 400ns to assert
"BUSY" */
1091    if ((stat = GET_STAT()) & BUSY_STAT) {
1092            __save_flags(flags);   /* local CPU only */
1093            ide__sti();            /* local CPU only */
1094            timeout += jiffies;
1095            while ((stat = GET_STAT()) & BUSY_STAT) {
1096                if (0 < (signed long)(jiffies - timeout)) {
1097                    __restore_flags(flags);   /* local CPU only
*/
1098                    *startstop = ide_error(drive, "status time-
out",stat);
1099                    return 1;
```

Message 4 states that IDE device driver had an error in the **start_request** routine, with the text of the message being **drive not ready for command**. Listing 8.6 shows that the source of this Syslog message is in the kernel source tree /usr/src/linux/drivers/ide/ide.c on line 1289.

Listing 8.6

ide.c (start_request)

```
1241 static ide_startstop_t start_request (ide_drive_t *drive,
struct request *rq)

1287    SELECT_DRIVE(hwif, drive);
1288    if (ide_wait_stat(&startstop, drive, drive->ready_stat,
BUSY_STAT|DRQ_STAT, WAIT_READY)) {
1289        printk("%s: drive not ready for command\n", drive-
>name);
1290        return startstop;
```

Message 5 states that IDE device driver issued a reset in the **reset_pollfunc** routine, with the text of the message being **reset: success**. Listing 8.7 shows that the source of this Syslog message is in the kernel source tree /usr/src/linux/drivers/ide/ide.c on lines 561 and 563.

Listing 8.7

ide.c (reset_pollfunc)

```
547 static ide_startstop_t reset_pollfunc (ide_drive_t *drive)
548 {
549    ide_hwgroup_t *hwgroup = HWGROUP(drive);
550    ide_hwif_t *hwif = HWIF(drive);
```

```
551    byte tmp;
552
553    if (!OK_STAT(tmp=GET_STAT(), 0, BUSY_STAT)) {
554        if (0 < (signed long)(hwgroup->poll_timeout -
jiffies)) {
555            ide_set_handler (drive, &reset_pollfunc, HZ/20,
NULL);
556            return ide_started;   /* continue polling */
557        }
558        printk("%s: reset timed-out, status=0x%02x\n",
hwif->name, tmp);
559        drive->failures++;
560    } else  {
561        printk("%s: reset: ", hwif->name);
562        if ((tmp = GET_ERR()) == 1) {
563            printk("success\n");
564            drive->failures = 0;
```

These types of messages are the first place to look to determine why the system is having a problem. Messages 1 through 5 show that there is an issue with the system's IDE hard drive /dev/hda.

Error Logging Subsystem for Event Logging

Telco and high-availability (HA) environments are two types of solutions that require a robust event delivery subsystem. The POSIX 1003.25 standard contains a specification for an event logging facility that meets these requirements.

The Event Logger uses the POSIX standard APIs to register clients for events, receive log events from applications and the kernel, and deliver event notifications to clients that registered for them. Events are stored in a persistent log that can be viewed and managed. The event logging framework provides APIs and utilities for displaying, registering for and taking actions when events are received, and managing events in the log.

The error logging facility components are part of the evlog package. Both the syslogd and evlog packages can be installed on a single system. Major components of error logging are discussed in the following sections.

The evlogd daemon starts during system initialization and monitors the special file /dev/error for new entries sent by the kernel or an application. The label of each new entry is checked against the contents of the Error Record Template Repository.

When a match is found, additional information about the system environment is added before the entry is added to the error log. Error entries are stored in two files; the default files are /var/evlog/eventlog and /var/evlog/privatelog.

Event Logging Interfaces

Event logging has two primary interfaces: the provider interface and the consumer interface. Log management is the secondary interface for event logging.

The provider interface is how software reports events. Commands executed from the command line and scripts are common providers. Each event needs a base set of information that must be provided to make the event and its data useful for analysis and acceptable for storage in the log.

Benefits of Event-Type Logging

The event logging system collects common information, such as a time stamp for the event, and adds it to the supplied provider data to create a log entry. The event logging system also has these additional features:

- It can take **printk**() and **syslog**() messages and create POSIX-compliant event record log entries.

- It can use specified thresholds to suppress logging of duplicate events being logged in rapid succession to minimize system performance degradation and reduce logging space.

- It can use specified criteria to screen events that are recorded to the log.

- It can use specified criteria to filter events that are read from the log.

- It can notify registered consumers when events match consumer criteria.

- The event buffer size can be configured.

- The following are true of the consumer interface:

  - Configurable event data can be retrieved from the log.

  - Configurable event records are displayed either in a standard format or in a customized format specified by the consumer.

  - You can register to be notified when events written to the log match consumer-specified criteria.

Log Management

Log management has methods for the following:

- Automatic removal of events from the log that are no longer needed, truncating the log, and reclaiming the space

- Event log size management

Different Types of Event Log Records

One of the new types of event log records that is available from event logging is to include binary data. This snippet of code allows binary data to be captured from the kernel:

```
evl_writek( facility, event_type, severity,
    "ushort", 0x1212,           /* type = unsigned short, value = 0x1212 */
    "3*uchar", 5, 20, 80,     /* 3 unsigned chars */
    "int[]", 20, int_array,   /* array of 20 integers */
    "string", "Binary example",
    "endofdata");
```

Managing the Event Log

The evlogmgr can be run as a cron job. A cron job is a program that lets Linux users execute commands or scripts (groups of commands) automatically at a specified time and date. It is normally used for sys admin commands. During event logging installation, the file evlogmgr is placed in the /etc/cron.d directory. This file contains the following:

```
# Everyday at 2:00 AM remove recds older than 30 days
0 2 * * * root /sbin/evlogmgr -c 'age > "30d"'

# Everyday at 1:00 AM remove recds w/ sev=DEBUG
0 1 * * * root /sbin/evlogmgr -c "severity=DEBUG"
```

This code schedules the **evlogmgr** command to perform the described actions. This is the default. See the evlogmgr man page for details on changing this feature.

Event Logging Utilities

The evlsend utility logs a POSIX-type event that contains an event type, severity, and the text of the event message.

The evlview utility lets you view events in real time or from a log file.

The evlnotify utility registers a command when a specified query match occurs on events.

The evlquery file is not a command. It provides query and filter expression rules for the evlview, evlconfig, evlnotify, and evlogmgr commands.

The evlfacility utility lists the contents of the event logging facility registry, replaces the entire facility registry, adds facilities (with options) to the facility registry, deletes facilities, and modifies an existing facility.

The **evlconfig** command lets you change the default settings for event logging.

The **evlogmgr** command performs log management on the event log, on the private log, or, optionally, on a specified log file. It can also specify which events are to be deleted. The space freed by deleted events is reused for undeleted events (a process called compaction) and the log file is truncated, thus reducing its overall size.

The **evlgentmpls** command generates formatting templates for event logging calls.

The **evltc** command reads the formatting template specification(s) in the source file and creates a binary template file for each specification.

Each of these event logging utilities has a man page with more complete descriptions and examples of how to set up different options for the utilities.

Remote Logging

This section describes the main components of remote event forwarding and logging.

The Event Consolidation Host collects events logged by multiple hosts in the network. It accepts events transmitted via UDP or TCP, but it logs events from a particular host only if its hostname is stored in the /etc/evlog.d/evlhosts file.

Forwarding Plug-ins can register with the evlogd daemon to read events from the evlogd event stream and provide alternative methods of processing and logging events.

Two plug-ins are available for forwarding events:

- **udp_rmtlog_be**, which transmits using UDP
- **tcp_rmtlog_be**, which transmits using TCP

User Datagram Protocol (UDP) is a communications protocol that offers a limited amount of service when messages are exchanged between computers in a network that uses Internet Protocol. UDP is an alternative to Transmission Control Protocol (TCP). Like TCP, UDP uses Internet Protocol to transmit a data unit from one computer to another. Unlike TCP, however, UDP does not divide a message into packets and reassemble it at the other end. Specifically, UDP doesn't sequence the packets that the data arrives in. This means that the application program that uses UDP must be able to make sure that the entire message has arrived and is in the right order. Network applications that want to save processing time because they have very small data units to exchange (and therefore very little message reassembling to do) may prefer UDP to TCP.

Setting up the Event Consolidator

The evlogrmtd daemon is installed when the main event logging software is installed in user space. evlogrmtd starts during bootup, opens the /etc/evlog.d/ evlhosts file, and, if hosts are listed, attempts to resolve each of the hostnames to an IP address.

Follow these steps to configure evlogrmtd:

1. Edit /etc/evlog.d/evlhosts to add an entry for each host that
    evlogrmtd is to accept events from. Each entry must specify the
    hostname—either the simple name or the fully qualified
    domain name—and a unique identifier for each host.

    The following are all valid entries:

Identifier	Hostname
1	mylinuxbox
10.128	mylinuxbox2

    The identifier is always specified first, followed by one or more spaces,
    followed by the hostname.

2. Edit /etc/evlog.d/evlogrmtd.conf, which contains the following:

```
Password=password
TCPPort=12000
UDPPort=34000
```

Password is used only by TCP clients to authenticate remote hosts when attempting to connect. If all remote hosts are using UDP, Password is ignored.

TCPPort must match the TCP port used by remote hosts to send events to the event consolidator.

UDPPort must match the UDP port used by remote hosts to send events to the event consolidator.

3. Restart the evlogrmtd daemon:

```
/etc/init.d/evlogrmt restart
```

Forwarding Syslog Messages to the Event Log

The **slog_fwd** command can be used to forward Syslog messages to the event log. This is a good way to try out event log and to start changing any scripts that are being used to parse Syslog messages to parse event log messages.

The following command can be issued to forward Syslog messages to the new event log:

```
# /sbin/slog_fwd
```

This forwards Syslog messages immediately and after every subsequent reboot. To disable Syslog forwarding, issue the following command:

```
# /sbin/slog_fwd -r
```

evlog Packages

The evlog package provides a set of tools to implement enterprise-level event logging, as defined by POSIX draft standard 1003.25. The evlog-devel package contains the header files and libraries to write applications for the evlog event logging system.

Summary

Logging can help you identify bugs, optimize performance, and more. Event logging provides a standard, centralized way for applications (and the operating system) to record important software and hardware events. The event-logging service stores events from various sources in a single collection called an event log. The Event Viewer allows you to view logs; the programming interface also lets a program examine the logs.

Credits

A big thank-you goes out to Rajarshi Das, Haren Myneni, Jim Keniston, Larry Kessler, Hien Nguyen, Nick Wilson, Kyle Petersen, Daniel Stekloff, and other developers for the development and support of Linux Event Logging for the Enterprise. A big thank-you goes out to Dr. Greg Wettstein, Stephen Tweedie, Juha Virtanen, Shane Alderton, and other developers for the development and support of syslogd.

Web Resource for Event Logging

URL	Description
http://evlog.sourceforge.net	Event logging web site

## Chapter 9

Linux Trace Toolkit

In this chapter

- Architecture Component Tasks   page 235
- Package and Installation   page 236
- Building the Kernel   page 240
- Building LTT User-Level Tools   page 242
- Data Acquisition   page 243
- Recording the Data   page 244
- Stopping Data Recording   page 244
- Ways to Analyze Tracing Processes   page 245
- Data Interpretation   page 248
- Tracing Example for Tarring a Subdirectory   page 253
- Data Reviewing Text Tools   page 256
- Summary   page 259
- Credits   page 259
- Web Resource for the Linux Trace Toolkit   page 259

An execution trace shows exactly what scheduling decisions are made, process switches, and how various management tasks are done. It captures how they are handled, how long they take, and to which process the processor has been allocated. The trace facility provides a dynamic way to gather system data. Application I/O latencies can also be identified, as well as the time when a specific application is actually reading from a disk. Tracing also can show certain types of locking issues.

Trace can be used to:

- Isolate and understand system problems.

- Observe system and application execution for measuring system performance.

- Perform bottleneck analysis when many processes are interacting and communicating with each other.

Linux Trace Toolkit (LTT) differs from using strace or gprof in that LTT provides a global view, including a view into the kernel and interrupts.

LTT is a suite of tools designed to capture an execution trace. By extracting program execution details from the operating system and interpreting them, you can see a view of the system's program execution. Tools to analyze the trace (both graphical viewing and text tools) are included in the LTT package.

This chapter describes how the tracing facility is implemented in the kernel and how to analyze data gathered by tracing. One of the key components of this tracing is that the kernel must have the tracing patch, and the patch must be enabled in the kernel configuration. The kernel support provides a number of default system events (see Table 9.1 for a complete list). Custom events are also supported. The performance impact of a functional tracing system is 2.5% for the system events. This means that if a program execution time is 200 seconds on a nontracing system, it will take 205 seconds on a system that has tracing enabled. This is a key issue with any type of tracing done at the kernel level: it must be implemented with low overhead.

Architecture Component Tasks

The toolkit is implemented in four parts. First, a Linux kernel allows events to be logged. Second, a Linux kernel module stores the events in its buffer and signals the trace daemon when it reaches a certain threshold. The daemon then reads the data from the module, which is visible from user space as a character device. Last, the data decoder takes the raw trace data and puts it in human-readable format while performing some basic and more advanced analysis. This decoder serves as the toolkit's graphic and command-line front end.

The process of tracing consists of the following components:

- Events are logged by having trace points in key components of the kernel. A trace point in the kernel has entry and exit. For a complete list of kernel events, see Table 9.1. Listing 9.1 shows an example of the trace point for capturing IRQ data. Line 443 is the entry trace point for the kernel's IRQ trace point. Line 460 is the exit trace point for the kernel's IRQ trace point.

  The IRQ processing for the x86 architecture is done in linux/arch/i386 /kernel/irq.c for the kernel. Lines 443 and 460 have been added to this routine to capture tracing data.

Listing 9.1

IRQ Trace Points

```
441    irq_enter(cpu, irq);
442
443    TRACE_IRQ_ENTRY(irq, !(user_mode(regs)));
444
445    status = 1;  /* Force the "do bottom halves" bit */
446
455    if (!(action->flags & SA_INTERRUPT))
456         __cli();
457
458    irq_exit(cpu, irq);
459
460    TRACE_IRQ_EXIT();
461
462 return status;
```

- A kernel trace driver that stores events in a data buffer.

- A trace daemon that uses the trace driver to be notified at specified points in time that a certain quantity of data is available to be read.

- A trace event data decoder that reads the captured trace and formats the data into a readable format.

Package and Installation

To use the LTT the kernel that is being run, the LTT kernel patch must be applied and the **CONFIG_TRACE** option must be enabled. One way to check if the LTT patch has been applied is to view the kernel's configuration file and check the "Kernel hacking" menu to see if there is a submenu called "Kernel events tracing support." The tracing driver, which is the kernel feature of LTT, can be built directly into the kernel or be built as a module. On the kernel configuration menu, shown in Figure 9.1, "Kernel events tracing support" is built directly into the kernel because the "y" option is selected.

FIGURE 9.1
The kernel configuration menu.

The LTT patch has not been accepted into the official kernel source tree hosted at www.kernel.org as of March 2005, so the web page for LTT provides several different patches for different kernel levels. If the kernel's level doesn't apply cleanly, check the mailing list for different patches.

> NOTE   Some Linux distributions already have the kernel LTT patch
> applied to their kernel and ship the user land tools for LTT.

Figure 9.2 shows the help screen for Kernel events tracing support.

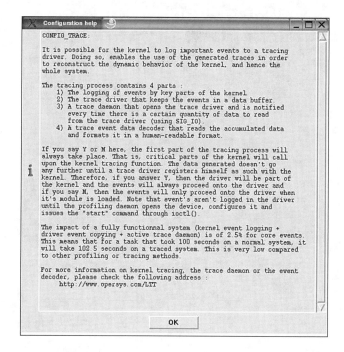

FIGURE 9.2
The Help menu for the tracing support option.

If the kernel that is being run doesn't have the LTT patch applied, it is possible to download the LTT package. That package has a directory called Patches, which has the kernel patch for the 2.6.9 kernel. For example, the ltt-0.9.6-pre4.tar.bz2 version of the LTT package expands to the ltt-0.9.6-pre4 base directory, and the kernel patches are located in the Patches subdirectory. The following steps show you how to apply the patch to a 2.6.9 kernel:

1. Change to the directory where the kernel source is (usually /usr/src/linux).

2. Use the **patch** command to apply the kernel change. The **—dry-run** option shows whether the patch applies, but it doesn't really apply the patch (see Figures 9.3 and 9.4). If the patch applies cleanly with no rejects, remove the **—dry-run** option and apply the patch.

FIGURE 9.3
Applying ltt-linux-2.6.9-vanilla-041214-2.2.patch.

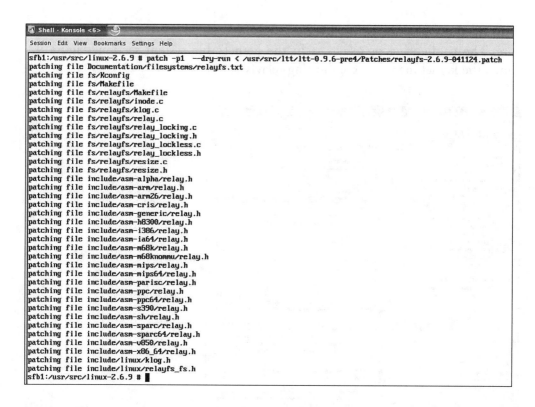

FIGURE 9.4
Applying relayfs-2.6.9-041124.patch.

In the 2.6.x level of the kernel, the patch for LTT also includes the relayfs feature. The configuring of relayfs is in the kernel's file system section. Figure 9.5 shows the kernel menu for configuring relayfs.

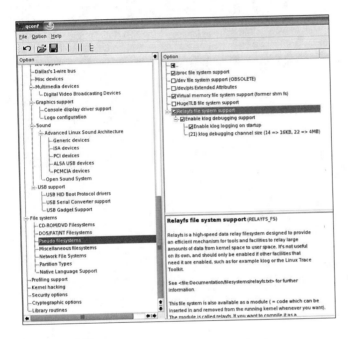

FIGURE 9.5
The relayfs kernel menu.

Building the Kernel

The following steps show you how to build the kernel (for i386):

1. Issue the **make xconfig** command.

2. Under "Kernel hacking," do the following:
   a. Select "y" for "Kernel events tracing support."
   b. Configure other kernel settings as needed.

3. Save and exit.

4. Issue the **make clean** command.

5. Issue the **make bzImage** command.

6. If modules need to be built, do the following:

   a. Issue the **make modules** command.

   b. Issue the **make modules_install** command.

7. Enter **cp arch/i386/boot/bzImage /boot/bzImage-2.6.9-ltt**.

8. Enter **cp System.map /boot/System.map-2.6.9-ltt**.

9. Enter **rm /boot/System.map && ln -s /boot/System. map-2.6.9-ltt /boot/System.map**.

10. If the system is using lilo as the boot loader, modify your configuration to boot from /boot/bzImage-2.6.9-ltt.

    For example, if you're using lilo, do the following:

    a. Modify /etc/lilo.conf.

    b. Run lilo to read the modified lilo.conf.

11. If the system is using grub as the boot loader, modify your configuration to boot from /boot/bzImage-2.6.9-ltt.

    For example, if you're using grub, modify /boot/grub/menu.lst.

12. Reboot.

The next step is to check the kernel's level and make sure that the LTT supported kernel is the one that is running. The **uname** command does not directly show that LTT support is built into the kernel, but the following example shows that level 2.6.9 of the kernel is running. Use the **uname -a** command to display the kernel's level. The output should be similar to the following:

```
Linux sfb1 2.6.9 #1 Fri Mar 25 05:08:30 UTC 2005 i686 i686 i386 GNU/Linux
```

To see if the application part of the LTT package is installed, use the **rpm** command. The **trace** command is part of the LTT package. You can use the -**qf** option to see which version of the LTT package is installed. Figure 9.6 shows that TraceToolkit-0.9.6pre2-38 is the version of the LTT user land tools installed on this system.

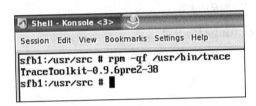

FIGURE 9.6
The version of the installed LTT package.

After the LTT package is installed, the following commands are available to start and view the trace data:

- **tracedaemon** is the user space daemon that communicates with the kernel.

- **tracevisualizer** is the graphical trace file viewer.

After you install the LTT package and ready the kernel for tracing, the system is ready to gather trace data. It is worth noting that if the trace daemon is not running, which means that no data is being collected, there is minimal overhead from having trace support in the kernel.

Since the overhead is minimal, LTT can be placed in a production enterprise environment to help isolate bottlenecks as many processes communicate information among themselves and across machines.

Building LTT User-Level Tools

The latest revision of the user tools for TraceToolkit is version 0.9.6-pre4, and the tar file that has this version is called ltt-0.9.6-pre4.tar.bz2. Using the **tar** command expands the source into the ltt-0.9.6-pre4 subdirectory. We'll use the standard **./configure**, **make**, and **make install** commands to build and install the user-level tools for LTT, as shown in Figure 9.7.

```
Shell - Konsole <3>
Session  Edit  View  Bookmarks  Settings  Help
sfb1:/usr/src/ltt/ltt-0.9.6-pre4 # ./configure && make && make install
checking build system type... i686-pc-linux-gnu
checking host system type... i686-pc-linux-gnu
checking target system type... i686-pc-linux-gnu
checking for a BSD-compatible install... /usr/bin/install -c
checking whether build environment is sane... yes
checking for gawk... gawk
checking whether make sets $(MAKE)... yes
checking whether to enable maintainer-specific portions of Makefiles... no
checking for gcc... gcc
checking for C compiler default output... a.out
checking whether the C compiler works... yes
checking whether we are cross compiling... no
checking for suffix of executables...
checking for suffix of object files... o
checking whether we are using the GNU C compiler... yes
checking whether gcc accepts -g... yes
checking whether gcc and cc understand -c and -o together... yes
checking for a BSD-compatible install... /usr/bin/install -c
checking for ld used by GCC... /usr/i586-suse-linux/bin/ld
checking if the linker (/usr/i586-suse-linux/bin/ld) is GNU ld... yes
checking for /usr/i586-suse-linux/bin/ld option to reload object files... -r
checking for BSD-compatible nm... /usr/bin/nm -B
checking whether ln -s works... yes
checking how to recognise dependant libraries... pass_all
checking command to parse /usr/bin/nm -B output... ok
checking how to run the C preprocessor... gcc -E
checking for ANSI C header files... yes
checking for sys/types.h... yes
checking for sys/stat.h... yes
checking for stdlib.h... yes
checking for string.h... yes
checking for memory.h... yes
checking for strings.h... yes
checking for inttypes.h... yes
checking for stdint.h... yes
checking for unistd.h... yes
checking dlfcn.h usability... yes
                                                                    Shell
```

FIGURE 9.7
Building and installing TraceToolkit tools.

Data Acquisition

Before data collection is started for the 2.6.x level of the kernel, the relayfs file system must be mounted.

A mount point must be used to mount the relayfs. The following example uses /mnt/relay as the mount point:

```
# mount -t relayfs nodev /mnt/relay
```

Collection of trace data starts and is transferred to user space when the tracer functionality in the kernel is started and the trace daemon connects to it through the device files or relayfs file system.

Several helper scripts call the trace daemon to start and stop tracing directly:

- **trace** *seconds filename*: The trace daemon is activated for *seconds*. The trace results are saved in two files. *filename*.trace stores the trace data, and *file name*.proc stores the /proc information at the start of the trace run. Both files are used to view the trace.

- **tracecore** *seconds filename*: The trace daemon is activated for *seconds*. The trace results are saved in the same two files as with **trace**, but only a core subset of events is saved.

- **tracecpuid** *seconds filename*: The trace daemon is activated for *seconds*. The trace results are saved in the same two files as with **trace**, but CPU identification is also included with each trace entry.

- **traceu** *filename*: The trace daemon is activated until it is killed. The trace results are saved in the same two files as with **trace**.

Recording the Data

If the tracer was built as a module, the kernel must load the module before data can be generated from the system. The following command can be used to load the tracer module:

```
# modprobe tracer
```

If the tracer was built directly into the kernel, you don't need this command.

The following command uses the trace script and records data for 20 seconds. The output is stored in files named trace1.trace and trace1.proc.

```
# trace 20 trace1
```

The following command uses the tracecpuid script, which adds the CPU identification and records data for 30 seconds. The output is stored in files named trace2.trace and trace2.proc. This option is useful if the system that needs to be traced is a symmetric multiprocessing (SMP) system.

```
# tracecpuid 30 trace2
```

The following command uses the traceu script, which doesn't have a fixed time period when the tracing will stop recording data. The output is stored in files named trace3.trace and trace3.proc.

```
# traceu trace3
```

Stopping Data Recording

Some of the scripts listed in the preceding section stop tracing after a specified time interval. Others allow tracing to run until the trace daemon process is stopped. You can use the following command to stop the trace daemon manually:

```
# pkill [tracedaemon]
```

The **ps** command can be used to find the process ID for the trace daemon. After you find it, you can use the **kill** command to stop the trace daemon:

```
# kill [tracedaemon pid]
```

Ways to Analyze Tracing Processes

Most of the time tracing needs to be done on a certain process to determine why that process isn't performing as expected. The LTT provides the framework for tracing, but there isn't a built-in way to start a trace when a process is created and to end the trace when the process exits.

Several methods exist to accomplish this task:

- For a one-time manual tracing, you can start and stop the tracing from a separate shell. Tracing is started, and then the process is started. Upon process exits, the trace daemon is killed. This method isn't easily automated.

- You can use a timed trace by using one of the helper scripts or by invoking the trace daemon with the -t option. This approach usually captures more tracing data and lets you automate tracing collection.

- You can start the trace daemon and then start the process of interest. Use the **pgrep** command or an equivalent to indicate that the process of interest has finished, and then kill the trace daemon.

A number of options control data acquisition, so it is worth viewing the man page for the trace daemon. One option that can limit the events being traced is having the trace daemon collect events by PID or group PID.

Table 9.1 lists the common kernel trace points that LTT can capture.

TABLE 9.1
Trace Points for the Kernel

Event Type	Event Subtype	Event Details
System call entry	N/A	System call ID, instruction counter
System call exit	N/A	None
Trap entry	N/A	Trap ID, instruction counter

(continues)

TABLE 9.1   (Continued)

Event Type	Event Subtype	Event Details
Trap exit	N/A	None
Interrupt entry	N/A	Interrupt ID, kernel-space occurrence
Interrupt exit	N/A	None
Scheduling change	N/A	Incoming process ID, outgoing process ID, outgoing process state
Kernel timer	N/A	None
Soft IRQ	Bottom half	Bottom half ID
	Soft IRQ	Bottom half ID
	Tasklet action	Address of function
	Tasklet hi-action	Address of function
Process	Creation of kernel thread	Thread start address, PID
	Fork or clone	PID of created process
	Exit	None
	Wait	PID waited on
	Signal	Signal ID, destination PID
	Wakeup	Process PID, state prior to wakeup
File system	Starting to wait for a data buffer	None
File system	End to the wait for a data buffer	None
	An exec occurred	Filename
	An open occurred	Filename, file descriptor
	A close occurred	File descriptor
	A read occurred	File descriptor, amount read
	A write occurred	File descriptor, amount written
	A seek occurred	File descriptor, offset

Event Type	Event Subtype	Event Details
	An ioctl occurred	File descriptor, command
	A select occurred	File descriptor, timeout
	A poll occurred	File descriptor, timeout
Timer	Timer expired	None
	Setting itimer occurred	Type, time
	Setting schedule timeout occurred	Time
Memory	Page allocated	Size order
	Page freed	Size order
	Swap in	Page address
	Swap out	Page address
	Page wait start	None
	Page wait end	None
Socket	Socket call has occurred	Call ID, socket ID
	Socket has been created	Socket type, ID of created socket
	Data has been sent to a socket	Socket type, amount sent
	Data has been read for a socket	Socket type, amount received
Interprocess communication	System V IPC call	Call ID, object ID
	Message queue has been created	Message queue ID, creation flags
	Semaphore has been created	Semaphore ID, creation flags
	Shared memory segment has been created	Shared memory ID, creation flags
Network	Incoming packet	Protocol type
	Outgoing packet	Protocol type

Data Interpretation

Data generated by tracing is provided in two files for each trace—filename.trace and filename.proc. You can view the trace using textual and graphical methods. The graphical method is called tracevisualizer.

tracevisualizer

The tracevisualizer program is LTT's data analysis component. It performs data interpretation on the acquired data and displays a graphical view of a trace. If the program is launched with no command-line arguments, it automatically launches the GUI and waits for the user to specify files to operate with.

If the tracevisualizer is launched without any command-line options, the window shown in Figure 9.8 is displayed.

FIGURE 9.8
The main tracevisualizer window.

tracevisualizer's main functionality is provided by the File menu. This pull-down contains the following actions:

- **Open Trace** displays the Open Trace window, which lets you enter the trace filename and proc filename. After you enter these names, the trace data is displayed.

- **Close Trace** closes the trace that was being displayed.

- **Dump To File** opens the Dump to File window for generating an output file.

- **Exit** terminates the program.

The following selections are available from the Tools menu:

- **Zoom In** magnifies the viewed area.

- **Zoom Out** decreases the viewed area's magnification.

- **Show Horizon** displays a series of horizontal lines in the background of the event graph.

- **Go to event** opens the Go to Event window, which lets you search for a particular event from the raw list of events.

- **View Time Frame** opens the View Time Frame window, which lets you specify a time frame in the current event graph.

The two other menus are Options and Help. The Options menu lets you change the trace's colors. The Help menu can be used to access the help information for LTT.

Event Graph

The Event Graph view shown in Figure 9.9 is from the ls -R command of the root file system. It is captured in the files trace001.log and trace001.proc. Figure 9.9 shows a sample of the event graph where the gettimeofday call was made. The left side of the window shows all the processes that were on the system while tracing was being collected.

FIGURE 9.9
The main tracevisualizer window, showing an event graph.

Process Analysis

The Process Analysis view, shown in Figure 9.10, shows all processes that were present while trace data was being acquired. Clicking a process displays details about it. By viewing each process, you get an overall view of the system.

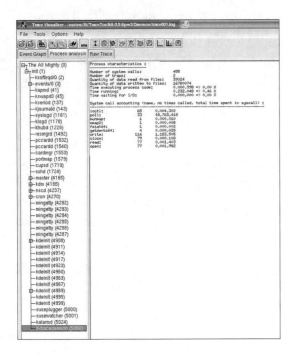

FIGURE 9.10
Process Analysis view.

Raw Trace

The Raw Trace view, shown in Figure 9.11, lists all the events that were logged by tracing the data.

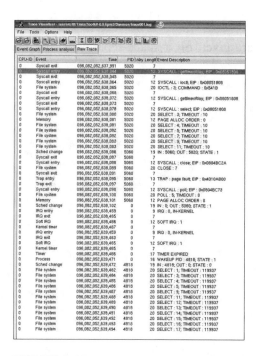

FIGURE 9.11
Raw Trace view.

A set of textual tools can be used to view trace data. The tracevisualizer also has a Dump to File option. We'll show that option as an example of looking at a tar of a subdirectory. The first thing that needs to happen to trace the tar command is to start the trace daemon.

Key tracevisualizer Options

The tracevisualizer command has a number of options that control the trace output. Some of these options are discussed next. (See the online HTML documentation for additional details. The help information is located in the /usr/share/doc/packages/TraceToolkit/Help/ subdirectory.)

-o (Omit Event Types)

Do not include any of the events that are given on a space-separated list. The event types can be any of the following:

- **START:** Trace start
- **SYS_ENTRY:** System call entry
- **SYS_EXIT:** System call exit
- **TRAP_ENTRY:** Trap entry
- **TRAP_EXIT:** Trap exit
- **IRQ_ENTRY:** Interrupt entry
- **IRQ_EXIT:** Interrupt exit
- **SCHED:** Schedule change
- **KTIMER:** Kernel timer
- **SIRQ:** Soft IRQ management
- **PROCESS:** Process management
- **FS:** File system management
- **TIMER:** Timer management
- **MEM:** Memory management
- **SOCKET:** Socket communications
- **IPC:** System V IPC communications
- **NET:** Network device management

-t (Event Types Tracing)

This includes only the specified events (a space-separated list of the same event types as for the -o option) in the output. This option can reduce the events that are captured.

-c (CPU ID Tracing)

This includes only events in the output that occurred on the specified CPU (numeric value). This option can be used to capture events that happen only on the specified CPU.

-p (PID Tracing)

This includes only events in the output that could be attributed to the specified PID in output. This option is useful to reduce the tracing on the system and to capture only data for the PID specified.

-a (Account Time Tracing)

This analyzes the trace and outputs the summary and translation to the output file.

Tracing Example for Tarring a Subdirectory

Now let's mount the relayfs file system and start the trace daemon with the parameters shown in Figure 9.12.

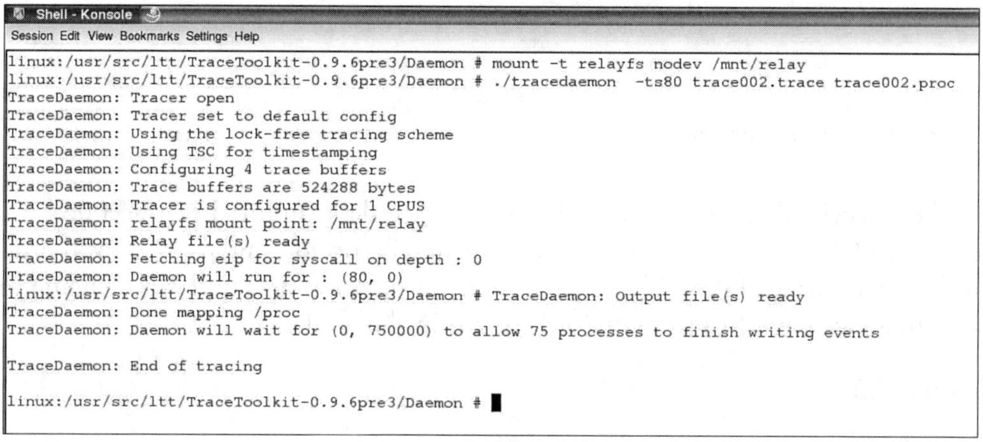

```
 Shell - Konsole
Session Edit View Bookmarks Settings Help
linux:/usr/src/ltt/TraceToolkit-0.9.6pre3/Daemon # mount -t relayfs nodev /mnt/relay
linux:/usr/src/ltt/TraceToolkit-0.9.6pre3/Daemon # ./tracedaemon  -ts80 trace002.trace trace002.proc
TraceDaemon: Tracer open
TraceDaemon: Tracer set to default config
TraceDaemon: Using the lock-free tracing scheme
TraceDaemon: Using TSC for timestamping
TraceDaemon: Configuring 4 trace buffers
TraceDaemon: Trace buffers are 524288 bytes
TraceDaemon: Tracer is configured for 1 CPUS
TraceDaemon: relayfs mount point: /mnt/relay
TraceDaemon: Relay file(s) ready
TraceDaemon: Fetching eip for syscall on depth : 0
TraceDaemon: Daemon will run for : (80, 0)
linux:/usr/src/ltt/TraceToolkit-0.9.6pre3/Daemon # TraceDaemon: Output file(s) ready
TraceDaemon: Done mapping /proc
TraceDaemon: Daemon will wait for (0, 750000) to allow 75 processes to finish writing events

TraceDaemon: End of tracing

linux:/usr/src/ltt/TraceToolkit-0.9.6pre3/Daemon # ▮
```

FIGURE 9.12
Tracing a tar of a subdirectory.

In Figure 9.13 tracing is done during the tarring of the /usr/src/chp9 directory.

```
linux:/usr/src # cd chp9
linux:/usr/src/chp9 # tar -cvf gg.tar .
./
./trace01.trace
./trace01.proc
./tracing01.jpg
./.xvpics/
./.xvpics/tracing01.jpg
./.xvpics/tracing02.jpg
./.xvpics/tracever01.jpg
./.xvpics/tracevisualizer01.jpg
./.xvpics/chp9-relayfs01.jpg
./.xvpics/chp9-graph01.jpg
./.xvpics/chp9-graph02.jpg
./.xvpics/chp9-graphrawtrace01.jpg
./tracing02.jpg
./trace02.trace
./trace1001.trace
./trace1001.proc
./tracever01.jpg
./test.trace
./test.proc
./test1.trace
./out302.proc
./out302.tgz
./out302.trace
./tracevisualizer01.jpg
./chp9-relayfs01.jpg
./chp9-graph01.jpg
./chp9-graph02.jpg
./chp9-graphrawtrace01.jpg
tar: ./gg.tar: file is the archive; not dumped
linux:/usr/src/chp9 #
```

FIGURE 9.13
Tarring the /usr/src/chp9 directory.

The tracevisualizer is started with the tar trace data captured in trace002.trace and trace002.proc. We can use the Dump to File option and view only the tar process that has a PID of 5125. The Dump to File option requires a filename to store the trace data. In Listing 9.2 it is stored in the tar.data file.

Listing 9.2

tar.data File

```
1   Trace start time: (1096157513, 774823)
2   Trace end time: (1096157593, 764048)
3   Trace duration: (79, 989225)
4
5   Number of occurrences of:
```

```
6        Events: 913072
7        Scheduling changes: 19092
8        Kernel timer tics: 79970
9        System call entries: 58949
10       System call exits: 58949
11       Trap entries: 1055
12       Trap exits: 1055
13       IRQ entries: 197527
14       IRQ exits: 197527
15       Bottom halves: 0
16       Timer expiries: 2870
17       Page allocations: 8978
18       Page frees: 12
19       Packets Out: 0
20       Packets In: 0
21
22
23 Tracing process 5125 only
24
25
###############################################################
26 Event           Time                    PID    Length
Description
27
###############################################################
28 Sched change   1,096,157,553,606,675    5125   19 IN : 5125;
OUT : 4801; STATE : 1
29 Syscall exit   1,096,157,553,606,676    5125   7
30 Trap entry     1,096,157,553,606,677    5125   13 TRAP : page
fault; EIP : 0x08067BB5
31 Trap exit      1,096,157,553,606,684    5125   7
32 Syscall entry  1,096,157,553,606,685    5125   12 SYSCALL :
getpid; EIP : 0x08067BBA
33 Syscall exit   1,096,157,553,606,685    5125   7
34 Syscall entry  1,096,157,553,606,687    5125   12 SYSCALL :
rt_sigp; EIP : 0x08067BF1
35 Syscall exit   1,096,157,553,606,688    5125   7
36 Trap entry     1,096,157,553,606,688    5125   13 TRAP : page
fault; EIP : 0x08067C30
```

Lines 1 through 20 are the summary section. Lines 28 through 36 are trace entry records. The first entry is sched change on line 28. From the tracing of the tar command you can see that it took a total of 10,775 microseconds (774,823 – 764,048 = 10,775). Now let's look at the number of high-level calls (see Figure 9.14). The trace shows that 4,958 syscalls occurred: 36 were opens, 2,381 were writes, and 4,863 were file system-related. Using grep on tar.data and wc, the numbers can be easily acquired from the trace data.

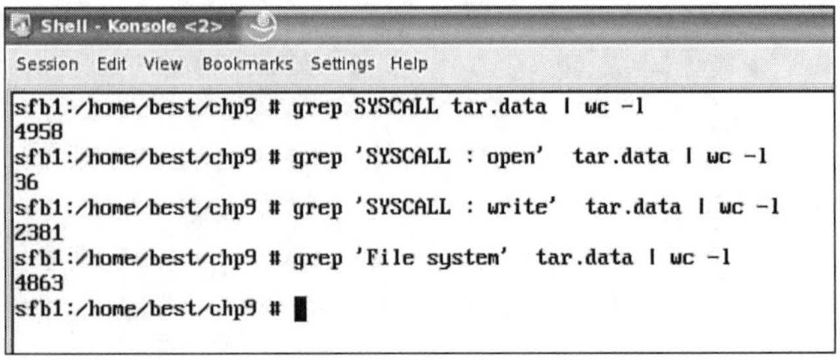

```
Shell - Konsole <2>

Session  Edit  View  Bookmarks  Settings  Help

sfb1:/home/best/chp9 # grep SYSCALL tar.data I wc -l
4958
sfb1:/home/best/chp9 # grep 'SYSCALL : open'  tar.data I wc -l
36
sfb1:/home/best/chp9 # grep 'SYSCALL : write'  tar.data I wc -l
2381
sfb1:/home/best/chp9 # grep 'File system'  tar.data I wc -l
4863
sfb1:/home/best/chp9 #
```

FIGURE 9.14
Commands used to capture total event numbers.

Data Reviewing Text Tools

Several scripts can be used to take the two binary trace files (*filename*.trace and *filename*.proc) and create an ASCII text file called *filename*.data. As soon as an ASCII text file exists, the trace data can be parsed by perl and python or other types of tools created for this type of parsing.

tracedcore *filename*

The script expects two files to exist: the binary trace file, usually named *filename*.trace, and the associated proc information for the trace, usually named *filename*.proc. The output is written to a file called *filename*.data.

traceanalyze *filename*

The script expects two files to exist: the binary trace file, usually named *filename*.trace, and the associated proc information for the trace, usually named *filename*.proc. The output is written to a file called *filename*.data. traceanalyze analyzes each process in the trace. If you used traceanalyze on the trace002.data tar example, the output would look similar to Figure 9.15 for the tar process (5125).

```
 Shell - Konsole
Session Edit View Bookmarks Settings Help
Analysis details:
        Process (5125, 5017): tar:
                Number of system calls: 4958
                Number of traps: 219
                Quantity of data read from files: 24015154
                Quantity of data written to files: 24033890
                Time executing process code: (0, 7921) => 0.01 %
                Time running: (1, 692588) => 2.12 %
                Time waiting for I/O: (0, 0) => 0.00 %
                System call usage:
                write:          2379    (4, 55051)
                readv:          1       (0, 2)
                writev:         2       (0, 63)
                socketcall:     4       (0, 122)
                getdents64:     4       (0, 10825)
                fcntl64:        2       (0, 3)
                lstat64:        30      (0, 227816)
                mmap2:          3       (0, 10)
                link:           1       (0, 1)
                sysctl:         1       (0, 4)
                :               1       (0, 1)
                munmap:         3       (0, 20)
                read:           2380    (8, 990700)
                close:          37      (0, 157)
                fstat64:        35      (0, 56)
                open:           36      (0, 41251)
                old_mmap:       12      (0, 54)
                brk:            4       (0, 3)
                newuname:       1       (0, 1)
                execve:         1       (0, 69606)
                ioctl:          1       (0, 2)
                setpgid:        1       (0, 2)
                rt_sigaction:   11      (0, 12)
                rt_sigprocmask: 5       (0, 5)
                getpid:         2       (0, 1)
        Process (5124, 5017): ls:
                Number of system calls: 140
                Number of traps: 203
                Quantity of data read from files: 15872
linux:/usr/src/ltt/TraceToolkit-0.9.6pre3/Visualizer/Scripts # 
```

FIGURE 9.15
traceanalyze output for trace002.data.

Figure 9.15 shows that most of the time is spent in performing I/O, with approximately equal parts in reads (24015154) and writes (24033890).

tracedump *filename*

The script expects two files to exist: the binary trace file, usually named *filename*.trace, and the associated proc information for the trace, usually named *filename*.proc. The output is written to a file called *filename*.data. The summary of the trace is written to the top of the *filename*.data file. A sample of the data produced by using tracedump on the tar example (trace002) is similar to Figure 9.16.

```
 Shell - Konsole
Session Edit View Bookmarks Settings Help
linux:/usr/src/ltt/TraceToolkit-0.9.6pre3/Visualizer/Scripts # ./tracedump trace002
linux:/usr/src/ltt/TraceToolkit-0.9.6pre3/Visualizer/Scripts # cat trace002.data | more
Trace start time: (1096157513, 774823)
Trace end time: (1096157593, 764048)
Trace duration: (79, 989225)

Number of occurences of:
        Events: 913072
        Scheduling changes: 19092
        Kernel timer tics: 79970
        System call entries: 58949
        System call exits: 58949
        Trap entries: 1055
        Trap exits: 1055
        IRQ entries: 197527
        IRQ exits: 197527
        Bottom halves: 0
        Timer expiries: 2870
        Page allocations: 8978
        Page frees: 12
        Packets Out: 0
        Packets In: 0


###################################################################
Event                 Time              PID    Length  Description
###################################################################
Syscall exit          1,096,157,513,774,823   N/A    7
Syscall entry         1,096,157,513,774,834   N/A    12      SYSCALL : creat; EIP : 0x0804BBFB
File system           1,096,157,513,774,872   N/A    34      OPEN : trace002.proc; FD : 7
Syscall exit          1,096,157,513,774,873   N/A    7
Trap entry            1,096,157,513,774,879   N/A    13      TRAP : page fault; EIP : 0x400DEA70
Trap exit             1,096,157,513,774,882   N/A    7
Syscall entry         1,096,157,513,774,883   N/A    12      SYSCALL : open; EIP : 0x08048881
File system           1,096,157,513,774,903   N/A    22      OPEN : /; FD : 8
Syscall exit          1,096,157,513,774,904   N/A    7
Syscall entry         1,096,157,513,774,905   N/A    12      SYSCALL : fstat64; EIP : 0x08048881
Syscall exit          1,096,157,513,774,906   N/A    7
Syscall entry         1,096,157,513,774,908   N/A    12      SYSCALL : fcntl64; EIP : 0x0804A806
Syscall exit          1,096,157,513,774,909   N/A    7
Trap entry            1,096,157,513,774,914   N/A    13      TRAP : page fault; EIP : 0x400DF2B0
Trap exit             1,096,157,513,774,914   N/A    7
```

FIGURE 9.16
tracedump on trace002.

The LTT also can add custom kernel trace events and user-level events. The LTT source code package has source code examples of both types of events; they are located in the TraceToolkit-0.x.xprex/Examples directory. Both custom kernel trace events and user-level events can be useful when additional tracing is needed in a kernel component or in an application to solve a performance issue.

Summary

This chapter gave an overview of the tool set available with the LTT and some of the views it offers. LTT can trace system events. You can do a tremendous amount of analysis with this type of detailed trace information.

LTT gives system administrators and developers all the information they need to reconstruct a system's behavior over a specified time period. Using LTT, you can see a graphical view of a system's dynamics, identify which application has access to the hardware during a specific time slice, and see what happens to an application when it receives or writes data. Application I/O latencies can also be identified, as well as the time when a specific application is reading from a disk. Tracing also helps you see certain types of locking issues.

Additional LTT information is available on your system. Start at the /usr/share/doc/packages/TraceToolkit/Help/index.html file after installing the LTT package.

Credits

A big thank-you goes out to Karim Yaghmour and other developers for the development and support of the Linux Trace Toolkit.

Web Resource for the Linux Trace Toolkit

URL	Description
http://opersys.com/	Linux Trace Toolkit

oprofile: a Profiler Supported by the Kernel

In this chapter

- Instrumentation   page 262
- Sampling   page 263
- oprofile: a System-Wide Profiler   page 263
- Utilities for oprofile   page 267
- General Profile Steps   page 268
- Examining a Single Executable's Profile   page 272
- Report Examples   page 276
- Saving Profiling Data   page 277
- Hardware Counters   page 277
- The Prospect Profiler   page 287
- Summary   page 288
- Web Resources for Profiling   page 289

This chapter covers profilers—software development tools designed to help analyze the performance of applications and the kernel. They can be used to identify sections of code that aren't performing as expected. They provide measurements of how long a routine takes to execute, how often it is called, where it is called from, and how much time it takes. Profiling is also covered in Chapter 1, "Profiling"; one profiler discussed in that chapter is called gprof. Another topic covered in this chapter is ways to minimize cache misses. Cache misses can be a cause of applications not performing as expected.

There are different ways to measure an application's performance while it runs. Depending on the method used, profiler results vary; this can affect your ability to optimize performance. Profiling methods can be divided into two categories: instrumentation and sampling. Let's take a look at each.

Instrumentation

Instrumentation profilers insert special code at the beginning and end of each routine to record when the routine starts and when it exits. With this information, the profiler can measure the time taken by the routine on each call. This type of profiler may also record which other routines are called from a routine. It can then display the time for the entire routine and also break it down into time spent locally and time spent on each call to another routine. gprof is an instrumentation profiler.

One possible drawback of instrumentation profiling is that, when a routine has a small number of code lines, another effect of instrumentation becomes important. Modern processors are quite dependent on order of execution for branch predictions and other CPU optimizations. Inevitably, inserting a timing operation at the start and end of a very small routine disturbs how it would execute in the CPU, absent the timing calls. If a small routine that is called thousands of times is hit by, say, a cache miss, an instrumentation profiler does not yield an accurate time comparison between this routine and larger routines. If this is ignored, a great deal of effort may be spent optimizing routines that are really not bottlenecks.

For a recap of instrumentation profilers, see Chapter 1, which covers gprof.

Sampling

To help address the limitations of instrumentation profilers, sampling profilers let applications run without any runtime modifications. Nothing is inserted, and all profiling work is done outside the application's process.

The operating system interrupts the CPU at regular intervals (time slices) to execute process switches. At that point, a sampling profiler records the currently executed instruction for the application it is profiling. This is as short an operation as can possibly be implemented: the contents of one CPU register are copied to memory. Using debug information linked to the application's executable, the profiler later correlates the recorded execution points with the routine and source code line they belong to. What the profiling finally yields is the frequency at which a given routine or source line was executing at a given period in the application's run, or over the entire run.

A sampling profiler is the perfect tool to isolate small, often-called routines that cause bottlenecks in program execution. The downside is that its evaluations of time spent are approximations. It is not impossible that a very fast routine should regularly execute at the sampling interrupts. To make sure that a given routine really is slow, you should run the application through the sampling profiler more than once. This chapter covers a sampling kernel profiler called oprofile.

oprofile: a System-Wide Profiler

oprofile is a low-overhead, system-wide profiler for Linux that uses performance-monitoring hardware on the processor to help find performance bottlenecks in both applications and the kernel. oprofile is a profiling system for Linux systems running the 2.2.x, 2.4.x, and 2.6.x kernels. This section focuses on using the oprofile support that is available for the 2.6.x kernel. The 2.6.8.1 kernel is used for the examples in this chapter. oprofile support has been accepted into the main kernel provided at www.kernel.org, so you don't need to apply a patch to the kernel. The first step is to check the kernel config and see if oprofile is enabled. One way to check the kernel config is to use the **make xconfig** command in the directory of the kernel's source tree—usually /usr/src/linux.

The oprofile kernel is enabled on the Profiling support menu. If Profiling isn't enabled, enable it and rebuild the kernel. Figure 10.1 shows the kernel configuration menu for oprofile; both options are set for profiling. The example shows that both profiling options will be built directly into the kernel.

FIGURE 10.1
The oprofile kernel menu.

Building the Kernel

The following steps show you how to build the kernel (for i386):

1. Issue the **make xconfig** command.

2. Under "General Setup," do the following:
    a. Select "Profiling support."
    b. Select "OProfile system profiling."
    c. Configure other kernel settings as needed.

3. Save and exit.

4. Issue the **make clean** command.

5. Issue the **make bzImage** command.

6. If modules need to be built, do the following:
   a. Issue the **make modules** command.
   b. Issue the **make modules_install** command.

7. Enter **cp arch/i386/boot/bzImage /boot/bzImage-2.6.8.1-oprofile**.

8. Enter **cp System.map /boot/System.map-2.6.8.1-oprofile**.

9. Enter **rm /boot/System.map && ln -s /boot/System.map-2.6.8.1-oprofile /boot/System.map**.

10. If the system is using lilo as the boot loader, modify your configuration to boot from /boot/bzImage-2.6.8.1-oprofile.

    For example, if you're using lilo, do the following:
    a. Modify /etc/lilo.conf.
    b. Run lilo to read the modified lilo.conf.

11. If the system is using grub as the boot loader, modify your configuration to boot from /boot/bzImage-2.6.8.1-oprofile.

    For example, if you're using grub, modify /boot/grub/menu.lst.

12. Reboot.

The next step is to check the kernel's level and make sure that the oprofile-supported kernel that was just built is the one running. The **uname -a** command displays the kernel's level. The output should be similar to the following:

```
Linux sfb1 2.6.8.1 #1 Fri Nov 26 10:08:30 UTC 2004 i686 i686 i386 GNU/Linux
```

At this point let's check to see if the kernel has oprofile support by running the following command:

```
# opcontrol —init
```

The oprofile /dev tree should be available as /dev/oprofile. The contents of /dev/oprofile should look similar to the following:

```
# ls /dev/oprofile

buffer          buffer_watershed  cpu_type  enable       stats
buffer_size     cpu_buffer_size   dump      kernel_only
```

The file /dev/oprofile/cpu_type contains a string to indicate the processor type oprofile will use.

cat /dev/oprofile/cpu_type displays the string.

oprofile is closely tied to the kernel and the processor architecture. Currently, oprofile supports these processors:

- Pentium Pro, Pentium II, Pentium III, Pentium 4

- Athlon, Hammer

- Itanium, Itanium 2

- IBM iSeries, IBM pSeries, IBM s390, IBM s390x

> NOTE **TIMER_INT** is a fallback mechanism for a processor without supported performance-monitoring hardware.

Listing 10.1 is a sample program that we'll profile using oprofile.

Listing 10.1

chp10-profile1.c

```
1   #include <pthread.h>
2   #include <dlfcn.h>
3   #include <dirent.h>
4
5   pthread_mutex_t mutex1 = PTHREAD_MUTEX_INITIALIZER;
6   void *
7   lookup_thread (void *handle)
8   {
9       while (1) {
10              pthread_mutex_lock( &mutex1 );
11              dlsym (handle, "main");
12              pthread_mutex_unlock( &mutex1 );
13      }
14
15      return NULL;
16  }
17
18
19  int
20  main (int argc, char **argv)
21  {
22      pthread_t loader;
23      DIR *d;
```

```
24      struct dirent *dent;
25      char *so;
26
27 pthread_create (&loader, NULL, lookup_thread, dlopen (NULL,
RTLD_NOW));
28 d = opendir ("/usr/lib");
29      while ((dent = readdir (d))) {
30              so = strstr (dent->d_name, ".so");
31              if (!so || so[3])
32                      continue;
33
34              printf ("%s\n", dent->d_name);
35              pthread_mutex_lock( &mutex1 );
36              dlopen (dent->d_name, RTLD_NOW | RTLD_GLOBAL);
37              pthread_mutex_unlock( &mutex1 );
38      }
39
40      printf ("we have finished!\n");
41      return 0;
42 }
```

We'll build chp10-profile1.c with the options shown in Figure 10.2.

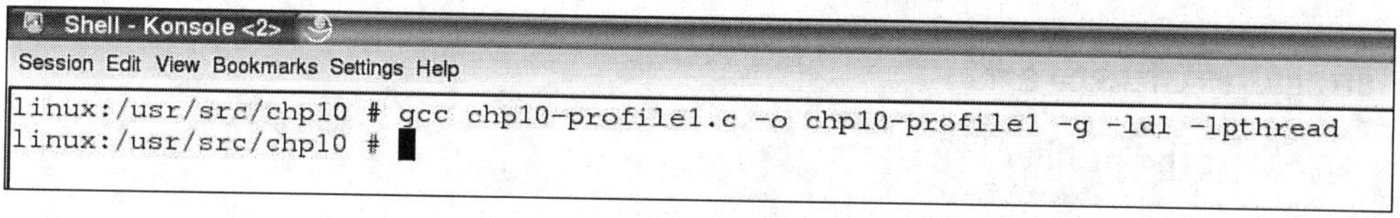

```
 Shell - Konsole <2>
Session Edit View Bookmarks Settings Help
linux:/usr/src/chp10 # gcc chp10-profile1.c -o chp10-profile1 -g -ldl -lpthread
linux:/usr/src/chp10 # █
```

FIGURE 10.2
Building chp10-profile1.c.

Utilities for oprofile

Five utilities help with oprofile, as described in the following list. The first and second are used to start and stop oprofile collection of data. The last three can be used to view oprofile data:

- opcontrol starts and stops the oprofile daemon and provides setup parameters.

   One useful parameter for opcontrol is —**save=filename**, which is used to start with a clean slate. Another parameter is —**dump**, which ensures that all the current profiling is flushed to the sample files before profiling data is analyzed.

See the opcontrol man page for more complete descriptions and examples of how to set up different options.

- oprof_start is a GUI program that is used to configure and control oprofile.

- opreport gives image- and symbol-based profile summaries for the whole system or a subset of binary images.

  See the opreport man page for more complete descriptions and examples of how to set up different options.

- opannotate outputs annotated source and/or assembly from profile data of an oprofile session.

  See the opannotate man page for more complete descriptions and examples of how to set up different options.

- opgprof can produce a gprof-format profile for a single binary.

  See the opgprof man page for more complete descriptions and examples of how to set up different options.

General Profile Steps

1. Start the profiler.

   Configure oprofile by setting up vmlinux:

   ```
   opcontrol --vmlinux=/path/to/where/vmlinux
   ```

   Once oprofile is configured, start the daemon:

   ```
   opcontrol --start
   ```

2. Now that the profiler is running, start the program to profile.

3. Stop the profiler:

   ```
   opcontrol --stop
   ```

4. Generate a profile summary:

   ```
   opreport -l /path/to/where/binary
   ```

   Or, if the binary was built with **-g**, annotated source can be viewed:

   ```
   opannotate -source -output-
   ```

```
dir=/path/to/where/annoatated-source
/path/to/where/binary
```

Or you can look at the summary of the various system components as a whole:

```
opreport
```

To reset the oprofile information before starting another profiler, use the following:

```
opcontrol —reset
```

Sample oprofile files are in the /var/lib/oprofile/samples/current directory. Each executable that has a sample is in that directory. The **find** command lets you see files that have the names of the executables that ran while the profiling occurred. Figure 10.3 shows sample output of **find** on the /var/lib/oprofile/samples/current directory on one of my systems.

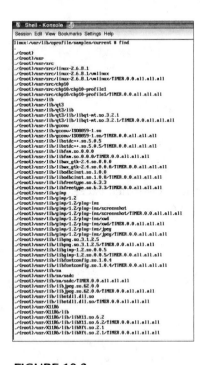

FIGURE 10.3
Executables that were profiled.

You can also use the GUI program oprof_start to control and configure oprofile, as shown in Figure 10.4.

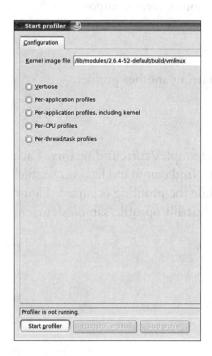

FIGURE 10.4
The oprof_start GUI program.

Now let's start oprofile and run chp10-profile1 as the program we'll collect data for (see Figure 10.5). After the chp10-profile1 program has finished execution, we'll stop oprofile using the —**stop** parameter (see Figure 10.6) and use opreport to view the profile data (see Figure 10.7).

```
Shell - Konsole
Session Edit View Bookmarks Settings Help
linux:/usr/src/chp10 # opcontrol --vmlinux=/usr/src/linux-2.6.8.1/vmlinux
linux:/usr/src/chp10 # opcontrol --start
Profiler running.
linux:/usr/src/chp10 # opcontrol --stop
Stopping profiling.
linux:/usr/src/chp10 # opreport -l /usr/src/chp10
CPU: CPU with timer interrupt, speed 598.199 MHz (estimated)
Profiling through timer interrupt
vma       samples  %        app name          symbol name
c0102510  41477    54.3206  vmlinux           default_idle
000080c0  25430    33.3045  ld-2.3.2.so       do_lookup
00013540  3504     4.5890   ld-2.3.2.so       strcmp
00008320  1045     1.3686   ld-2.3.2.so       do_lookup_versioned
08183850  258      0.3379   XFree86           miRegionOp
c0150ea0  253      0.3313   vmlinux           check_poison_obj
0000a2a0  122      0.1598   libpthread.so.0   __pthread_alt_unlock
000013e0  121      0.1585   libdl.so.2        _dlerror_run
c01183f0  102      0.1336   vmlinux           finish_task_switch
c0106c00  96       0.1257   vmlinux           handle_IRQ_event
0000a140  92       0.1205   libpthread.so.0   __pthread_alt_lock
00074ec0  81       0.1061   libc.so.6         _int_malloc
00008900  79       0.1035   ld-2.3.2.so       _dl_lookup_symbol_internal
c03b2a80  75       0.0982   vmlinux           unix_poll
c033a730  70       0.0917   vmlinux           i8042_interrupt
080c5400  68       0.0891   XFree86           XYToWindow
0000d540  67       0.0877   ld-2.3.2.so       _dl_catch_error_internal
00008050  65       0.0851   ld-2.3.2.so       _dl_elf_hash
c0150cd0  61       0.0799   vmlinux           poison_obj
000590b0  56       0.0733   konsole.so        TEWidget::setImage(ca const*, int, int)
0000a6a0  54       0.0707   ld-2.3.2.so       _dl_relocate_object_internal
c0153b30  54       0.0707   vmlinux           kfree
00064770  50       0.0655   konsole.so        TEScreen::getCookedImage()
000070e0  49       0.0642   libpthread.so.0   _GI___pthread_mutex_unlock
c0190a20  49       0.0642   vmlinux           do_select
0010dd80  48       0.0629   libc.so.6         _dl_sym
c0175330  47       0.0616   vmlinux           fget
00009300  43       0.0563   libpthread.so.0   pthread_getspecific
00073fe0  42       0.0550   libc.so.6         __malloc
00006ef0  41       0.0537   libpthread.so.0   _GI___pthread_mutex_lock
00006dc0  38       0.0498   ld-2.3.2.so       _dl_map_object_internal
New  Shell
```

FIGURE 10.5
oprofile for the chp10-profile1 program.

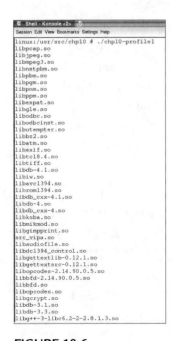

FIGURE 10.6
Stopping chp10-profile1.

```
Shell - Konsole <2>
Session Edit View Bookmarks Settings Help
linux:/usr/src/chp10/output # opreport
CPU: CPU with timer interrupt, speed 598.199 MHz (estimated)
Profiling through timer interrupt
    43211 49.0010 vmlinux
    30449 34.5289 ld-2.3.2.so
    11791 13.3709 chp10-profile1
      782  0.8868 XFree86
      459  0.5205 libqt-mt.so.3.2.1
      423  0.4797 libpthread.so.0
      365  0.4139 libc.so.6
      187  0.2121 libdl.so.2
      128  0.1452 konsole.so
       70  0.0794 libX11.so.6.2
       42  0.0476 kdeinit
       32  0.0363 libXft.so.2.1
       30  0.0340 oprofiled
       28  0.0318 libkdecore.so.4.1.0
       24  0.0272 appletproxy
       24  0.0272 libmcop.so.1.0.0
       18  0.0204 libstdc++.so.5.0.5
       15  0.0170 bash
       15  0.0170 libglib-1.2.so.0.0.10
       12  0.0136 libkdeui.so.4.1.0
       10  0.0113 kwin.so
        9  0.0102 libartsflow.so.1.0.0
        8  0.0091 libXrender.so.1.2
        6  0.0068 libgdk-1.2.so.0.9.1
        5  0.0057 libkparts.so.2.1.0
        5  0.0057 clock_panelapplet.so
        4  0.0045 klaptopdaemon.so
        4  0.0045 keramik.so
        4  0.0045 ISO8859-1.so
        2  0.0023 libreadline.so.4.3
        2  0.0023 artsd
        2  0.0023 kdesktop.so
        2  0.0023 libkdefx.so.4.1.0
        2  0.0023 libmcop_mt.so.1.0.0
        1  0.0011 libXext.so.6.4
        1  0.0011 libkonq.so.4.1.0
        1  0.0011 libkickermain.so.1.0.0
        1  0.0011 gimp-1.2
        1  0.0011 gpg-agent
```

FIGURE 10.7
opreport running on the data collected for profiling chp10-profile1.

The chp10-profile1 is in the third location. You see that there were 11,791 samples for chp10-profile1, the application executable. The second column shows the relative amount of time spent by the system's various executables. For the chp10-profile1 executable, the time was 13.3709.

Examining a Single Executable's Profile

Let's view the chp10-profile1 program in more detail. This requires debugging information to map the address in the program back to the source code. Thus, gcc's **-g** option should be used when producing executables. The gcc **-g** option adds the mapping information needed by the debugger to map addresses back to line numbers.

> NOTE Most programs are distributed without debugging information to save space, so if detailed profiling information is needed, the program needs to be rebuilt with the **-g** option.

For the chp10-profile1 program, you can find where it spends its time using different opreport options.

One useful option for opreport is —**long-filenames**, which outputs full path names instead of base names.

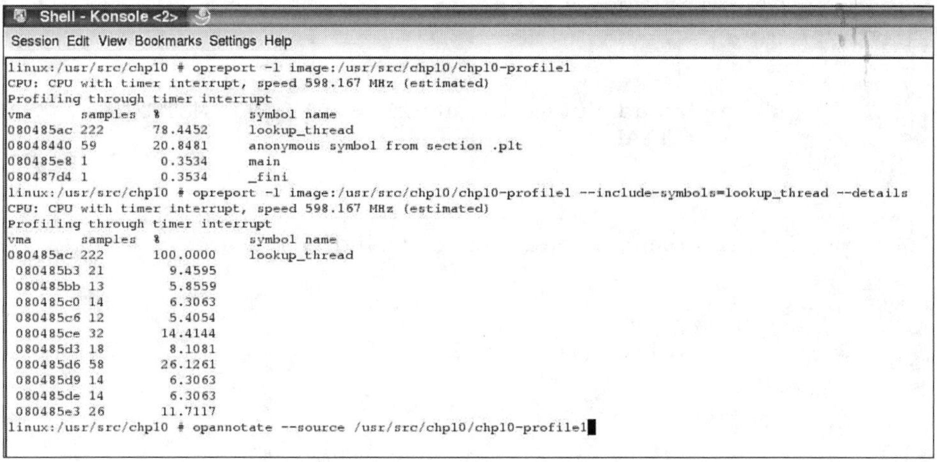

```
Shell - Konsole <2>
Session Edit View Bookmarks Settings Help
linux:/usr/src/chp10 # opreport -l image:/usr/src/chp10/chp10-profile1
CPU: CPU with timer interrupt, speed 598.167 MHz (estimated)
Profiling through timer interrupt
vma       samples    %           symbol name
080485ac 222        78.4452     lookup_thread
08048440 59         20.8481     anonymous symbol from section .plt
080485e8 1          0.3534      main
080487d4 1          0.3534      _fini
linux:/usr/src/chp10 # opreport -l image:/usr/src/chp10/chp10-profile1 --include-symbols=lookup_thread --details
CPU: CPU with timer interrupt, speed 598.167 MHz (estimated)
Profiling through timer interrupt
vma       samples    %           symbol name
080485ac 222        100.0000    lookup_thread
 080485b3 21         9.4595
 080485bb 13         5.8559
 080485c0 14         6.3063
 080485c6 12         5.4054
 080485ce 32        14.4144
 080485d3 18         8.1081
 080485d6 58        26.1261
 080485d9 14         6.3063
 080485de 14         6.3063
 080485e3 26        11.7117
linux:/usr/src/chp10 # opannotate --source /usr/src/chp10/chp10-profile1
```

FIGURE 10.8
Viewing chp10-profile using -l option.

You can see that most of the time is spent in the **lookup_thread** subroutine. To get the detailed view of the addresses in the particular function in the executable, use the -**include-symbols=lookup_thread** option. The samples can be related back to the original source code with the **opannotate** command.

For each file used to build the executable, an equivalent file is annotated with the sample counts for each line. The created file also has information at the end describing the processor and the events the counters measured. Listing 10.2 shows the annotation from the chp10-profile1 program. It shows the **lookup_thread** subroutine from the created file. You can see that most of the samples are for the loop in the **lookup_thread** function. You also can see that lookup_thread had 17 samples and the time was 0.0223.

Listing 10.2

Annotation from chp10-profile1.c

```
        :#include <pthread.h>

            :#include <dlfcn.h>

            :#include <dirent.h>

            :

            :pthread_mutex_t mutex1 = PTHREAD_MUTEX_
              INITIALIZER;

            :void *

            :lookup_thread (void *handle)

            :{

            :  while (1) {

            :            pthread_mutex_lock( &mutex1 );

            :            dlsym (handle, "main");

            :            pthread_mutex_unlock( &mutex1 );

            :}

            :

            :  return NULL;
/* lookup_thread total:      17   0.0223 */
            :}

            :

            :
   2  0.0026 :int

            :main (int argc, char **argv)

   5  0.0065 :{

            :  pthread_t loader;

  10  0.0131 :  DIR *d;
```

```
              :      struct dirent *dent;

              :      char *so;

              :

              :      pthread_create (&loader, NULL,
lookup_thread, dlopen (NULL, RTLD_NOW));

              :

              :      d = opendir ("/usr/lib");

              :      while ((dent = readdir (d))) {

              :              so = strstr (dent->d_name, ".so");

              :              if (!so || so[3])

              :                      continue;

              :

              :              printf ("%s\n", dent->d_name);

              :              pthread_mutex_lock( &mutex1 );

              :              dlopen (dent->d_name, RTLD_NOW |
                                  RTLD_GLOBAL);

              :              pthread_mutex_unlock( &mutex1 );

              :      }

              :

              :      printf ("we have finished!\n");

              :      return 0;

              :}
/*
 * Total samples for file : "/usr/src/chp10/chp10-profile1.c"
 *
 *      17    0.0223
 */


/*
 * Command line: opannotate —source —output-
dir=/usr/src/chp10/output —source-dir=/usr/src/chp10
```

```
*
* Interpretation of command line:
* Output annotated source file with samples
* Output all files
*
* CPU: CPU with timer interrupt, speed 598.199 MHz (estimated)
* Profiling through timer interrupt
*/
```

Report Examples

The following are some examples of output after the profile of chp10-profile1. The reports have been abridged for readability.

System-Wide Binary Image Summary

```
# opreport —exclude-dependent
CPU: CPU with timer interrupt, speed 1694.72 MHz (estimated)
Profiling through timer interrupt
   120768 52.2588 ld-2.3.2.so
    89847 38.8786 vmlinux
    13648  5.9058 chp10-profile1
     1891  0.8183 libpthread.so.0
     1055  0.4565 libc.so.6
    ...
```

You see that ld-2.3.2.so has 120,768 samples. The second column shows that the relative amount of time the system spent in the ld-2.3.2.so executable was 52.2588. The data shows that most of the time spent in this program was in ld-2.3.2.so, which is part of glibc.

System-Wide Symbol Summary, Including Per-Application Libraries

The system-wide summary shows which routines are being called, as well as the percentage of time spent in those routines. You can see that the top two routines are **do_lookup** and **strcmp**. The **default_idle** routine isn't a concern, since this summary shows that the kernel is waiting or idle.

```
# opreport —symbols —image-path=/lib/modules/2.6.8.1/kernel/
CPU: CPU with timer interrupt, speed 1694.72 MHz (estimated)
Profiling through timer interrupt
vma       samples %       image name    app name      symbol name
000080c0 105043  48.3007 ld-2.3.2.so   ld-2.3.2.so   do_lookup
c0102510 87905   40.4204 vmlinux       vmlinux       default_idle
00013540 12073    5.5514 ld-2.3.2.so   ld-2.3.2.so   strcmp
00008320 1711     0.7867 ld-2.3.2.so   ld-2.3.2.so   do_lookup_versioned
```

```
0000a2a0 522        0.2400  libpthread.so.0  libpthread.so.0   __pthread_alt_unlock
000013e0 519        0.2386  libdl.so.2       libdl.so.2         _dlerror_run
0000d540 444        0.2042  ld-2.3.2.so      ld-2.3.2.so
_dl_catch_error_internal
0000a140 425        0.1954  libpthread.so.0  libpthread.so.0   __pthread_alt_lock
00008900 344        0.1582  ld-2.3.2.so      ld-2.3.2.so
_dl_lookup_symbol_internal
...
```

You see that the first entry has a virtual memory address (vma) of 000080c0, there are 105,043 samples for ld-2.3.2.so, the image name is ld-2.3.2.so, the app name is ld-2.3.2.so, and the symbol name is **do_lookup**.

Saving Profiling Data

The —**save**=*xxx* option for **opcontrol** allows the data to be saved for future reference. This allows the data from multiple experiments to be saved separately. It should be noted that there is a need to avoid modifying the executables. oprofile cannot perform the analysis if the executable has been changed. oprofile needs both the saved sample files and the unchanged executable.

Thus, for the chp10-profile1 example, the data could be saved with the following command:

```
opcontrol —save=chp10-profile1
```

The addition of **session:chp10-profile1** specifies the session saved by this **opcontrol**. Thus, the commands used earlier to analyze chp10-profile1 would now be as follows:

```
opreport session:chp10-profile1 —long-filenames

opreport session:chp10-profile1 -l image:/usr/src/chp10/chp10-profile1

opreport -l session:chp10-profile1 image:/usr/src/chp10/chp10-profile1 —include-
symbols=Lookup_thread -details

opannotate session:chp10-profile1 —source /usr/src/chp10/chp10-profile1
```

Hardware Counters

This section looks at the hardware performance counters available through some processors. A performance counter is the part of a microprocessor that measures and gathers performance-relevant events on the microprocessor. The number and type of available events differ significantly between existing microprocessors.

These counters impose no overhead on the system, but since there are only a few of them and there are more than a few interesting things to measure, they have been designed so that they can be configured through software. oprofile can configure the performance counters.

One performance area of concern is cache misses. The following section describes different types of coding areas that can cause cache misses. oprofile is used to show how some simple examples can avoid cache misses.

Minimizing Cache Misses

Most CPUs have first-level instruction and data caches on chip, and many have second-level caches that are bigger but somewhat slower. Memory accesses are much faster if the data is already loaded into the first-level cache. When your program accesses data that isn't in one of the caches, a *cache miss* occurs. This causes a block of consecutively addressed words, including the data your program just accessed, to be loaded into the cache. Since cache misses are costly, you should try to minimize them by following these suggestions:

- Keep frequently accessed data together. Store and access frequently used data in flat, sequential data structures and avoid pointer indirection. This way, the most frequently accessed data remains in the first-level cache as much as possible.

- Access data sequentially. Each cache miss brings in a block of consecutively addressed words of needed data. If the program is accessing data sequentially, each cache miss brings in n words (where n is system-dependent). If the program is accessing only every nth word, it constantly brings in unneeded data, degrading performance.

- Avoid simultaneously traversing several large buffers of data, such as an array of vertex coordinates and an array of colors within a loop, since there can be cache conflicts between the buffers. Instead, pack the contents sequentially into one buffer whenever possible. If you are using vertex arrays, try to use interleaved arrays.

- Some frame buffers have cache-like behaviors as well. It is a good idea to group geometry so that the drawing is done to one part of the screen at a time. Using triangle strips and polylines tends to do this while simultaneously offering other performance advantages.

Padding and Aligning Structures

Some compilers (or compiler options) automatically pad structures.

Referencing a data structure that spans two cache blocks may incur two misses, even if the structure itself is smaller than the block size. Padding structures to a multiple of the block size and aligning them on a block boundary can eliminate these "misalignment" misses, which generally show up as conflict misses. Padding is easily accomplished in C by declaring extra pad fields, as shown in Example 1. Alignment is a little more difficult, since the structure's address must be a multiple of the cache block size. Aligning statically declared structures generally requires compiler support. The programmer can align dynamically allocated structures using simple pointer arithmetic, as shown in Example 2. Note that some dynamic memory allocators (for example, some versions of **malloc**()) return cache block aligned memory.

Example 1: Padding Structures in C

```
/* old declaration of a 12-byte structure */

struct a_struct {

      int a1,a2,a3;
};

/* new declaration of structure padded to 16-byte block size */

struct a_struct {

      int a1,a2,a3; char pad[4];
};
```

Example 2: Aligning Structures in C

```
/* original allocation does not guarantee alignment */

ap = (struct a_struct *)

malloc(sizeof(struct a_struct)*SIZE);

/* new code to guarantee alignment of structure. */

ap = (struct a_struct *)

malloc(sizeof(struct a_struct)*(SIZE+1));

ap = ((int) ap + 15)/16)*16
```

Packing

Packing is the opposite of padding. By packing an array into the smallest space possible, the programmer increases locality, which can reduce both conflict and capacity misses. In Example 3, the programmer observes that the elements of array value are never greater than 255, and hence could fit in type unsigned char, which requires 8 bits, instead of unsigned int, which typically requires 32 bits. For a machine with 16-byte cache blocks, the code shown in Example 4 permits 16 elements per block rather than four, reducing the maximum number of cache misses by a factor of 4.

Example 3: An Unpacked Array in C

```
/* old declaration of an array of unsigned integers. */

unsigned int values[100000];

/* loop sequencing through values */

for (i=0; i<100000; i++)

    values[i] = i % 256;
```

Example 4: Packed Array Structures in C

```
/* new declaration of an array of unsigned characters. */
/* valid if 0 <= value <= 255 */

unsigned char values[100000];

/* loop sequencing through values */

for (i=0; i<100000; i++)

    values[i] = i % 256;
```

Loop Grouping

Numeric programs often consist of several operations on the same data, coded as multiple loops over the same arrays and shown in Example 5. By combining these loops, a programmer increases the program's temporal locality and frequently reduces the number of capacity misses. Example 6 combines two doubly nested loops so that all operations are performed on an entire row before moving on to the next.

Example 5: Separate Loops

```
for (i=0; i < N; i++)

    for (j=0; j < N; j++)

        a[i][j] = 1/b[i][j]*c[i][j];

for (i=0; i < N; i++)

    for (j=0; j < N; j++)

        d[i][j] = a[i][j]+c[i][j];
```

Example 6: Combined Loop

```
for (i=0; i < N; i++)

    for (j=0; j < N ;j++) {

        a[i][j] = 1/b[i][j]*c[i][j];
        d[i][j] = a[i][j]+c[i][j];
    }
```

Blocking

Blocking is a general technique for restructuring a program to reuse chunks of data that fit in the cache and hence reduce capacity misses.

The analysis and transformation techniques described here can help a programmer develop algorithms that minimize cache misses. However, cache misses result from the complex interaction between algorithm, memory allocation, and cache configuration; when the program is executed, the programmer's expectations may not match exactly what the processor does. We'll use oprofile with Examples 2 and 3 and see cache misses be reduced by the techniques just shown. oprofile helps provide the insight necessary for programmers to select program transformations that improve cache behavior.

For the Intel Pentium Pro, Pentium II, and Pentium III, the **CPU_CLOCK_UNHALTED** counter can be used to get time-based measurements. For the Pentium 4, the **GLOBAL_POWER_EVENTS** counter provides time-based measurements. The **TIMER_INT** counter provides time-based sampling using a periodic interrupt on processors without supporting performance-monitoring hardware. The hot spots can be checked for common performance problems. Both

Intel and AMD have produced documents that describe in detail techniques for optimizing code for their processors. These documents are listed in the section "Web Resources for Profiling." Here are a few of the different types of processor performance counters that can be viewed:

- Memory references and data cache misses

- Misaligned memory accesses

- Branch misprediction

- Instruction cache misses

We'll focus on data cache misses.

Data Cache Misses

Processor speed has increased at a much greater rate than memory access speed. As a result, each data cache miss is becoming significantly more expensive on current processors than on older processors. A cache miss that requires access to main memory on a 3 GHz Pentium 4 costs about 100 clock cycles. To have good processor performance, the cache miss rate needs to be low. Table 10.1 shows the processor events related to cache misses.

TABLE 10.1
Data Cache Miss Events

Processor	Event
Pentium Pro/Pentium II/Pentium III	**DCU_MISS_OUTSTANDING**
Pentium 4 (HT and non-HT)	**BSQ_CACHE_REFERENCE**
Athlon/Hammer	**DATA_CACHE_MISSES**
Itanium 2	**L1D_READ_MISSES**

To check the performance counters available on your system, use the **op_help** command, as shown in Figure 10.9. Before the **op_help** command can be issued, the **opcontrol --init** command needs to be used to initialize oprofile. The processor in this system is an Intel Pentium 4.

FIGURE 10.9
opcontrol --init used to initialize oprofile.

The performance counter we'll use for cache misses is called
BSQ_CACHE_REFERENCE. It's shown in Figure 10.10.

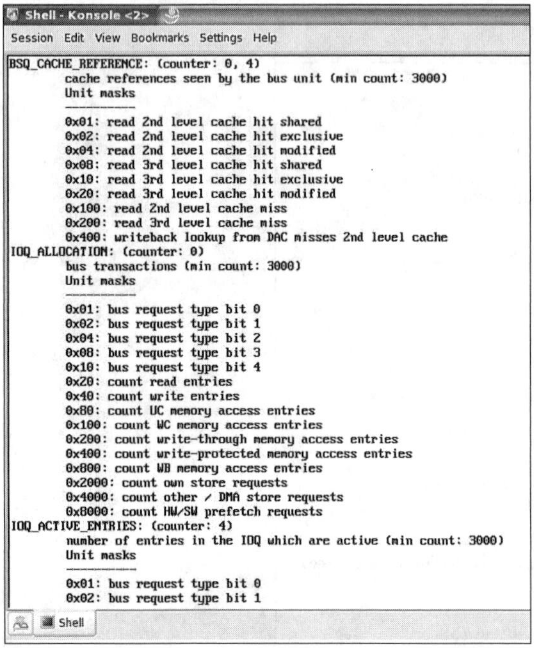

FIGURE 10.10
The cache misses performance counter.

We start with the sample program shown in Listing 10.3. We'll measure the cache misses with oprofile and then change the program's line 3 to have char instead of int and see that cache misses are reduced. The following command can be used to build the chp10-sample1 program:

```
# gcc chp10-sample1.c -o chp10-sample1 -g
```

Listing 10.3

chp10-sample1 Program 100000 Values Using int

```
1 int main (int argc, char **argv)
2 {
3   unsigned int values[100000];
4   int i;
5   for (i=0; i < 100000; i++){
6     values[i] = i % 256;
7     printf(" i is %d \n",i);
8   }
9 };
```

So now let's set up oprofiler and start it with the **--start** option, execute the sample program (chp10-sample1), and stop oprofile with the **--stop** parameter, as shown in Figure 10.11. Next we'll view the high-level results of profiling chp10-sample1 by issuing the **opreport** command.

FIGURE 10.11
oprofiler on chp10-sample1.

From the output of oprofile using opreport (the last line), you can see that chp10-sample1 has three samples. The following command can be used to build the chp10-sample2 program:

```
# gcc chp10-sample2.c -o chp10-sample2 -g
```

In Listing 10.4, line 3 has been changed from **unsigned int values** to **unsigned char values**. This does packing, which will be shown to reduce data cache misses.

Listing 10.4

chp10-sample2 Program 100000 Values Using char

```
1 int main (int argc, char **argv)
2 {
3   unsigned char values[100000];
4   int i;
5   for (i=0; i < 100000; i++){
6     values[i] = i % 256;
7     printf(" i is %d \n",i);
8   }
9 };
```

oprofiler is set up to use the data cache misses counter **BSQ_CACHE_ REFERENCE** and to start oprofiler with the **--start** option, as shown in Figure 10.12. We'll execute the sample program (chp10-sample2) and stop the oprofile with **--stop**. Using the **opreport** command, we can view the results of profiling chp10-sample2.

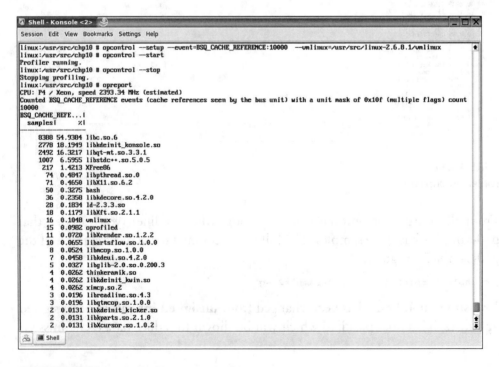

FIGURE 10.12
Viewing chp10-sample2.

Figure 10.13 shows that chp10-sample2 has one sample for data cache misses. You can see that a simple change in the declaration of a variable from int to char has reduced data cache misses from three to one.

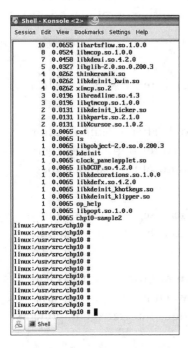

FIGURE 10.13
Viewing chp10-sample2.

Additional profilers are available. One of these open-source profilers is Prospect, which uses the support from the kernel that oprofile provides.

The Prospect Profiler

Prospect is an instruction-pointer-sampling, flat profiler for obtaining code profiles in a nonintrusive way for Linux systems. Profiles can be obtained (both symbol-level and assembly-level) without undue requirements for the target application. For example, there is no need to specially instrument the application, and there is no need to rebuild or relink. In fact, the only requirement is that the application not be stripped. Shared libraries escape even this requirement for the most part.

Both user and kernel profiles are output for every process that ran on the system in the defined time interval. More in-depth kernel profiles are also available. Prospect creates a process-centric view of the system. It answers questions such as "Where and how are my applications spending their time?" and "Where is the kernel spending its time?". Prospect collects profile samples using oprofile.

Summary

Before you dive into specific optimization techniques, here are some basic heuristics to remember about optimizing code:

- Don't optimize for optimization's sake; do so only after a demonstration that the optimization is necessary. Verify the need for optimization with proven timing techniques or a reliable execution profiler that identifies specific performance issues.

- Optimizations should be applied carefully; otherwise, bugs can be introduced. Remember that slow, robust code is better than faster, unstable code.

- After performing an optimization, profile again to prove that it has had the desired effect. This is especially necessary when implementing optimizations in a system of software in which various integrated components have or share optimizations.

Design problems typically spring up because developers need to produce speedy code. Moreover, in their haste, they can neglect solid design principles for perceived (and unrealized) performance improvements. This might result in faster code, but it also produces inefficient code and designs that lack robustness and extensibility. The bigger issue is this: applications designed in this manner require that developers predict potential performance problems without the benefit of the working code that produces measurable execution paths.

A good rule for producing fast code is to optimize only what is being executed. Time spent optimizing code that does not have a substantial impact on performance is wasted. Typically, 80 to 90 percent of an application's execution time is spent executing only 20 to 30 percent of its code. The 20 to 30 percent of your code that needs improvement is best found by using performance profilers.

Web Resources for Profiling

URL	Description
http://oprofile.sourceforge.net/	oprofile
http://sourceforge.net/projects/prospect	Prospect
http://www.amd.com/us-en/assets/ content_type/	AMD64 Software
DownloadableAssets/dwamd_25112.pdf	Optimization Guide
http://developer.intel.com/design/pentiumii/ manuals/245127.htm	Intel Architecture Optimization Reference Manual
http://www.intel.com/design/pentium4/ manuals/index_new.htm	Intel Architecture Software Developer's Manuals IA-32
ftp://download.intel.com/design/Pentium4/	manuals/24896611.pdf IA-32 Intel Architecture Optimization Reference Manual
http://www.intel.com/design/itanium2/ manuals/251110.htm	Intel Itanium 2
ftp://download.intel.com/design/Itanium2/ manuals/25111003.pdf	Processor Reference Manual for Software Development and Optimization

Chapter 11

User-Mode Linux

In this chapter

- UML: Introduction to the Kernel and Root File System   page 293
- Patching and Building the Kernel   page 296
- Building the Kernel   page 303
- Root Image   page 304
- File Systems   page 305
- Setting up a gdb Session   page 306
- Booting UML   page 307
- A Typical gdb Session   page 307
- GDB Thread Analysis   page 308
- Tips   page 310
- UML Utilities   page 312
- Summary   page 313
- Credits   page 314
- Web Resources for User-Mode Linux   page 314

One of the largest efforts involved with software engineering is testing the software to make sure that it works as designed. Testing can require several different types of system configurations and could require multiple instances of Linux. One way to create this type of environment is to use a virtual machine.

User-Mode Linux (UML) is a fully functional Linux kernel. It runs its own scheduler and virtual memory (VM) system, relying on the host kernel for hardware support. It includes virtual block, network, and serial devices to provide an environment that is almost as full-featured as a hardware-based machine. UML cannot destroy the host machine. Furthermore, the UML block devices, also called disks, can be files on the native Linux file system, so you cannot affect the native block devices. This is very useful when you're testing and debugging block operations.

Each UML instance is a complete virtual machine that's all but indistinguishable from a real computer. All of them run as a normal user on the host. They give you root-level access, the ability to start daemons, the ability to run text and graphical applications, full networking, and almost all of the other capabilities of a Linux system. The only exception is that you can't directly address hardware inside UML, so the UML environment provides virtual network adapters, virtual X Window displays, and virtual drives.

The virtual machine can be configured through the command line, which allows memory and devices to be configured. The kernel, and hence any programs running under UML, runs as a software process of the real/host Linux system rather than directly under the hardware. UML can give you complete root access, and the same programs can be run that would normally be run on a Linux server. UML is a good way to experiment with new Linux kernels and distributions and to learn the internals of Linux without risking the system's main setup.

UML has been used in the following ways:

- As a system administration tool
- As an inexpensive dedicated hosting environment
- For server consolidation
- As a secure, isolated environment
- To test applications

- In college classes

- For kernel development and debugging

This chapter covers the advantages that UML can provide in the area of kernel development and debugging. UML offers the advantage of source-level kernel debugging using gdb. Using gdb, you can view kernel data structures. kdb is another kernel debugger that can't directly show the kernel data structures. For additional information about kdb, see Chapter 13, "Kernel-Level Debuggers (kgdb and kdb)."

UML is not the right environment to use in some cases:

- Developing and testing disk device drivers

- Developing and testing network device drivers

- Developing and testing other hardware devices

Currently UML is supported only on the x86 architecture.

UML: Introduction to the Kernel and Root File System

Getting a minimal UML system up and running requires a UML kernel and a root file system to boot it on. The UML tools aren't needed for basic UML use, but they are needed for networking, managing copy-on-write (COW) file system files, and using the management console.

Before building a UML kernel and root file system, let's download a prebuilt UML kernel and root file system. The host system needs to be running a 2.4.x level of the kernel to run this prebuilt UML. The kernel on my machine is from the SuSE 9.0 release, and it has a 2.4.21 kernel. The UML rpm is named user_mode_linux-2.4.19.5um-0.i386.rpm, and it contains the following files:

- /usr/bin/jailtest

- /usr/bin/linux (an executable binary that is the UML kernel)

- /usr/bin/tunctl

- /usr/bin/uml_mconsole

- /usr/bin/uml_moo

- /usr/bin/uml_net

- /usr/bin/uml_switch

- /usr/lib/uml/config

- /usr/lib/uml/modules-2.2.tar

- /usr/lib/uml/modules-2.4.tar

- /usr/lib/uml/port-helper

The next step is to uncompress the root image. In this example the root image is called root_fs.rh-7.2-server.pristine.20020312.bz2. Once the root image is uncompressed, you can start the UML kernel, which is named linux.

The commands shown in Figure 11.1 show the installation of the rpm, the setting up of the root image, and the starting of the UML kernel with the root file system image.

FIGURE 11.1
Installing the UML rpm, setting up the root image, and booting the UML kernel.

When the **linux** command is executed, the terminal shows that a new Linux operating system is booting. Figure 11.2 shows the booted system, ending with a login prompt. Logging in with the user root and the password root gives you access to the operating system.

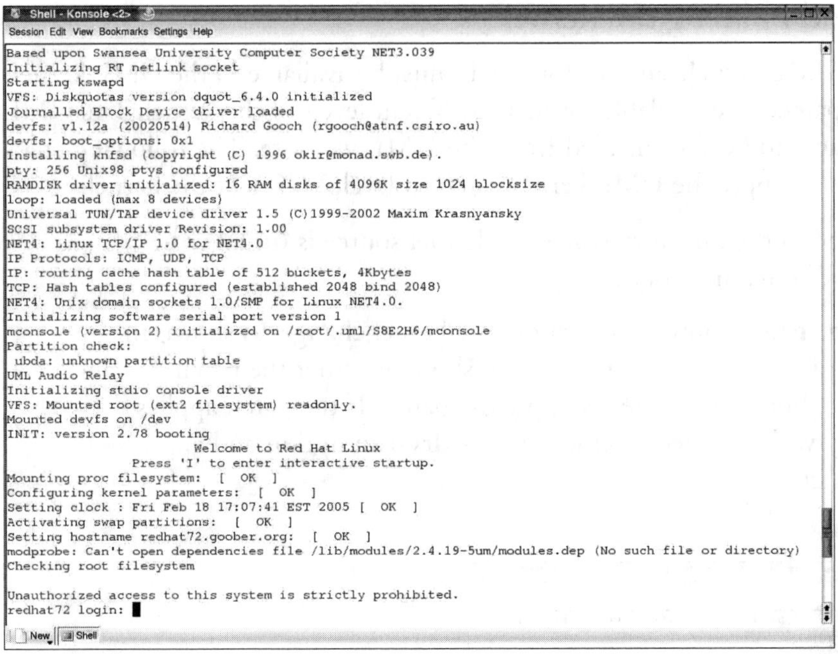

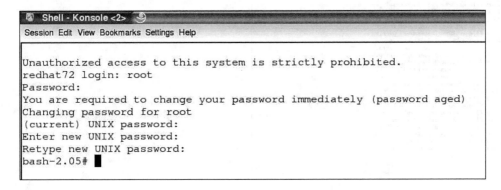

FIGURE 11.2
The UML kernel booting up.

The login requires the root password to be changed, and bash will be set up. Figure 11.3 shows UML ready to function as a Linux system.

```
Unauthorized access to this system is strictly prohibited.
redhat72 login: root
Password:
You are required to change your password immediately (password aged)
Changing password for root
(current) UNIX password:
Enter new UNIX password:
Retype new UNIX password:
bash-2.05# █
```

FIGURE 11.3
Logging into the UML system.

The next section shows you how to patch, configure, and build a UML kernel.

Patching and Building the Kernel

To build a UML kernel, support for UML must be available in the UML kernel. UML kernel patches are available for many different levels of the kernel. The UML patch is available to be downloaded from the UML web site. The following steps show you how to apply the UML kernel patch to level 2.6.8.1 of the kernel:

1. Change to the directory where the kernel source is (usually the /usr/src/linux directory).

2. Use the **patch** command to apply the kernel change, as shown in Figure 11.4. The —**dry-run** option shows whether the patch applies, but it doesn't really apply the patch. If the patch applies cleanly with no rejects, remove the —**dry-run** option and apply the patch.

FIGURE 11.4
The UML patch being applied to the kernel.

There are no rejects when applying the patch, so the —dry-run option can be removed and the patch is applied to the kernel.

UML Kernel Options

UML is enabled through the UML-specific options menu. If UML isn't enabled, enable it and rebuild the kernel. Figure 11.5 shows the kernel configuration menu for UML. Fourteen options are available for UML. Other versions of UML might have more or fewer configuration options:

- **Tracing thread support** controls whether tracing thread support is compiled into UML.

- **Separate Kernel Address Space support** controls whether skas (separate kernel address space) support is compiled in.

- **Networking support** adds kernel networking support.

- **Kernel support for ELF binaries** allows your kernel to run ELF binaries.

- **Kernel support for MISC binaries** allows plug wrapper-driven binary formats to run in the kernel. It is useful for programs that need an inte-preter to run, like Java, Python, .NET, and Emacs-Lisp. It's also useful if you need to run DOS executables under the Linux DOS emulator (DOSEMU).

- **Support for host-based filesystems** allows for host-based file system support.

- **Host filesystem** allows a UML user to access files stored on the host.

- **HoneyPot ProcFS** is a file system that allows UML /proc entries to be overridden, removed, or fabricated from the host. Its purpose is to allow a UML to appear to be a physical machine by removing or changing any thing in /proc that gives away a UML's identity.

- **Management console** is a low-level interface to the kernel; it is similar to the kernel SysRq interface.

- **2G/2G host address space split** causes UML to load itself in the top .5 GB of that smaller process address space of the kernel. Most Linux machines are configured so that the kernel occupies the upper 1 GB (0xc0000000 to 0xffffffff) of the 4 GB address space and processes use the lower 3 GB (0x00000000 to 0xbfffffff). However, some machines are configured with a 2 GB/2 GB split, with the kernel occupying the upper 2 GB (0x80000000 to 0xffffffff) and processes using the lower 2 GB

(0x00000000 to 0x7fffffff). The prebuilt UML binaries on the UML web site will not run on 2 GB/2 GB hosts because UML occupies the upper .5 GB of the 3 GB process address space (0xa0000000 to 0xbfffffff). Obviously, on 2 GB/2 GB hosts, this is right in the middle of the kernel address space, so UML doesn't even load—it immediately segfaults. Turning on this option allows UML to load correctly in this kernel configuration.

- **Symmetric multi-processing support** enables UML SMP support. UML implements a virtual SMP by allowing as many processes to run simultaneously on the host as there are virtual processors configured.

- **Highmem support** adds the UML arch support for highmem.

- **/proc/mm support** is used to support skas mode.

- **Real-time Clock** makes UML time deltas match wall clock deltas. This should normally be enabled. The exception would be if you are debugging with UML and spend long times with UML stopped at a break point. In this case, when UML is restarted, it calls the timer enough times to make up for the time spent at the break point.

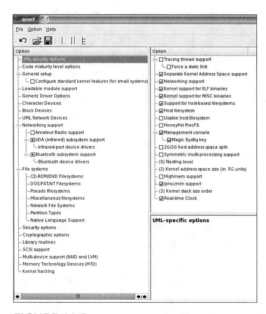

FIGURE 11.5
The UML-specific options kernel menu.

The UML menu in Figure 11.5 shows that all the UML options that are turned on will be built directly into the kernel. A check mark in the configuration menu means that the option will be built directly into the kernel. A period in the configuration menu means that the option will be built as a module for the kernel. No mark in the configuration menu means that the option hasn't been turned on.

UML can be used as a debugging mechanism (source code debugging for kernel-level code using gdb) for systems running on 2.4.x and 2.6.x kernels. This section is focused on using the UML support that is available for the 2.6.x kernel. The 2.6.8.1 kernel is used for the examples in this chapter. The steps listed in the section "Building the Kernel" build the UML kernel that will run on the Linux host system.

Some Linux distributions have added the UML patch to their kernel for both the 2.4.x and 2.6.x levels of the kernel and provide a UML kernel with the distribution. The first step is to check the kernel config and see if UML is enabled. One way to do so is to use the **make xconfig ARCH=um** command in the directory of the kernel source tree, usually in the /usr/src/linux directory.

The UML kernel is enabled on the "UML-specific options" support menu. Enable the UML options and build the kernel.

The UML network devices are enabled on the UML Network Devices menu, as shown in Figure 11.6. The main menu option is Virtual network device. If this option is enabled, seven transport options are available. Versions of UML other than the one shown here might have more or fewer configuration options.

The following transport types are available for a UML virtual machine to exchange packets with other hosts:

- Ethertap
- TUN/TAP
- SLIP
- Switch daemon
- Multicast
- pcap
- SLiRP

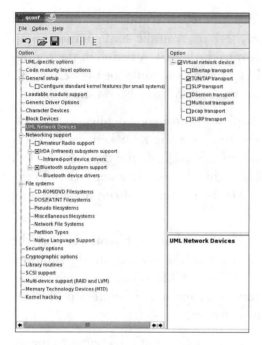

FIGURE 11.6
The UML Network Devices kernel menu.

The TUN/TAP, Ethertap, SLIP, and SLiRP transports allow a UML instance to exchange packets with the host. They may be directed to the host, or the host may just act as a router to provide access to other physical or virtual machines.

Once the virtual network device is enabled, the following options are available:

- **Ethertap transport** allows a single running UML to exchange packets with its host over one of the host's Ethertap devices, such as /dev/tap0. Ethertap provides packet reception and transmission for user space programs. It can be viewed as a simple Ethernet device that, instead of receiving packets from a network wire, receives them from user space. Ethertap can be used for anything from AppleTalk to IPX to even building bridging tunnels.

- **TUN/TAP transport** allows a UML instance to exchange packets with the host over a TUN/TAP device. TUN/TAP provides packet reception and transmission for user space programs. It can be seen as a simple point-to-point or Ethernet device that, instead of receiving packets from physical media, receives them from the user space program and instead of sending packets via physical media writes them to the user space program.

- **SLIP transport** allows a running UML to network with its host over a point-to-point link.

- **Daemon transport** allows one or more running UMLs on a single host to communicate with each other but not with the host.

- **Multicast transport** allows multiple UMLs to talk to each other over a virtual Ethernet network.

- **pcap transport** makes a pcap packet stream on the host look like an Ethernet device inside UML. This is useful for making UML act as a network monitor for the host. libcap must be installed in order to build the pcap transport into UML.

- **SLiRP** allows a running UML to network by invoking a program that can handle SLIP encapsulated packets.

The UML menu in Figure 11.6 shows that all the UML options that are turned on will be built directly into the kernel.

Kernel debugging is enabled on the Kernel hacking menu, as shown in Figure 11.7. Six options are available for UML, as shown in the figure. Other versions of UML might have more or fewer configuration options:

- **Debug memory allocations** has the kernel do limited verification on memory allocation as well as poisoning memory on free to catch use of freed memory.

- **Debug spinlocks usage** has the kernel catch missing spinlock initialization and certain other kinds of spinlock errors.

- **Enable kernel debugging symbols** are included in the UML kernel binary.

- **Enable ptrace proxy** enables a debugging interface, which allows gdb to debug the kernel without needing to attach to kernel threads.

- **Enable gprof support** allows profiling the UML kernel with the gprof utility.

- **Enable gcov support** allows code coverage data for the UML session.

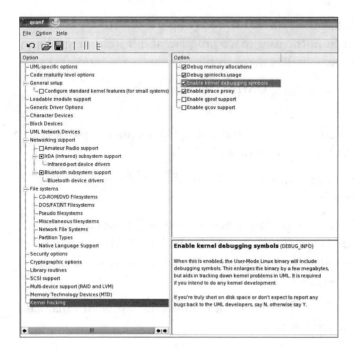

FIGURE 11.7
The UML Kernel hacking menu.

To use gdb with the UML kernel, make sure that both Enable kernel debugging symbols (**CONFIG_DEBUGSYM**) and Enable ptrace proxy (**CONFIG_PT_PROXY**) are turned on. These compile the kernel with **-g** and enable the ptrace proxy so that gdb works with UML, respectively.

The UML menu in Figure 11.7 shows that all the UML options turned on will be built directly into the UML kernel.

UML can be configured to support gcov.

gcov support

gcov allows code coverage to be done on kernel-level code. gcov can help determine how well your test suites exercise your code. One indirect benefit of gcov is that its output can be used to identify which test case provides coverage for each source file. With that information, a subset of the test suite can be selected to verify that changes in the program can be run. Thorough code coverage during testing is one measurement of software quality. For more information about gcov, see Chapter 2, "Code Coverage."

UML also can be configured to support gprof.

gprof support

gprof allows profiling to be done on kernel-level code. Profiling displays where a program is spending its time and which functions are called while the program is being executed. With profile information, you can determine which pieces of the program are slower than expected. These sections of the code could be good candidates to be rewritten to make the program execute faster. Profiling is also the best way to determine how often each function is called. With this information you can determine which function will give you the most performance boost by changing the code to perform faster. For more information about gprof, see Chapter 1, "Profiling."

Building the Kernel

The following steps show you how to build the UML kernel:

1. Issue the **make xconfig ARCH=um** command.

2. Under "UML-specific options," select the options that are needed for UML.

3. Under "UML Network Devices," select the options that are needed for UML.

4. Under "Kernel hacking," select the options that are needed for UML.

5. Configure other kernel settings as needed.

6. Save and exit.

7. Issue the **make clean** command.

8. Issue the **make linux ARCH=um** command.

   The result is the binary file named linux in this directory.

> NOTE   If kernel modules are required, they must be installed inside the
> UML. One way to do this is described next. In this example, the root file
> system for the UML is called root_fs, and the mount point is called mnt.

9.   If modules need to be built, do the following:

   a.   Issue the **make modules ARCH=um** command.

   b.   Issue the **mount root_fs mnt -o loop** command.

   c.   Issue the **make modules_install**
        `INSTALL_MOD_PATH=/path/to/uml/mnt ARCH=um` command.

   d.   Issue the **umount mnt** command.

   The UML kernel is named linux. For this example you'll copy the
   UML kernel to the /usr/src/uml subdirectory.

10. Issue the **cp /usr/src/linux/linux /usr/src/uml/linux** command.

Root Image

UML needs a root image. Several are available on the UML web site. The root
image is the file system that UML kernel will be booted on. Here are some of the
root images available on the UML web site:

- Slackware 8.1

- Debian 3.0

- Debian 2.2

- Red Hat 9.0

- Red Hat 7.1

- Mandrakelinux 8.0

- Mandrakelinux 8.2

If one of these root images is unacceptable, you can create a new root image based
on another distribution. umlbuilder is a tool for creating root images. It installs a
Linux distribution for use with UML.

Download the Debian 3.0 root image from the UML project download page, and use this in the following examples. First you extract the image using the **bunzip2** command, and then you loopback mount the image to check the layout of the root image. The exact steps are shown in Figure 11.8.

```
Session Edit View Bookmarks Settings Help
linux-009041085120:/usr/src/uml # bunzip2 -c Debian-3.0r0.ext2.bz2 > root_fs.ext2
linux-009041085120:/usr/src/uml # ls -all
total 84042
drwxr-xr-x  2 root root       120 Feb 15 14:24 .
drwxr-xr-x  7 root root       248 Feb 15 12:09 ..
-rw-r--r--  1 root root 23106438 Feb 15 12:33 Debian-3.0r0.ext2.bz2
-rw-r--r--  1 root root 62862336 Feb 15 14:24 root_fs.ext2
linux-009041085120:/usr/src/uml # mkdir /mnt.ext2
linux-009041085120:/usr/src/uml # mount root_fs.ext2 /mnt.ext2 -o loop,ro
linux-009041085120:/usr/src/uml # cd /mnt.ext2
linux-009041085120:/mnt.ext2 # ls -all
total 62
drwxr-xr-x  20 root root  1024 Mar 13  2003 .
drwxr-xr-x  23 root root   536 Feb 15 14:29 ..
drwxr-xr-x   2 root root  2048 Jul 27  2002 bin
drwxr-xr-x   2 root root  1024 Jul 27  2002 boot
drwxr-xr-x   2 root root  1024 Jul 27  2002 cdrom
drwxr-xr-x   8 root root 25600 Jul 27  2002 dev
drwxr-xr-x  35 root root  2048 Mar 27  2003 etc
drwxr-xr-x   2 root root  1024 Jul 27  2002 floppy
drwxrwsr-x   2 root    50  1024 Feb  8  2002 home
drwxr-xr-x   2 root root  1024 Jul 27  2002 initrd
drwxr-xr-x   5 root root  4096 Jul 27  2002 lib
drwx------   2 root root 12288 Jul 27  2002 lost+found
drwxr-xr-x   2 root root  1024 Feb  8  2002 mnt
drwxr-xr-x   2 root root  1024 Jul 27  2002 opt
drwxr-xr-x   2 root root  1024 Feb  8  2002 proc
drwxr-xr-x   2 root root  1024 Mar 14  2003 root
drwxr-xr-x   2 root root  2048 Jul 27  2002 sbin
drwxrwxrwt   2 root root  1024 Mar 27  2003 tmp
drwxr-xr-x  12 root root  1024 Jul 27  2002 usr
drwxr-xr-x  13 root root  1024 Jul 27  2002 var
linux-009041085120:/mnt.ext2 # cd ..
linux-009041085120:/ # umount /mnt.ext2
linux-009041085120:/ # 
```

FIGURE 11.8
The Debian 3.0 root image.

File Systems

When UML is running, you can access the host file system as well as all other file systems that are passed in as command-line arguments. Each file system file is considered a unique device/partition in UML.

Swap Partition

The commands shown in Figure 11.9 create a 0.5 GB swap partition called **swap_fs** that is used by the UML instance.

```
Session Edit View Bookmarks Settings Help
linux-009041085120:/usr/src/uml # dd if=/dev/zero of=swap_fs seek=500 count=1 bs=1M
1+0 records in
1+0 records out
linux-009041085120:/usr/src/uml # ls
.   ..  Debian-3.0r0.ext2.bz2  root_fs.ext2  swap_fs
linux-009041085120:/usr/src/uml # mkswap -f swap_fs
Setting up swapspace version 1, size = 525332 kB
linux-009041085120:/usr/src/uml # ls -all
total 85571
drwxr-xr-x  2 root root       144 Feb 15 14:57 .
drwxr-xr-x  7 root root       248 Feb 15 12:09 ..
-rw-r--r--  1 root root  23106438 Feb 15 12:33 Debian-3.0r0.ext2.bz2
-rw-r--r--  1 root root  62862336 Feb 15 14:24 root_fs.ext2
-rw-r--r--  1 root root 525336576 Feb 15 14:58 swap_fs
linux-009041085120:/usr/src/uml # █
```

FIGURE 11.9
Creating the swap_fs file.

Setting up a gdb Session

You now have the UML kernel built with symbols, which allows the UML kernel to be debugged with gdb. The standard gdb commands can be used to set break points, view a back trace, and view variables.

Instead of typing commands to set up the gdb session every time, you can have gdb read input parameters by creating a file called .gdbinit. This file would be placed in the kernel subdirectory where the UML kernel is started from. In Figure 11.9, that would be /usr/src/uml directory. Listing 11.1 shows a sample .gdbinit file. Line 1 sets the linux file as the symbol file. Line 2 places a break point on panic. Line 3 places a break point on stop. Line 4 sets gdb's output to display hexadecimal.

Listing 11.1
.gdbinit Start File for gdb

```
1 symbol-file linux
2          b panic
3          b stop
4 set output-radix 16
```

Booting UML

Running the UML kernel (linux) program boots the user-mode kernel and brings up the system stored in the file root_fs. The UML looks for the root file system located in the current working directory, or the location of root_fs can be passed to the command line that loads the user-mode kernel. **ubd***x*, where *x* is 0 to *n*, is a virtual disk for UML.

If gdb is required to debug a UML kernel, the **debug** parameter is included on the UML command line. So to start the UML kernel, the root image is root_fs.ext2 and the swap file is swap_fs. The UML command would look like this:

```
linux debug ubd0=root_fs.ext2 ubd1=swap_fs
```

A Typical gdb Session

Let's start debugging by placing a break point in the **jfs_create** routine, which is called when a file is created in a JFS file system. Once you have the break point set, you copy a file to the JFS, and the break point is hit.

First you press Ctrl-C to enter the gdb session. To see if any breaks are set, use the **info breakpoints** command, as shown in Figure 11.10. In this session, no break points are set. Now let's use gdb to do a source listing inside the JFS routine called **jfs_create**; this routine is located in /usr/src/linux-2.6.8-1/fs/jfs/namei.c. You then place a breakpoint on line 110:

```
110    iplist[0] = dip;
```

```
Shell No. 2 - Konsole
(gdb) info breakpoints
No breakpoints or watchpoints.
(gdb) list fs/jfs/namei.c:110
105              tblk = tid_to_tblock(tid);
106              tblk->xflag |= COMMIT_CREATE;
107              tblk->ino = ip->i_ino;
108              tblk->u.ixpxd = JFS_IP(ip)->ixpxd;
109
110              iplist[0] = dip;
111              iplist[1] = ip;
112
113              /*
114               * initialize the child XAD tree root in-line in inode
(gdb) break fs/jfs/namei.c:110
Breakpoint 3 at 0xc01d3f50: file fs/jfs/namei.c, line 110.
(gdb) cont
Continuing.
[New Thread 11704]
[Switching to Thread 11704]

Breakpoint 3, jfs_create (dip=0xcac7a6e8, dentry=0xc9424968, mode=0x4, nd=0xc92cbf68) at fs/jfs/namei.c:110
110              iplist[0] = dip;
(gdb) print ip.i_ino
$8 = 0x5
(gdb) print tblk
$9 = (struct tblock *) 0xd880018c
(gdb) print tblk.xflag
$10 = 0x400
(gdb) print tblk.ino
$11 = 0x5
(gdb) x/20xw 0xd880018c
0xd880018c:     0x00000400      0x00000000      0x00000000      0x00000000
0xd880019c:     0x00000000      0xd75aa518      0x00000000      0x1d244b3c
0xd88001ac:     0x00000000      0x0000000a      0xc02d53d5      0x00000000
0xd88001bc:     0x00000000      0xd88001c0      0xd88001c0      0x00000004
0xd88001cc:     0x00000000      0x00000000      0x00000000      0x00000000
(gdb) cont
Continuing.
█
```

```
    Shell     Shell No. 2     Shell No. 3
```

FIGURE 11.10

gdb session 1: a break point in **jfs_create** and viewing variables.

You then use four **print** commands to show the values of the variables **ip->i_ino**, **tblk**, **tblk->xflag**, and **tblk->ino**. Finally, you look at 20 words of the **tblk** structure by using the **x/20xw** command with the address 0xd880018c.

GDB Thread Analysis

In Linux, a single program may have more than one thread of execution. The precise semantics of threads differ from one operating system to another, but in general the threads of a single program are akin to multiple processes—except that they share one address space (that is, they can all examine and modify the same variables). On the other hand, each thread has its own registers and execution stack, and perhaps private memory.

GDB provides these facilities for debugging multithread programs. Some of the thread-related commands are as follows:

- **info threads** displays all existing threads.

- **thread** *thread* # switches to another thread.

- **thread apply** [*thread* #] [**all**] *args* applies a command to a list of threads.

- Thread-specific breakpoints

Let's look at gdb's capability to switch between threads and view where each thread is on the system. You'll see how to view a thread. The first gdb command you use is **info threads**. This command displays all the threads on the system. Suppose you're looking for one JFS thread, and from **thread info** the thread number turns out to be 18. To view thread 18, first you use the gdb command **thread 18**, and then you use the **where** command to get a back trace for this thread. The exact gdb commands are as follows:

- **info threads** displays the program's threads.

- **thread 18** switches to that thread.

- **where** displays a back trace for thread 18.

Checking where each thread is can be an effective way to determine which thread (or threads) are causing the system to hang. One thing to look for is when one thread is holding a semaphore and the other thread is waiting on that semaphore. Another area of interest is when one thread has a lock that the other thread is waiting for.

Using UML for Development and Testing

I used UML to develop and test one of file systems available for Linux—Journaled File System (JFS). UML provided a source-level debugging environment using gdb, and using UML helped reduce the amount of time it took to port this file system to Linux. During the development of JFS, I was traveling a significant amount of time, presenting JFS at conferences. Usually the conferences were three days long plus two days of travel time, so without UML I could have lost a week of development time. With UML I could develop and test file system code on my laptop computer and not worry about having a bad change in the file system, which could have caused the system to stop booting. I've actually written and tested code using UML in an airplane while the person next to me was watching a movie on his notebook computer—two very different uses of a notebook computer.

Most developers have a development system and one or more test machines. UML's major advantage is that it eliminates the need for a separate test machine. Also, UML can boot faster than a physical machine. An average UML environment can boot and display the login prompt in less than 20 seconds!

Another file system where UML was used successfully for development and testing is the Lustre File System. The Lustre File System team uses UML to develop and test this cluster file system. Lustre File System is a next-generation cluster file system whose goal is to serve clusters with tens of thousands of nodes, that have petabytes of storage, that move hundreds of GBps, and that provide a state-of-the-art security and management infrastructure. This type of kernel development is a good fit for debugging in the UML environment because very few supercomputers are available to the Lustre team; using a virtual machine helps create a similar environment. The Lustre team has created a very good how-to guide for debugging with UML. It is available at https://wiki.clusterfs.com/lustre/LustreUML.

Tips

Consoles and Serial Lines

UML uses xterms for the virtual consoles that are run at boot time, so make sure that the UML terminal has **$DISPLAY** set properly (along with the proper **xhost/xauth** permissions). You have several options for configuring UML consoles and serial lines. You can find a how-to for configuring serial lines and consoles at http://user-mode-linux.sourceforge.net/input.html.

UML Networking Support

UML's networking support is quite flexible and comprehensive. There are several different approaches to allow UML(s) to access the network. One way to get both your host and UML on the net is to use a bridge and to use the TUN/TAP transport configuration option. You can find a description of these different ways at http://user-mode-linux.sourceforge.net/networking.html.

Root Image

Running multiple instances of UML, on the same or different Linux hosts, requires a separate root_fs image file for each running UML, because Linux writes to it. One nice feature of UML is that the root image is a file. If it is damaged beyond repair, a new copy of the root image can be created, and the system can be back up in seconds.

Adding File Systems

Like the root file system, the second file system is also a file in your Linux host. Figure 11.11 shows the commands to create a 100 MB file system called root_fs_second.

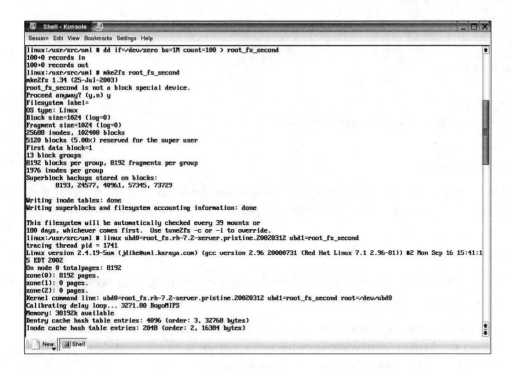

FIGURE 11.11
Creating an additional root file system.

To use the second file system in the UML session, add an extra command-line option each time UML is started (**ubd1=root_fs_second**). Figure 11.12 shows one way to mount the second file system as soon as UML is running: log in as root and mount the file system. To see the space available, use the **df** command. It shows that the /second file system has 100 MB.

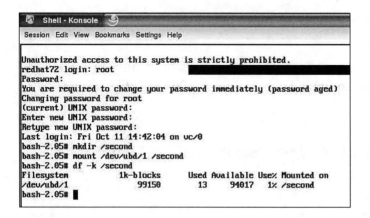

FIGURE 11.12
Using the additional root file system in UML.

Shutting Down

Simply log in as root and type **halt**. Messages are displayed, and the original shell prompt (before running the UML kernel) returns.

UML Utilities

Five UML utilities facilitate networking (among other things) between the UML virtual system and the host Linux system:

- **uml_mconsole** is the UML management console. It's a low-level interface to the kernel, somewhat like the SysRq interface to the kernel. The mconsole interface provides the following functions:

  - Displays the kernel version.

  - Adds and removes devices.

  - Halts or reboots the machine.

- Sends SysRq commands.
- Pauses and resumes the UML.
- Creates online backups without shutting down the UML.
- Receives notifications of events of interest from within UML.
- Monitors the UML's internal state.
- **uml_moo** merges a copy-on-write (COW) file with its backing file.
- **uml_mkcow** creates a new COW file.
- **uml_net** sets up the various transports and provides a UML instance with network access to the host, other machines on the local net, and the rest of the network.
- **uml_switch** is the switch daemon, which provides a mechanism for creating a totally virtual network.

Summary

One of the key features of UML is that different UML instances on the same machine can run different distributions, different virtual hardware configurations, and even different versions of the kernel if the need arises.

UML runs the same executables as the host, with the exception of a few utilities that need hardware access. Because of how UML is designed, each instance can be a replacement for a physical box.

As a virtual machine, UML requires virtualized hardware and comes with a complete set of drivers, including the following:

- Consoles and serial lines
- Virtual disks
- Networking
- A special interface for managing a UML from the host

The benefit of UML from a debugging point of view is that it lets you do kernel development and debugging at the source code level using gdb. The UML technology can be a powerful tool to reduce the time that is needed to debug a kernel problem and development kernel-level features.

With UML, you can greatly speed up the testing phase, because you need less hardware and the network setup goes much faster. You can also demonstrate new features more easily, because a simple notebook computer suffices to demonstrate large networks.

Credits

A big thank-you goes out to Jeff Dike and other developers for the development and support of UML. Dike is the author and maintainer of UML.

Web Resources for User-Mode Linux

URL	Description
http://user-mode-linux.sourceforge.net/	The UML kernel home page has complete documentation, how-tos, FAQs, papers, presentations, source code, and mailing lists.
http://usermodelinux.org/	UML community page
http://user-mode-linux.sourceforge.net/ UserModeLinux-HOWTO.html#toc4	UML how-to
http://user-mode-linux.sourceforge.net/ uses.html	UML uses
http://user-mode-linux.sourceforge.net/ networking.html	Setting up the UML network
http://user-mode-linux.sourceforge.net/ input.html	Setting up the UML serial line and consoles
http://edeca.net/articles/bridging/index.html	UML bridge how-to
http://umlbuilder.sourceforge.net/ commandline.shtml	UML builder
https://wiki.clusterfs.com/lustre/LustreUML	Lustre File System UML guide

## Chapter 12

Dynamic Probes

In this chapter

- Unique Aspects of Dynamic Probes   page 318
- General Steps for Using Probes   page 318
- Kprobes: Kernel Dynamic Probes   page 319
- Probe Example for sys_open   page 324
- Makefile for a Basic Kernel Module   page 326
- Finding Kprobes That Are Active on the System   page 328
- Finding an Offset in sys_open   page 328
- Jumper Probes   page 329
- Uses of Kprobes   page 330
- Successful Employment of Dprobes   page 331
- Summary   page 331
- Credits   page 331
- Web Resource for Dynamic Probes   page 331

Dynamic probes (Dprobes) allow debugging in environments without rebuilding. They offer a technique for acquiring diagnostic information without custom-building the component. Dynamic probes can also be used as a tracing mechanism for both user and kernel space. They can be used to debug software problems that are encountered in a production environment and that can't be re-created in a test lab environment. Dprobes can be used particularly in production environments where the use of an interactive debugger is either undesirable or unavailable. Dprobes also can be used during the code development phase to cause faults or error injections into code paths that are being tested.

The Dprobes facility inserts software probes dynamically into executing code. When a probe fires, a user-written probe handler executes. A probe handler can access registers, data structures, and memory. A probe can be inserted within the kernel and user space code. A probe is defined relative to a module and not to a storage address or process.

The probe can acquire data and use it as input for a trace record. The trace record could be passed to the system's tracing mechanism. This chapter focuses on kernel dynamic probes (Kprobes), which are probes that can be inserted into the kernel. For additional information about user space Dprobes, view the web site for Dprobes, http://sourceforge.net/projects/dprobes/.

Figure 12.1 shows the major components of Dprobes and the relationships between them. The kernel part of Dprobes contains the Probe Manager [1] and the Dprobes Event Handler (DPEH) [2]. The Probe Manager does the following:

- Accepts requests to register and deregister probes.

- Saves the probe definitions for each probed module in a per-module probe object. The probe object [3] is made up of the following parts:

  - The set of probe programs for this module

  - The local variable array

  - Probe records for each probe defined for that module

- Probe insertion causes code to be modified in memory. Probes are inserted whenever a page within a probed module is loaded into memory.

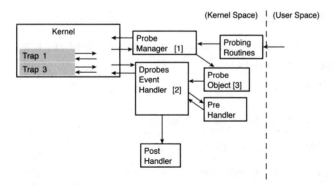

FIGURE 12.1
Probe components.

The Dprobes Event Handler handles a probe event notification. Module execution causes an event notification when a probed location executes.

Figure 12.2 shows the probe mechanism. The probe mechanism starts by placing a break point [1] into the source so that instruction replacement can occur. The next event is to do single-stepping (SS) [2] or emulation [3], during which the processor interrupts are disabled. The commit to the log [4] is done, and the break point [5] is reinstated.

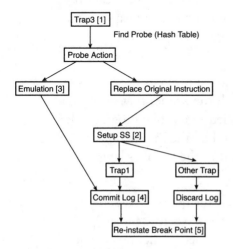

FIGURE 12.2
The probe mechanism.

Unique Aspects of Dynamic Probes

A probe can be placed almost anywhere in executable code (kernel and applications). A probe has the following characteristics:

- It has read/write access to hardware registers.

- It has read/write access to resident physical memory.

- It is available to all processes executing the code.

- It is enabled while running under a debugger.

- Data collected from a probe can be directed to a system trace buffer.

- Watch point probes are available on Intel x86 processors; these probes can be specified to be enabled on specific types of accesses to memory.

General Steps for Using Probes

The general steps for using dynamic probes are as follows:

1. Narrow down the problem such that the source code that needs to be debugged has been identified. The source code could be an executable program, a shared library, or kernel code.

2. Identify the probe locations. Listing 12.1 shows a probe location in the kernel for the **sys_open** routine. For a complete explanation of where probe locations can occur, see the man page for dprobes.lang.

3. Specify the actions to be taken when a given probe is fired. This is the probe handler part of each probe. All the probes that need to work on a given module must be specified in a probe program file. The format of the probe program file and all the instructions available for a probe handler are detailed in the dprobes.lang(8) man page.

4. Run the program to be debugged or wait for the probed code locations to be activated. When the probes are activated, the probe handlers run and logs are collected, as per the instructions in the probe handlers.

5. Examine the log and repeat the steps as needed.

Now let's place a probe in the **sys_open** kernel routine located in the /usr/src/linux/fs/open.c file. A typical probe needs a probe handler, and in this example it is called **probe_handler_open**. The **addr** field is set to the kernel **sys_open** routine, which allows the probe mechanism in the kernel to insert the Kprobe for the **sys_open** routine. After the Kprobe structure is set up, the Kprobe must be registered. The registration is done using the **register_kprobe** call.

Listing 12.1

High-Level Usage for Adding a Kprobe

```
static int probe_handler_open(struct kprobe *p, struct pt_regs
*regs)
{
        ... do the probe commands ...
}
struct kprobe kp = {
        .addr = sys_open,
        .pre_handler = probe_handler_open
};
register_kprobe(&kp);
```

Kprobes: Kernel Dynamic Probes

The Kprobes option can be set in the kernel to enable debugging without the need to constantly reboot your system when the next step of the debug process needs to happen. Designed to be lightweight and nondisruptive, Kprobes can reduce the time needed to debug a problem. Kprobes provides a mechanism in the kernel to insert break points into a running kernel and collect debug information.

Kprobes works on systems running 2.4.x and 2.6.x kernels. This section focuses on using the Kprobe support that is available for the 2.6.x kernel. The 2.6.9 kernel is used for the examples in this chapter. The support of Kprobes was accepted into main kernel (www.kernel.org) during the 2.6.9 development cycle. You don't need to apply a patch to the kernel to have the functionality of Kprobes if your kernel's base is 2.6.9 or later.

Some Linux distributions have added the Kprobes patch to their kernel for both the 2.4.x and 2.6.x levels of the kernel. The first step is to check the kernel config and see if Kprobes is enabled in the kernel. One way to do so is to use the **make xconfig** command in the directory of the kernel source tree, usually /usr/src/linux. Kprobes kernel enablement is on the Kernel hacking support menu, as shown in

Figure 12.3. If the Kprobes option isn't enabled, enable it and rebuild the kernel.
Figure 12.3 shows that the Kprobes option will be built directly into the kernel.

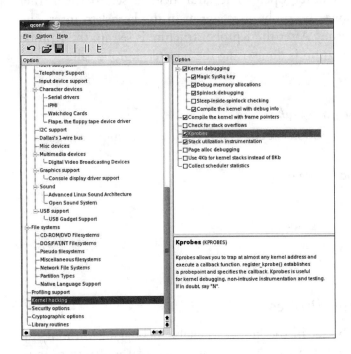

FIGURE 12.3
The Kprobe kernel menu.

Building the Kernel

The following steps show you how to build the kernel (for i386):

1. Issue the **make xconfig** command.

2. Under "Kernel hacking," do the following:
   a. Select "Kprobes."
   b. Configure other kernel settings as needed.

3. Save and exit.

4. Issue the **make clean** command.

5. Issue the **make bzImage** command.

6. If modules need to be built, do the following:
    a. Issue the **make modules** command.
    b. Issue the **make modules_install** command.

7. Enter **cp arch/i386/boot/bzImage /boot/bzImage-2.6.9-kprobe**.

8. Enter **cp System.map /boot/System.map-2.6.9-kprobe**.

9. Enter **rm /boot/System.map && ln -s /boot/System. map-2.6.9-kprobe System.map**.

10. If the system is using lilo as the boot loader, modify your configuration to boot from /boot/bzImage-2.6.9-kprobe.

    For example, if you're using lilo, do the following.
    a. Modify /etc/lilo.conf.
    b. Run lilo to read the modified lilo.conf.

11. If the system is using grub as the boot loader, modify your configuration to boot from /boot/bzImage-2.6.9-kprobe.

    For example, if you're using grub, modify /boot/grub/menu.lst.

12. Reboot.

The next step is to check the kernel's level and make sure that kernel just built with Kprobe support is the one that is running. The **uname** command does not directly show that Kprobe support is built into the kernel, but the following example shows that level 2.6.9 of the kernel is running. Use the **uname -a** command to display the kernel's level. The output should be similar to the following:

```
Linux sfb1 2.6.9 #1 Tue Nov 30 10:19:04 PST 2004 i686 i686 i386 GNU/Linux
```

Kprobe Interfaces

Kprobes can also be used in test and development environments. During testing, the probe may inject or simulate errors. In development, debugging code (such as a **printk**) can be quickly inserted without having to recompile code being tested.

With each probe, a corresponding probe event handler address is specified. Probe handlers run as extensions to the system break point interrupt handler and are designed to have no dependence on additional system facilities.

One of the features of Dprobes is the dpcc compiler. It allows probe points to be created using a C-like language. Variables and data structures can be referenced in the code that needs to be captured or probed. The probe point definition is inserted into the source code without the need to recompile the original source code.

Registering and Unregistering Kprobes

There are two Kprobe interfaces: **register_probe** and **unregister_probe**.

The probe location is created during the registration process. A callback address is used to handle the event. When the event is triggered, the routine's address is executed. Three callback addresses are defined for the probing module:

- The probe-event handler address, called as the probed instruction, is about to execute. When returning, Kprobes single-step the probed instruction.

- The post-execution handler address, called when the single-stepping event completes.

- The fault handler address, called if an exception is generated for any instruction within the fault handler or when Kprobes single-step the probed instruction.

register_probe

register_probe passes a Kprobe structure with the following fields:

```
struct kprobe {
        struct hlist_node hlist;

        /* location of the probe point */
        kprobe_opcode_t *addr;

        /* Called before addr is executed. */
        kprobe_pre_handler_t pre_handler;

        /* Called after addr is executed */
        kprobe_post_handler_t post_handler;

        /* ... called if executing addr causes a fault (eg. page fault).
         * Return 1 if it handled fault, otherwise kernel will see it. */
        kprobe_fault_handler_t fault_handler;

        /* ... called if break point trap occurs in probe handler.
         * Return 1 if it handled break, otherwise kernel will see it. */
        kprobe_break_handler_t break_handler;
```

```
    /* Saved opcode (which has been replaced with break point) */
    kprobe_opcode_t opcode;

    /* copy of the original instruction */
    kprobe_opcode_t insn[MAX_INSN_SIZE];
};
```

addr

The address contains the location of the probe point. The probe point must be at an instruction boundary.

pre_handler

The **pre_handler** function is called when the probe instruction is about to be executed.

post_handler

The **post_handler** function is called on completion of successful execution of the probed instruction.

fault_handler

The **fault_handler** function is called if any software exceptions occur:

- While executing inside the **probe_handler**
- When single-stepping the probed instruction

The Kprobe structure is required to be in resident memory for as long as the probe remains active. Both the **addr** and **pre_handler** fields are required. The **post_handler** and **fault_handler** are optional. For more information about the Kprobe structure, see the /include/linux/kprobes.h file in the kernel source tree.

unregister_probe

unregister_probe also requires a Kprobe structure. All registered probes must be explicitly unregistered before the probe handler module is removed.

Listing 12.2 contains the source for the **sys_open** kernel routine located in the /usr/src/linux/fs/open.c file. It creates a Kprobe for the **sys_open** routine. The Kprobe is set up at the start of the **sys_open** routine.

Listing 12.2

sys_open Source Code

```
1   asmlinkage long sys_open(const char __user * filename, int
flags, int mode)
2   {
3       char * tmp;
4       int fd, error;
5
6   #if BITS_PER_LONG != 32
7       flags |= O_LARGEFILE;
8   #endif
9       tmp = getname(filename);
10      fd = PTR_ERR(tmp);
11      if (!IS_ERR(tmp)) {
12              fd = get_unused_fd();
13              if (fd >= 0) {
14                      struct file *f = filp_open(tmp, flags,
mode);
15                      error = PTR_ERR(f);
16                      if (IS_ERR(f))
17                              goto out_error;
18                      fd_install(fd, f);
19              }
20  out:
21              putname(tmp);
22      }
23      return fd;
24
25  out_error:
26      put_unused_fd(fd);
27      fd = error;
28      goto out;
29  }
30  EXPORT_SYMBOL_GPL(sys_open);
```

Probe Example for sys_open

The first step is to specify the address of the symbol in which to insert the probe. The symbol in this example is the **sys_open** kernel routine, shown in Listing 12.3 and located in the /usr/src/linux/fs/open.c file.

There are at least three ways to get the address of a symbol for the kernel:

- Use the /proc/kallsyms file entry.
- Use the **nm** command on the kernel.
- Use the kernel's System.map.

Each of these methods is shown in Figure 12.4. All these methods return c01569c0 as the symbol address for **sys_open**. The c01569c0 address is what the Kprobe **addr** field is set to.

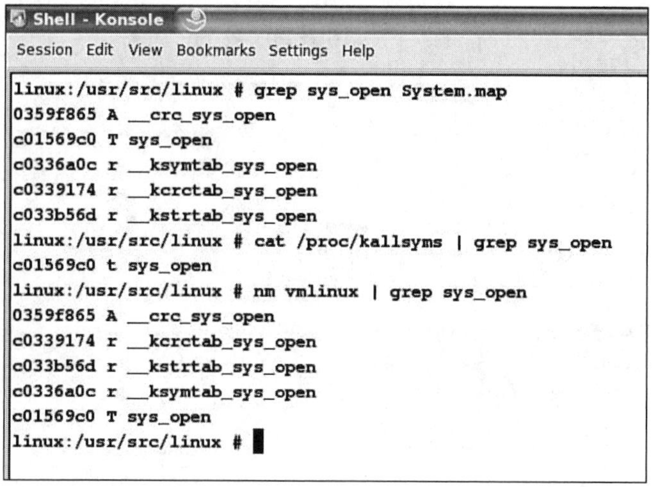

```
Shell - Konsole
Session  Edit  View  Bookmarks  Settings  Help
linux:/usr/src/linux # grep sys_open System.map
0359f865 A __crc_sys_open
c01569c0 T sys_open
c0336a0c r __ksymtab_sys_open
c0339174 r __kcrctab_sys_open
c033b56d r __kstrtab_sys_open
linux:/usr/src/linux # cat /proc/kallsyms | grep sys_open
c01569c0 t sys_open
linux:/usr/src/linux # nm vmlinux | grep sys_open
0359f865 A __crc_sys_open
c0339174 r __kcrctab_sys_open
c033b56d r __kstrtab_sys_open
c0336a0c r __ksymtab_sys_open
c01569c0 T sys_open
linux:/usr/src/linux #
```

FIGURE 12.4
Getting the address of a symbol in the kernel.

The sample module shown in Listing 12.3 creates a Kprobe for the **sys_open** routine. The Kprobe fires each time an open for a file is done in the kernel. Line 5 defines the pre-handler. Line 10 defines the post-handler. Line 14 defines the fault handler. The address for **sys_open** is 0xc01569c0 and is set on Line 25. The probe is registered on Line 26 and unregistered on Line 33.

Listing 12.3

Sample Module for a Kprobe for the sys_open Routine

```
1   #include <linux/module.h>
2   #include <linux/kprobes.h>
3
4   struct kprobe kpb;
5   int handler_pre_sys_open(struct kprobe *p, struct pt_regs
*regs) {
6       printk("sys_open pre_handler: p->addr=0x%p\n", p->addr);
7       return 0;
8   }
9
```

```
10  void handler_post_sys_open(struct kprobe *p, struct pt_regs
*regs, unsigned long flags){
11      printk("post_handler_sys_open: p->addr=0x%p\n", p->addr);
12  }
13
14 int handler_fault_sys_open(struct kprobe *p, struct pt_regs
*regs, int trapnr) {
15      printk("fault_handler_sys_open: p->addr=0x%p\n", p-
>addr);
16      return 0;
17 }
18
19 int init_module(void)
20 {
21      kpb.fault_handler = handler_fault_sys_open;
22      kpb.pre_handler = handler_pre_sys_open;
23      kpb.post_handler = handler_post_sys_open;
24
25      kpb.addr = (kprobe_opcode_t *) 0xc01569c0;
26      register_kprobe(&kpb);
27      printk(" register kprobe \n");
28      return 0;
29 }
30
31 void cleanup_module(void)
32 {
33      unregister_kprobe(&kpb);
34      printk("unregister kprobe\n");
35 }
36 MODULE_LICENSE("GPL");
```

Makefile for a Basic Kernel Module

A simple makefile for compiling the **chp12-kprobe_sys_open** module could have one line:

```
obj-m += chp12-kprobe_sys_open.o
```

The module is compiled by issuing the **make** command, as shown in Figure 12.5. The 2.6 kernel uses a new naming convention for kernel modules; modules now have a .ko extension (in place of the old .o extension). Additional details about makefiles for kernel modules are available in the linux/Documentation/kbuild/makefiles.txt file.

```
Shell - Konsole
Session  Edit  View  Bookmarks  Settings  Help
linux:/usr/src/chp12 # make -C /usr/src/linux  SUBDIRS=$PWD modules
make: Entering directory `/usr/src/linux-2.6.9'
  CC [M]  /usr/src/chp12/chp12-kprobe_sys_open.o
  Building modules, stage 2.
  MODPOST
  CC      /usr/src/chp12/chp12-kprobe_sys_open.mod.o
  LD [M]  /usr/src/chp12/chp12-kprobe_sys_open.ko
make: Leaving directory `/usr/src/linux-2.6.9'
linux:/usr/src/chp12 # insmod ./chp12-kprobe_sys_open.ko
linux:/usr/src/chp12 # rmmod chp12-kprobe_sys_open
linux:/usr/src/chp12 # █
```

FIGURE 12.5
Building, loading, and unloading the **chp12-kprobe_sys** module.

To insert the Kprobe module into the kernel, use the **insmod** command. Once the Kprobe for **sys_open** has collected the needed data, it can be removed from the kernel with **rmmod**. Figure 12.5 shows examples of both inserting and removing the Kprobe module.

After the Kprobe is registered, any file that the kernel opens is captured on the console or by running dmesg.

Figure 12.6 shows sample output for the Kprobe that was placed on the **sys_open** call. In this example the Kprobe for **sys_open** is writing the messages to the /var/log/messages file.

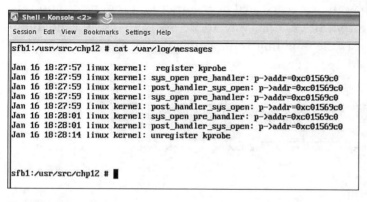

```
Shell - Konsole <2>
Session  Edit  View  Bookmarks  Settings  Help
sfb1:/usr/src/chp12 # cat /var/log/messages

Jan 16 18:27:57 linux kernel:  register kprobe
Jan 16 18:27:59 linux kernel: sys_open pre_handler: p->addr=0xc01569c0
Jan 16 18:27:59 linux kernel: post_handler_sys_open: p->addr=0xc01569c0
Jan 16 18:27:59 linux kernel: sys_open pre_handler: p->addr=0xc01569c0
Jan 16 18:27:59 linux kernel: post_handler_sys_open: p->addr=0xc01569c0
Jan 16 18:28:01 linux kernel: sys_open pre_handler: p->addr=0xc01569c0
Jan 16 18:28:01 linux kernel: post_handler_sys_open: p->addr=0xc01569c0
Jan 16 18:28:14 linux kernel: unregister kprobe


sfb1:/usr/src/chp12 # █
```

FIGURE 12.6
Output of the **sys_open** Kprobe.

Finding Kprobes That Are Active on the System

First the kernel must have Magic SysRq Key support configured (see Figure 12.3 for the menu where this option is configured for the kernel).

The **echo** command can be used to enable SysRq key support, as shown in Figure 12.7. To display the Kprobes active on the system, press Alt-SysRq-w. The example of /var/log/messages in Figure 12.7 shows that the **sys_open** Kprobe is the only active Kprobe on the system.

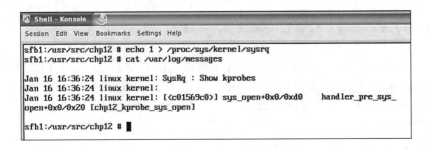

FIGURE 12.7
Displaying the Kprobes on a system.

Finding an Offset in sys_open

The first Kprobe that we created was for the beginning of the **sys_open** routine (Listing 12.3). A Kprobe can also be created at an offset in a routine. To do this, you need to determine the offset. One way to do so is to use the **objdump** command. Figure 12.8 uses the **objdump** command with the -D option and pipes the output to a file named open.dump.

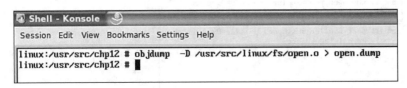

FIGURE 12.8
objdump for the open.o file.

The output from **objdump** for **sys_open** is shown in Listing 12.4.

Listing 12.4

Disassembly of sys_open

```
00000680 <sys_open>:
     680:    55                          push    %ebp
     681:    57                          push    %edi
     682:    56                          push    %esi
     683:    53                          push    %ebx
     684:    83 ec 24                    sub     $0x24,%esp
     687:    8b 44 24 38                 mov     0x38(%esp),%eax
     68b:    e8 fc ff ff ff              call    68c <sys_open+0xc>
     690:    3d 18 fc ff ff              cmp     $0xfffffc18,%eax
     695:    89 c3                       mov     %eax,%ebx
     697:    89 c5                       mov     %eax,%ebp
     699:    0f 97 c0                    seta    %al
     69c:    25 ff 00 00 00              and     $0xff,%eax
     6a1:    85 c0                       test    %eax,%eax
     6a3:    0f 85 82 00 00 00           jne     72b
<sys_open+0xab>
     6a9:    8d 74 24 04                 lea     0x4(%esp),%esi
```

To insert a probe in the last line of Listing 12.4 at offset 0x6a9, you must calculate the relative address from the start of **sys_open**, which is 0x680. You do this by subtracting 0x680 from 0x6a9 (which equals 0x029) and then adding this to the **sys_open** address (0xc01569c0 + 0x029 = 0xc01569e9). To use the same information captured in the Kprobe shown in Listing 12.3, line 25 would be changed to line 25a. The address changes from 0xc01569c0 to 0xc01569e9:

```
25    kpb.addr = (kprobe_opcode_t *) 0xc01569c0;
```

```
25a   kpb.addr = (kprobe_opcode_t *) 0xc01569e9;
```

Jumper Probes

Jumper probes (Jprobes) are a type of Kprobe in which the probe can be placed on a function entry point. This allows access to the parameters of the function that is being probed. The probe handler routine must have the same prototype as the function being probed.

Listing 12.5 places a Jprobe on the **sys_open** kernel routine located in the /usr/src/linux/fs/open.c file. A typical probe needs a probe handler, and in this example it is called **jp_sys_open**. The **addr** field is set to the kernel **sys_open** address, which allows the probe mechanism in the kernel to insert the Jprobe for the **sys_open** routine. After the Jprobe structure is set up, the Jprobe must be registered using the **register_jprobe** call.

Listing 12.5

High-Level Usage for Adding a Jprobe

```
static int jp_sys_open(const char __user * filename, int flags,
int mode)
{
        ... do the probe commands ...
        jprobe_return();
        return 0;
}
struct jprobe jp = {
        .addr = sys_open,
        .entry = jp_sys_open
};
register_jprobe(&jp);
```

Uses of Kprobes

A Kprobe can be used to trigger a dump when a specific set of circumstances occurs. This is one of the most powerful aspects of Kprobes—being able to watch for a rare set of conditions and to get a snapshot of the system when they occur.

dpcc, the Linux Trace Toolkit (LTT), and Dprobes provide the infrastructure to do all-points-addressable dynamic tracing. This combination is a very powerful facility. You can easily generate a set of probe points from the **nm** output. From that, within minutes you can have a functional execution trace of a driver or module. Dynamic probes are aimed at solving the following problems:

- Extreme debugging where problem re-creation cannot be forced

- Highly available systems where debugging has to be done (for reasons of complexity you need to force a reproduction) on a production/live system

- As an alternative to inserting a temporary **printf** or **printk** where rebuild time can be saved (this especially applies to kernel development)

Successful Employment of Dprobes

Dprobes and Kprobes in Linux have been successfully used to solve development problems in the following areas:

- Development of Dprobes
- Kernel development
- Debugging races and timing-sensitive problems
- Ad-hoc profiling
- Large-scale (internal) instrumentation

Summary

Kprobes can reduce the amount of time it takes to solve a problem. They do not disrupt the environment, and they allow debugging in environments without rebuilding. Kprobes let you acquire diagnostic information without custom-building the component. Dprobes also can be used as a tracing mechanism for both user and kernel space. They can be used to debug software problems you encounter in a production environment that cannot be re-created in a test lab environment. Dprobes and Kprobes can be used particularly in production environments where the use of an interactive debugger is either undesirable or unavailable. Dprobes also can be used during the development phase to cause faults or error injections into code paths that are being tested. Kprobe technology can be a powerful weapon to reduce the time needed to debug a problem.

Credits

A big thank-you goes out to Suparna Bhattacharya, Michael Grundy, Richard J. Moore, Prasanna S. Panchamukhi, Bharata B. Rao, Vamsi Krishna Sangavarapu, Maneesh Soni, Subodh Soni, Thomas Zanussi, and other developers for the development and support of Dprobes and Kprobes.

Web Resource for Dynamic Probes

URL	Description
http://sourceforge.net/projects/dprobes/	Dprobes and Kprobes

## Chapter 13

Kernel-Level Debuggers (kgdb and kdb)

In this chapter

- kgdb   page 335
- kdb   page 348
- Summary   page 368
- Credits   page 369
- Web Resources for kgdb and kdb   page 369

This chapter covers two debuggers: kgdb and kdb. Both are kernel-level debuggers. kgdb is an extension to gdb that allows the gdb debugger to debug kernel-level code. One key feature of kgdb is that it allows source-code-level debugging of kernel-level code. The kdb debugger allows kernel-level debugging but does not provide source-level debugging. The kernel source available at www.kernel.org doesn't include either of these debuggers.

The reason for this is that the maintainer of Linux, Linus Torvalds, believes that having a debugger built into the kernel causes developers of the kernel source code to take shortcuts and not thoroughly understand the code they are fixing or adding new functionality to.

The following quote from Torvalds concerns adding kdb to the kernel:

The debugger is akin to giving the rabbits *a bazooka. The poor wolf doesn't get any sharper teeth. Yeah, it sure helps against wolves.*

They explode in pretty patterns of red drops flying everywhere. *Cool.*

But it doesn't help against a rabbit gene pool that is slowly deteriorating because there is nothing to keep them from breeding, and no Darwin to make sure that it's the fastest and strongest that breeds. You mentioned how NT has the nicest debugger out there. Contemplate it.

Most kernel developers don't share this view and patch the kernel to include one of the debuggers. The first kernel-level debugger I patched into the kernel was kgdb when I started to port the Journaled File System (JFS) to Linux in 1999. It sure beats debugging a major component of the system with **printk**.

Some distributions support both of the kernel debuggers, and one is enabled and the other isn't. Both SuSE SLES 8 and SuSE SLES 9 default kernel config have kdb built in. Currently Red Hat doesn't include kdb in its kernel.

Figure 13.1 shows a Kernel hacking menu that has both debuggers available, but neither is currently configured to be built for this kernel.

FIGURE 13.1
A Kernel hacking menu showing both debuggers.

The kernel config shown in Figure 13.1 has four configuration options for kgdb: KGDB: Remote (serial) kernel debugging with gdb, KGDB: Thread analysis, KGDB: Console messages through gdb, and KGDB: Enable kernel asserts. The number of configuration options can change for each version of kgdb.

The kernel config shown in Figure 13.1 has five configuration options for kdb: Built-in Kernel Debugger support, KDB modules, KDB off by default, Support for USB Keyboard in KDB, and Load all symbols for debugging is required for kdb. The number of configuration options can change per version of kdb.

kgdb

The kgdb functionality (remote host Linux kernel debugger through gdb) provides a mechanism to debug the Linux kernel using gdb. kgdb is an extension of the kernel that allows a connection to a machine running the kgdb-extended kernel when gdb is running on a remote host machine. gdb can stop the kernel and break points can be set, data can be examined, and so on (similar to how you would use gdb on an application program). For more details about gdb, see Chapter 3, "GNU

Debugger (gdb)." One of the primary features of this patch is that the remote host running gdb connects to the target machine (running the kernel to be debugged) during the boot process. This allows debugging as early as possible.

Two machines are required to use kgdb—a development machine and a test machine. A serial line (null-modem cable) connects the machines through their serial ports. The kernel to be debugged runs on the test machine; gdb runs on the development machine.

First check to see if kgdb is available in the kernel config by looking at the Kernel hacking menu. If it isn't, the next section shows you how to enable kgdb by first applying the kgdb patches to the kernel.

kgdb Kernel Patching

The first step is to apply the kgdb patch to the kernel by downloading the patch from the kgdb web site (http://kgdb.sourceforge.net/). kgdb provides patches for several levels of the kernel.

The following example uses the kgdb patch that has been created for the 2.6.7 level of the kernel. The patch is called linux-2.6.7-kgdb-2.2.tar.bz2. The first step is to unzip the patch using the **bunzip2** command. You also can use tar's **j** option to unzip the patch. The next step is to expand the tar file using tar's **xvf** options. Figure 13.2 shows these steps.

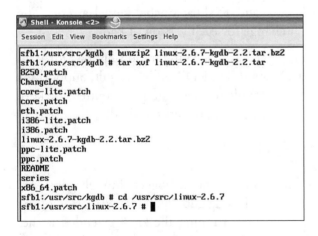

FIGURE 13.2
Expanding the kernel patch for kgdb.

The next step is to apply the needed patches. In this example you'll build the kgdb for the i386 architecture. There are also kernel patches that apply to the PowerPC architecture. The i386 patches should be applied in the following order:

1. core-lite.patch

2. i386-lite.patch

3. 8250.patch

4. eth.patch

5. i386.patch

6. core.patch

Figure 13.3 shows the commands to apply the first three.

```
Shell - Konsole
Session  Edit  View  Bookmarks  Settings  Help
sfb1:/usr/src/linux-2.6.7 # patch -p1  < /usr/src/kgdb/core-lite.patch
patching file Documentation/DocBook/Makefile
patching file Documentation/DocBook/kgdb.tmpl
patching file Makefile
patching file include/linux/debugger.h
patching file include/linux/kgdb.h
patching file kernel/Kconfig.kgdb
patching file kernel/Makefile
patching file kernel/kgdb.c
patching file kernel/sched.c
sfb1:/usr/src/linux-2.6.7 # patch -p1 < /usr/src/kgdb/i386-lite.patch
patching file arch/i386/Kconfig
patching file arch/i386/kernel/Makefile
patching file arch/i386/kernel/irq.c
patching file arch/i386/kernel/kgdb.c
patching file arch/i386/kernel/nmi.c
patching file arch/i386/kernel/signal.c
patching file arch/i386/kernel/traps.c
patching file arch/i386/mm/fault.c
patching file include/asm-i386/kgdb.h
patching file include/asm-i386/processor.h
patching file include/asm-i386/system.h
sfb1:/usr/src/linux-2.6.7 # patch -p1 < /usr/src/kgdb/8250.patch
patching file drivers/serial/8250.c
patching file drivers/serial/Makefile
patching file drivers/serial/kgdb_8250.c
patching file drivers/serial/serial_core.c
patching file kernel/Kconfig.kgdb
sfb1:/usr/src/linux-2.6.7 #
```

FIGURE 13.3
Applying the core-lite, i386-lite, and 8250 patches.

Figure 13.4 shows the commands to apply the next three patches.

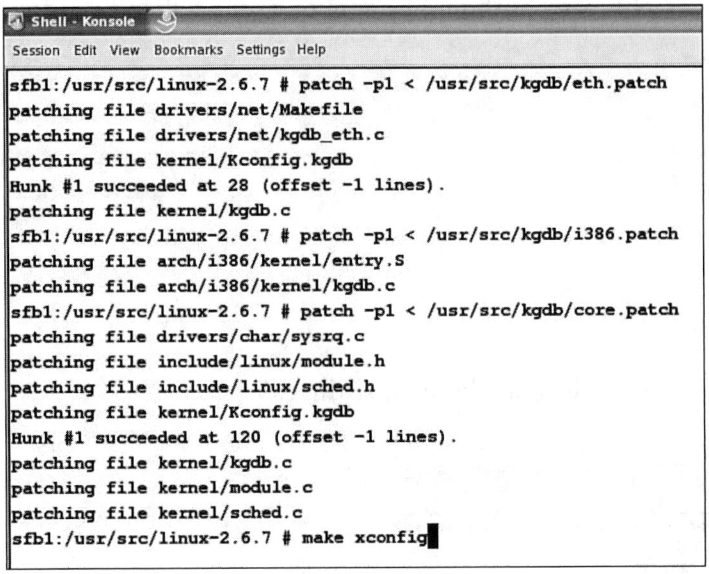

```
sfb1:/usr/src/linux-2.6.7 # patch -p1 < /usr/src/kgdb/eth.patch
patching file drivers/net/Makefile
patching file drivers/net/kgdb_eth.c
patching file kernel/Kconfig.kgdb
Hunk #1 succeeded at 28 (offset -1 lines).
patching file kernel/kgdb.c
sfb1:/usr/src/linux-2.6.7 # patch -p1 < /usr/src/kgdb/i386.patch
patching file arch/i386/kernel/entry.S
patching file arch/i386/kernel/kgdb.c
sfb1:/usr/src/linux-2.6.7 # patch -p1 < /usr/src/kgdb/core.patch
patching file drivers/char/sysrq.c
patching file include/linux/module.h
patching file include/linux/sched.h
patching file kernel/Kconfig.kgdb
Hunk #1 succeeded at 120 (offset -1 lines).
patching file kernel/kgdb.c
patching file kernel/module.c
patching file kernel/sched.c
sfb1:/usr/src/linux-2.6.7 # make xconfig
```

FIGURE 13.4
Applying the eth, i386, and core patches.

The next step is to configure the kernel. One way to do that is to use the **make xconfig** command.

Figure 13.5 shows the kgdb options that are turned on for the kernel you'll build. The first selection allows kgdb to be used over a serial port or Ethernet. You'll turn on the serial port and then set 115200 as the baud rate and set ttyS0 as the serial port. One other option to check in your kernel config is to make sure that the serial port is configured. The serial port configuration is set in the Character devices menu in the Serial drivers section.

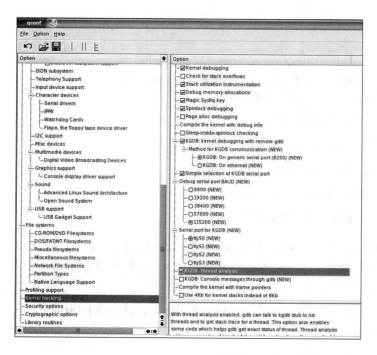

FIGURE 13.5
The Kernel hacking menu showing the kgdb options.

Building the Kernel

The following steps show you how to build the kernel (for i386):

1. Issue the **make xconfig** command.

2. Under "General Setup," select the following:
   a. Select "Kernel hacking."
   b. Select "KGDB: Remote (serial) kernel debugging with gdb."
   c. Select options for kgdb (see Figure 13.1 for the additional options).
   d. Configure other kernel settings as needed.

3. Save and exit.

4. The kernel makefile in the same directory where .config resides (which is /usr/src/linux-2.6.7 in this example) must be checked for the following changes:

HOSTCFLAGS = -Wall -Wstrict-prototypes -O2 -fomit-frame-pointer
changed to:
HOSTCFLAGS = -Wall -Wstrict-prototypes -O2 **-g -ggdb**
The **-g** flag inserts symbolic debugging information. Removing
-fomit-frame-pointer lets you do stack traces.

5. Issue the **make clean** command.

6. Issue the **make bzImage** command.

7. If modules need to be built, do the following:

    a. Issue the **make modules** command.

    b. Issue the **make modules_install** command.

The modules that were just built won't be run on the development machine, but
the **make modules_install** option places the modules in a fixed place to pull all of
them from.

Listing 13.1 is an example of a script that transfers the kernel and modules you
built on your development machine to the test machine.

A few items need to be changed for your setup:

- **best@sfb**—User ID and machine name

- **/usr/src/linux-2.6.7**—Directory of your kernel source tree

- **bzImage-2.6.7**—Name of the kernel that will be booted on the test
  machine

- **scp and rsync**—Must be allowed to run on the machine the kernel was
  built on

Run this on the test machine:

Listing 13.1

Script to Pull the Kernel and Modules to Test the Machine

```
1 set -x
2 scp best@sfb:/usr/src/linux-2.6.7/arch/i386/boot/bzImage
/boot/bzImage-2.6.7
3 scp best@sfb:/usr/src/linux-2.6.7/System.map
/boot/System.map-2.6.7
4 rm -rf /lib/modules/2.6.7
5 rsync -a best@sfb:/lib/modules/2.6.7 /lib/modules
6 chown -R root /lib/modules/2.6.7
```

After the kernel has been placed on the test machine, the serial connection between the development and test machines should be checked.

Checking the Null Modem Serial Cable Setup

The following steps can be used to check your serial connection between the two systems. You'll use the **stty** command, as shown in Figures 13.6 and 13.7, which lets you change and print the terminal setting. For detailed information on stty, view the man page by typing **man stty**. In this example, the serial connection on both machines uses /dev/ttyS0. You'll set the baud rate to 115200 and use the file called test to send data to the test machine. The file test has two lines of data—**test1** and **test2**. The two machines are set up correctly since **test1** and **test2** are sent successfully.

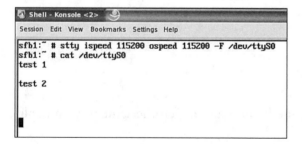

FIGURE 13.6
The development machine: data being sent to the test machine.

```
Shell - Konsole <2>
Session  Edit  View  Bookmarks  Settings  Help
sfb1:~ # stty ispeed 115200 ospeed 115200 -F /dev/ttyS0
sfb1:~ # cat /dev/ttyS0
test 1

test 2
```

FIGURE 13.7
The test machine: data being received from the development machine.

One common problem is that the null-modem cable could be connected to the wrong serial port. If the data does not come across, switch the port to the second serial port connection, and this could enable the serial connection.

Once the serial connection to the development and test machines has been verified, the next step is to enable kgdb through the boot loader of the test machine.

Booting the Kernel

The kgdb kernel command-line option **kgdbwait** makes kgdb wait for the gdb connection during the booting of a kernel. The second kernel command option, **kgdb8250**, is used to configure the serial port. The port number and speed can be overridden on the command line by using this option:

```
kgdb8250=portnumber, speed
```

where *portnumber* is the COM port and supported *speed*s are 9600, 19200, 38400, 57600, and 115200.

Here's an example:

```
kgdbwait kgdb8250=0,115200
```

Connecting gdb

If you used **kgdbwait**, kgdb prints the message **Waiting for connection from remote gdb...** on the console and waits for a connection from gdb. At this point the connection is made through kgdb to gdb.

Here's an example:

```
% gdb ./vmlinux
(gdb) set remotebaud 115200
(gdb) target remote /dev/ttyS0
```

After the connection, debugging the kernel can happen the same way an application is debugged using gdb.

If your system uses lilo as the boot loader, add the **append** line to lilo. Here's a sample lilo entry:

```
 image=/boot/bzImage-2.6.7
label=gdb267
read-only
root=/dev/sda8
append="kgdbwait kgdb8250=0,115200"
```

Run lilo and reboot.

If your system uses grub as the boot loader, add the two kgdb keywords to the kernel entry.

Here's a sample grub entry:

```
title kgdb-2.6.7
    kernel (hd1,2)/boot/bzImage-2.6.7 root=/dev/hdb3
kgdbwait kgdb8250=0,115200 vga=0x314 splash=silent desktop showopts
    initrd (hd1,2)/boot/initrd
```

After the kgdb keywords have been added to the kernel entry for kgdb, reboot the system and select the kgdb-2.6.7 kernel entry to boot that kernel.

A Typical gdb Session

Now that you have the development and test machines set up correctly through their serial ports, let's see some of the gdb commands that can be used to set break points, view a back trace, and view variables.

Instead of typing commands to set up the gdb session every time, it is possible to have gdb read input parameters by creating a file called .gdbinit. This file would be placed in the kernel subdirectory where gdb will be started on the development machine. In this example gdb is started in the /usr/src/linux-2.6.7 directory. Listing 13.2 shows a sample .gdbinit file. Line 1 sets the baud rate to 115200. Line 2 sets vmlinux as the symbol file. Line 3 sets the serial port to /dev/ttyS0. Line 4 sets gdb's output to display hexadecimal.

Listing 13.2

.gdbinit Start File for gdb

```
1  set remotebaud 115200
2  symbol-file vmlinux
3  target remote /dev/ttyS0
4  set output-radix 16
```

Now you're ready to start the gdb program on the development machine by changing to the directory where the kernel source tree starts. In this example, the kernel source tree is at /usr/src/linux-2.6.7. To start gdb, type **gdb**.

If everything is working, the test machine will stop during the boot process. Enter the gdb command **cont** to continue the boot process.

Using kgdb to Stop and View the Kernel Source

To stop kernel execution, press Ctrl-C on the gdb terminal. gdb sends a stop message to the kernel gdb, which takes control of the kernel and contacts gdb. gdb then presents a command prompt and waits for user input. The kernel is stopped, and all processors are controlled by kernel gdb routines. gdb commands can be entered now.

Listing 13.3 shows the code you'll put a break point in. This code is part of the mount code of the JFS. The source code is in the kernel and is located in the /usr/src/linux-2.6.7/fs/jfs/jfs_mount.c file.

Listing 13.3

jfs_mount.c Code

```
81   int jfs_mount(struct super_block *sb)
82   {
83       int rc = 0;     /* Return code   */
84       struct jfs_sb_info *sbi = JFS_SBI(sb);
85       struct inode *ipaimap = NULL;
86       struct inode *ipaimap2 = NULL;
87       struct inode *ipimap = NULL;
88       struct inode *ipbmap = NULL;
89       /*
90        * read/validate superblock
91        * (initialize mount inode from the superblock)
92        */
93       if ((rc = chkSuper(sb))) {
94             goto errout20;
95       }
```

After you set the break point on the development machine and use the **cont** command to start the kernel running again, you mount a JFS file system on the test machine. The **mount** command causes the break point to be hit, and gdb stops the system.

Figure 13.8 shows the lines in the .gdbinit file that are used as parameters to gdb. You'll start gdb and press Ctrl-C to set the first break point in the **jfs_mount** routine. Once the break is hit, you'll use back trace (**bt**) with 6 as the number of traces you want to see. The back trace shows that **jfs_mount** has the following calling structure:

```
do_add_mount -> do_kern_mount -> jfs_get_sb -> get_sb_sdev -> jfs_fill_super ->
jfs_mount
```

NOTE   The -> designates which routine is being called.

```
sfb1:/usr/src/linux-2.6.7 # cat .gdbinit
set remotebaud 115200
symbol-file vmlinux
target remote /dev/ttyS0
set output-radix 16
sfb1:/usr/src/linux-2.6.7 # gdb
GNU gdb 6.1
Copyright 2004 Free Software Foundation, Inc.
GDB is free software, covered by the GNU General Public License, and you are
welcome to change it and/or distribute copies of it under certain conditions.
Type "show copying" to see the conditions.
There is absolutely no warranty for GDB.  Type "show warranty" for details.
This GDB was configured as "i686-pc-linux-gnu".
Using host libthread_db library "/lib/tls/libthread_db.so.1".
breakpoint () at kernel/kgdb.c:1212
1212            atomic_set(&kgdb_setting_breakpoint, 0);
(gdb) cont
Continuing.
[New Thread 32768]

Program received signal SIGTRAP, Trace/breakpoint trap.
breakpoint () at kernel/kgdb.c:1212
1212            atomic_set(&kgdb_setting_breakpoint, 0);
(gdb) break jfs_mount
Breakpoint 1 at 0xc01d669c: file jfs_incore.h, line 182.
(gdb) cont
Continuing.
[New Thread 6232]
[Switching to Thread 6232]

Breakpoint 1, jfs_mount (sb=0xd75aa518) at jfs_incore.h:182
182            return sb->s_fs_info;
(gdb) bt 6
#0  jfs_mount (sb=0xd75aa518) at jfs_incore.h:182
#1  0xc01d2e28 in jfs_fill_super (sb=0xd75aa518, data=0x0, silent=0x0) at fs/jfs/super.c:417
#2  0xc01627bf in get_sb_bdev (fs_type=0xc030b340, flags=0x0, dev_name=0xcac02000 "/dev/hdb1", data=0x0,
    fill_super=0xc01d2d70 <jfs_fill_super>) at fs/super.c:668
#3  0xc01d308d in jfs_get_sb (fs_type=0xc030b340, flags=0x0, dev_name=0xcac02000 "/dev/hdb1", data=0x0)
    at fs/jfs/super.c:505
#4  0xc01629b0 in do_kern_mount (fstype=0xcac9d000 "jfs", flags=0x0, name=0xcac02000 "/dev/hdb1", data=0x0)
    at fs/super.c:781
#5  0xc017de4b in do_add_mount (nd=0xcabf1f50, type=0xcac9d000 "jfs", flags=0x0, mnt_flags=0x1000,
    name=0xcac02000 "/dev/hdb1", data=0x0) at fs/namespace.c:738
(More stack frames follow...)
```

FIGURE 13.8
.gdbinit: starting gdb and setting a break point in **jfs_mount**.

The next gdb session, shown in Figure 13.9, places a break point in the **jfs_create** routine, which is called when a file is created in a JFS file system. After the break point is set, you'll copy a file to the JFS file system, and the break point will be hit.

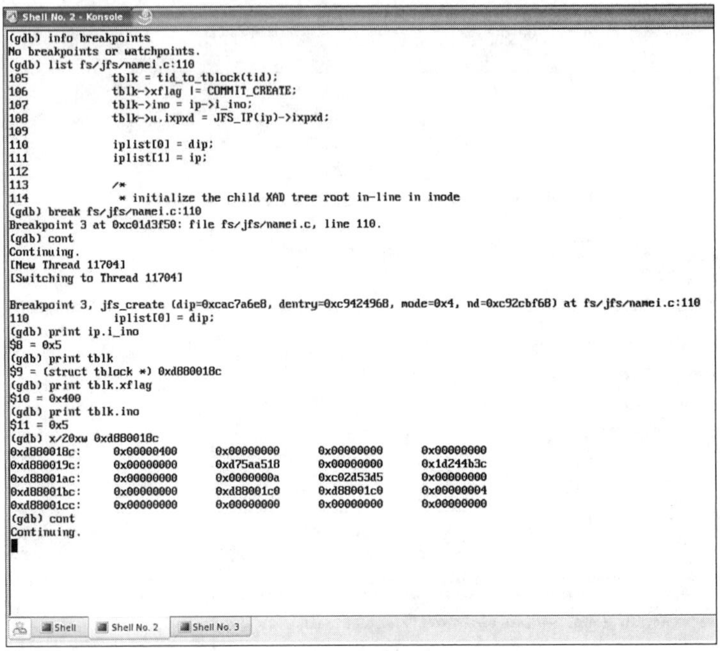


```
(gdb) info breakpoints
No breakpoints or watchpoints.
(gdb) list fs/jfs/namei.c:110
105             tblk = tid_to_tblock(tid);
106             tblk->xflag |= COMMIT_CREATE;
107             tblk->ino = ip->i_ino;
108             tblk->u.ixpxd = JFS_IP(ip)->ixpxd;
109
110             iplist[0] = dip;
111             iplist[1] = ip;
112
113             /*
114              * initialize the child XAD tree root in-line in inode
(gdb) break fs/jfs/namei.c:110
Breakpoint 3 at 0xc01d3f50: file fs/jfs/namei.c, line 110.
(gdb) cont
Continuing.
[New Thread 11704]
[Switching to Thread 11704]

Breakpoint 3, jfs_create (dip=0xcac7a6e8, dentry=0xc9424968, mode=0x4, nd=0xc92cbf68) at fs/jfs/namei.c:110
110             iplist[0] = dip;
(gdb) print ip.i_ino
$8 = 0x5
(gdb) print tblk
$9 = (struct tblock *) 0xd880018c
(gdb) print tblk.xflag
$10 = 0x400
(gdb) print tblk.ino
$11 = 0x5
(gdb) x/20xw 0xd880018c
0xd880018c:     0x00000400      0x00000000      0x00000000      0x00000000
0xd880019c:     0x00000000      0xd75aa518      0x00000000      0x1d244b3c
0xd88001ac:     0x00000000      0x0000000a      0xc02d53d5      0x00000000
0xd88001bc:     0x00000000      0xd88001c0      0xd88001c0      0x00000004
0xd88001cc:     0x00000000      0x00000000      0x00000000      0x00000000
(gdb) cont
Continuing.
```

FIGURE 13.9
A break point in **jfs_create** and viewing variables.

First you'll press Ctrl-C to enter the gdb session. To check if any breaks are set, use the **info breakpoints** command. In this session no break points are set. Now use gdb to do a source listing inside the JFS routine called **jfs_create.** This routine is located in /usr/src/linux-2.6.7/fs/jfs/namei.c. You'll then place a break point on line 110:

```
110   iplist[0] = dip;
```

You'll use four **print** commands to show the value of the variables **ip->i_ino, tblk, tblk->xflag**, and **tblk->ino**. Finally, you'll look at 20 words of the **tblk** structure by using the **x/20xw** command with the address 0xd880018c.

gdb Thread Analysis

In Linux, a single program may have more than one thread of execution. The precise semantics of threads differ from one operating system to another, but in general the threads of a single program are akin to multiple processes—except that they share one address space (that is, they can all examine and modify the same variables). On the other hand, each thread has its own registers and execution stack, and perhaps private memory.

gdb provides these facilities for debugging multithread programs. Some of the thread-related commands are as follows:

- **info threads** displays all existing threads.
- **thread** *thread* # switches to another thread.
- **thread apply** [*thread #*] [**all**] *args* applies a command to a list of threads.
- Thread-specific break points
- Automatic notification of new threads

Let's look at gdb's capability to switch between threads and view where each thread is on the system. You'll see how to view two threads. The first gdb command you'll use is **info threads**. This command displays all the threads on the system. Suppose you're looking for two JFS threads, and from **thread info** the thread numbers turn out to be 8 and 14. To view thread 8, you'll use the gdb command **thread 8** and use the **where** command to get a back trace for this thread. The exact gdb commands are as follows:

- **info threads** displays the program's threads.
- **thread 8** switches to that thread.
- **where** displays a back trace for thread 8.
- **thread 14** switches to that thread.
- **where** displays a back trace for thread 14.

Checking where each thread is can be an effective way to determine which thread or threads are causing the system to hang. Some things to look for are if one thread is holding a semaphore and the other thread is waiting on that semaphore. Another area of interest is when one thread has a lock that the other thread is waiting for.

kdb

The Linux kernel debugger (kdb) is a patch for the Linux kernel. It lets you examine kernel memory and data structures while the system is operational. A key feature of kdb is that it requires only one machine to use the debugger. kdb also can be set up to use two machines, which would be connected through serial ports. kdb does not allow source-level debugging like kgdb. Additional commands to format and display essential system data structures given an identifier or address of the data structure can be added to kdb. The current command set allows the control of kernel operations, including the following:

- Single-stepping a processor
- Stopping upon execution of a specific instruction
- Stopping upon access (or modification) of a specific virtual memory location
- Stopping upon access to a register in the input-output address space
- Stack back trace for the current active task as well as for all other tasks (by process ID [PID])
- Instruction disassembly

First, check to see if kdb is available in the kernel config by looking at the Kernel hacking menu. If it isn't, the next section shows you how to enable kdb by first applying the kdb patches to the kernel.

kdb Kernel Patching

The first step of applying the kdb patch to the kernel is to download the patch from the kdb web site (http://oss.sgi.com/projects/kdb/). kdb provides patches for several levels of the kernel.

The following example uses the kdb patch that has been created for the 2.6.9 level of the kernel. The patches are called kdb-v4.4-2.6.9-rc4-common.1.bz2 and kdb-v4.4-2.6.9-i386.1.bz2. The first step is to unzip both patches using the **bzip2** command with the -**d** option.

Figure 13.10 shows the command to apply the first of two patches (kdb-v4.4-2.6.9-rc4-common-1).

FIGURE 13.10

Patching the kernel with the first of two kdb patches.

Figure 13.11 shows the command to apply the second of two patches (kdb-v4.4-2.6.9-rc4-i386-1).

FIGURE 13.11

Patching the kernel with the second of two kdb patches.

The next step is to configure the kernel. One way to do that is to use the **make xconfig** command.

Figure 13.12 shows the kdb options that are turned on for the kernel you'll build. It is also recommended that "Compile the kernel with frame pointers" be turned on. This flag is in the Kernel hacking section.

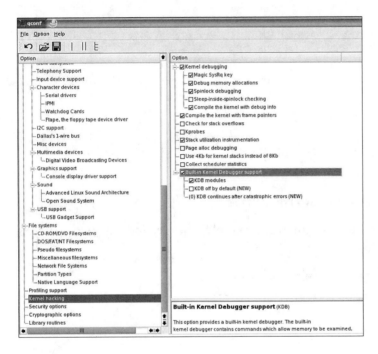

FIGURE 13.12
The Kernel hacking menu showing the kdb options.

One other option to check in your kernel config is if kdb will be used over a serial port. The serial port configuration is set in the Character devices menu in the Serial drivers section.

Building the Kernel

The following steps show you how to build the kernel (for i386):

1. Issue the **make xconfig** command.

2. Under "Kernel hacking," select the following:
    a. Select "Built-in Kernel Debugger support."
    b. Select "KDB modules."
    c. Configure other kernel settings as needed.

3. Save and exit.

4. Issue the **make clean** command.

5. Issue the **make bzImage** command.

6. If modules need to be built, do the following:
    a. Issue the **make modules** command.
    b. Issue the **make modules_install** command.

7. Enter **cp arch/i386/boot/bzImage /boot/bzImage-2.6.9-kdb**.

8. Enter **cp System.map /boot/System.map-2.6.9-kdb**.

9. Enter **rm /boot/System.map && ln -s /boot/System. map-2.6.9-kdb System.map**.

10. If the system is using lilo as the boot loader, modify your configuration to boot from /boot/bzImage-2.6.8.1-kdb.

    For example, if you're using lilo, do the following.
    a. Modify /etc/lilo.conf.
    b. Run lilo to read the modified lilo.conf.

11. If the system is using grub as the boot loader, modify your configuration to boot from /boot/bzImage-2.6.8.1-kdb.

    For example, if you're using grub, modify /boot/grub/menu.lst.

12. Reboot.

The next step is to check the kernel's level and make sure that the kdb supported kernel is the one that is running. The **uname** command does not directly show that kdb support is built into the kernel, but the following example shows that we are running level 2.6.9 of the kernel. The **uname -a** command displays the kernel's level. The output should be similar to the following:

```
Linux sfb1 2.6.9 #1 Fri Nov 26 05:08:30 UTC 2004 i686 i686 i386 GNU/Linux
```

kdb Activation

kdb can be activated by configuring it at kernel build time.

If kdb off by default (**CONFIG_KDB_OFF**) was not selected during kernel configuration, kdb is active by default.

The runtime options are as follows:

- Activate it by passing the **kdb=on** flag to the kernel during boot.

- Turn it on or off through the /proc file system entry.

  To enable kdb through the /proc, use this command:

  ```
  # echo "1" > /proc/sys/kernel/kdb
  ```

  To disable kdb through the /proc, use this command:

  ```
  # echo "0" > /proc/sys/kernel/kdb
  ```

If kdb is needed during boot, specify the **kdb=early** flag to the kernel during boot. This allows kdb to be activated during the boot process.

kdb is invoked in the following ways:

- Pressing the Pause key on the keyboard manually invokes kdb.

- Whenever there is an Oops or kernel panic.

- If kdb is set up through a serial port between two machines, pressing Ctrl-A invokes kdb from the serial console. Several programs can be used to communicate with kdb through a serial port, such as minicom and kermit.

> NOTE The key sequence Ctrl-A has been changed in version 4.4 of kdb. It is now Esc-KDB.

Using kdb Via a Serial Console Port

The following steps assume that lilo is the boot loader. If your system uses another boot loader, the commands should be added to that boot loader.

1. Add **serial = 0,115200n8** to the file /etc/lilo.conf.

2. Add **append="console=ttyS0,115200"** to the file /etc/lilo.conf.

3. A user space program must be reading from the serial port to see

characters coming down the line; this is a restriction of the Linux
serial layer. A sample entry in /etc/inittab that does this is as follows:

```
Add S1:23:respawn:/sbin/getty -L ttyS1 115200 vt100 to the file
/etc/inittab.
```

4. Connect the serial port to the other computer via a null modem
   cable.

5. Run a terminal tool (minicom or kermit) on the other computer
   and start the connection.

6. Reboot the computer with kdb.

7. Enter kdb by pressing Ctrl-A on the terminal tool's console.

8. Enter some kdb commands to check to see if kdb is working.

kdb has 10 man pages available; the kdb kernel patch places them in the
/Documentation/kdb directory. The overall man page for kdb is located in the
kdb.mm file. You can access it using the following commands:

```
# cd /usr/src/linux-2.6.9/Documentation/kdb
# man ./kdb.mm
```

kdb Commands

When kdb is enabled, a kernel Oops causes the debugger to be invoked, and the
keyboard LEDs blink. Once the kdb prompt is displayed, you can enter kdb commands. Table 13.1 describes some of the commands.

TABLE 13.1
kdb Commands

Command	Description
bp *name*	Sets a break point, where *name* is the name of the kernel routine.
bt	Displays a back trace.
bta	Displays a back trace for all processes.
btp *PID*	Gets a back trace of a particular process, where *PID* is the process ID.
di *name*	Disassemble instructions for a routine, where *name* is the name of the kernel routine.

(continues)

TABLE 13.1
kdb Commands (Continued)

Command	Description
dmesg	Displays the kernel log buffer.
go	Exits the debugger.
help?	Displays help for the debugger.
md *address*	Displays memory, where *address* is the memory address.
ps	Displays a list of processes.

If the system will be run in graphical mode with kdb enabled, it is recommend that kdb be set up to use a serial console so that the kdb prompt can be seen.

kdb Debug Sessions

Now let's look at some real problems where kdb was useful in showing where the problem in the kernel occurred. The first session looks at a problem while a volume snapshot is created on an XFS volume. The second session shows a problem in the JFS file system. The third session is a system that is hanging, and the problem turned out to be in the BIOS for the system. We'll look at some of the structures in the IDE device driver while walking through this session.

kdb Debug Session 1

The following bug showed up while a volume snapshot of an XFS volume was being created. kdb is entered because the kernel has hit a system panic or Oops. The system has stopped because the Extended Instruction Pointer (EIP) register is invalid (0xb800). The instruction pointer is the memory address of the next instruction the processor will load and execute.

```
Entering kdb (current=0xd600e000, pid 940) Oops: Oops
due to oops @ 0xb800
eax = 0xffffffff ebx = 0xd600e000 ecx = 0x0000b800 edx = 0xc018fd25
esi = 0x00000008 edi = 0xd600e000 esp = 0xd600ff0c eip = 0x0000b800
ebp = 0xd600ff30 xss = 0x00000018 xcs = 0x00000010 eflags = 0x00010086
xds = 0x00000018 xes = 0x00000018 origeax = 0xffffffff &regs = 0xd600fed8
```

The **ps** command can be used to list the system's processes when the system went into kdb. In this case we know that PID 940 is the process that caused the Oops, so that process could be the most important process to solve this problem. The * next to the **lvcreate** process shows that this is the running process when the Oops occurred.

```
kdb> ps
Task Addr   Pid        Parent     [*] cpu  State Thread     Command
0xd7fe2000  00000001   00000000    1  000  stop  0xd7fe2270 init
0xc163c000  00000002   00000001    1  000  stop  0xc163c270 keventd
0xc1638000  00000003   00000000    1  000  stop  0xc1638270 ksoftirqd_CPU0
0xc1636000  00000004   00000000    1  000  stop  0xc1636270 kswapd
0xc1634000  00000005   00000000    1  000  stop  0xc1634270 bdflush
0xc1632000  00000006   00000000    1  000  stop  0xc1632270 kupdated
0xd7ec4000  00000007   00000001    1  000  stop  0xd7ec4270 mdrecoveryd
0xd7eae000  00000008   00000001    1  000  stop  0xd7eae270 raid5d
0xd7228000  00000156   00000001    1  000  stop  0xd7228270 kreiserfsd
0xd7022000  00000159   00000001    1  000  stop  0xd7022270 pagebuf_daemon
0xd630c000  00000522   00000001    1  000  stop  0xd630c270 dhcpcd
0xd6fce000  00000658   00000001    1  000  stop  0xd6fce270 syslogd
0xd630a000  00000663   00000001    1  000  stop  0xd630a270 klogd
0xd61a2000  00000683   00000001    1  000  stop  0xd61a2270 portmap
0xd617c000  00000711   00000001    1  000  stop  0xd617c270 rpc.statd
0xd6108000  00000823   00000001    1  000  stop  0xd6108270 crond
0xd651c000  00000860   00000001    1  000  stop  0xd651c270 atd
0xd7986000  00000867   00000001    1  000  stop  0xd7986270 login
0xd627a000  00000868   00000001    1  000  stop  0xd627a270 mingetty
0xd6194000  00000869   00000001    1  000  stop  0xd6194270 mingetty
0xd613e000  00000870   00000001    1  000  stop  0xd613e270 mingetty
0xd6400000  00000871   00000001    1  000  stop  0xd6400270 mingetty
0xd60e4000  00000872   00000001    1  000  stop  0xd60e4270 mingetty
0xd6284000  00000873   00000001    1  000  stop  0xd6284270 mgetty
0xd67f2000  00000876   00000867    1  000  stop  0xd67f2270 bash
0xd600e000  00000940   00000876    1  000  run   0xd600e270*lvcreate
```

The **bt** command shows the back trace for the current process:

```
kdb> bt
   EBP        EIP          Function(args)
0xd600ff30 0x0000b800 <unknown>+0xb800 (0x1)
                         kernel <unknown> 0x0 0x0 0x0
         0xc011ce83 dequeue_signal+0x43 (0xd600e560, 0xd600ff30,
0xd600e560, 0xd600ffc4, 0xc01392ff)
                         kernel .text 0xc0100000 0xc011ce40 0xc011cef0
         0xc01069b9 do_signal+0x59 (0x11, 0xbfffec40, 0xbfffebb0, 0x8, 0x11)
                         kernel .text 0xc0100000 0xc0106960 0xc0106c00
         0xc0106d54 signal_return+0x14
                         kernel .text 0xc0100000 0xc0106d40 0xc0106d58
```

The actual Oops can be produced by letting the system continue by using the **go** command in kdb:

```
kdb> go
Oops: 0000
CPU:    0
EIP:    0010:[<0000b800>]    Not tainted
EFLAGS: 00010086
eax: ffffffff   ebx: d600e000   ecx: 0000b800   edx: c018fd25
esi: 00000008   edi: d600e000   ebp: d600ff30   esp: d600ff0c
ds: 0018   es: 0018   ss: 0018
Process lvcreate (pid: 940, stackpage=d600f000)
Stack: c011ce83 00000001 00000000 00000000 c01069b9 d600e560 d600ff30 d600e560
       d600ffc4 c01392ff 00000282 d604ab40 d600e000 00000011 c1672144 c011de97
       00000011 d600e568 00000000 d600ff70 d600ffa4 c011e252 00000011 d600ff90
Call Trace: [<c011ce83>] [<c01069b9>] [<c01392ff>] [<c011de97>] [<c011e252>]
   [<c0106d54>]

Code:  Bad EIP value.
-- --
```

kdb is correctly reporting the current EIP, but the kernel has taken a branch into an invalid address. The code that seems to have caused this problem is in the **dequeue_signal** routine. **objdump** can be used to view the code in the kernel.

The **objdump** command is as follows:

```
#  objdump -d —start-addr=0xc011ce40 —stop-address=0xc011ce90 vmlinux
```

The call instruction just before 0xc011ce83 is an indirect call via ecx:

```
dequeue_signal(sigset_t *mask, siginfo_t *info)
{
        int sig = 0;

#if DEBUG_SIG
printk("SIG dequeue (%s:%d): %d ", current->comm, current->pid,
        signal_pending(current));
#endif

        sig = next_signal(current, mask);
        if (sig) {
               if (current->notifier) {
                      if (sigismember(current->notifier_mask, sig)) {
                             if (!(current->notifier)(current-
>notifier_data)) {   <=== failing here
                                    current->sigpending = 0;
                                    return 0;
                            }
```

The problem is caused by the **current->notifier** being corrupt. The next step is to find out how this happened.

The only place that the notifier is set is in **block_all_signals()**, so one way to determine which routine is calling the **dequeue_signal** with bad data is to patch the kernel. The following kernel patch was used to find that routine. We used the back trace to find out why it is passing a bad pointer:

```
-- kernel/signal.c.orig   Tue Dec  9 10:15:50 2001
+++ kernel/signal.c        Tue Jan  8 01:28:12 2002
@@ -155,6 +155,8 @@ block_all_signals(int (*notifier)(void *
 {
     unsigned long flags;

+     if (notifier && (unsigned long)notifier < 0xc0000000)
+           BUG();
     spin_lock_irqsave(&current->sigmask_lock, flags);
     current->notifier_mask = mask;
     current->notifier_data = priv;
```

A quick scan through the kernel found only Direct Rendering Manager (DRM) code using **block_all_signals**. The **block_all_signals()/unblock_all_signals()** interface allows drivers to react nicely to signals that happen to a process that owns the driver data. It provides direct rendering lock handling.

If the bug is a bad notifier, the Oops is timing-dependent. The notifier routine is called only if a signal happens between **block_all_signals()** and **unblock_all_signals()**, and that does not always occur.

A timing problem was found in the DRM code. The correct notifier was set up for the **dequeue_signal** routine, and the Oops was fixed.

kdb Debug Session 2

This kdb session shows a JFS problem during the booting of the system. The boot processing passes the root volume to the file system to see if the file system claims the volume. The JFS file system wasn't checking for this condition and would Oops the system. The Oops causes kdb to be entered.

```
NET4: Unix domain sockets 1.0/SMP for Linux NET4.0.
fatfs: bogus cluster size
fatfs: bogus cluster size
ToDo: Parse mount options: "<NULL>"
Mount JFS Failure: 22
Unable to handle kernel NULL pointer dereference at virtual address 00000004
 printing eip:
```

```
c0157db7
*pde = 00000000

Entering kdb (current=0xc1228000, pid 1) Oops: Oops
due to oops @ 0xc0157db7
eax = 0x00000000 ebx = 0xc12349a0 ecx = 0xc12349a0 edx = 0x00000000
esi = 0xc034cb40 edi = 0xc7f63120 esp = 0xc1229ef8 eip = 0xc0157db7
ebp = 0xc034dd60 xss = 0x00000018 xcs = 0x00000010 eflags = 0x00010246
xds = 0x00000018 xes = 0x00000018 origeax = 0xffffffff &regs = 0xc1229ec4
```

The **bt** command shows a back trace for the PID 1 process, which is the process that is causing the Oops:

```
kdb> bt
    EBP        EIP          Function(args)
0xc034dd60 0xc0157db7 fat_clear_inode+0x17 (0xc12349a0)
                           kernel .text 0xc0100000 0xc0157da0 0xc0157dc4
          0xc0140deb clear_inode+0xb3 (0xc12349a0)
                           kernel .text 0xc0100000 0xc0140d38 0xc0140e1c
          0xc0141767 iput+0x147 (0xc12349a0, 0xc1234a44, 0x0, 0x0, 0xc12349a0)
                           kernel .text 0xc0100000 0xc0141620 0xc014177c
          0xc0162938 jfs_read_super+0x160 (0xc127e400, 0x0, 0x1)
                           kernel .text 0xc0100000 0xc01627d8 0xc0162954
          0xc01330a5 read_super+0x109 (0x306, 0xc7f63120, 0xc034dd60, 0x1, 0x0)
                           kernel .text 0xc0100000 0xc0132f9c 0xc0133114
          0xc0366fb4 mount_root+0x164
                           kernel .text.init 0xc0360000 0xc0366e50
0xc03671c0
          0xc0360992 do_basic_setup+0x3a
                           kernel .text.init 0xc0360000 0xc0360958
0xc03609a0
          0xc0105007 init+0x7
                           kernel .text 0xc0100000 0xc0105000 0xc0105150
          0xc0105457 kernel_thread+0x23
                           kernel .text 0xc0100000 0xc0105434 0xc0105464
```

You see the list of processes using the **ps** command. This system is early in the booting process, so only eight processes have started in the system so far:

```
kdb> ps
Task Addr  Pid       Parent    [*] cpu State Thread      Command
0xc1228000 00000001 00000000  0   000 run   0xc1228260*swapper
0xc1230000 00000002 00000001  0   000 stop  0xc1230260 keventd
0xc7f9e000 00000003 00000001  0   000 stop  0xc7f9e260 kswapd
0xc7f9c000 00000004 00000001  0   000 stop  0xc7f9c260 kreclaimd
0xc7f9a000 00000005 00000001  0   000 stop  0xc7f9a260 bdflush
0xc7f98000 00000006 00000001  0   000 stop  0xc7f98260 kupdated
0xc7f70000 00000007 00000001  0   000 stop  0xc7f70260 jfsIO
0xc7f6e000 00000008 00000001  0   000 stop  0xc7f6e260 jfsCommit
```

From the **bt** output you see that the **fat_clear_inode** routine, which is shown in Listing 13.4, is called by **clear_inode**. The call to **fat_clear_inode** is wrong. The correct call is shown in Listing 13.5, which is **jfs_clear_inode**. Each file system has a **clear_inode** routine.

What was causing this problem is that the table shown in Listing 13.6 for the JFS file system didn't have the **jfs_clear_inode** set in the table when the **clear_inode** call was done on the file system. So the solution was to have the table for the JFS operation set up **jfs_clear_inode**, and the Oops was fixed.

The FAT file system used this routine to clear the inode. It is called by the Virtual File System (VFS) **clear_inode** method.

Listing 13.4

fat_clear_inode

```
void fat_clear_inode(struct inode *inode)
{
        if (is_bad_inode(inode))
                return;
        lock_kernel();
        spin_lock(&fat_inode_lock);
        fat_cache_inval_inode(inode);
        list_del(&MSDOS_I(inode)->i_fat_hash);
        spin_unlock(&fat_inode_lock);
        unlock_kernel();
}
```

The JFS file system uses this routine to clear the inode. It is called by the VFS **clear_inode** method.

Listing 13.5

jfs_clear_inode

```
void jfs_clear_inode(struct inode *inode)
{
        struct jfs_inode_info *ji = JFS_IP(inode);

        jFYI(1, ("jfs_clear_inode called ip = 0x%p\n", inode));

        if (ji->active_ag != -1) {
                printk(KERN_ERR "jfs_clear_inode, active_ag =
%d\n",
                        ji->active_ag);
                printk(KERN_ERR "i_ino = %ld, i_mode = %o\n",
```

```
                     inode->i_ino, inode->i_mode);
        }

        ASSERT(list_empty(&ji->mp_list));
        ASSERT(list_empty(&ji->anon_inode_list));

        if (ji->atlhead) {
                jERROR(1, ("jfs_clear_inode: inode %p has
anonymous tlocks\n",
                           inode));
                jERROR(1, ("i_state = 0x%lx, cflag = 0x%lx\n",
                           inode->i_state, ji->cflag));
        }

        free_jfs_inode(inode);
```

Listing 13.6 shows the routines for the JFS Super Block operations. The **clear_inode** routine was the one that caused the Oops in this example. **clear_inode** is an optional method, called when VFS clears the inode.

Listing 13.6

Call Table for Super Block File System Operations

```
static struct super_operations jfs_super_operations = {
        .read_inode           = jfs_read_inode,
        .dirty_inode          = jfs_dirty_inode,
        .write_inode          = jfs_write_inode,
        .clear_inode          = jfs_clear_inode,
        .delete_inode         = jfs_delete_inode,
        .put_super            = jfs_put_super,
        .write_super_lockfs   = jfs_write_super_lockfs,
        .unlockfs             = jfs_unlockfs,
        .statfs               = jfs_statfs,
        .remount_fs           = jfs_remount,
};
```

kdb Debug Session 3

This example shows a rather complex debugging example in which a system is in a hung state waiting on disk I/O to be completed. With the help of kdb we were able to look at the IDE device driver subsystem. The debug session for this problem took several days. kdb helped reduce that time by providing a way to view this system in a very hung state. Several processes were created after the system was hung trying to log in through ssh and seeing why the system wasn't working as expected.

Three kdb commands can be used to start looking at hard kernel problems—
dmesg, **ps**, and **bta**. In the **dmesg** output you should look for any unusual messages
that the kernel has written. The **ps** command shows you all the processes on the system. The **bta** command provides a back trace of where the process is waiting on the
system. For this example, since the system we are looking at is hanging, the back
traces were useful information to determine which processes are hanging.

List All Processes (ps)

The serial connection to this kdb session was done using an AIX system. The **cu**
command was used to connect with the Linux system that is showing the hang.

This system has over 200 processes. The process list from **ps** has been shortened
for this example:

```
Script command is started on Fri Sep  3 01:52:59 GMT 2004.
# cu -ml tty0
Connected

Entering kdb (current=0xc03e8000, pid 0) on processor 0 due to Keyboard Entry
[0]kdb> ps
Task Addr   Pid        Parent      [*] cpu  State Thread       Command
0xc1c0e000  00000001   00000000    0   000  stop  0xc1c0e370   init
0xf7500000  00000002   00000001    0   000  stop  0xf7500370   migration_CPU0
0xf7906000  00000003   00000001    0   000  stop  0xf7906370   keventd
0xf7904000  00000004   00000001    0   000  stop  0xf7904370   ksoftirqd_CPU0
0xf790e000  00000005   00000001    0   000  stop  0xf790e370   kswapd
0xf790c000  00000006   00000001    0   000  stop  0xf790c370   bdflush
0xf790a000  00000007   00000001    0   000  stop  0xf790a370   kupdated
0xf7908000  00000008   00000001    0   000  stop  0xf7908370   kinoded
0xc1c18000  00000011   00000001    0   000  stop  0xc1c18370   mdrecoveryd
0xc1c10000  00000185   00000001    0   000  stop  0xc1c10370   srcmstr
0xc2b50000  00000465   00000001    0   000  stop  0xc2b50370   httpd
0xc2970000  00000752   00000001    0   000  stop  0xc2970370   syslogd
0xc2962000  00000755   00000001    0   000  stop  0xc2962370   klogd
0xc2956000  00000790   00000001    0   000  stop  0xc2956370   khubd
0xc28f6000  00000903   00000001    0   000  stop  0xc28f6370   xinetd
0xc28d6000  00000916   00000001    0   000  stop  0xc28d6370   sshd
0xc2fa0000  00001196   00000001    0   000  stop  0xc2fa0370   xfs
0xc32d4000  00001221   00000001    0   000  stop  0xc32d4370   atd
0xc32cc000  00001236   00000001    0   000  stop  0xc32cc370   nscd
0xc2cea000  00001241   00001236    0   000  stop  0xc2cea370   nscd
0xc2ce0000  00001242   00001241    0   000  stop  0xc2ce0370   nscd
0xc2836000  00001243   00001241    0   000  stop  0xc2836370   nscd
0xc2ce4000  00001244   00001241    0   000  stop  0xc2ce4370   nscd
0xc32c8000  00001245   00001241    0   000  stop  0xc32c8370   nscd
0xc2cd8000  00001246   00001241    0   000  stop  0xc2cd8370   nscd
0xc328e000  00001292   00000001    0   000  stop  0xc328e370   cron
```

```
0xc236a000 00001296 00000001  0  000   stop   0xc236a370 mingetty
0xc2358000 00001297 00000001  0  000   stop   0xc2358370 agetty
0xc329a000 00001298 00000001  0  000   stop   0xc329a370 initCIMOM
0xc3294000 00001299 00000001  0  000   stop   0xc3294370 startServer
0xc328a000 00001300 00000001  0  000   stop   0xc328a370 CommandControll
0xc3286000 00001301 00000001  0  000   stop   0xc3286370 startCSPEvent
0xc3280000 00001303 00000001  0  000   stop   0xc3280370 startFNMTrace
0xc327c000 00001304 00000001  0  000   stop   0xc327c370 startHDWR_SVR
0xc3276000 00001305 00000001  0  000   stop   0xc3276370 su
0xc3272000 00001306 00000001  0  000   stop   0xc3272370 su
0xc326e000 00001307 00000001  0  000   stop   0xc326e370 su
0xc3264000 00001309 00000001  0  000   stop   0xc3264370 java
0xc3258000 00001310 00000001  0  000   stop   0xc3258370 runccfw
0xc324a000 00001311 00001304  0  000   stop   0xc324a370 hdwr_svr
0xc3224000 00001319 00001303  0  000   stop   0xc3224370 tracelogd
0xc3234000 00001321 00001299  0  000   stop   0xc3234370 java
0xc3238000 00001322 00001321  0  000   stop   0xc3238370 java
0xc321a000 00001323 00001322  0  000   stop   0xc321a370 java
```

Back Trace for All Processes (bta)

The **bta** command is used to display a back trace for each process on the system. The list of back traces has been shortened for this example. Thirty-two processes are stuck waiting for I/O. The list of PIDs that are hanging is shown next. Looking at each back trace helped determine which processes were hanging and what they were waiting on. This system had over 200 processes, so it was time-consuming to determine if a process was hanging or in a normal sleep condition. An example of a process in a normal sleep condition is the process with PID 2. It is shown next.

Back Trace for PID 2

PID 2 has done a **context_switch**. This is a normal state where a process would be waiting in the kernel.

```
Stack traceback for pid 2
ESP         EIP          Function (args)
0xf7501f50 0xc0121afe context_switch+0xae (0xc041d880, 0xf7500000,
                                           0xc1c0e000, 0xc041d880,
                                           0xf7500000)
                        kernel .text 0xc0100000 0xc0121a50 0xc0121c6d
0xf7501f88 0xc011fcd7 schedule+0x147 (0xf7500346, 0xc030f8d4, 0x0,
                                      0xc1c0ff30, 0xc041e224)
                        kernel .text 0xc0100000 0xc011fb90 0xc011fdf0
0xf7501fac 0xc0121885 migration_thread+0x355
                        kernel .text 0xc0100000 0xc0121530 0xc0121890
0xf7501ff4 0xc010758e arch_kernel_thread+0x2e
                        kernel .text 0xc0100000 0xc0107560 0xc01075a0
Enter <q> to end, <cr> to continue:
```

A List of "Stuck" PIDs on the Hung Machine

In this system, 32 processes are waiting on I/O. The following list shows the PID, the process name, and the condition or routine that the process is waiting on:

```
pid 6        bdflush         __get_request_wait
pid 7        kupdated        ___wait_on_page
pid 752      syslogd         __wait_on_buffer
pid 1297     agetty          ___wait_on_page
pid 1311     hdwr_svr        __down
pid 4796     java            __wait_on_buffer
pid 4802     java            rwsem_down_failed
pid 4861     java            rwsem_down_failed
pid 10328    java            __wait_on_buffer
pid 16008    rmcd            __down
pid 16010    rmcd            __down
pid 16041    IBM.DMSRMd      do_no_page
pid 16047    IBM.LparCmdRMd  do_no_page
pid 16086    IBM.AuditRMd    do_no_page
pid 3078     IBM.ServiceRMd  __get_request_wait
pid 12330    java            ___wait_on_page
pid 12428    cat             ___wait_on_page
pid 12564    mandb           __lock_page
pid 16309    grep            ___wait_on_page
pid 18451    find            __lock_page
pid 26888    java            __down
pid 27503    login.krb5      __down
pid 27525    telnetd         __down
pid 27526    login.krb5      __down
pid 27527    telnetd         __down
pid 27528    login.krb5      __down
pid 27550    sshd            __wait_on_buffer
pid 27571    telnetd         __down
pid 27572    login.krb5      __down
pid 27597    login.krb5      __down
pid 27599    login.krb5      __down
pid 27702    sshd            __lock_page
```

We'll show four PIDs that are stuck waiting for I/O—6, 7, 752, and 1311:

```
[0]kdb> bta

Stack traceback for pid 6
ESP         EIP         Function (args)
0xf790ddc8 0xc0121afe context_switch+0xae (0xc041d880, 0xf790c000, 0xca02e000,
0xc041d880, 0xf790c000)
                                kernel .text 0xc0100000 0xc0121a50 0xc0121c6d
0xf790de00 0xc011fcd7 schedule+0x147 (0xc04ac904, 0x0, 0x0, 0xf790c000, 0x0)
                                kernel .text 0xc0100000 0xc011fb90 0xc011fdf0
0xf790de24 0xc01fd89d __get_request_wait+0xfd (0xc04ac904, 0x1, 0xf7596900,
0xc2422b40, 0x1)
                                kernel .text 0xc0100000 0xc01fd7a0 0xc01fd8a0
```

```
0xf790de80 0xc01fdd53 __make_request+0x283 (0xc04ac904, 0x1, 0xc2422b40, 0x0,
0x0)
                       kernel .text 0xc0100000 0xc01fdad0 0xc01fe210
0xf790dedc 0xc01fe309 generic_make_request+0xf9 (0x1, 0xc2422b40)
                       kernel .text 0xc0100000 0xc01fe210 0xc01fe360
0xf790df08 0xc01fe3b7 submit_bh+0x57 (0x1, 0xc2422b40)
                       kernel .text 0xc0100000 0xc01fe360 0xc01fe420
0xf790df24 0xc015285c write_locked_buffers+0x2c (0xf790df44, 0x20, 0x20,
0xf75cbae0, 0xf75cb9e0)
                       kernel .text 0xc0100000 0xc0152830 0xc0152870
0xf790df38 0xc0152979 write_some_buffers+0x109 (0x0, 0x0, 0x18, 0x10f00,
0xc1c0ff9c)
                       kernel .text 0xc0100000 0xc0152870 0xc01529c0
0xf790dfd8 0xc0156959 bdflush+0xc9
                       kernel .text 0xc0100000 0xc0156890 0xc0156980
0xf790dff4 0xc010758e arch_kernel_thread+0x2e
                       kernel .text 0xc0100000 0xc0107560 0xc01075a0


Stack traceback for pid 7
ESP        EIP        Function (args)
0xf790bee8 0xc0121afe context_switch+0xae (0xc041d880, 0xf790a000, 0xc03e8000,
0xc041d880, 0xf790a000)
                       kernel .text 0xc0100000 0xc0121a50 0xc0121c6d
0xf790bf20 0xc011fcd7 schedule+0x147 (0xc11d8100, 0x0, 0xf790a000, 0xc1c002cc,
0xc1c002cc)
                       kernel .text 0xc0100000 0xc011fb90 0xc011fdf0
0xf790bf44 0xc013c7d9 __wait_on_page+0x79 (0xc11d8100, 0x1, 0xc2f569a0,
0xc2f569a8)
                       kernel .text 0xc0100000 0xc013c760 0xc013c800
0xf790bf7c 0xc013c3d7 filemap_fdatawait+0x77 (0xc2f56a54, 0x0)
                       kernel .text 0xc0100000 0xc013c360 0xc013c400
0xf790bf94 0xc016bf9e __sync_one+0x9e (0xc2f569a0, 0x0)
                       kernel .text 0xc0100000 0xc016bf00 0xc016c046
0xf790bfac 0xc016a5c3 sync_unlocked_inodes+0x63 (0x0, 0xf790a664)
                       kernel .text 0xc0100000 0xc016a560 0xc016a600
0xf790bfc0 0xc01566e8 sync_old_buffers+0x28 (0xc03d78c0, 0xc0105000, 0x8e000,
0x0, 0x10f00)
                       kernel .text 0xc0100000 0xc01566c0 0xc0156770
0xf790bfd0 0xc0156a7d kupdate+0xfd
                       kernel .text 0xc0100000 0xc0156980 0xc0156ac0
0xf790bff4 0xc010758e arch_kernel_thread+0x2e
                       kernel .text 0xc0100000 0xc0107560 0xc01075a0
Stack traceback for pid 752
ESP        EIP        Function (args)
0xc2971cf8 0xc0121afe context_switch+0xae (0xc041d880, 0xc2970000, 0xc03e8000,
0xc041d880, 0xc2970000)
                       kernel .text 0xc0100000 0xc0121a50 0xc0121c6d
0xc2971d30 0xc011fcd7 schedule+0x147 (0x0, 0x0, 0xc2970000, 0xf6505670,
0xf6505670)
                       kernel .text 0xc0100000 0xc011fb90 0xc011fdf0
0xc2971d54 0xc01527ce __wait_on_buffer+0x6e
```

```
                            kernel .text 0xc0100000 0xc0152760 0xc0152800
0xc2971d8c 0xc0153c8c bread+0x7c (0x307, 0x80255, 0x1000)
                            kernel .text 0xc0100000 0xc0153c10 0xc0153ca0
0xc2971da0 0xc01a114f ext2_get_branch+0x6f (0xc296cd40, 0x2, 0xc2971e10,
0xc2971de0, 0xc2971ddc)
                            kernel .text 0xc0100000 0xc01a10e0 0xc01a11c0
0xc2971dc0 0xc01a144c ext2_get_block+0x8c (0xc23344e0, 0xc1978f50, 0xe2b, 0xe3a,
0xc013877b)
                            kernel .text 0xc0100000 0xc01a13c0 0xc01a17c0
0xc2971eac 0xc013f5a9 do_generic_file_write+0x3f9
                            kernel .text 0xc0100000 0xc013f1b0 0xc013f990
0xc2971f04 0xc013fa2b generic_file_write+0x9b
                            kernel .text 0xc0100000 0xc013f990 0xc013fa60
Enter <q> to end, <cr> to continue:

Stack traceback for pid 1311
ESP        EIP         Function (args)
0xc324bc9c 0xc0121afe context_switch+0xae (0xc041d880, 0xc324a000, 0xf7904000,
0xc041d880, 0xf75f2448)
                            kernel .text 0xc0100000 0xc0121a50 0xc0121c6d
0xc324bcd4 0xc011fcd7 schedule+0x147 (0x1, 0xc324a000, 0xd6539dc8, 0xf75f2454,
0x0)
                            kernel .text 0xc0100000 0xc011fb90 0xc011fdf0
0xc324bcf8 0xc0107f42 __down+0x82
                            kernel .text 0xc0100000 0xc0107ec0 0xc0107f90
0xc324bd2c 0xc01080ec __down_failed+0x8 (0x0, 0xc02a5a82)
                            kernel .text 0xc0100000 0xc01080e4 0xc01080f0
0xc324bd3c 0xc019ecd4 ext2_bg_num_gdb+0x64 (0xc2b84c00, 0xc29fec00, 0xc29fec00,
0xebacf260, 0xc29fec00)
                            kernel .text 0xc0100000 0xc019ec70 0xc019ed30
0xc324bd50 0xc2b33bb1 [epca]receive_data+0x1af (0xc3140ba0, 0xc164a390, 0x0,
0x2a, 0x0)
                            epca .text 0xc2b30060 0xc2b33a02 0xc2b33c6a
0xc324bf1c 0xc013f5a9 do_generic_file_write+0x3f9
                            kernel .text 0xc0100000 0xc013f1b0 0xc013f990
0xc324bf74 0xc013fa2b generic_file_write+0x9b
                            kernel .text 0xc0100000 0xc013f990 0xc013fa60
0xc324bf98 0xc01510d3 sys_write+0xa3 (0x3, 0x40014000, 0x3c, 0x3c, 0x40014000)
                            kernel .text 0xc0100000 0xc0151030 0xc0151190
0xc324bfc4 0xc01095af system_call+0x33
                            kernel .text 0xc0100000 0xc010957c 0xc01095b4
[0]more>
```

Looking at the machine in its current state, it appears that the IDE interface has an I/O in flight and that a timer is running against it. Since the processing on an I/O timeout is to read a register and just restart the timer, it looks like we are endlessly looping in this code path. Using the kdb we were able to verify this by exiting kdb and checking the **ide_hwgroup_t** structure before and after. The pointer to the current request had not changed, the timer had been modified to some point in the future, and the **ide_hwgroup** "busy" bit was still set.

ide_hwgroup_t is used to attach requests for **IDE_TASK_CMDS**. It is located in the /usr/src/linux/include/linux/ide.h file. The structure is shown in Listing 13.7.

Listing 13.7

ide_hwgroup_t Structure

```
typedef struct hwgroup_s {
    ide_handler_t     *handler;      /* irq handler, if active */
    volatile int       busy;         /* BOOL: protects all fields
below */
    int                sleeping;     /* BOOL: wake us up on timer
expiry */
    ide_drive_t       *drive;        /* current drive */
    ide_hwif_t        *hwif;         /* ptr to current hwif in
linked list */
    struct request    *rq;           /* current request */
    struct timer_list timer;         /* failsafe timer */
    struct request    wrq;           /* local copy of current
write rq */
    unsigned long      poll_timeout; /* timeout value during long
polls */
    ide_expiry_t      *expiry;       /* queried upon timeouts */
} ide_hwgroup_t;

/* structure attached to the request for IDE_TASK_CMDS */
```

After some analysis, an area where this hang could be happening is the IDE device driver. One of the places to look is the **ide_hwgroup_t** structure, which is shown in Listing 13.7. The address of the **ide_hwgroup_t** structure is 0xf7520e60. You can use the **md** command to display this structure. The current request from **ide_hwgroup_t** has the value of f7596a80, and it appears in bold. The timer is highlighted and has the value of 00f877e7:

```
[0]kdb> md f7520e60
0xf7520e60 c021d7f0 00000001 00000000 c04ac904   ..........?
0xf7520e70 c04ac8c0 f7596a80 c0454dd0 c0454dd0   ?J?jY??ME?
0xf7520e80 00f877e7 f7520e60 c020f6e0 c0454400   ..`.R??DE?
0xf7520e90 00000000 f7595c20 c04ac924 00000000   .... \Y??...
0xf7520ea0 ffffffff 00000000 00000063 00000004   ?....c.......
0xf7520eb0 00000000 00000000 00000000 00000000   .............
0xf7520ec0 00000000 00000000 00000000 00000000   .............
0xf7520ed0 00000000 00000000 f7595da0 c04aca68   ........ ]Y??
[0]kdb>
0xf7520ee0 00000000 00000000 00000000 00000000   .............
0xf7520ef0 00000000 c021e0d0 00000000 00000000   ....p!?.......
```

```
0xf7520f00 00000000 00000000 00000000 00000000    ...............
0xf7520f10 00000000 00000000 00000000 00000000    ...............
0xf7520f20 00000000 00000000 00000000 00000000    ...............
0xf7520f30 00000000 00000000 00000000 00000000    ...............
0xf7520f40 00000000 00000000 00000000 00000000    ...............
0xf7520f50 00000000 00000000 00000000 00000000    ...............
```

```
[0]kdb> go
```

The system is allowed to continue, and after 5 seconds, we break back into kdb. Looking at **ide_hwgroup_t** again, we see that the request remains the same, 0xf7596a80, and that the timer is highlighted. The value getting incremented is 00f87bcf – 00f877e7 = 3e8.

```
[0]kdb> md f7520e60
0xf7520e60 c021d7f0 00000001 00000000 c04ac904    ..........?
0xf7520e70 c04ac8c0 f7596a80 c0454df0 d31cbf58    ?J?jY???..
0xf7520e80 00f87bcf f7520e60 c020f6e0 c0454400    .???DE?
0xf7520e90 00000000 f7595c20 c04ac924 00000000    .... \Y??...
0xf7520ea0 ffffffff 00000000 00000063 00000004    ?....c.......
0xf7520eb0 00000000 00000000 00000000 00000000    ...............
0xf7520ec0 00000000 00000000 00000000 00000000    ...............
0xf7520ed0 00000000 00000000 f7595da0 c04aca68    ........ ]Y??
[0]kdb>
0xf7520ee0 00000000 00000000 00000000 00000000    ...............
0xf7520ef0 00000000 c021e0d0 00000000 00000000    ....p!?.......
0xf7520f00 00000000 00000000 00000000 00000000    ...............
0xf7520f10 00000000 00000000 00000000 00000000    ...............
0xf7520f20 00000000 00000000 00000000 00000000    ...............
0xf7520f30 00000000 00000000 00000000 00000000    ...............
0xf7520f40 00000000 00000000 00000000 00000000    ...............
0xf7520f50 00000000 00000000 00000000 00000000    ...............
```

```
[0]kdb> go
```

The system is allowed to continue, and after 45 seconds, we break back into kdb. Looking at **ide_hwgroup_t**, which is at address 0xf7520e60, you see that the request remains the same: 0xf7596a80. This request is in an infinite loop, and this is what is causing the system to hang.

```
[0]kdb> md f7520e60
0xf7520e60 c021d7f0 00000001 00000000 c04ac904    .........?
0xf7520e70 c04ac8c0 f7596a80 c03e3808 d31cbf58    ?J?jY???..
0xf7520e80 010e74cf f7520e60 c020f6e0 c0454400    ...`.R??DE?
0xf7520e90 00000000 f7595c20 c04ac924 00000000    .... \Y??...
0xf7520ea0 ffffffff 00000000 00000063 00000004    ?....c.......
0xf7520eb0 00000000 00000000 00000000 00000000    ...............
0xf7520ec0 00000000 00000000 00000000 00000000    ...............
0xf7520ed0 00000000 00000000 f7595da0 c04aca68    ........ ]Y??
```

```
[0]kdb>
0xf7520ee0 00000000 00000000 00000000 00000000          ..............
0xf7520ef0 00000000 c021e0d0 00000000 00000000          ....p!?.......
0xf7520f00 00000000 00000000 00000000 00000000          ..............
0xf7520f10 00000000 00000000 00000000 00000000          ..............
0xf7520f20 00000000 00000000 00000000 00000000          ..............
0xf7520f30 00000000 00000000 00000000 00000000          ..............
0xf7520f40 00000000 00000000 00000000 00000000          ..............
0xf7520f50 00000000 00000000 00000000 00000000          ..............
```

Listing 13.8 is part of the **ide_timer_expiry** routine located in /usr/src/linux/drivers/ide/ide.c file. This is where this system is looping forever.

Listing 13.8

ide_timer_expiry

```
if ((expiry = hwgroup->expiry) != NULL) {
                /* continue */
                if ((wait = expiry(drive)) != 0) {
                        /* reset timer */
                        hwgroup->timer.expires   = jiffies +
wait;
                        add_timer(&hwgroup->timer);

spin_unlock_irqrestore(&io_request_lock, flags);
                        return;
                }
        }
```

Now for the root of the problem. The possible causes of an I/O timeout could be a hardware problem, or perhaps the Serviceworks chipset driver has a bug in it.

This problem turned out to be a BIOS problem. When the customer updated its BIOS from version 1.06 to 1.07, the problem was fixed.

Summary

kgdb and kdb are powerful tools for performing kernel debugging. kgdb requires two machines to debug the kernel. It also allows source-level-type debugging, similar to debugging an application with gdb. kdb requires only one machine, but it can't do source-code-level debugging.

Credits

A big thank-you goes out to Keith Owens and other developers for the development and support of kdb. A big thank-you goes out to Amit S. Kale and the other developers for the development and support of kgdb.

Web Resources for kgdb and kdb

URL	Description
http://kgdb.sourceforge.net/	kgdb web site
http://www.gnu.org/doc/book7.html	Debugging with GDB: The GNU Source-Level Debugger
http://oss.sgi.com/projects/kdb/	SGI's kdb (built-in kernel debugger)
http://www.kernel.org	Kernel source tree

## Chapter 14

Crash Dump

In this chapter

- Kernel Configuration   page 374
- Patching and Building the Kernel   page 376
- General Crash Dump Steps   page 379
- LKCD Commands   page 385
- System Panic and Crash Dump Taken   page 386
- Netdump: The Network Crash Dump Facility from Both the Client and Server   page 391
- diskdump: a Crash Dump Facility   page 392
- Viewing an mcore Crash Dump   page 393
- Summary   page 410
- Credits   page 411
- Web Resources for Crash Dump   page 411

Linux can support a crash dump in several ways—through Linux Kernel Crash Dump (LKCD), through Netdump and Diskdump, and through mcore.

SUSE Linux Enterprise Server includes LKCD functionality to provide crash dump support. Red Hat Enterprise Linux includes Netdump and Diskdump functionality to provide crash dump support.

A crash dump is designed to meet the needs of end users, support personnel, and system administrators who need a reliable method of detecting, saving, and examining system problems. There are many benefits to having a bug report and dump of the problem, since the dump provides a significant amount of information about the system's state at the time of the problem.

The primary objectives of a crash dump are to incorporate kernel crash dump functionality into the Linux kernel and to provide Linux crash analysis tools that can help determine the cause of a system crash.

With Linux, the traditional method of debugging a system crash has been to analyze the details of the Oops message sent to the system console at the time of the crash. The Oops message, which contains details of the system failure, such as the contents of the CPU registers, can then be passed to the ksymoops utility. (Running ksymoops is required only on the 2.4.x kernel and below. With the 2.6.x kernel and above, the kernel does this functionality.) ksymoops converts the code instructions and stack values to kernel symbols, which produces a back trace. In many cases, this is enough information for the developer of the failing line of code to determine a possible cause of why the code has failed. For more complete descriptions of Oops message analysis and the ksymoops utility, see Chapter 7, "System Error Messages."

As the kernel becomes increasingly complex, enabling it to run on larger enterprise-class systems, from mainframes to supercomputers, it becomes increasingly difficult to determine a crash's cause solely by analyzing an Oops message. (The Oops message will and can be used to indicate what has caused the crash.) In enterprise computing, having a facility to analyze the events leading up to a crash is a requirement.

Another driving factor for having crash dump is the need for systems availability. Therefore, dumping lets customers maximize their system uptime and not spend time on hands-on problem diagnosis.

Being able to generate system crash dumps is a standard part of just about every flavor of UNIX available today. With LKCD or Netdump and Diskdump, Linux also has this now.

lcrash is the system crash analysis tool for analyzing Linux system crash dumps for dumps created with LKCD. crash is the system crash analysis tool for Netdump, Diskdump, and mcore. Both lcrash and crash contain a significant number of features for displaying information about the events leading up to a system crash in an easy-to-read manner. lcrash and crash have two primary modes of operation: crash dump report generation and crash dump interactive analysis.

The crash dump report contains selected pieces of information from the kernel that are considered useful to determine what caused the crash. The report includes the following information:

- General system information

- Type of crash

- Dump of the system buffer, which contains the latest messages printed via the kernel's **printk** function

- CPU summary

- Kernel stack trace leading up to the system PANIC

- Disassembly of instructions before and after the instructions that caused the crash

The crash dump interactive analysis is a set of commands invoked via the command line that provides access to a wide range of kernel internal data. The following is a sample of some of the commands provided:

- **stat** displays pertinent system information and the contents of the system buffer, which contains the latest messages printed via the kernel's **printk** function.

- **vtop** displays virtual-to-physical address mappings for both kernel and application virtual addresses.

- **task** displays relevant information for selected tasks or all tasks running at the time of the crash.

- **trace** displays a kernel stack back trace for selected tasks or for all tasks running on the system.

- **dis** disassembles a routine and displays one or more machine instructions.

LKCD creates files in the /var/log/dump directory. To save crash dumps to a different location, change the **DUMPDIR** value in the /etc/sysconfig/dump file. If the default location /var/log/dump is used to save dumps, LKCD can easily exceed multiple gigabytes in this directory, so be sure that space is available in this directory.

Kernel Configuration

Crash dump support is available for the 2.4.x and 2.6.x versions of the kernel. The LKCD kernel functionality hasn't been accepted into the mainline kernel provided at www.kernel.org. But most if not all Linux distributions provide LKCD functionality in their kernel. One way to see if LKCD kernel support is available in the kernel that your distribution ships is to view the kernel configuration. If the kernel that is running on your system doesn't have LKCD support, several kernel patches are available from the LKCD web site that can be used to enable this function in your kernel.

Patching the LKCD kernel support is easy. You'll see how to use the 2.6.8.1 kernel.

One way to check the kernel config is to use the **make xconfig** command in the directory of the kernel source tree, usually /usr/src/linux.

Crash Dump Kernel Options

The crash dump kernel is enabled on the Kernel hacking support menu, as shown in Figure 14.1. If crash dump isn't enabled, enable it and rebuild the kernel. Seven options are available for crash dump in the 6.0.0 version of LKCD. Other versions of LKCD might have fewer configuration options. The added features for version 6.0.0 from 4.x versions are **CRASH_DUMP_NETDEV**, **CRASH_DUMP_ MEMDEV**, and **CRASH_DUMP_SOFTBOOT**. If one of these features looks interesting in your environment, that could be a reason to move up to version 6.0.0.

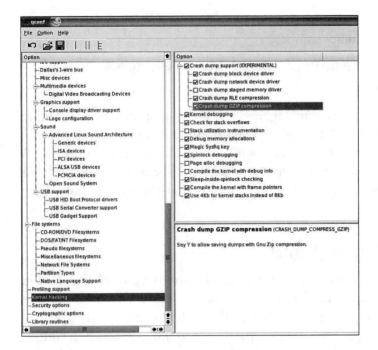

FIGURE 14.1
The crash dump kernel menu.

The first option is **CRASH_DUMP**; it must be enabled to have any part of kernel crash dump support.

Once **CRASH_DUMP** is enabled, the following options are available:

- **CRASH_DUMP_BLOCKDEV** lets you save crash dumps directly to a disk device.

- **CRASH_DUMP_NETDEV** lets you save crash dumps over a network device.

- **CRASH_DUMP_MEMDEV** lets you save crash dumps intermediately in spare memory pages that will be written to disk later.

- **CRASH_DUMP_SOFTBOOT** lets a crash dump be preserved in memory pages across a soft reboot and written out to disk thereafter.

- **CRASH_DUMP_COMPRESS_RLE** lets you save dumps with Run Length Encoding compression.

- **CRASH_DUMP_COMPRESS_GZIP** lets you save dumps with GNU Zip compression.

The crash dump kernel menu in Figure 14.1 shows that all the crash dump options that are turned on will be built directly into the kernel. A check mark in the configure menu means that the option will be built directly into the kernel. A period in the configure menu means that the option will be built as a module for the kernel. No mark in the configure menu means that the option hasn't been turned on.

Patching and Building the Kernel

If your kernel doesn't have the LKCD kernel patch applied, you can download it. It is a good practice to match the LKCD kernel patch version to the LKCD user utilities version. For example, version 6.0.0 of the LKCD kernel patch is named lkcd-6.0.0_2.6.8.1.patch.gz. The utilities patch for 6.0.0 is named lkcdutils-6.0.0.tar.gz. Follow these steps to apply the LKCD kernel patch to a 2.6.8.1 level of the kernel:

1. Change to the directory where the kernel source is (usually the /usr/src/linux directory).

2. Use the **patch** command to apply the kernel change, as shown in Figure 14.2. The **—dry-run** option shows if the patch applies, but it doesn't really apply the patch. If the patch applies cleanly with no rejects, remove the **—dry-run** option and apply the patch.

There are no rejects when applying the patch, so the **—dry-run** option can be removed, and the patch is applied to the kernel.

FIGURE 14.2
The LKCD patch being applied to the kernel.

Building the Kernel

The following steps show you how to build the kernel (for i386):

1. Issue the **make xconfig** command.

2. Under "General Setup," do the following:
    a. Select "Kernel hacking."
    b. Select "Crash dump support."
    c. Select options for the crash dump (see the "Crash Dump Kernel Options" section for descriptions of the additional options).
    d. Configure other kernel settings as needed.

3. Save and exit.

4. Issue the **make clean** command.

5. Issue the **make bzImage** command.

6. If modules need to be built, do the following:
   a. Issue the **make modules** command.
   b. Issue the **make modules_install** command.

7. Issue the **cp arch/i386/boot/bzImage /boot/bzImage-2.6.8.1-lkcd** command.

8. Issue the **cp System.map /boot/System.map-2.6.8.1-lkcd** command.

   kerntypes is a file containing kernel type information that lcrash needs to properly access kernel data in the system memory image. The default kerntypes is /boot/Kerntypes, which provides access to kernel type information when analyzing a live system.

9. Issue the **cp init/kerntypes.o /boot/Kerntypes-2.6.8.1-lkcd** command.

10. Issue the **rm /boot/System.map && ln -s /boot/System. map-2.6.8.1-lkcd System.map** command.

11. Issue the **rm /boot/Kerntypes && ln -s /boot/Kerntypes- 2.6.8.1-lkcd Kerntypes** command.

12. If the system is using lilo as the boot loader, modify your configuration to boot from /boot/bzImage-2.6.8.1-lkcd.

    For example, if you're using lilo, do the following:
    a. Modify /etc/lilo.conf.
    b. Run lilo to read the modified lilo.conf.

13. If the system is using grub as the boot loader, modify your configuration to boot from /boot/bzImage-2.6.8.1-lkcd.

    For example, if you're using grub, modify /boot/grub/menu.lst.

14. Reboot.

The next step is to check the level of the kernel and make sure that the LKCD supported kernel is the one that is running. The **uname** command does not directly show that LKCD support is built into the kernel, but the following example shows that we are running level 2.6.8.1 of the kernel. The **uname -a** command displays the kernel's level. The output should be similar to the following:

```
Linux sfb1 2.6.8.1 #1 Wed Oct 27 02:08:30 UTC 2004 i686 i686 i386 GNU/Linux
```

General Crash Dump Steps

The following are the general crash dump steps:

1. Determine what level of dump is needed:

    8—All memory on the system
    4—Only used memory
    2—Kernel memory
    1—Dump header
    0—Do nothing

2. Create a partition on which the dump will be created. You'll use the /dev/hda3 partition for the dump. The amount of memory that needs to be dumped determines the partition size. For example, if the system has 1 GB and the dump level is 8, a partition of 1 GB is needed.

3. Create a symlink:

    ```
    ln -s /device/partition number
    ```

    Here's an example:

    ```
    ln -s /dev/hda3 /dev/vmdump
    ```

4. Edit /etc/sysconfig/dump and set the **DUMP_LEVEL** to 8.

5. Run **/sbin/lkcd config**.

> NOTE **/sbin/lkcd config** needs to be run every time the system is rebooted. Sample patches in the LKCD package add **lkcd config** and **lkcd save** to various sysinit startup scripts.

6. Run dmesg to see that lkcd is configured. There should be six messages about lkcd. Output from dmesg should be similar to the following:

    ```
    dump: Registering dump compression type 0x0
    dump: mbank[0]: type:1, phys_addr: 0 ... fe73fff
    dump: Crash dump driver initialized
    dump: dump_compress = 0
    dump: dump_blk_shift:12, PAGE_SHIFT:12
    dump:dump device 0x343 opened: Ready to take a save
    or core dump
    ```

7. Enable sys-request:

```
echo "1" > /proc/sys/kernel/sysrq.
```

8. Trigger the dump:

```
echo "c" > /proc/sysrq-trigger
```

or

Press Alt-SysRq-C.

The dump starts. Depending on whether **DUMP_PANIC** is set, the system either reboots or is placed back into your shell.

9. To save the dump, run **/sbin/lkcd save**.

This copies the dump from the partition to /var/log/dump/*n* starting at *n* = 0.

10. You can display the dump using the lcrash program.

In step 4, the variables are configured for the Linux crash dump. Listing 14.1 is a sample dump file where the dump variables are set. Eight variables can be set. They are set on lines 23, 35, 45, 62, 81, 92, 103, and 114. The dump variables are described on the line or lines that precede them.

The dump file shown in Listing 14.1 is from version 4.1_1 of lkcdutils. This is the version of lkcdutils that ships with SuSE 9.0.

Listing 14.1

A Sample Dump File Located at /etc/sysconfig/dump

```
1  ## Path:          System/Kernel/LKCD
2  ## Description:  Linux Kernel Crash Dump (LKCD) options
3  ## Type:          integer(0:1)
4  ## Default:       1
5  #
6  # Copyright 1999 Silicon Graphics, Inc. All rights reserved.
7  #
8  # This file contains the configuration variables for Linux
kernel crash
9  # dumps.  The file should reside in /etc/sysconfig/dump,
permissions
10 # set to 0755.  There are currently six variables defined
in this file:
11 #
12 #      DUMP_ACTIVE
13 #      DUMPDEV
14 #      DUMPDIR
15 #      DUMP_SAVE
16 #      DUMP_LEVEL
```

```
17 #       DUMP_COMPRESS_PAGES
18 #
19 # Each one is documented below.
20 # ───────────────────────────────────-
21 # DUMP_ACTIVE indicates whether the dump process is active
or not. If
22 # this variable is 0, the dump kernel process will not be
activated.
23 DUMP_ACTIVE="1"
24
25 ## Type:        string
26 ## Default:     /dev/vmdump
27 #
28 # DUMPDEV represents the name of the dump device.  It is
typically
29 # the primary swap partition on the local system, although
any disk
30 # device can be used.  Please be EXTRA careful when
defining this
31 # value, as one false slip can cause all kinds of problems.
32 #
33 # Currently, a link is created from /dev/vmdump to the
right device;
34 # rename this to the exact device to dump to if that's what
you want.
35 DUMPDEV="/dev/vmdump"
36
37 ## Type:        string
38 ## Default:     /var/log/dump
39 #
40 # DUMPDIR is the location where crash dumps are saved.  In
that
41 # directory, a file called 'bounds' will be created, which
is
42 # the current index of the last crash dump saved.  The
'bounds'
43 # file will be updated with an incremented once a new crash
dump or
44 # crash report is saved.
45 DUMPDIR="/var/log/dump"
46
47 ## Type:        list(0,1,2,4,8)
48 ## Default:     8
49 #
50 # DUMP_LEVEL has a number of possible values:
51 #
52 #      DUMP_NONE (0):  Do nothing; just return if called.
53 #    DUMP_HEADER (1):  Dump the dump header and first 128K
bytes out.
54 #      DUMP_KERN (2):  Everything in DUMP_HEADER and kernel
pages only.
```

```
55 #       DUMP_USED (4):   Everything except kernel free pages.
56 #        DUMP_ALL (8):   All memory.
57 #
58 # For now, either DUMP_NONE, DUMP_HEADER, or DUMP_ALL are
valid until
59 # someone comes along and adds page typing, at which time
DUMP_KERN and
60 # DUMP_USED should be added.  NOTE:  You must use the
numeric value, not
61 # the name of the variable.
62 DUMP_LEVEL="8"
63
64 ## Type:         integer(0:2)
65 ## Default:      0
66 #
67 # DUMP_COMPRESS indicates which compression mechanism the
kernel should
68 # attempt to use for compression — the new method is not to
use dump
69 # compression unless someone specifically asks for it.
There are multiple
70 # types of compression available.  For now, if you 'mod-
probe dump_rle',
71 # the dump_rle.o module will be installed, which enables RLE
compression
72 # of the dump pages.  The RLE compression algorithm used in
the kernel
73 # gives (on average) 40% compression of the memory image,
which can
74 # vary depending on how much memory is used on the system.
There are
75 # also other compression modules coming (such as GZIP).
The values for
76 # DUMP_COMPRESS are currently:
77 #
78 #    DUMP_COMPRESS_NONE(0):  Don't compress this dump.
79 #     DUMP_COMPRESS_RLE(1):  Use RLE compression.
80 #    DUMP_COMPRESS_GZIP(2):  Use GZIP compression.
81 DUMP_COMPRESS="0"
82
83 ## Type:         list(0,1)
84 ## Default:      0
85 #
86 # DUMP_FLAGS are the flag parameters to use when configuring
system dumps.
87 # There are multiple values coming, but for now, the only
valid value is
88 # DUMP_FLAGS_NONDISRUPT.   The table includes:
89 #
90 #         DUMP_FLAGS_NONE(0):  No flags are required.
91 #    DUMP_FLAGS_NONDISRUPT(1):  Do not reboot after dumping;
```

```
continue running.
92 DUMP_FLAGS="0"
93
94 ## Type:        list(0,1)
95 ## Default:     1
96 #
97 # DUMP_SAVE defines whether to save the memory image to
disk or not.
98 # If the value is 1, the vmcore image is stored, and a
crash report
99 # is created from the saved dump.  If it is not set to 1,
only a crash
100# report will be created, and the dump will not be saved.
This option
101# can be used on systems that do not want their disk space
consumed
102# by large crash dump images.
103 DUMP_SAVE="1"
104
105## Type:        integer
106## Default:     5
107#
108# PANIC_TIMEOUT represents the timeout (in seconds) before
reboot after a
109# panic occurs.  Typically this is set to 0 on the system,
which means the
110# kernel sits and spins until someone resets the machine.
This is not the
111# preferred action if we want to recover the dump after the
reboot.
112# ——————————————————————————————————-
113#
114PANIC_TIMEOUT="5"
```

In step 9 you save the dump using the **lkcd save** option. Figure 14.3 shows sample output from **lkcd save**.

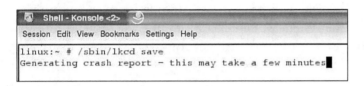

FIGURE 14.3
Sample output from lkcd save.

The last step is to make sure that lcrash can view the crash dump. lcrash has three inputs—the System.map file, the dump file, and Kerntypes. The dump for the example shown in Figure 14.4 is located in /var/log/dump/0, and the dump file is named dump.0. The simple operation for checking to see if the dump is valid is to use lcrash's **trace** option.

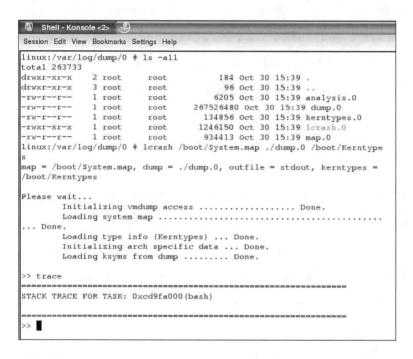

FIGURE 14.4
lcrash: viewing a dump.

The **trace** option shows that the bash process was running when the dump was taken. This is correct since the system was at a bash prompt when the dump was triggered by using the **echo "c" > /proc/sysrq-trigger** command.

LKCD Commands

Table 14.1 is a brief overview of **lcrash** commands.

TABLE 14.1
lcrash Commands

Command	Description
base	Displays a number in binary, octal, decimal, and hex.
deftask	Sets/displays the default task.
dis	Disassembles code.
dump	Displays values starting at the kernel virtual address.
findsym	Displays information for each requested symbol name.
help/?	Displays help information.
history	Displays the current history of past commands issued.
ldcmds	Dynamically loads a library of lcrash commands.
load	Loads a macro from a file or a directory.
mktrace	Constructs a stack back trace from scratch using an arbitrary stack address.
mmap	Displays relevant information for each entry in mmap_list.
module	Displays a list of loaded modules and module symbols.
namelist	Adds/lists opened namelists.
page	Displays relevant information from the page structure for each entry in page_list.
print	Evaluates an expression and prints the result.
quit	Exits lcrash.
report	Displays a crash dump report.
savedump	Creates a live dump or reduces a dump size.

(continues)

TABLE 14.1
lcrash Commands   (Continued)

Command	Description
sizeof	Displays the size of data types in bytes.
stat	Displays system statistics and the system buffer, which contains the latest messages printed via the kernel's **printk**.
strace	Displays all complete and unique stack traces.
symtab	Adds/removes/lists symbol table information.
task	Displays relevant information for each entry in task_list.
trace	Displays a stack trace for each task included in task_list.
unload	Unloads a file or directory.
vi	Starts a vi session for a file.
vtop	Displays the virtual-to-physical memory mapping for each entry in vaddr_list.
walk	Displays a linked list of kernel structures or memory blocks.
whatis	Displays, in C-like fashion, detailed information about kernel types.

System Panic and Crash Dump Taken

Now let's view a sample system panic and a crash dump that has been taken. This system has been set up in /etc/sysconfig/dump to reboot after a crash. The first step after the system has been rebooted is to save the crash dump. Once the crash dump has been saved, you can look at what caused the system's panic using lcrash to view the dump, as shown in Figure 14.5.

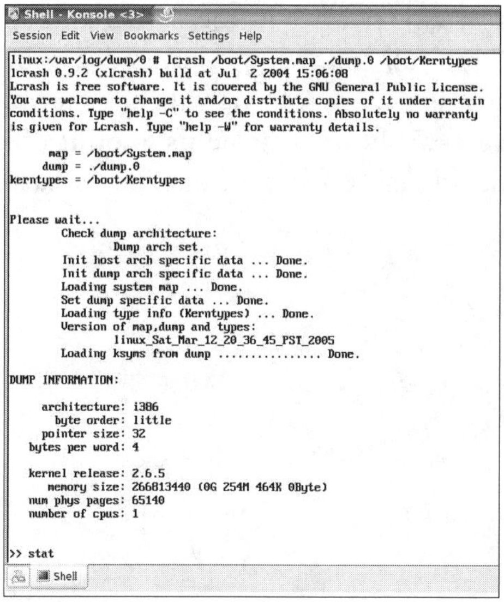

```
Shell - Konsole <3>
Session Edit View Bookmarks Settings Help
linux:/var/log/dump/0 # lcrash /boot/System.map ./dump.0 /boot/Kerntypes
lcrash 0.9.2 (xlcrash) build at Jul  2 2004 15:06:08
Lcrash is free software. It is covered by the GNU General Public License.
You are welcome to change it and/or distribute copies of it under certain
conditions. Type "help -C" to see the conditions. Absolutely no warranty
is given for Lcrash. Type "help -W" for warranty details.

      map = /boot/System.map
     dump = ./dump.0
kerntypes = /boot/Kerntypes


Please wait...
        Check dump architecture:
                Dump arch set.
        Init host arch specific data ... Done.
        Init dump arch specific data ... Done.
        Loading system map ... Done.
        Set dump specific data ... Done.
        Loading type info (Kerntypes) ... Done.
        Version of map,dump and types:
                linux_Sat_Mar_12_20_36_45_PST_2005
        Loading ksyms from dump ................ Done.

DUMP INFORMATION:

     architecture: i386
       byte order: little
     pointer size: 32
   bytes per word: 4

   kernel release: 2.6.5
      memory size: 266813440 (0G 254M 464K 0Byte)
   num phys pages: 65140
   number of cpus: 1


>> stat
Shell
```

FIGURE 14.5
Viewing a crash dump with lcrash.

The first command we'll use to check on what caused the crash dump is **stat**, which displays the latest kernel messages printed. Figure 14.6 shows the output from the **stat** command.

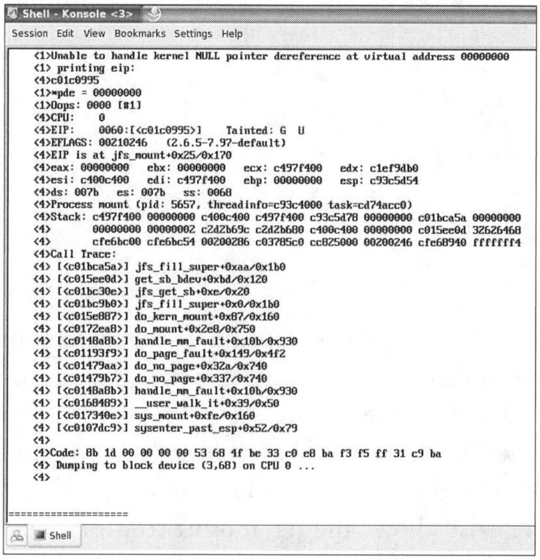

```
Shell - Konsole <3>
Session Edit View Bookmarks Settings Help
    <1>Unable to handle kernel NULL pointer dereference at virtual address 00000000
    <1> printing eip:
    <4>c01c0995
    <1>*pde = 00000000
    <1>Oops: 0000 [#1]
    <4>CPU:    0
    <4>EIP:    0060:[<c01c0995>]    Tainted: G  U
    <4>EFLAGS: 00210246   (2.6.5-7.97-default)
    <4>EIP is at jfs_mount+0x25/0x170
    <4>eax: 00000000   ebx: 00000000   ecx: c497f400   edx: c1ef9db0
    <4>esi: c400c400   edi: c497f400   ebp: 00000000   esp: c93c5d54
    <4>ds: 007b   es: 007b   ss: 0068
    <4>Process mount (pid: 5657, threadinfo=c93c4000 task=cd74acc0)
    <4>Stack: c497f400 00000000 c400c400 c497f400 c93c5d78 00000000 c01bca5a 00000000
    <4>       00000000 00000002 c2d2b69c c2d2b680 c400c400 00000000 c015ee0d 32626468
    <4>       cfe6bc00 cfe6bc54 00200286 c03785c0 cc825000 00200246 cfe68940 fffffff4
    <4>Call Trace:
    <4> [<c01bca5a>] jfs_fill_super+0xaa/0x1b0
    <4> [<c015ee0d>] get_sb_bdev+0xbd/0x120
    <4> [<c01bc30e>] jfs_get_sb+0xe/0x20
    <4> [<c01bc9b0>] jfs_fill_super+0x0/0x1b0
    <4> [<c015e887>] do_kern_mount+0x87/0x160
    <4> [<c0172ea8>] do_mount+0x2e8/0x750
    <4> [<c0148a8b>] handle_mm_fault+0x10b/0x930
    <4> [<c01193f9>] do_page_fault+0x149/0x4f2
    <4> [<c01479aa>] do_no_page+0x32a/0x740
    <4> [<c01479b7>] do_no_page+0x337/0x740
    <4> [<c0148a8b>] handle_mm_fault+0x10b/0x930
    <4> [<c0168489>] __user_walk_it+0x39/0x50
    <4> [<c017340e>] sys_mount+0xfe/0x160
    <4> [<c0107dc9>] sysenter_past_esp+0x52/0x79
    <4>
    <4>Code: 8b 1d 00 00 00 00 53 68 4f be 33 c0 e8 ba f3 f5 ff 31 c9 ba
    <4> Dumping to block device (3,68) on CPU 0 ...
    <4>


===================
Shell
```

FIGURE 14.6
output from **stat**.

The dump was taken because there was a NULL pointer in the kernel and an Oops was created. Figure 14.6 shows that the null pointer was created by the **jfs_mount** routine. The offset into this routine is 0x25. You can view the **jfs_mount** routine by using lcrash's **dis** command. Figure 14.7 shows that the **jfs_mount** offset 0x25 is the line that caused the kernel panic. In Figure 14.7, the line that is causing the panic is as follows:

```
jfs_mount+37 movl 0x0, ebx
```

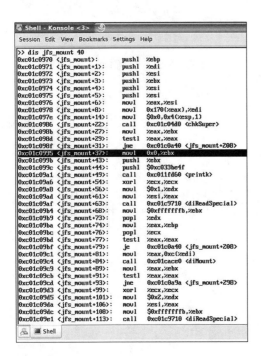

FIGURE 14.7
output from **dis jfs_mount**.

Next you need to determine which line of code is causing the problem in **jfs_mount**. The Oops tells you that the problem is caused by the instruction at offset 25 of the **jfs_mount**. The objdump utility is one way to view the jfs_mount.o file and look at offset 25. objdump is used to disassemble a module function and see what assembler instructions are created by the C source code. Figure 14.8 shows what is displayed from objdump. Figure 14.9 shows the **jfs_mount** routine. Next we can look at the C code for **jfs_mount** and see that the null pointer was caused by line 98.

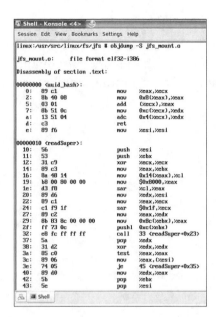

```
 Shell - Konsole <4>
Session  Edit  View  Bookmarks  Settings  Help

linux:/usr/src/linux/fs/jfs # objdump -S jfs_mount.o

jfs_mount.o:     file format elf32-i386

Disassembly of section .text:

00000000 <uuid_hash>:
   0:   89 c1              mov    %eax,%ecx
   2:   8b 40 08           mov    0x8(%eax),%eax
   5:   03 01              add    (%ecx),%eax
   7:   8b 51 0c           mov    0xc(%ecx),%edx
   a:   13 51 04           adc    0x4(%ecx),%edx
   d:   c3                 ret
   e:   89 f6              mov    %esi,%esi

00000010 <readSuper>:
  10:   56                 push   %esi
  11:   53                 push   %ebx
  12:   31 c9              xor    %ecx,%ecx
  14:   89 c3              mov    %eax,%ebx
  16:   8a 48 14           mov    0x14(%eax),%cl
  19:   b8 00 80 00 00     mov    $0x8000,%eax
  1e:   d3 f8              sar    %cl,%eax
  20:   89 d6              mov    %edx,%esi
  22:   89 c1              mov    %eax,%ecx
  24:   c1 f9 1f           sar    $0x1f,%ecx
  27:   89 c2              mov    %eax,%edx
  29:   8b 83 8c 00 00 00  mov    0x8c(%ebx),%eax
  2f:   ff 73 0c           pushl  0xc(%ebx)
  32:   e8 fc ff ff ff     call   33 <readSuper+0x23>
  37:   5a                 pop    %edx
  38:   31 d2              xor    %edx,%edx
  3a:   85 c0              test   %eax,%eax
  3c:   89 06              mov    %eax,(%esi)
  3e:   74 05              je     45 <readSuper+0x35>
  40:   89 d0              mov    %edx,%eax
  42:   5b                 pop    %ebx
  43:   5e                 pop    %esi

 Shell
```

FIGURE 14.8
Assembler listing of **jfs_mount**.

```
 Shell - Konsole <4>
Session  Edit  View  Bookmarks  Settings  Help

00000620 <jfs_mount>:
 620:   55                 push   %ebp
 621:   57                 push   %edi
 622:   56                 push   %esi
 623:   53                 push   %ebx
 624:   56                 push   %esi
 625:   56                 push   %esi
 626:   89 c6              mov    %eax,%esi
 628:   8b b8 70 01 00 00  mov    0x170(%eax),%edi
 62e:   c7 44 24 04 00 00 00  movl $0x0,0x4(%esp)
 635:   00
 636:   e8 45 fb ff ff     call   180 <chkSuper>
 63b:   89 c3              mov    %eax,%ebx
 63d:   85 c0              test   %eax,%eax
 63f:   0f 85 ab 00 00 00  jne    6f0 <jfs_mount+0xd0>
 645:   8b 1d 00 00 00 00  mov    0x0,%ebx
 64b:   53                 push   %ebx
 64c:   68 05 00 00 00     push   $0x5
 651:   e8 fc ff ff ff     call   652 <jfs_mount+0x32>
 656:   31 c9              xor    %ecx,%ecx
 658:   ba 01 00 00 00     mov    $0x1,%edx
 65d:   89 f0              mov    %esi,%eax
 65f:   e8 fc ff ff ff     call   660 <jfs_mount+0x40>
 664:   bb fb ff ff ff     mov    $0xfffffffb,%ebx
 669:   5a                 pop    %edx
 66a:   89 c5              mov    %eax,%ebp
 66c:   59                 pop    %ecx
 66d:   85 c0              test   %eax,%eax
 66f:   74 7f              je     6f0 <jfs_mount+0xd0>
 671:   89 47 0c           mov    %eax,0xc(%edi)
 674:   e8 fc ff ff ff     call   675 <jfs_mount+0x55>
 679:   89 c3              mov    %eax,%ebx
 67b:   85 c0              test   %eax,%eax
 67d:   0f 85 c7 00 00 00  jne    74a <jfs_mount+0x12a>
 683:   31 c9              xor    %ecx,%ecx
 685:   ba 02 00 00 00     mov    $0x2,%edx
 68a:   89 f0              mov    %esi,%eax
 68c:   bb fb ff ff ff     mov    $0xfffffffb,%ebx

 Shell
```

FIGURE 14.9
Assembler listing of **jfs_mount** showing the **jfs_mount** routine.

The crash dump was created by the mount to the JFS file system. The **jfs_mount** routine was changed to add the three lines shown in bold in Listing 14.2. Listing 14.2 lists the code that was modified in the source of the usr/src/linux/jfs/fs/jfs_mount.c file to create a segmentation fault at line 98 by creating a null pointer exception.

Listing 14.2

Modified jfs_mount.c Code

```
68  /*
69   * NAME: jfs_mount(sb)
70   *
71   * FUNCTION: vfs_mount()
72   *
73   * PARAMETER: sb       - super block
74   *
75   * RETURN:-EBUSY       - device already mounted or open for
write
76   *           -EBUSY       - cvrdvp already mounted
77   *           -EBUSY       - mount table full
78   *           -ENOTDIR    - cvrdvp not directory on a device
mount
79   *           -ENXIO      - device open failure
80   */
81  int jfs_mount(struct super_block *sb)
82  {
83     int rc = 0;    /* Return code */
84     struct jfs_sb_info *sbi = JFS_SBI(sb);
85     struct inode *ipaimap = NULL;
86     struct inode *ipaimap2 = NULL;
87     struct inode *ipimap = NULL;
88     struct inode *ipbmap = NULL;
89     int *ptr;    /* line 1 added */
90     /*
91      * read/validate superblock
92      * (initialize mount inode from the superblock)
93      */
94     if ((rc = chkSuper(sb))) {
95            goto errout20;
96     }
97     ptr = 0;                         /* line 2 added */
98     printk(" jfs %d \n", *ptr);   /* line 3 added */
```

So we have changed the JFS file system code to create a NULL pointer reference by adding the three bold lines of code to the mount code of JFS. If we mount the file system using /dev/hda1 as the JFS device and /jfs as the mount point, a segment failure is displayed, and the crash dump is taken.

Netdump: The Network Crash Dump Facility from Both the Client and Server

In Red Hat Linux Advanced Server 2.1 and above, Red Hat, Inc. provided its first crash dump facility. Unlike traditional crash dump facilities, this facility dumps memory images to a centralized server via the network. Two tasks are involved in using netdump: setting up the netdump server, and allowing the clients to send dumps to the server.

Server

One requirement of the server is that there be sufficient free disk space to store each dump. The crash dump images and files are written to the /var/crash directory.

The netdump-server package needs to be installed on the server. There is a way to limit the number of concurrent dump operations that are permitted to be sent to the server. For example, if you want to set the limit to 10, set **max_concur-rent_dumps=10** in the /etc/netdump.conf file. A README file that comes with the netdump-server package explains that a password needs the client to authenticate itself with the server.

The netdump server is enabled using the following command:

```
# chkconfig netdump-server on
```

This causes it to be started automatically on subsequent boots. The service can also be started by using the following command:

```
# netdump-server start
```

The netdump server is now ready to receive network crash dump images.

A set of scripts runs when system events occur. They go in /var/crash/scripts, and sample scripts are in the directory /usr/share/doc/netdump-server*/ example_scripts/. The man page for netdump-server explains the uses of these scripts. One key feature is that reports of system crashes can notify a system administrator.

Client

The client must have a network device that supports netdump. Some of the supported drivers are 3c59x, eepro100, e100, tlan, and tulip.

The netdump package needs to be installed on the client. Edit the file /etc/sysconfig/netdump and add a line like **NETDUMPADDR**=*x.x.x.x*, where *x.x.x.x* specifies the address of the netdump server.

The netdump client and server must authenticate themselves with the server. One way to do this is to have the netdump init script send a dynamic random key to the server. To do that, the netdump service can propagate and be prepared to give the netdump user's password on the netdump server. This needs to be done only once when the client is set up. This sets up the netdump server to allow connections to provide the dynamic random key to the server each time the module is loaded on the client.

Enable the netdump client to start with the following command:

```
# chkconfig netdump on
```

This causes it to be started automatically on subsequent boots. The service can be started by using the following command:

```
# netdump start
```

Once a netdump is created on the server, the crash utility can be used to view that dump.

diskdump: a Crash Dump Facility

In Red Hat Linux Enterprise Server 3 Update 3 and above, Red Hat, Inc. provided diskdump as another crash dump facility.

diskdump lets you create a kernel dump on a single system without sending the dump to a server like netdump does. Diskdump creates files identical in format to the netdump core files and can be analyzed with the same tools. Like netdump, diskdump requires device driver support. The SCSI disk series controllers (aic7xxx/aic79xx) are supported. For additional support device drivers, see the README file in the /usr/share/doc/diskdump-* directory.

A diskdump is created in a two-stage process and works similarly to UNIX-style traditional disk dumps. The first step is when the kernel crash happens. The system-related information and the current memory are stored to a reserved partition on a supported disk.

On the next reboot, when the system restarts, the diskdump init scripts create a dump file from the saved information on the reserved partition. This file is stored in the /var/crash/ directory.

General Steps to Configure diskdump

Here are the general steps to configure diskdump:

1. Load the diskdump module.

2. The diskdump reserved partition can be specified in /etc/syscon-fig/diskdump. The **DEVICE** option specifies which partition the dump will be placed on. The following example uses /dev/sdb1:

    DEVICE=/dev/sdb1

3. Initialize the partition for use:

    ```
    # service diskdump initialformat
    ```

    > WARNING Any data on this partition will be lost.

4. Add the service to run on startup, and then start the service:

    ```
    # chkconfig diskdump o
    ```

    ```
    # service diskdump start
    ```

The diskdump service is now configured. At the next system crash, the dump will be saved to the reserved partition.

Viewing an mcore Crash Dump

Now let's look at a crash dump taken by having mcore functionality on a system. mcore allows a system to take a crash dump when a panic occurs on the system. The crash program can be used to view dumps created by mcore, Netdump, and Diskdump. You'll use crash to look at a panic in the ext3 file system. The crash program takes two parameters—the vmlinux file and the crash dump. The vmlinux file is created when the kernel is built. It is created in the /usr/src/linux directory. The crash dump shown in the example is called lcore.cr.56. This dump was created on a 32-bit PowerPC system. The crash dump shown in the example identifies that the ext3 file system has a problem in the file /usr/src/linux/fs/ext3/balloc.c. The source for ext3 **load_block_bitmap** is shown in Listing 14.3.

Listing 14.3

ext3 File System balloc.c Source

```
112 /*
113 * load_block_bitmap loads the block bitmap for a blocks
group.
114 *
115 * It maintains a cache for the last bitmaps loaded. This
cache is
116 * managed with a LRU algorithm.
117 *
118 * Notes:
119 * 1/ There is one cache per mounted file system.
120 * 2/ If the file system contains less than
EXT3_MAX_GROUP_LOADED groups,
121 *    this function reads the bitmap without maintaining an
LRU cache.
122 *
123 * Return the slot used to store the bitmap, or a -ve error
code.
124 */
125 static int __load_block_bitmap (struct super_block * sb,
126                                 unsigned int
block_group)
127 {
128    int i, j, retval = 0;
129    unsigned long block_bitmap_number;
130    struct buffer_head * block_bitmap;
131
132    if (block_group >= sb->u.ext3_sb.s_groups_count)
133            ext3_panic (sb, "load_block_bitmap",
134                        "block_group >= groups_count - "
135                        "block_group = %d, groups_count =
%lu",
136                        block_group, sb-
>u.ext3_sb.s_groups_count);
```

Line 133 is where the dump says that the panic is coming from. Listing 14.4 shows the viewing of the dump using the crash program. You'll see some important crash commands that can help you view system information and solve this problem with the help of the mcore crash dump. This crash dump and other problems reported on the same subject lead to the solution to this file system problem.

Listing 14.4

Viewing a Dump with crash

```
root@winesap crash-3.3-28]# ./crash vmlinux lcore.cr.56

crash 3.3-28
```

```
Copyright (C) 2002, 2003  Red Hat, Inc.
Copyright (C) 1998-2002  Hewlett-Packard Co
Copyright (C) 1999, 2002  Silicon Graphics, Inc.
Copyright (C) 1999, 2000, 2001, 2002  Mission Critical Linux,
Inc.
This program is free software, covered by the GNU General
Public License and you are welcome to change it and/or distrib-
ute copies of it under certain conditions.  Enter "help copy-
ing" to see the conditions. This program has absolutely no war-
ranty.  Enter "help warranty" for details.

GNU gdb Red Hat Linux (5.2.1-4)
Copyright 2002 Free Software Foundation, Inc.
GDB is free software, covered by the GNU General Public
License, and you are welcome to change it and/or distribute
copies of it under certain conditions.
Type "show copying" to see the conditions.
There is absolutely no warranty for GDB.  Type "show warranty"
for details.
This GDB was configured as "powerpc-unknown-linux-gnu"...


please wait... (gathering task table data) KERNEL: vmlinux
      DUMPFILE: lcore.cr.56
          CPUS: 1
          DATE: Thu Mar  3 06:49:56 2005
        UPTIME: 00:03:03
  LOAD AVERAGE: 0.61, 0.29, 0.11
         TASKS: 38
      NODENAME: open3c1
       RELEASE: 2.4.19-146
       VERSION: #1 Fri Feb 18 23:31:27 UTC 2005
       MACHINE: ppc   (unknown Mhz)
        MEMORY: 128 MB
         PANIC: "EXT3-fs panic (device ide0(3,1)):
load_block_bitmap: block_group >= groups_count - block_group =
524287, groups_count = 7"
           PID: 1937
       COMMAND: "java"
          TASK: c6ace000
           CPU: 0
         STATE: TASK_RUNNING (PANIC)
```

The **sys** command shows general information about the system. Listing 14.5 shows that the system was just booted, because the uptime is 3 minutes and 3 seconds. The system has 128 MB of memory. The listing also shows other general information.

```
crash> sys
```

Listing 14.5

Viewing the System Information Using the sys Command

```
       KERNEL: vmlinux
     DUMPFILE: lcore.cr.56
         CPUS: 1
         DATE: Thu Mar  3 06:49:56 2005
       UPTIME: 00:03:03
 LOAD AVERAGE: 0.61, 0.29, 0.11
        TASKS: 38
     NODENAME: open3c1
      RELEASE: 2.4.19-146
      VERSION: #1 Fri Feb 18 23:31:27 UTC 2005
      MACHINE: ppc   (unknown Mhz)
       MEMORY: 128 MB
        PANIC: "EXT3-fs panic (device ide0(3,1)):
load_block_bitmap: block_group
>= groups_count - block_group = 524287, groups_count = 7"
```

The **mach** command shows general information about the hardware. As shown in Listing 14.6, the processor is ppc, and there is one CPU. The listing also shows other general information about the hardware.

```
crash> mach
```

Listing 14.6

Viewing the Machine Information Using the mach Command

```
       MACHINE TYPE: ppc
        MEMORY SIZE: 128 MB
               CPUS: 1
    PROCESSOR SPEED: (unknown)
                 HZ: 100
          PAGE SIZE: 4096
      L1 CACHE SIZE: 32
 KERNEL VIRTUAL BASE: c0000000
 KERNEL VMALLOC BASE: c9000000
  KERNEL STACK SIZE: 8192
```

The **bt** command shows the back trace of the process that was running when the panic occurred. From the call trace, you can see that the panic occurred when a sys_unlink operation was being done on one of the ext3 file systems, as shown in Listing 14.7.

```
crash> bt
```

Listing 14.7

Getting a Back Trace Using the bt Command

```
PID: 1937    TASK: c6ace000  CPU: 0    COMMAND: "java"
 #0 [c6acfb10]  crash_save_current_state at c000e5ac
 #1 [c6acfbb0]  ext3_free_blocks at c006aa68
 #2 [c6acfbd0]  ext3_free_blocks at c006ac9c
 #3 [c6acfc80]  ext3_clear_blocks at c0070518
 #4 [c6acfce0]  ext3_free_data at c0070798
 #5 [c6acfd40]  ext3_free_branches at c0070a88
 #6 [c6acfda0]  ext3_free_branches at c00708f0
 #7 [c6acfe00]  ext3_truncate at c0070e44
 #8 [c6acfe80]  ext3_delete_inode at c006e26c
 #9 [c6acfea0]  iput at c005b294
#10 [c6acfec0]  d_delete at c0059560
#11 [c6acfed0]  vfs_unlink at c0050890
#12 [c6acff00]  sys_unlink at c0050af8
#13 [c6acff40]  ret_from_syscall_1 at c0005edc
syscall [c00] exception frame:
R0:  0000000a  R1:  7ffff430  R2:  00000000  R3:  10270ea0
R4:  00000000  R5:  1005cb38  R6:  00000019  R7:  10270ea0
R8:  00000000  R9:  0ffcb3dc  R10: 1005cb34  R11: 7ffff3f0
R12: 48044488  R13: 1001f620  R14: 00000001  R15: 1005c918
R16: 00000000  R17: 00000002  R18: 300e3b20  R19: 1014f984
R20: 1005cab0  R21: 0000000d  R22: 1003d210  R23: 1005caf4
R24: 00000000  R25: 00000000  R26: 00000006  R27: 00000000
NIP: 0fec935c  MSR: 0000f032  OR3: 10270ea0  CTR: 0fc5c15c
LR:  0fe60d2c  XER: 20000000  CCR: 28044482  MQ:  00000000
DAR: 30242fcc DSISR: 42000000      Syscall Result: 00000000
```

The **ps** command shows the processes on the system. Listing 14.8 shows that 37 processes were on this system when the panic occurred.

```
crash> ps
```

Listing 14.8

Viewing the Processes on the System Using the ps Command

PID	PPID	CPU	TASK	ST	%MEM	VSZ	RSS	COMM
0	0	0	c0166430	RU	0.0	0	0	[swap- per]
1	0	0	c03f6000	IN	0.2	488	228	init
2	1	0	c03ea000	IN	0.0	0	0	

```
[keventd]
    3       1   0   c03e6000   IN   0.0        0        0
[ksoftirqd_CPU0]
    4       1   0   c03e4000   IN   0.0        0        0   [kswapd]
    5       1   0   c03e2000   IN   0.0        0        0   [bdflush]
    6       1   0   c03e0000   IN   0.0        0        0
[kupdated]
   19       1   0   c7858000   IN   0.0        0        0
[kjournald]
   76       1   0   c7de2000   IN   0.0        0        0
[kjournald]
   78       1   0   c7df6000   IN   0.0        0        0
[kjournald]
  179       1   0   c7dc0000   IN   0.0        0        0
[kjournald]
  295       1   0   c7ba8000   IN   0.4     1384      544   agetty
  296       1   0   c7bb6000   IN   0.4     1460      528   lnxrelm
  297       1   0   c7bdc000   IN   1.1     2856     1384
lnxsysdaemon
  298       1   0   c018a000   IN   0.4     1392      492
i2caccessdm
  359     297   0   c6eda000   IN   0.3     1356      360   sysdaemon
  685       1   0   c137c000   IN   0.5     1512      644   syslogd
  688       1   0   c11e8000   RU   0.8     1940     1072   klogd
  711       1   0   c7ce6000   IN   1.2     4292     1588   sshd
  713       1   0   c7ca8000   IN   0.5     1672      704   cron
 1235     711   0   c76be000   IN   1.8     5408     2324   sshd
 1236    1235   0   c6dde000   IN   1.4     3248     1868   bash
 1898    1897   0   c743e000   IN   0.4     1436      580   ncwd
 1899    1898   0   c72b2000   IN   2.1    11340     2780
niStartServers
 1930    1899   0   c77ba000   IN   2.1    11340     2780
niStartServers
 1931    1930   0   c70ac000   IN   2.1    11340     2780
niStartServers
 1932    1930   0   c7708000   IN   2.1    11340     2780
niStartServers
 1933    1930   0   c72ce000   IN   2.1    11340     2780
niStartServers
 1937    1898   0   c6ace000   RU  10.9    35460    14344   java
 1953    1937   0   c6358000   IN  10.9    35460    14344   java
 1954    1953   0   c6354000   IN  10.9    35460    14344   java
 1955    1953   0   c6344000   IN  10.9    35460    14344   java
 1956    1953   0   c633e000   IN  10.9    35460    14344   java
 1957    1953   0   c61ee000   IN  10.9    35460    14344   java
 1958    1953   0   c61ec000   IN  10.9    35460    14344   java
 1959    1953   0   c61e8000   IN  10.9    35460    14344   java
 1960    1953   0   c5baa000   IN  10.9    35460    14344   java
```

The **bt** command lets you display a process's back trace. Listing 14.9 looks at a Java process that has a PID of 1960. The back trace shows that the **crash_save_current_state** routine is where this process stopped. The **crash_save_current_state** routine was called by the **sys_rt_sigsuspend** routine.

```
crash> bt 1960
```

Listing 14.9

Viewing the Back trace for Process 1960 Using the bt Command

```
PID: 1960     TASK: c5baa000  CPU: 0    COMMAND: "java"
 #0 [c5babee0] crash_save_current_state at c000e5ac
 #1 [c5babf10] sys_rt_sigsuspend at c0009404
 #2 [c5babf40] ret_from_syscall_1 at c0005edc
syscall [c00] exception frame:
R0:   000000b2    R1:  7ebff1a0   R2:  00000000   R3:  00000004
R4:   00000008    R5:  7ebff1c8   R6:  00000008   R7:  000000d0
R8:   7ebffc00    R9:  00000000   R10: 00000000   R11: 00000000
R12:  28042488    R13: 1001f620   R14: 00000001   R15: 1026648c
R16:  00000000    R17: 10046e50   R18: 1025d178   R19: 1025d008
R20:  10266574    R21: 00000003   R22: 1025cff8   R23: 7ebff308
R24:  1025d34c    R25: 00000000   R26: 00001010   R27: ffffffff
R28:  10046e50    R29: 0ffcb388   R30: 0ffcb254   R31: 7ebffc00
NIP:  0fe3a640    MSR: 0000d032   OR3: 7ebff1c8   CTR: 00000000
LR:   0fe39324    XER: 20000000   CCR: 38042488   MQ:  00000000
DAR:  7ebffc80  DSISR: 42000000         Syscall Result: fffffffc
```

The **mount** command shows the file systems that are mounted (see Listing 14.10):

```
crash> mount
```

Listing 14.10

Viewing the File Systems That Are Mounted Using the mount Command

VFSMOUNT	SUPERBLK	TYPE	DEVNAME	DIRNAME
c05ff120	c05fd000	rootfs	rootfs	/
c05ff360	c7b10000	ext3	/dev/root	/
c05ff320	c05fd400	proc	proc	/proc
c05ff3a0	c03bf000	devpts	devpts	/dev/pts
c05ff3e0	c03bfe00	ext3	/dev/hda8	/curr_lic
c05ff420	c7b10200	ext3	/dev/hda9	/persist
c05ff460	c7b10400	ext3	/dev/hda1	/var/log
c05ff4a0	c7b10600	shm	shmfs	/dev/shm

The **log** command shows system messages that were in the system buffer when the system took a system dump:

```
crash> log
```

The log information was the most helpful to solve this problem. It showed that the ext3 file systems weren't having the file system checker (fsck) run before the file systems are mounted. It was run only once. From Listing 14.10 you know that this system has four ext3 file systems mounted. Therefore, the message **EXT3-fs: recovery complete** should be seen four times, but the log shown in Listing 14.11 shows it only once. So because the file system checker (fsck) wasn't run on the ext3 file system, the file system wasn't in a consistent state, and that caused the ext3 panic in the **load_block_bitmap** routine shown in Listing 14.3. Another issue with this system configuration was that the file systems weren't umounted at shutdown or fsck wasn't run on bootup. As soon as both of these changes were done to the system scripts, this ext3 panic never occurred again.

Listing 14.11

Viewing the System Buffer Information Using the log Command

```
Setting up ppc_ide_md
Memory BAT mapping: BAT2=128Mb, BAT3=0Mb, residual: 0Mb
Total memory = 128MB; using 256kB for hash table (at c01c0000)
 map_page IOBASE returned 0
 map_page INTS returned 0
 Internal registers found at 0x30040000.
 map_page BAR24 returned 0
 map_page INTREGSBASE returned 0
Linux version 2.4.19-146 (root@build3) (gcc version 3.2.3) #1
Fri Feb 18 23:31:27 UTC 2005
crash_pages=451
crash_init(ptov(PFN_PHYS(0x40000000)), ptov(0x00000000),
ptov(0x401c3000))
crash_init (crash_va: c0430000)
crash_dump_header c0430000 {
    magic[0]            = 0
    map                 = c7a23000
    map_pages           = 5
    data_pages          = 5ca
    compr_units         = 4b
    boot_reserved_start = c0430000
    boot_reserved_end   = c05f3000
Specific Linux Setup Routines Executing.
Boot arguments: console=ttyS0,38400 rw
Cache Enabled.
On node 0 totalpages: 32768
```

```
zone(0): 32768 pages.
zone(1): 0 pages.
zone(2): 0 pages.
Kernel command line: console=ttyS0,38400 rw
pldinte 00000000 pldints 00000000 twints 00004000
pldintemsk 00000ffd pldintsmsk 0000ffff twmsk ffffffff
todmod:rw_ds1337: wait for i2c bus initialization
todmod:time_init: We failed updating 0x0E
Turning on EE bit: Enabling IRQs
IRQs ENABLED!
Calibrating delay loop... 1998.84 BogoMIPS
Memory: 121592k available (1272k kernel code, 412k data, 72k
init, 0k highmem)
Dentry cache hash table entries: 16384 (order: 5, 131072 bytes)
Inode cache hash table entries: 8192 (order: 4, 65536 bytes)
Mount-cache hash table entries: 2048 (order: 2, 16384 bytes)
Buffer-cache hash table entries: 8192 (order: 3, 32768 bytes)
Page-cache hash table entries: 32768 (order: 5, 131072 bytes)
POSIX conformance testing by UNIFIX
PCI: Probing PCI hardware
Linux NET4.0 for Linux 2.4
Based upon Swansea University Computer Society NET3.039
Initializing RT netlink socket
Starting kswapd
Journalled Block Device driver loaded
pty: 256 Unix98 ptys configured
Serial driver version 5.05c (2001-07-08) with MANY_PORTS
SHARE_IRQ SERIAL_PCI enabled
ttyS00 at 0xff900000 (irq = 44) is a 16550A
Uniform Multi-Platform E-IDE driver Revision: 6.31
ide: Assuming 50MHz system bus speed for PIO modes; override
with idebus=xx
hda: SMART ATA FLASH, ATA DISK drive
ide0 at 0xff880000-0xff880007,0xff88001c on irq 45
hda: 4029984 sectors (2063 MB) w/1KiB Cache, CHS=3998/16/63
Partition check:
hda: [PTBL] [1999/32/63] hda1 hda2 < hda5 hda6 hda7 hda8 hda9
>
SLIP: version 0.8.4-NET3.019-NEWTTY (dynamic channels, max=256)
(6 bit encapsulation enabled).
CSLIP: code copyright 1989 Regents of the University of
California.
SLIP linefill/keepalive option.
RAMDISK driver initialized: 16 RAM disks of 4096K size 1024
blocksize
loop: loaded (max 8 devices)
NET4: Linux TCP/IP 1.0 for NET4.0
IP Protocols: ICMP, UDP, TCP
IP: routing cache hash table of 1024 buckets, 8Kbytes
TCP: Hash tables configured (established 8192 bind 16384)
NET4: Unix domain sockets 1.0/SMP for Linux NET4.0.
```

```
RAMDISK: Compressed image found at block 0
Freeing initrd memory: 4096k freed
VFS: Mounted root (ext2 filesystem).
hda: hda1 hda2 < hda5 hda6 hda7 hda8 hda9 >
hda: hda1 hda2 < hda5 hda6 hda7 hda8 hda9 >
hda: hda1 hda2 < hda5 hda6 hda7 hda8 hda9 >
kjournald starting.  Commit interval 5 seconds
EXT3 FS 2.4-0.9.18, 14 May 2002 on ide0(3,5), internal journal
EXT3-fs: recovery complete.
EXT3-fs: mounted filesystem with ordered data mode.
VFS: Mounted root (ext3 filesystem).
Trying to move old root to /initrd ... failed
Unmounting old root
Trying to free ramdisk memory ... okay
Freeing unused kernel memory: 72k init
In REBOOT:  current process init (1)
with parent swapper (0) and grandparent swapper (0).
kjournald starting.  Commit interval 5 seconds
EXT3-fs warning: maximal mount count reached, running e2fsck is
recommended
EXT3 FS 2.4-0.9.18, 14 May 2002 on ide0(3,6), internal journal
EXT3-fs: mounted filesystem with ordered data mode.
kjournald starting.  Commit interval 5 seconds
EXT3 FS 2.4-0.9.18, 14 May 2002 on ide0(3,8), internal journal
EXT3-fs: mounted filesystem with ordered data mode.
kjournald starting.  Commit interval 5 seconds
EXT3 FS 2.4-0.9.18, 14 May 2002 on ide0(3,9), internal journal
EXT3-fs: mounted filesystem with ordered data mode.
journald starting.  Commit interval 5 seconds
EXT3-fs warning: maximal mount count reached, running e2fsck is
recommended
EXT3 FS 2.4-0.9.18, 14 May 2002 on ide0(3,7), internal journal
EXT3-fs: mounted filesystem with ordered data mode.
kjournald starting.  Commit interval 5 seconds
EXT3-fs warning: maximal mount count reached, running e2fsck is
recommended
EXT3 FS 2.4-0.9.18, 14 May 2002 on ide0(3,7), internal journal
EXT3-fs: mounted filesystem with ordered data mode.
kjournald starting.  Commit interval 5 seconds
EXT3-fs warning: maximal mount count reached, running e2fsck is
recommended
EXT3 FS 2.4-0.9.18, 14 May 2002 on ide0(3,6), internal journal
EXT3-fs: mounted filesystem with ordered data mode.
kjournald starting.  Commit interval 5 seconds
EXT3-fs warning: maximal mount count reached, running e2fsck is
recommended
EXT3-fs: mounted filesystem with ordered data mode.
kjournald starting.  Commit interval 5 seconds
EXT3-fs warning: maximal mount count reached, running e2fsck is
recommended
EXT3 FS 2.4-0.9.18, 14 May 2002 on ide0(3,1), internal journal
```

```
EXT3-fs: mounted filesystem with ordered data mode.
Kernel panic: EXT3-fs panic (device ide0(3,1)):
load_block_bitmap: block_group >
= groups_count - block_group = 524287, groups_count = 7

 save_core: started on CPU0
```

The **runq** command displays the tasks on the run queue (see Listing 14.12):

```
crash> runq
```

Listing 14.12

Viewing the System Run Queue Using the runq Command

```
PID: 688     TASK: c11e8000   CPU: 0    COMMAND: "klogd"
PID: 1937    TASK: c6ace000   CPU: 0    COMMAND: "java"
```

The **dis** command displays the assembler instructions for a routine. Listing 14.13 shows the **crash_save_current_state** routine.

```
crash> dis crash_save_current_state
```

Listing 14.13

Displaying the crash_save_current_state Routine Using the dis Command

```
0xc000e578 <crash_save_current_state>:    stwu     r1,-16(r1)
0xc000e57c <crash_save_current_state+4>:           mflr     r0
0xc000e580 <crash_save_current_state+8>:           lis      r9,
-16359
0xc000e584 <crash_save_current_state+12>:          stw
r0,20(r1)
0xc000e588 <crash_save_current_state+16>:          stw
r1,616(r3)
0xc000e58c <crash_save_current_state+20>:          stw      r1,
-15812(r9)
0xc000e590 <crash_save_current_state+24>:          sync
0xc000e594 <crash_save_current_state+28>:          bl
0xc0025260 <save_core>
0xc000e598 <crash_save_current_state+32>:          li       r3,1
0xc000e59c <crash_save_current_state+36>:
    bl   0xc000e5b0 <crash_halt_or_reboot>
0xc000e5a0 <crash_save_current_state+40>:          lwz
r0,20(r1)
0xc000e5a4 <crash_save_current_state+44>:          addi
r1,r1,16
0xc000e5a8 <crash_save_current_state+48>:          mtlr     r0
0xc000e5ac <crash_save_current_state+52>:          blr
```

The **files** command displays the task's current root directory and working directories and then displays information about each open file descriptor (see Listing 14.14):

```
crash> files
```

Listing 14.14

Displaying File Information Using the files Command

```
PID: 1937    TASK: c6ace000   CPU: 0    COMMAND: "java"
ROOT: /      CWD: /persist/dc
  FD      FILE       DENTRY       INODE     TYPE         PATH
   0    c7d7e940    c7a9da60    c7b2b200    CHR     /dev/console
   1    c7c8d4a0    c12a0e20    c1145580    REG     /var/log/star.out
   2    c7c8d4a0    c12a0e20    c1145580    REG     /var/log/star.out
   3    c6d0f6c0    c69e79e0    c699c900    REG     /opt/IBMJava2-ppc-
142/jre/lib/core.jar
   4    c7d7ea40    c1146240    c720d740    REG
/curr_lic/etc/nearcwd.conf
   5    c7d7eac0    c11462c0    c69c4040    REG
/var/lock/nearcwd.lock
   6    c7d7eb40    c11464c0    c69c4200    SOCK    socket:/[2345]
   7    c7c8d4a0    c12a0e20    c1145580    REG     /var/log/star.out
   8    c7c8d3a0    c69e7a60    c699cac0    REG     /opt/IBMJava2-ppc-
142/jre/lib/graphics.jar
   9    c7c8d0a0    c69e7ae0    c699cc80    REG     /opt/IBMJava2-ppc-
142/jre/lib/security.jar
  10    c13522e0    c69e7b60    c699ce40    REG     /opt/IBMJava2-ppc-
142/jre/lib/server.jar
  11    c13521e0    c69e7be0    c66a9040    REG     /opt/IBMJava2-ppc-
142/jre/lib/xml.jar
  12    c1352960    c69e7c60    c66a9200    REG     /opt/IBMJava2-ppc-
142/jre/lib/charsets.jar
  13    c6d0fc40    c69e7ce0    c66a93c0    REG     /opt/IBMJava2-ppc-
142/jre/lib/ibmcertpathprovider.jar
  14    c1352360    c69e7d60    c66a9580    REG     /opt/IBMJava2-ppc-
142/jre/lib/ibmjaaslm
  15    c13524e0    c69e7de0    c66a9740    REG     /opt/IBMJava2-ppc-
142/jre/lib/ibmjcefw.jar
  16    c13523e0    c69e7e60    c66a9900    REG     /opt/IBMJava2-ppc-
142/jre/lib/ibmjgssprovider.jar
  17    c1352560    c69e7ee0    c66a9ac0    REG     /opt/IBMJava2-ppc-
142/jre/lib/ibmjssefips.jar
  18    c1352460    c69e7f60    c66a9c80    REG     /opt/IBMJava2-ppc-
142/jre/lib/ibmjsseprovider.jar
  19    c6d0fcc0    c65db0a0    c66a9e40    REG     /opt/IBMJava2-ppc-
142/jre/lib/ibmorb.jar
```

```
 20   c7c8d9a0   c65db120   c6533040   REG    /opt/IBMJava2-ppc-
142/jre/lib/ibmorbapi.jar
 21   c6d0fbc0   c65db1a0   c6533200   REG    /opt/IBMJava2-ppc-
142/jre/lib/ibmpkcs.jar
 22   c6d0fec0   c65db220   c65333c0   FIFO   pipe:/[2599]
 23   c6d0fe40   c65db220   c65333c0   FIFO   pipe:/[2599]
 24   c6d0ff40   c65db3a0   c6533740   REG    /opt/IBMJava2-ppc-
142/jre/lib/ext/dumpfmt.jar
 25   c13525e0   c65db420   c6533900   REG    /opt/IBMJava2-ppc-
142/jre/lib/ext/gskikm.jar
 26   c1352260   c65db4a0   c6533ac0   REG    /opt/IBMJava2-ppc-
142/jre/lib/ext/ibmjcefips.jar
 27   c1352660   c65db520   c6533c80   REG    /opt/IBMJava2-ppc-
142/jre/lib/ext/ibmjceprovider.jar
 28   c13526e0   c65db5a0   c6533e40   REG    /opt/IBMJava2-ppc-
142/jre/lib/ext/ibmjsseprovider2.jar
 29   c1352760   c65db620   c6235040   REG    /opt/IBMJava2-ppc-
142/jre/lib/ext/ibmpkcs11impl.jar
 30   c13527e0   c65db6a0   c6235200   REG    /opt/IBMJava2-ppc-
142/jre/lib/ext/indicim.jar
 31   c1352860   c65db720   c62353c0   REG    /opt/IBMJava2-ppc-
142/jre/lib/ext/jaccess.jar
 32   c13529e0   c65db7a0   c6235580   REG    /opt/IBMJava2-ppc-
142/jre/lib/ext/ldapsec.jar
 33   c1352a60   c65db820   c6235740   REG    /opt/IBMJava2-ppc-
142/jre/lib/ext/oldcertpath.jar
 34   c1352ae0   c65db8a0   c6235900   REG
/curr_lic/home/essni/lib/ibmjsse.jar
 35   c1352b60   c65db920   c6235ac0   REG
/curr_lic/home/essni/lib/hwmcaapi.jar
 36   c1352be0   c65dba20   c6235c80   REG
/curr_lic/home/essni/lib/ESSNINode.jar
 37   c1352c60   c65dbaa0   c6235e40   REG
/curr_lic/home/essni/lib/logger.jar
 38   c1352ce0   c65dbc20   c6055200   REG
/curr_lic/home/essni/etc/ni_SM_ESSNI.properties
 39   c5e6d0a0   c5e728c0   c6055580   REG
/curr_lic/config/masterComponents.pro
 40   c5e6d3a0   c65dbc20   c6055200   REG
/curr_lic/home/essni/etc/ni_SM_ESSNI.properties
```

The **task** command displays a task's complete **task_struct** contents for PID 1937, which is the process that was running when the crash dump was taken (see Listing 14.15):

```
crash> task
```

Listing 14.15

Displaying Task Information Using the task Command

```
PID: 1937    TASK: c6ace000    CPU: 0    COMMAND: "java"
struct task_struct {
  state = 0,
  flags = 0,
  sigpending = 0,
  addr_limit = {
    seg = 0
  },
  exec_domain = 0xc0168b98,
  need_resched = 1,
  ptrace = 0,
  lock_depth = -1,
  counter = 0,
  nice = 0,
  policy = 0,
  mm = 0xc7be99a0,
  processor = 0,
  cpus_runnable = 1,
  cpus_allowed = 4294967295,
  run_list = {
    next = 0xc0168ab0,
    prev = 0xc11e803c
  },
  sleep_time = 18328,
  next_task = 0xc6358000,
  prev_task = 0xc72ce000,
  active_mm = 0xc7be99a0,
  local_pages = {
    next = 0xc6ace054,
    prev = 0xc6ace054
  },
  allocation_order = 0,
  nr_local_pages = 0,
  binfmt = 0xc016ae48,
  exit_code = 0,
  exit_signal = 17,
  pdeath_signal = 0,
  personality = 0,
  did_exec = -1,
  pid = 1937,
  pgrp = 1937,
  tty_old_pgrp = 0,
  session = 1898,
  tgid = 1937,
  leader = 0,
  p_opptr = 0xc743e000,
  p_pptr = 0xc743e000,
```

```
p_cptr = 0xc6358000,
p_ysptr = 0x0,
p_osptr = 0xc72b2000,
thread_group = {
  next = 0xc6ace0a8,
  prev = 0xc6ace0a8
},
pidhash_next = 0x0,
pidhash_pprev = 0xc0191718,
wait_chldexit = {
  lock = <incomplete type>,
  task_list = {
    next = 0xc6ace0b8,
    prev = 0xc6ace0b8
  }
},
vfork_done = 0x0,
rt_priority = 0,
it_real_value = 0,
it_prof_value = 0,
it_virt_value = 0,
it_real_incr = 0,
it_prof_incr = 0,
it_virt_incr = 0,
real_timer = {
  list = {
    next = 0x0,
    prev = 0x0
  },
  expires = 65075,
  data = 3333218304,
  function = 0xc0019e2c <it_real_fn>
},
times = {
  tms_utime = 79,
  tms_stime = 33,
  tms_cutime = 3,
  tms_cstime = 2
},
start_time = 18089,
per_cpu_utime = {79},
per_cpu_stime = {2141},
min_flt = 2515,
maj_flt = 1665,
nswap = 0,
cmin_flt = 451,
cmaj_flt = 2100,
cnswap = 0,
swappable = -1,
uid = 0,
euid = 0,
```

```
  suid = 0,
  fsuid = 0,
  gid = 0,
  egid = 0,
  sgid = 0,
  fsgid = 0,
  ngroups = 0,
  groups = {0, 0, 0, 0, 0, 0, 0, 0, 0, 0, 0, 0, 0, 0, 0, 0, 0,
0, 0,
      0, 0, 0, 0, 0, 0, 0, 0, 0, 0, 0, 0, 0},
  cap_effective = 3758096127,
  cap_inheritable = 0,
  cap_permitted = 3758096127,
  keep_capabilities = 0,
  user = 0xc0169a24,
  rlim = {{
      rlim_cur = 4294967295,
      rlim_max = 4294967295
    }, {
      rlim_cur = 4294967295,
      rlim_max = 4294967295
    }, {
      rlim_cur = 4294967295,
      rlim_max = 4294967295
    }, {
      rlim_cur = 2093056,
      rlim_max = 4294967295
    }, {
      rlim_cur = 0,
      rlim_max = 4294967295
    }, {
      rlim_cur = 4294967295,
      rlim_max = 4294967295
    }, {
      rlim_cur = 1024,
      rlim_max = 1024
    }, {
      rlim_cur = 1024,
      rlim_max = 1024
    }, {
      rlim_cur = 4294967295,
      rlim_max = 4294967295
    }, {
      rlim_cur = 4294967295,
      rlim_max = 4294967295
    }, {
      rlim_cur = 4294967295,
      rlim_max = 4294967295
    }},
  used_math = 0,
  comm = "java\0va2-ppc-14",
```

```
    link_count = 0,
    total_link_count = 0,
    tty = 0x0,
    locks = 1,
    semundo = 0x0,
    semsleeping = 0x0,
    thread = {
      ksp = 3333225072,
      regs = 0xc6acff50,
      fs = {
        seg = 1
      },
      pgdir = 0xc7029000,
      fpexc_mode = 0,
      last_syscall = 10,
      fpr = {0, 17.25, 0, 0, 0, 0, 0, 0, 0, 0, 0,
4503599627370496, 65536,
        4503601774854144, 0, 0, 0, 0, 0, 0, 0, 0, 0, 0, 0, 0, 0,
0, 0, 0, 0, 0},
      fpscr_pad = 4294443008,
      fpscr = 2181464064,
      dbat4u = 0,
      dbat4l = 0,
      dbat5u = 0,
      dbat5l = 0,
      dbat6u = 0,
      dbat6l = 0,
      dbat7u = 0,
      dbat7l = 0,
      priv_anchor = 0
    },
    fs = 0xc7bf6400,
    files = 0xc74ab060,
    namespace = 0xc05fe200,
    sigmask_lock = <incomplete type>,
    sig = 0xc6c2cac0,
    blocked = {
      sig = {2147483648, 0}
    },
    pending = {
      head = 0x0,
      tail = 0xc6ace3c8,
      signal = {
        sig = {0, 0}
      }
    },
    sas_ss_sp = 0,
    sas_ss_size = 0,
    notifier = Cannot access memory at address 0x0
```

The **help** command shows you all the commands that are available for crash (see Listing 14.16):

```
crash> help
```

Listing 14.16

Displaying the Commands Available for crash Using the help Command

*	files	mod	runq
union			
alias	foreach	mount	search
vm			
ascii	fuser	net	set
vtop			
bt	gdb	p	sig
waitq			
btop	help	ps	struct
whatis			
dev	irq	pte	swap
wr			
dis	kmem	ptob	sym
q			
eval	list	ptov	sys
exit	log	rd	task
extend	mach	repeat	timer

```
crash version: 3.3-28    gdb version: Red Hat Linux (5.2.1-4)
For help on any command above, enter "help <command>".
For help on input options, enter "help input".
For help on output options, enter "help output".
```

You end the crash program using the **quit** command:

```
crash> quit
```

Summary

The crash dump functionality inside the kernel provides a method for the system to take a system dump if a panic occurs in the system. The analysis tools (lcrash and crash) let you view the system dump. The back trace option can be a key command to find the cause of the panic in a crash dump. It shows the exact system calls that occurred during the panic call. Having a crash dump of a problem can greatly reduce the time it takes to solve a system crash problem.

Credits

A big thank-you goes out to Matt D. Robinson and other developers for the development and support of LKCD. A big thank-you goes out to David Anderson and other developers for the development and support of crash.

Web Resources for Crash Dump

URL	Description
http://lkcd.sourceforge.net/	LKCD
http://people.redhat.com/anderson/	crash

Index

SYMBOLS

./configure command, Valgrind installation, 99
/boot directory layout, 188-189
/etc/syslog.conf configuration file, 213
/proc file system, 112
   administrative applications, 113
   entries, 114-116
   interfaces, 112
   relationship with sysctl functions, 112
   utilities
      /proc/vmstat file, 146
      /sys/kernel file, 140-143
      /sys/vm file, 144-145
      buddyinfo file, 117
      bus directory, 118
      cmdline file, 121
      cpuinfo file, 122
      dev/fs file, 138
      diskstats file, 122-126
      free file, 134
      interrupts file, 127
      kallsyms file, 128
      kcore file, 128
      kmsg file, 128
      loadavg file, 129
      lsdev file, 128
      meminfo file, 129
      mpstat, 134
      net directory, 135-136
      slabinfo file, 136
      stat file, 137
      sys directory, 138
      sysrq-trigger file, 145
      vmstat, 131-133
   Web resources, 149
/proc/mm support option (UML configuration), 298
/proc/vmstat file, 146
/sys/kernel file, 140-143
/sys/vm file, 144-145
-l hostlist option (syslogd daemon), 213
1000 memory overrun, 97
2.5.1 pre5, kernel mailing list Oops, 204-207

2G/2G host address space split option (UML configuration), 297
3c59x network driver, kernel mailing list Oops, 200-204

A

a option
   Account Time Tracing, 253
   unlimit gdb command, 63
acquisition of data, LTT (Linux Trace Toolkit), 243-244
action field (syslog.conf configuration file), 215
activation
   kdb debugger, 352
   serial console port, 352-353
addr field (register_probe interface), 323
Address Resolution Protocol (ARP cache), 178
   ARP table, 135
   manipulation, 179
administrative applications (/proc file system), 113
Akkerman, Wichert, 201
aligning structures, performance counters, 279
Alt-SysRq-command, 145
an option (netstat command), 181
analysis
   Oops messages, 190-195, 372
   tracing processes, LTT (Linux Trace Toolkit), 245
applications
   debugging
      Dprobes, 316-331
      gdb, 54-76
      memory management debugging, 82-109
      symbols that increase executable size, 77
      techniques, 78-79
   Kprobes, 330-331
   trace, 234
   UML (User-Mode Linux), 292
architecture component tasks, LTT (Linux Trace Toolkit), 235
ARP (Address Resolution Protocol) cache, 178
   ARP table, 135
   manipulation, 179
arp command, 179

arrays, 280
assembly code, generation of by gcc –s option, 199-200
attach command, 56

B

b option
    gprof profiler, 17
    sar utility, 126
back traces
    magic key sequence, 174-176
    PID 2, 362
backtrace command, 60
binary interface, 112
bio_alloc( ) routine, 205
blocking technique, performance counters, 281, 285-287
bogomips entry (cpuinfo file, /proc file system), 122
booting UML (User-Mode Linux), 307
branch coverage, 40
break 30 command, 46
break 36 command, 48
break command, 60
break points, 54
BSQ_CACHE_REFERENCE counter, 283
bt command, 355, 397
    back traces, 396
    viewing the back trace for process 1960, 399
bta (Back Trace for All Processes) kdb command, 362
buddyinfo file, 117
buffer overruns, 82
building the kernel
    crash dumps, 376-378
    kdb debugger, 350-351
    kgdb debugger, 339-341
    Kprobes, 320-321
    LTT (Linux Trace Toolkit), 240-242
    Oops message analysis, 193-195
    UML (User-Mode Linux), 296-304
        configuration options, 297-299
        gcov support, 302
        gprof support, 303
        Kernel hacking menu, 301
        transports, 299-301
        UML Network Devices menu, 299
Built-in Kernel Debugger support option, 335
bunzip2 command, 98, 336
bus directory (/proc file system), 118
bus error messages, 79
busy waiting, 202
bzip2 command, 348

C

c option (CPU ID tracing)
    tracevisualizer program, 253
    unlimit gdb command, 63
cache misses
    data cache misses, 282
    performance counters, 278
cache profiling (Valgrind), 106-109
call graphs, 14
call stacks, 55
called functions (kprof), 31
calloc( ) function, memory management, 83
cg_annotate command, 108
character-based interface (/proc file system), 112
checkers (memory-management)
    Electric Fence package, 93-96
    MEMWATCH, 84-86
    Valgrind, 97
        cache profiling, 106-109
        finding memory errors, 101-106
        installation, 98-101
        limitations, 109
    Web resources, 81, 109-111
    YAMD package, 86-93
clear_inode method (VFS), 359
client requirements, Netdump, 391-392
clock( ) function, execution time, 6, 9-10
cmdline file, 121
code coverage analysis, 38
    gcov
        branch coverage, 40
        gcc options, 41-42, 51
        loop coverage, 40
    logic errors, 39-40
combined loops (performance counters), 281
commands
    ./configure, 99
    arp, 179
    bt, 355, 396-399
    bunzip2, 98, 336
    bzip2, 348
    cg_annotate, 108
    cont, 344
    cp, 189
    cp /usr/src/linux/linux /usr/src/uml/linux, 304
    crash dump interactive analysis, 373-374
    date, 4
    diff, 202
    dis, 403
    echo, 152
    evlconfig, 229
    evlgentmpls, 229

evlogmgr, 228-229
evltc, 229
files, 404-405
gdb, 56-60, 74
    break 30, 46
    break 46, 48
    cont, 48-49
    list, 46-48
    print array, 46
    print array[0], 49
    quit, 48-49
    run 1, 46, 49
    set array=0, 46
    set array[0]=0, 49
    step, 48-49
go, 356
help, 410
info breakpoints, 307, 346
info gprof, 15
info threads, 309
kdb
    bta command, 362
    dmesg command, 361
    ps command, 361
kdb debugger, 353-354
kill, 245
lcrash commands, 385-386
linux, 294
ln, 190
log, 400-403
logger (Syslog), 218-219
logrotate, 221
mach, 396
make, 99
make bzImage, 265, 320
make clean, 265, 320
make install, 88, 99
make modules, 265, 321
make modules_install, 265, 321
make xconfig, 263, 320
make xconfig ARCH=um, 299, 303
man gprof, 15
man ps, 154
md, 366
mount, 344, 399
mount root_fs mnt -o loop, 304
netstat, 180-182
nm, 189
objdump, 356
opannotate, 273
opcontrol --init, 282
op_help, 282
patch, 202, 296
perror, 188, 208-209

pgrep bash, 169
ps, 116, 245, 397-398
quit, 410
rpm, 16
run-yamd, 92
runq, 403
slog_fwd, 231
stat, 387
stty, 341
sys, 395-396
tar, 98
task, 405, 409
thread, 309
thread apply, 309
time, 5-6
tracedaemon, 242
tracevisualizer, 242, 251
umount mnt, 304
uname, 321
uname -a, 265
valgrind ls -all, 100
compilation of programs (gdb), 59
compile-time flags (MEMWATCH), 85
config file, 189
configuration
    Diskdump, 393
    kernel configuration, crash dumps, 374-376
    network interface, ifconfig utility, 178
    UML (User-Mode Linux), 297-299
CONFIG_DEBUGSYM debugging symbol, 302
CONFIG_PT_PROXY debugging symbol, 302
consoles (UML), 310
consumer interface, 227
cont array command, 48
cont command, 49, 60, 344
copy-on-write (COW) file system files, 293
core files, debugging applications with gdb, 63-65
core-file command, 64
COW (copy-on-write) file system files, 293
Cox, Alan, 201
cp /usr/src/linux/linux /usr/src/uml/linux
    command, 304
cp command, 189
cpuinfo file, 122
CPU_CLOCK_UNHALTED counter, 281
crash dumps, 372
    Diskdump, 392-393
    interactive analysis, 373-374
    kernel configuration, 374-376
    lcrash commands, 385-386
    mcore crash dump, 393-405, 410
    Netdump, 391-392
    patching and building the kernel, 376-378
    report generation, 373

sample system panic and crash dump taken, 386, 390

steps, 379-384

Web resources, 411

crash tool, 373

CRASH_DUMP option (LKCD kernel crash dump), 375

CRASH_DUMP_BLOCKDEV option (LKCD kernel crash dump), 375

CRASH_DUMP_COMPRESS_GZIP option (LKCD kernel crash dump), 376

CRASH_DUMP_COMPRESS_RLE option (LKCD kernel crash dump), 376

CRASH_DUMP_MEMDEV option (LKCD kernel crash dump), 375

CRASH_DUMP_NETDEV option (LKCD kernel crash dump), 375

CRASH_DUMP_SOFTBOOT option (LKCD kernel crash dump), 375

cron job, 228

D

Daemon transport, UML packet exchange, 301

data (LTT)

acquisition, 243-244

interpretation, 248-253

recording, 244

reviewing, 256-259

saving, oprofile, 277

data cache misses, 282

Data Display Debugger. See ddd

date command, 4

dbench program execution time, 4

ddd (Data Display Debugger), 54

features, 66

installation, 66-67

invocation, 67

dead code, 38-39

Debian 3.0 root image, 305

debuggers, 334-335

kdb, 348

activation, 352-353

building the kernel, 350-351

commands, 353-354

debug sessions, 354-368

kernel patching, 348-350

Web resources, 369

kgdb, 335

building the kernel, 339-341

checking the null modem serial cable setup, 341-343

gdb sessions, 343

gdb thread analysis, 347

kernel patching, 336-338

stopping kernel execution, 344-346

Web resources, 369

debugging applications

Dprobes, 316

characteristics, 318

DPEH (Dprobes Event Handler), 317

general steps, 318-319

Kprobes, 319-331

Probe Manager, 316

Web resources, 331

gdb, 54

commands, 56-59

compiling program to be debugged, 59

core files, 63-65

GUIs (graphical user interfaces), 54, 65-76

installation, 55

invocation, 60-63

operations, 54-55

memory management, 82

Electric Fence package, 93-96

errors, 83-84

libc (library calls), 82-83

MEMWATCH, 84-86

Valgrind, 97-109

YAMD package, 86, 91-93

printf( ) statements, 54

symbols, 77

Syslog, 222-226

techniques, 78-79

delete command (gdb), 60

dev/fs file (/proc file system), 138

development

machines, kgdb requirement, 336

UML file systems, 309

diff command, 202

Direct Rendering Manager (DRM), 357

dis command, 403

disk space (Syslog), 219-220

Diskdump, 372, 392-393

diskstats file, 122-126

iostat utility, 122-125

information reported, 123-124

measurements of tuning results, 125-126

sample output, 124

x option, 124

sar utility, 126

dlopen( ) function, 156

dlsysm( ) function, 156

dmap_pmap_verify( ) routine, 108

DMEMWATCH compile-time flag, 85

dmesg kdb command, 361

DMW_STDIO compile-time flag, 85

dpcc, 330

DPEH (Dprobes Event Handler), 317

Dprobes (dynamic probes), 316
  characteristics, 318
  DPEH (Dprobes Event Handler), 317
  general steps, 318-319
  Kprobes, 319
    applications, 330-331
    building the kernel, 320-321
    creating at an offset in a routine, 328-329
    finding active Kprobes, 328
    interfaces, 321-322
    Jprobes, 329-330
    makefile for a basic kernel module, 326
    registering and unregistering, 322-324
    sys_open sample, 324-326
  Probe Manager, 316
  Web resources, 331
DRM (Direct Rendering Manager), 357
dumping traffic on a network (tcpdump), 179
dynamic probes. See Dprobes

E

echo command, 152
EIP (Extended Instruction Pointer) register, 354
Eldredge, Nate, YAMD package, 86
Electric Fence package, 93-96
entries (/proc file system), 114-116
error messages, 188
  config files, 189
  event logging, 212-213, 226
    evlog packages, 231
    evlogd daemon, 226
    evlogmgr command, 228
    evlogrmtd daemon, 230-231
    features, 227
    forwarding Syslog messages to event log, 231
    interfaces, 227
    log management, 228
    log records, 228
    remote logging, 229-230
    utilities, 228-229
    Web resources, 232
  kernel files, 188-189
  Oops messages
    analysis, 190-195
    applying gdb to display jfs_mount, 199
    generation of assembly code by gcc –s option, 199-200
    kernel mailing lists, 200-207
    processing using ksymoops, 196-198
    Web resources, 209
  perror command, 208-209
  Syslog, 212-226
  system.map, 189-190

Error Record Template Repository, 226
Ethereal, browsing network traffic, 180
Ethertap transport, UML packet exchange, 300
Event Consolidation Host, 229
Event Graph (tracevisualizer program), 249
Event Handler (Dprobes). See DPEH
event logging, 212-213, 226
  evlog packages, 231
  evlogd daemon, 226
  evlogmgr command, 228
  evlogrmtd daemon, 230-231
  features, 227
  forwarding Syslog messages to event log, 231
  interfaces, 227
  log management, 228
  log records, 228
  remote logging, 229-230
  utilities, 228-229
  Web resources, 232
evlconfig command, 229
evlfacility utility, 229
evlgentmpls command, 229
evlnotify utility, 229
evlog packages, 231
evlogd daemon, 226
evlogmgr command, 228-229
evlogrmtd daemon, 230-231
evlquery utility, 229
evltc command, 229
evlview utility, 229
executable size (programs), 77
execution time, 2
  clock( ) function, 6, 9-10
  date command, 4
  gettimeofday( ) function, 11-13
  gprof profiler, 13-14
    b option, 17
    field descriptions, 28-31
    for loops/if statements, 20, 26
    fprofile-arcs option, 18
    ftest-coverage option, 18
    kprof, 31-32
    pg gcc option, 15-16
  stopwatch method, 3
  time command, 5-6
execution traces, 234
  applications, 234
  LTT (Linux Trace Toolkit), 234
    analyzing tracing processes, 245
    architecture component tasks, 235
    building the kernel, 240-242
    building user-level tools, 242
    data acquisition, 243-244
    data recording, 244

data reviewing text tools, 256-259
interpretation of data, 248-253
package and installation, 236-240
tarring a subdirectory sample, 253-256
Web resources, 259
Extended Instruction Pointer (EIP) register, 354

F

f option (Event Types Tracing), tracevisualizer
    program, 252
facility code, 215
fault_handler function, 323
features
    ddd (Data Display Debugger), 66
    event logging, 227
    Insight, 70-71
field descriptions (gprof profiler), 28-31
fields (/proc file system)
    dev/fs file, 138-139
    mpstat utility, 134
    stat file, 137-138
    /sys/kernel file, 140-142
    /sys/vm file, 144
file systems, (UML), 305, 311
files command, 404-405
flat profile view, 31
flat profiles, 13-14
for loops, 20, 26
Forwarding Plug-ins, 229
forwarding Syslog messages to event log, 231
fprofile-arcs (gcc option), 41
fprofile-arcs option (gprof profiler), 18
frames (stack frames), 55
free files, 134
free( ) function, memory management, 83
fscklog_init( ) function, 101
ftest-coverage option (gcc), 42
ftest-coverage option (gprof profiler), 18
functions
    clock( ), 6, 9-10
    gettimeofday( ), 11-13
    memory management, 83
    sqrt( ), 20

G

g compiler option (gdb), 59
g option (Electric Fence package), 94
gcc options
    gcov, 41-42, 51
    -fprofile-arcs option, 41
    -ftest-coverage option, 42
    −s option, generation of assembly code,
      199-200
    gprof profiler, 15-16

gcov
    code coverage analysis
      branch coverage, 40
      gcc options, 41-42, 51
      loop coverage, 40
    logic errors, 39-40
    UML support, 302
gdb (GNU debugger), 54
    commands, 46-48, 56-60, 74
    compiling program to be debugged, 59
    core files, 63-65
    displaying jfs_mount code, 199
    GUIs (graphical user interfaces), 54, 65
      ddd, 66-67
      Insight, 70-76
    installation, 55
    invocation, 60-63
    operations, 54-55
    sessions, 343
    thread analysis, 347
    UML sessions, 306-308
    UML thread analysis, 308
    Web resources, 53, 80
gdb executable_file corefile command (gdb), 56
gettimeofday( ) function, 11-13
GLOBAL_POWER_EVENTS counter, 281
GNU debugger. *See* gdb
go command, 356
gprof profiler
    performance tuning, 13-14
      -b option, 17
      field descriptions, 28-31
      for loops/if statements, 20, 26
      fprofile-arcs option, 18
      ftest-coverage option, 18
      kprof, 31-32
      pg gcc option, 15-16
    UML support, 303
graph view (kprof), 31
graphical user interfaces. *See* GUIs
Graphviz, 32
GUIs (graphical user interfaces), 54
    ddd, 54, 66-67
    Insight, 54, 70-76

H

h option (syslogd daemon), 213
hardware counters, 277
    aligning structures, 279
    cache misses, loop grouping, 278-287
    packing arrays, 280
    padding structures, 279
hardware watch points, 54-55
help command, 410

hierarchical profile view (kprof), 31
Highmem support option (UML configuration), 298
HoneyPot ProcFS option (UML configuration), 297
Host filesystem option (UML configuration), 297
HUP signals, 213

I

ide_hwgroup_t structure, 365
ide_timer_expiry routine, 368
if statements, 20, 26
ifconfig utility, 178
info breakpoints command, 307, 346
info gprof command, 15
info threads command, 74, 309
initial_processing( ) routine, 101
Insight, 54
    features, 70-71
    installation, 71-76
installation
    ddd (Data Display Debugger), 66-67
    gdb, 55
    Insight, 71-76
    kprof, 32
    LTT (Linux Trace Toolkit), 236-240
    Valgrind, 98-101
    YAMD package, 88
instrumentation profilers, 262
interactive analysis, crash dump commands, 373-374
interfaces
    event logging, 227
    Kprobes, 321-322
    /proc file system, 112
interpretation of data, LTT (Linux Trace Toolkit), 248-253
interrupts files, 127
invocation
    ddd (Data Display Debugger), 67
    gdb, 60-63
ioctl call, 173
iostat utility, 122-125
    information reported, 123-124
    measurements of tuning results, 125-126
    sample output, 124
    x option, 124
IRQ trace points, 235

J

JFS (Journaled File System), 188, 309
    jfs_mount code
        applying gdb to display jfs_mount, 199
        modifying code to create Oops messages, 191-192
jfs_mount code, 191-192

Journaled File System. See JFS
Jprobes (jumper probes), 329-330

K

kallsyms files, 128
kcore files, 128
kdb debugger, 348
    activation, 352-353
    building the kernel, 350-351
    commands, 353-354
    debug sessions, 354-368
    kernel patching, 348-350
    Web resources, 369
KDB modules option, 335
KDB off by default option, 335
kernel
    building, 264-265
    configuration, crash dumps, 374-376
    files, 188-189
    LTT (Linux Trace Toolkit), 240-242
    mailing lists (Oops messages), 200
        2.5.1-pre5, 204-207
        3c59x network driver, 200-204
    UML, 292
        applications, 292
        booting, 307
        consoles and serial lines, 310
        file systems, 305, 309-311
        gdb sessions, 306-308
        gdb thread analysis, 308
        introduction to kernel and root file system, 293-295
        limitations, 293
        networking support, 310
        patching and building kernel, 296-304
        root images, 304, 311
        shutting down, 312
        utilities, 312-313
        Web resources, 314
Kernel Dynamic Probes. See Kprobes
Kernel hacking menu, 301, 334
Kernel support for ELF binaries option (UML configuration), 297
Kernel support for MISC binaries option (UML configuration), 297
kernel-level debuggers, 334-335
    kdb, 348
        activation, 352-353
        building the kernel, 350-351
        commands, 353-354
        debug sessions, 354-368
        kernel patching, 348-350
        Web resources, 369

kgdb, 335
    building the kernel, 339-341
    checking the null modem serial cable setup,
       341-343
    gdb sessions, 343
    gdb thread analysis, 347
    kernel patching, 336-338
    stopping kernel execution, 344-346
    Web resources, 369
kgdb debugger, 335
    building the kernel, 339-341
    checking the null modem serial cable setup,
       341-343
    gdb sessions, 343
    gdb thread analysis, 347
    kernel patching, 336-338
    stopping kernel execution, 344-346
    Web resources, 369
kgdb8250 option (kgdb kernel command-line
    option), 342
KGDB: Console messages through gdb option, 335
KGDB: Enable kernel asserts option, 335
KGDB: Remote (serial) kernel debugging with gdb
    option, 335
KGDB: Thread analysis option, 335
kgdbwait option (kgdb kernel command-line
    option), 342
kill command, 245
klogd utility, 213, 217-218
kmsg files, 128
Kprobes (Kernel Dynamic Probes), 319
    applications, 330-331
    building the kernel, 320-321
    creating at an offset in a routine, 328-329
    finding active Kprobes, 328
    interfaces, 321-322
    Jprobes, 329-330
    makefile for a basic kernel module, 326
    registering and unregistering, 322-324
    sys_open sample, 324-326
kprof, 31-32
ksymoops, 196-198

L

lcrash commands, 385-386
lcrash tool, 373
lefence option (Electric Fence package), 94
libc (library calls), 82
    calloc( ) function, 83
    free( ) function, 83
    malloc( ) function, 83
    realloc( ) function, 83
library calls. *See* libc
lilo boot loader, 321

limitations
    UML (User-Mode Linux), 293
    Valgrind, 109
Lindh, Johan, MEMWATCH package, 84
linux command, 294
Linux Kernel Crash Dump. *See* LKCD
Linux Trace Toolkit. *See* LTT
list command, 46-48, 60, 75
list of callers (kprof), 31
listings
    add.c file, 200
    add.s file, 200
    annotation from chp10_profile 1 program,
       273-276
    annotation of one entry of cachegrind, 108
    benefits profiling has on small programs, 15
    call table for super block file system
       operations, 360
    complex use of profiling, 26-27
    creating a patch, 202
    creating a thread with pthread_create, 72
    demonstration of gdb's features, 57
    disassembly of sys_open routine, 329
    displaying commands available for crash using
       help command, 410
    displaying crash_save_current_state routine
       using dis command, 403
    displaying file information using files command,
       404-405
    displaying task information using task
       command, 405-409
    dump file, 380-383
    Electric Fence makefile for malloc_test.c, 94-95
    Electric Fence malloc_test-fixed.c, 96
    ext3 file system balloc.c source, 393-394
    fat_clear_inode, 359
    fix to bio.c, 205-207
    fix to pnp_bios.c, 202-204
    gcov after five tests, 50-51
    gcov after running application with input 1000,
       44-45
    gcov output, 19, 25-26
    gcov-enabled program, 42-43
    gdbinit start file for gdb, 306, 343
    getting a back trace using bt command, 396-397
    gprof output, 17-21
    high-level usage for adding a Kprobe, 318-319
    ide_hwgroup_t structure, 366
    ide_timer_expiry routine, 368
    IRQ trace points, 235
    jfs_clear_inode, 359
    jfs_mount.c code, 344
    Jprobe for sys_open routine, 330
    Kprobe for sys_open routine, 325-326

logrotate.conf file, 221-222
makefile for sampleclock program, 6-7
measuring cache misses with oprofile, 284
MEMWATCH memory sample, 84-85
modified jfs_mount.c code, 191-192, 390
Oops directly from /var/log/messages, 195
Oops messages after processing by ksymoops, 196
oprofile sample program, 266-267
portion of validate_super( ) routine, 105
ps command showing a deadlock in JFS, 165-166
ps-test.c, 157
ps-test2.c, 160
pseudocode for timing write code, 12-13
sampleclock, 6-7, 9
sampletime code, 11-12
script to pull kernel and modules to test machine (kgdb), 340
source for Syslog message, 224-226
sqrt function, 20-21
start of the strace on mkfs, 173
Syslog message, 223-224
syslog.conf file, 215, 217
system call, 167
sys_open source code, 323-324
tar.data file, 254-255
valgrind-1.c, 101
valgrind-2.c, 103-104
viewing a dump with crash, 394-395
viewing file systems mounted using mount command, 399
viewing system buffer information using log command, 400-403
viewing system processes using ps command, 397-398
viewing system run queue using runq command, 403
viewing the back trace for process 1960 using bt command, 399
viewing the machine information using mach command, 396
viewing the system information using sys command, 395-396
YAMD memory sample, 87
LKCD (Linux Kernel Crash Dump), 372
crash dump kernel options, 374-376
evaluating support for, 374
general crash dump steps, 379-384
lcrash commands, 385-386
patching and building the kernel, 376-378
sample system panic and crash dump taken, 386-390
ln commands, 190
Load all symbols for debugging option, 335
loadavg files, 129

log command, 400-403
log files, 215
management (Syslog), 221
event logging, 228
log records, 228
logger command, 218-219
logic errors, code coverage analysis, 39-40
logrotate command, 221
loop coverage, 40
loop grouping, performance counters, 280-281
lsdev files, 128
lsof tool, 176
lspci utility, 118, 121
lsusb utility, 118
LTT (Linux Trace Toolkit), 234, 330
analyzing tracing processes, 245
architecture component tasks, 235
building the kernel, 240-242
building user-level tools, 242
data acquisition, 243-244
data recording, 244
data reviewing text tools
traceanalyze filename, 257
tracedump filename, 258-259
tradedcore filename, 256
interpretation of data, 248-253
package and installation, 236-240
tarring a subdirectory sample, 253-256
Web resources, 259
Lustre File System, 310

M

mach command, 396
magic key sequence, back traces, 174-176
Magic SysRq, 145
make bzImage command, 265, 320
make clean command, 265, 320
make command, 99
make install command
installing YAMD, 88
Valgrind installation, 99
make modules command, 265, 321
make modules_install command, 265, 321
make xconfig ARCH=um command, 299, 303
make xconfig command, 263, 320
malloc( ) error conditions, 46
malloc( ) function, 83
man gprof command, 15
man ps command, 154
management, event logs (evlogmgr command), 228
Management console option (UML configuration), 297
mcore crash dump, 393-410
md command, 366

meminfo files, 129
memory corruption, 82
memory leaks, 82
memory management debugging, 82
    Electric Fence package, 93-96
    errors, 83-84
    libc (library calls), 82
        calloc( ) function, 83
        free( ) function, 83
        malloc( ) function, 83
        realloc( ) function, 83
    MEMWATCH, 84-86
    Valgrind, 97
        cache profiling, 106-109
        finding memory errors, 101-106
        installation, 98-101
        limitations, 109
    Web resources, 81, 109-111
    YAMD package, 86, 91-93
memory overruns, 97
MEMWATCH, 84, 86
messages, syslogd daemon, 217
mount command, 344, 399
mount root_fs mnt -o loop command, 304
Mozilla, 116
mpstat (/proc file system), 134
Multicast transport, UML packet exchange, 301
mutex objects, 156
MySQL error code, perror utility, 208-209

N

net directory (/proc file system), 135-136
Netdump, 372, 391-392
netstat command, 180-182
network debugging tools, 178
    arp command, 179
    ethereal, 180
    ifconfig utility, 178
    netstat command, 180-182
    tcpdump program, 179
Networking support option (UML configuration),
    297, 310
nm command, 189
null modem serial cable setup, 341-343

O

o option (Omit Event Types), tracevisualizer
    program, 252
objdump command, 356
Oops messages (panic messages), 188-190
    analysis, 190-195, 372
    applying gdb to display jfs_mount, 199

    generation of assembly code by gcc –s option,
        199-200
    kernel mailing lists
        2.5.1-pre5, 204-207
        3c59x network driver, 200-204
    processing using ksymoops, 196-198
    Web resources, 209
opannotate command, 273
opannotate utility, 268
opcontrol -init command, 282
opcontrol utility, 267
open dialog box (kprof), 33
OpenOffice, 116
operations, gdb, 54-55
opgprof utility, 268
opreport utility, 268
oprofile kernel profiler, 263
    building the kernel, 264-265
    hardware counters, 277
        aligning structures, 279
        blocking technique, 281-287
        cache misses, 278
        loop grouping, 280-281
        packing arrays, 280
        padding structures, 279
    oprof_start utility, 268
    profile steps, 268-272
    reports, 276-277
    saving data, 277
    single executable profiles, 272-273
    utilities, 267-268
op_help command, 282
overruns (memory), 97

P

p option (PID tracing), tracevisualizer program, 253
packing arrays, performance counters, 280
padding structures, performance counters, 279
panic messages. *See* Oops messages
patch command, 202, 296
patching kernel, 376-278
    kdb, 348-350
    kgdb, 336-338
    UML (User-Mode Linux), 296
        configuration options, 297-299
        gcov support, 302
        gprof support, 303
        Kernel hacking menu, 301
        transports, 299-301
        UML Network Devices menu, 299
pcap transport, UML packet exchange, 301
Perens, Bruce, 93

performance counters, 277
    aligning structures, 279
    blocking technique, 281-287
    cache misses, 278
    loop grouping, 280-281
    packing arrays, 280
    padding structures, 279
performance tuning
    profiling methods, 2
        clock( ) function, 6, 9-10
        date command, 4
        gettimeofday( ) function, 11-13
        gprof profiler, 13-20, 26-32
        stopwatch method, 3
        time command, 5-6
    steps, 2
perror command, 188, 208-209
pg gcc option (gprof profiler), 15-16
pgrep -u root httpd (pgrep utility), 168
pgrep -u root,best (pgrep utility), 168
pgrep bash command, 169
pgrep utility, 168-169
PID 2, back trace, 362
POSIX 1003.25 standard, 226
post_handler function, 323
pre_handler function, 323
print array command, 46
print array[0] command, 49
print command, 60
Print Screen key, 145
printf( ) statements, 54
printk( ) messages, 227
Probe Manager (Dprobes), 316
Process Analysis view (tracevisualizer program), 250
process-specific subdirectories (/proc file system
    entries), 114
    /proc/vmstat file, 146
    /sys/kernel file, 140-143
    /sys/vm file, 144-145
    buddyinfo file, 117
    bus directory, 118
    cmdline file, 121
    cpuinfo file, 122
    dev/fs file, 138
    diskstats file, 122-126
    free file, 134
    interrupts file, 127
    kallsyms file, 128
    kcore file, 128
    kmsg file, 128
    loadavg file, 129
    lsdev file, 128
    meminfo file, 129
    mpstat, 134

    net directory, 135-136
    slabinfo file, 136
    stat file, 137
    statm, 116
    sys directory, 138
    sysrq-trigger file, 145
    vmstat, 131-133
processes
    task_struct data structure, 152-153
    tools, 154
        pgrep utility, 168-169
        ps (process status) program, 154-157, 165-167
        pstree, 169
        top utility, 170
processor entry (cpuinfo file, /proc file system), 122
processors, hardware counters, 277
    aligning structures, 279
    blocking technique, 281-287
    cache misses, 278
    loop grouping, 280-281
    packing arrays, 280
    padding structures, 279
profiling, 2, 262
    clock( ) function, 6, 9-10
    date command, 4
    gettimeofday( ) function, 11-13
    gprof profiler, 13-14
        b option, 17
        field descriptions, 28-31
        for loops/if statements, 20, 26
        fprofile-arcs option, 18
        ftest-coverage option, 18
        kprof, 31-32
        pg gcc option, 15-16
    instrumentation profilers, 262
    sampling profilers
        oprofile, 263-287
        Prospect, 287-288
    stopwatch method, 3
    time command, 5-6
    Web resources, 289
Profiling support menu, 264
programs
    compilation, 59
    identifying crashes, 79
Prospect profiler, 287-288
provider interface (event logging), 227
ps (List All Processes) kdb command, 361
ps (process status) program, 154-157, 165
    displaying syscall currently executed, 166
    ps au option, 154-156
    starting a new process, 167
ps au option (ps program), 154-156
ps command, 116, 245, 397-398

ps-test2, 162
pstree utility, 169
pthread_mutex_lock( ) function, 156
pthread_mutex_unlock( ) function, 156

Q-R

quit command, 48-49, 61, 410

R (runnable) state of tasks, 156
r option (syslogd daemon), 213
Raw Trace view (tracevisualizer program), 250
Real-time Clock option (UML configuration), 298
real-time performance, 2
    clock( ) function, 6, 9-10
    date command, 4
    gettimeofday( ) function, 11-13
    gprof profiler, 13-14
        b option, 17
        field descriptions, 28-31
        for loops/if statements, 20, 26
        fprofile-arcs option, 18
        ftest-coverage option, 18
        kprof, 31-32
        pg gcc option, 15-16
    stopwatch method, 3
    time command, 5-6
realloc( ) function, memory management, 83
receive (RX) errors, ifconfig utility, 178
recording data, LTT (Linux Trace Toolkit), 244
registering Kprobes, 322-323
register_probe interface, 322-323
remote logging
    event logging, 229-230
    syslogd daemon, 214
reports
    generation, crash dumps, 373
    oprofile kernel profiler, 276-277
resources (Web resources)
    /proc file system, 149
    crash dumps, 411
    Dprobes, 331
    event logging, 232
    GNU Debugger, 53, 80
    kdb debugger, 369
    kgdb debugger, 369
    LTT (Linux Trace Toolkit), 259
    memory checkers, 81, 109-111
    Oops messages, 209
    profiling, 289
    system tools, 185
reviewing data, LTT text tools, 256
    traceanalyze filename, 257
    tracedcore filename, 256
    tracedump filename, 258-259

root file system (UML), 293-295
root images (UML), 304, 311
rpm (UML), 293
rpm command, 16
run 1 command, 46, 49
run command, 56, 60-61, 74
run-yamd command, 92
runq command, 403
RX (receive) errors, ifconfig utility, 178

S

S (sleeping) state of tasks, 156
s domainlist option (syslogd daemon), 213
sampling profilers, 263
    oprofile, 263
        building the kernel, 264-265
        hardware counters, 277-287
        profile steps, 268-272
        reports, 276-277
        saving data, 277
        single executable profiles, 272-273
        utilities, 267-268
    Prospect, 287-288
    Web resources, 289
sar utility, 126
segmentation fault - core dumped messages, 79
selector field (syslog.conf configuration file), 214-215
Separate Kernel Address Space support option
    (UML configuration), 297
separate loops, performance counters, 281
serial cable setup, 341-343
serial console port, 352-353
serial lines, UML (User-Mode Linux), 310
server requirements, Netdump, 391
set array=0 command, 46
set array[0]=0 command, 49
severity code (syslog.conf selector field), 214
Seward, Julian, Valgrind, 97
sharp profiles, 13
shutting down UML (User-Mode Linux), 312
single executable profiles, 272-273
slabinfo file (/proc file system), 136
SLIP transport, UML packet exchange, 301
SLiRP transport, UML packet exchange, 301
slog_fwd command, 231
sourcename files, 42
spinlock, 202
sqrt function, 20-21
SRAM (static RAM), 106
stack frames, 55
starting OpenOffice, 116
stat command, 387
stat file (/proc file system), 137

static RAM (SRAM), 106
statm entry (/proc file system), 116
Steinberg, Udo A., 204
step command, 48-49
steps
    crash dumps, 379-380, 384
    profiling, 268, 272
stopwatch, 3
strace, 170-174
strip command, 78
stty command, 341
Support for host-based filesystems option (UML
    configuration), 297
Support for USB Keyboard in KDB option, 335
SUSE Linux Enterprise Server, LKCD
    functionality, 372
swap partition, UML (User-Mode Linux), 306
swap_fs swap partition, 306
symbols (debugging), 77
Symmetric multi-processing support option (UML
    configuration), 298
sys command, 395-396
sys directory (/proc file system), 138
sysctl functions, 112
Syslog, 212
    changing messages, 217
    debugging using messages, 222-226
    disk space, 219-220
    klogd, 217-218
    log file management, 221
    logger command, 218-219
    options, 213
    remote logging, 214
    syslog.conf configuration file, 214-215
syslog( ) messages, 227
syslog.conf configuration file, 214-215
syslogd daemon, 213
    changing messages, 217
    debugging using messages, 222-226
    disk space, 219-220
    klogd, 217-218
    log file management, 221
    logger command, 218-219
    options, 213
    remote logging, 214
    syslog.conf configuration file, 214-215
SysRq key, 145
sysrq-trigger file (/proc file system), 145
system call, 167
system error messages
    config files, 189
    kernel files, 188-189

Oops messages
    analysis, 190-195
    applying gdb to display jfs_mount, 199
    generation of assembly code by gcc –s option,
        199-200
    kernel mailing lists, 200-207
    processing using ksymoops, 196-198
    Web resources, 209
perror command, 208-209
system.map, 189-190
system information (/proc file system), 112
    /proc/vmstat file, 146
    /sys/kernel file, 140-143
    /sys/vm file, 144-145
    administrative applications, 113
    buddyinfo file, 117
    bus directory, 118
    cmdline file, 121
    cpuinfo file, 122
    dev/fs file, 138
    diskstats file, 122-126
    entries, 114-116
    free file, 134
    interfaces, 112
    interrupts file, 127
    kallsyms file, 128
    kcore file, 128
    kmsg file, 128
    loadavg file, 129
    lsdev file, 128
    meminfo file, 129
    mpstat, 134
    net directory, 135-136
    relationship with sysctl functions, 112
    slabinfo file, 136
    stat file, 137
    sys directory, 138
    sysrq-trigger file, 145
    vmstat, 131-133
    Web resources, 149
system panic, crash dump, 386-390
system tools, 152
    crash, 373
    lcrash, 373
    lsof, 176
    magic key sequence, 174-176
    network debugging tools, 178
        arp command, 179
        ethereal, 180
        ifconfig utility, 178
        netstat command, 180-182
        tcpdump program, 179

processes, 152-154
    pgrep utility, 168-169
    ps (process status) program, 154-157, 165-167
    pstree, 169
    top utility, 170
strace, 170-174
task states, 153
Web resources, 185
system.map, 189-190

T

tap option (netstat command), 182
tar command, 98
tarring a subdirectory sample (LTT), 253-256
task command, 405, 409
task states, 153
TASK_DEAD, 153
TASK_INTERRUPTIBLE, 153
TASK_RUNNING, 153
TASK_STOPPED, 153
task_struct data structure, 152-153
TASK_UNINTERRUPTIBLE, 153
TASK_ZOMBIE, 153
TCP (Transmission Control Protocol), 230
tcpdump program, 179
test machines, 336
test suites, 38
testing UML file systems, 309
thread 1 command, 75
thread 2 command, 75
thread 3 command, 75
thread 4 command, 75
thread analysis, 308, 347
thread apply command, 309
thread command, 309
time command, 5-6
TIMER_INT counter, 281
tools, 152
    crash, 373
    lcrash, 373
    lsof, 176
    magic key sequence, 174-176
    network debugging tools, 178
        arp command, 179
        ethereal, 180
        ifconfig utility, 178
        netstat command, 180-182
        tcpdump program, 179
    processes, 152-154
        pgrep utility, 168-169
        ps (process status) program, 154-157, 165-167
        pstree, 169
        top utility, 170

strace, 170-174
task states, 153
Web resources, 185
top utility, 170
trace facility, 234
    applications, 234
    LTT (Linux Trace Toolkit), 234
        analyzing tracing processes, 245
        architecture component tasks, 235
        building the kernel, 240-242
        building user-level tools, 242
        data acquisition, 243-244
        data recording, 244
        data reviewing text tools, 256-259
        interpretation of data, 248-253
        package and installation, 236-240
        tarring a subdirectory sample, 253-256
        Web resources, 259
trace seconds filename script, 243
traceanalyze filename script, 257
tracecore seconds filename script, 244
tracecpuid seconds filename script, 244
tracedaemon command, 242
tracedcore filename script, 256
tracedump filename script, 258-259
traceu filename script, 244
tracevisualizer command, 242, 251
tracevisualizer program, LTT data interpretation, 248-249
    a option (Account Time Tracing), 253
    c option (CPU ID tracing), 253
    Event Graph, 249
    f option (Event Types Tracing), 252
    o option (Omit Event Types), 252
    p option (PID tracing), 253
    Process Analysis view, 250
    Raw Trace view, 250
Tracing thread support option (UML configuration), 297
Transmission Control Protocol (TCP), 230
transmit (TX) errors, 178
transports (UML packet exchange), 299-301
TUN/TAP transport, UML packet exchange, 300
TX (transmit) errors, 178

U

UDP (User Datagram Protocol), 230
ulimit command, 63
UML (User-Mode Linux), 292
    applications, 292
    booting, 307
    consoles and serial lines, 310

file systems, 305
  adding, 311
  development and testing, 309
gdb sessions, 306-308
gdb thread analysis, 308
introduction to kernel and root file system, 293-295
limitations, 293
networking support, 310
patching and building kernel, 296-304
  configuration options, 297-299
  gcov support, 302
  gprof support, 303
  Kernel hacking menu, 301
  transports, 299-301
  UML Network Devices menu, 299
root images, 304, 311
shutting down, 312
utilities, 312-313
Web resources, 314
UML Network Devices menu, 299
uml_mconsole utility, 312
uml_mkcow utility, 313
uml_moo utility, 313
uml_net utility, 313
uml_switch utility, 313
umount mnt command, 304
uname -a command, 265
uname command, 321
unregistering Kprobes, 322-324
unregister_probe interface, 323-324
User Datagram Protocol (UDP), 230
user-level tools, LTT (Linux Trace Toolkit), 242
User-Mode Linux. See UML
utilities
  /proc file system, 114
    /proc/vmstat file, 146
    /sys/kernel file, 140-143
    /sys/vm file, 144-145
    buddyinfo file, 117
    bus directory, 118
    cmdline file, 121
    cpuinfo file, 122
    dev/fs file, 138
    diskstats file, 122-126
    free file, 134
    interrupts file, 127
    kallsyms file, 128
    kcore file, 128
    kmsg file, 128

loadavg file, 129
lsdev file, 128
meminfo file, 129
mpstat, 134
net directory, 135-136
slabinfo file, 136
stat file, 137
statm, 116
sys directory, 138
sysrq-trigger file, 145
vmstat, 131-133
event logging, 228-229
oprofile kernel profiler, 267-268
UML (User-Mode Linux), 312-313

V

Valgrind, 97
  cache profiling, 106-109
  finding memory errors, 101-106
  installation, 98-101
  limitations, 109
valgrind ls –all install command, 100
validate_super( ) routine, 105
VFS (Virtual File System), 359
VM (virtual memory) systems, 292
vmlinux file, 188
vmlinuz file, 188
vmstat (/proc file system), 131-133

W-Z

Web resources
  /proc file system, 149
  crash dumps, 411
  Dprobes, 331
  event logging, 232
  GNU Debugger, 53, 80
  kdb debugger, 369
  kgdb debugger, 369
  LTT (Linux Trace Toolkit), 259
  memory checkers, 81, 109-111
  Oops messages, 209
  profiling, 289
  system tools, 185
  UML (User-Mode Linux), 314
where command, 75

x option (iostat utility), 124

YAMD package, 86-93

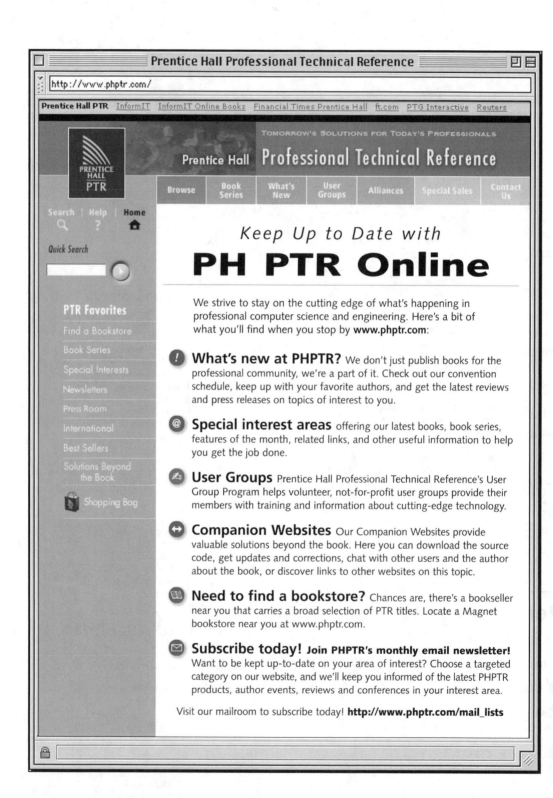